CHINA'S SEARCH FOR DEMOCRACY

CHINA'S SEARCH FOR DEMOCRACY

THE STUDENT AND MASS MOVEMENT OF 1989

Edited by **SUZANNE OGDEN**
KATHLEEN HARTFORD
LAWRENCE SULLIVAN
DAVID ZWEIG

An East Gate Book

M. E. Sharpe, Inc.
Armonk, New York
London, England

An East Gate Book

Copyright © 1992 by M. E. Sharpe, Inc.

Available in the United Kingdom and Europe from M. E. Sharpe,
Publishers, 3 Henrietta Street, London WC2E 8LU.

Library of Congress Cataloging-in-Publication Data

China's search for democracy : the student mass movement of 1989 /
edited by Suzanne Ogden . . . [et al.].
p. cm
Includes bibliographical references.
ISBN 0-87332-723-3 (cloth)
ISBN 0-87332-724-1 (paper)
1. China—Politics and government—1976– 2. Students—
China—Political activity. I. Ogden, Suzanne.
DS779.26.C47355   1991
320.951—dc20
91-26768
CIP

Printed in the United States of America

The paper used in this publication meets the minimum requirements
of American National Standard for Information Sciences—
Permanence of Paper for Printed Library Materials, ANSI Z39.48-1984.

MV (c) 10 9 8 7 6 5 4 3 2
MV (p) 10 9 8 7 6 5 4 3 2

To all those Chinese who dared to write, act,
and speak out during the spring of 1989

Contents

Foreword

The events of the Beijing Spring of 1989 naturally aroused enormous interest among the China specialists affiliated with the Fairbank Center for East Asian Research at Harvard University. The Center is a focus of activity for over one hundred associates teaching and doing research at the various universities and colleges in the greater Boston area, and from April through the summer of that year there were daily exchanges about the remarkable events unfolding in Tiananmen Square. Joining them in the seminars and debates were Chinese students and intellectuals, and recent returnees from China who had either participated in or witnessed the student movement. In the aftermath of the tragic events of June 4, much of the activity was organized by an independent China Scholars Coordinating Committee, which aimed to spread information and mobilize opinion about the crackdown and its aftermath.

Aside from these activities, however, some affiliates felt strongly that their main contribution should be through their metier, scholarship. This book, a product of their commitment, has entailed the sacrifice of considerable time and energy that normally would have been devoted to ongoing individual research projects.

The collaborators provide a full background to the Beijing Spring and incisive commentary on it in their chapters, but their main aim has been to document what the prodemocracy demonstrators were saying and doing during their heady days of occupation of the square. The profusion, indeed confusion, of voices recaptured in this extraordinary collection of documents proves yet again that actors in historic events rarely have a clear grasp of their situation and alternative courses of action.

This is a unique record of a seminal political event of the twentieth century and is required reading for anyone wanting to understand the history of modern China and the spread of the prodemocracy movement, worldwide.

Roderick MacFarquhar, Director
Fairbank Center for East Asian Research
Harvard University
January 1991

Preface

The world sat spellbound as the drama of China's popular movement unfolded in the spring of 1989. The first such Chinese movement to be captured by the modern mass media, this upsurge of protest and participation, which occupied the literal center-stage of China's own political theater, also moved into tens of millions of homes around the globe, courtesy of satellite television transmission. As the pictorial images flickered past, images of the movement itself began to lodge in the imagination of those outside China: earnest young students petitioning for democracy and justice, "people power," nonviolent protests paralyzing a heretofore all-powerful state-party-military apparatus, and so on. Such images helped generate the intensity of international outrage over the eventual crackdown on the movement, and the outpouring of support for the movement's participants and sympathizers in exile.

And yet, like most images, these gross oversimplifications are highly misleading. After the June crackdown, outside observers began asking such questions as: Was a crackdown inevitable? What was the point of no return? On what terms could a withdrawal from Tiananmen Square have occurred after the hunger strike began? Would it have made a difference? Could a viable, modern democratic movement sustain itself in the Chinese environment? Just what did "democracy" mean in a Chinese context? How did ordinary Chinese view the movement, its goals, and its methods? These questions were in fact being posed by some of the movement's participants and onlookers during that spring of 1989, and even before the movement began in mid-April. The answers offered varied widely, however, and prompted a wide range of responses to the popular movement. Attempts to channel it sometimes went in diametrically opposed directions. Moreover, as participation in the movement expanded, many began to act without any clear idea of its broader meaning and often at cross-purposes with other participants. Like most mass social movements, in other words, China's "Beijing Spring" of 1989 was complex, convoluted, and often contradictory.

Already many books dissecting the movement and its tragic demise have been written, some by firsthand observers, some by participants, some by outside experts. All offer windows on an understanding of the events of that spring. But the panorama, we believe, deserves a wider perspective, and therefore we have chosen to present the picture of the movement by combining our own analyses of the events with the diverse and contradictory voices of the democracy movement, speaking for themselves—eloquently, passionately, brazenly, in confusion, and even in despair. From the thousands of handbills, wall posters, songs, poems, speeches, and slogans that the movement generated, we have translated some as most significant, some as most representative, and some as capturing the complicated flavor of the times. These documents preach morality, argue points of law, denounce those in power, search for the roots of China's problems and the route out of them, and sometimes (quite literally) sing with the emotions of the students, workers, and other participants in the mass movement of spring 1989.

Because those who feel comfortable wielding pen or microphone are most likely to be at the forefront in such a protest movement, most of the documents were generated by China's well-educated college students. Nevertheless, workers and ordinary citizens from all backgrounds did organize, speak out, and write their own statements of position and appeals for action. We are fortunate to have had access to many of the documents they generated. Needless to say, since the impetus for this student-initiated mass movement was to demand change, most of the participants wrote documents of criticism and protest. The voices of those who might have sided with the Chinese Communist party leadership are muted, but there is no lack of those critical of the movement's leadership, tactics, or strategy while sympathizing with its basic goals.

Our collection includes no Chinese Communist party leadership documents. An excellent collection of these may be found in a companion volume to this one, edited by Michel Oksenberg, Lawrence R. Sullivan, and Marc Lambert, *Beijing Spring, 1989, Confrontation and Conflict: The Basic Documents* (Armonk, NY: M. E. Sharpe, 1990). Many of the developments in the popular movement came as a response to officially issued pronouncements or leaders' speeches concerning the movement and the party-state's handling of it. Thus, anyone desiring a complete view of the evolution of events in the spring of 1989 should read both volumes.

The documents herein are broadly grouped in chronological sections, which in turn are sometimes arranged topically in order to make particular issues, and commentaries on them, more comprehensible to the general reader. Many of the documents included in this collection are undated and could only be assigned to a particular period because of contextual clues. Some documents cover topics that spanned the entire period, and therefore documents in some sections refer back to events highlighted in an earlier section. Because we considered it essential to provide a sense of the context in which the movement arose, our first section concerns the months leading up to the emergence of the movement in mid-April.

The editors as a group selected appropriate documents, with the assistance of Zheng Shiping, our translator. Without him, the work would be far less complete and certainly far less interesting. Suzanne Ogden served in the role of senior editor and project director. Each editor also took the major responsibility for winnowing and editing the documents in one or two of six chronological sections, and wrote the introduction(s) to those sections. These introductory analyses speak not only to the major issues raised in the documents themselves, but also to issues on which the documents are silent but which are crucial to understanding why the movement took the shape it did in a particular period.

We spent long hours of discussion and debate over the meaning of the student-led mass movement, its twists and turns, and the significance of these documents. In the end, however, each author bears individual responsibility for his or her own introductory analyses. Despite the editors' own passionate feelings about various issues concerning the popular movement, they have tried to present dispassionate, objective, and scholarly analyses. That these analyses sometimes differ among themselves as to interpretation and perspective is an indication of the complexity of the movement itself, and the range of informed judgments that may be made. We have deliberately chosen not to resolve such differences or paper them over, because we believe that the documents themselves will permit readers to balance the views presented in the analytical essays and to come to their own conclusions on the dynamics of the movement.

To some extent, our differences reflect the many differences within the Chinese popular movement. The participants in that movement disagreed among themselves in evaluating the dynamics of the movement, its potential for success, and what actually happened. Their objectives quite often diverged and sometimes clashed. Intellectuals (including students) and workers could unite in condemning corruption among the Communist party and government leadership, and see a free press as a partial corrective to such ills. Yet when it came to the pursuit of *democracy*, they might come to both theoretical and tactical parting of ways. Workers were characteristically more interested in bread-and-butter issues; students, on the other hand, discouraged workers' direct participation in the movement for a considerable time, claiming no interest in forming a broader movement. Older intellectuals, many of whom had participated in the heyday of the Cultural Revolution and suffered from its excesses, others of whom had been victimized in earlier mass movements or campaigns, frequently took more cautious, more theoretical tacks than did the students themselves. Students from outside Beijing often had a different perspective from students in Beijing institutions. Students from the elite Beijing institutions might differ substantially from those in lower-status colleges and institutes. The broader the participation, in fact, the more diversity and divergence could be expected. And the stronger the sense of crisis, the more tension-ridden and acrimonious the differences could become.

The editors' and the documents' diverging opinions also surround the issue of the "inevitability" of the outcome: Just where was the crucial turning point? What tactical or strategic choice might have resolved the confrontation with the CCP leadership without a violent crackdown? Each of the editors makes a bid to establish a different period as the one in which the crucial, no-return decisions were made or missed, the one that determined the denouement. From a broader perspective, one might of course contend that these several decisive turning points add up to an "overdetermined" outcome and help to explain the savagery of the regime's final (and ongoing) response.

In one respect, the editors have been in agreement: we had to confront the question of the reliability and accuracy of any given document. Myths may be reported as self-evident facts; numbers may be bandied about like magic talismans; and the wildest of tenthhand rumors may be garbed in the guise of firsthand observation. The documents may not be accurate records of history understood as "events"; nonetheless, they helped to shape that history, and in a very real sense they *are* the history. The documents give us a sense of what the environment was; for those intimately involved in the making of their own history, these documents and others like them in large part created the environment. The Chinese authors of these documents, whether correct or incorrect in their factual assertions, whether attempting detached analysis or purposely fomenting anger with false information and rumor, reached hundreds, thousands, even millions of their fellow citizens, undermined old shibboleths, and shaped new beliefs. In doing so they shaped actions and thus helped to create a new history for the People's Republic of China.

After the June 4 massacre, the Chinese authorities launched a massive repression campaign that has still not halted. International and Chinese reactions to the movement's violent suppression and the subsequent arrests, trials, executions, "administrative" (i.e., without trial) sentences, and "political study" sessions have not abated. Prison sentences were imposed on some of the popular movement's major leaders as this preface went to press. We have chosen, however, to end the volume's coverage with June 4. Hindsight, action-reaction cycles, government actions, subsequent discoveries, the treatment of activists, the attempt to reimpose ideological controls over the populace as a whole—all are important in their own right. But, in an effort to include only the content of what happened during the most recent flourishing of China's search for democracy, the editors have left this work for others to do. We trust that it will not be too long before there is another, happier story to tell.

Suzanne Ogden   Kathleen Hartford
Professor and Chair   Associate Professor and Chair
Department of Political Science   Department of Political Science
Northeastern University   University of Massachusetts, Boston

Acknowledgments

The authors obtained the bulk of the documents from two sources: the Hong Kong Federation of Students (HKFS) and the October Review Society, also located in Hong Kong. Robin D. S. Yates of Dartmouth College brought back the documents from the HKFS in August 1989, and we are indebted both to him and to Ng Kwok-wa, the general secretary of the HKFS, for making them available. We are also indebted to Robin Munro of Asia Watch, who supplied many of the documents that were subsequently published by the October Review Society.

The editors are especially grateful to Zheng Shiping of Yale University for translating the hundreds of documents included herein, and for being an important participant in our discussions; to Nancy Hearst, the librarian at Harvard's Fairbank Center for East Asian Research, for compiling the bibliography; to Nancy Liu for translating several documents; and to Ding Xueliang of Harvard University for supplying additional documents.

Finally, we wish to thank the Fairbank Center for East Asian Research at Harvard University, our publisher M. E. Sharpe, Northeastern University, and the Fletcher School of Law and Diplomacy at Tufts University for their generous financial support, without which this book would not have been possible.

List of Documentary Sources and Abbreviations

We have used the abbreviations listed below for our major Chinese sources. Please note that the romanization reflects the preferred spelling of those Chinese who produced the sources in Hong Kong, Taiwan, or the People's Republic of China.

Jinxin dongpo de wushiliu tian (The soul-stirring 56 days) (Beijing: Dadi Publishers, 1989). Abbreviated as *56 Days*.

Documents supplied by Hong Kong Federation of Students, courtesy of Robin D. S. Yates and Ng Kwok-wa. Abbreviated as HKFS.

Chung-kuo min-yun yuan tzu-liao ching hsuan: Ta tzu pao, hsiao tzu pao, ch'uan-tan, min-k'an (Carefully selected original documents from China's democracy movement: Large- and small-character posters, handbills, and unofficial publications (Hong Kong: October Review Publishing House, no. 1, June 25, 1989). Also known as October Review Special Documents. Abbreviated as ORSD, 1.

Chung-kuo min-yun yuan tzu-liao ching hsuan: Ta tzu pao, hsiao tzu pao, ch'uan-tan, min-k'an (Carefully selected original documents from China's democracy movement: Large- and small-character posters, handbills, and unofficial publications) (Hong Kong: October Review Publishing House, no. 2, November 1989). Also known as October Review Special Documents. Abbreviated as ORSD, 2.

Shih-yueh p'ing-lun: Si-yueh hsueh-yun t'eh-k'an (October Review special issue on the April student movement) (Hong Kong: October Review Publishing House, May 4, 1989). Also known as October Review Special Issue. Abbreviated as ORSI.

For Tiananmen 1989, compiled by Lien-ho pao (Taipei: Lien-ching Publishing Company, 1989). Abbreviated as *Tiananmen 1989*.

CHINA'S
SEARCH FOR
DEMOCRACY

Sketch Map of Beijing City Centre

Source: Beijing Review, June 26–July 2, 1989, p. 17 (with additions by Marc Lambert).

I

Summer 1988–Spring 1989
The Ferment Before the "Turmoil"

Economic Crisis, Social Change, Cultural
Disintegration, and Political Stagnation

Kathleen Hartford

> *Mao Zedong huai shi huai*
> *Dan yikuai zhi yikuai.*
> *Deng Xiaoping hao shi hao,*
> *Dan yikuai zhi yimao.*
>
> Mao Zedong was bad, real bad,
> But with a buck you knew what you had.
> Deng Xiaoping is fine, real fine,
> But a buck is only worth a dime.
>
> —Popular rhyme current in China in late 1988–early 1989

China hovered on the brink of crisis for a long time before going over the edge. After ten years of economic reform, rapid growth, proliferating ties with the outside world, and high hopes, by 1988 the country was in the slough of despair. While in objective terms most Chinese had never had it so good, many felt that they had never had it so bad. As the economy careened out of control, the economic reforms ground to a halt and the national leadership grew ever more divided over the route to take next. Political reform seemed stillborn, while rampant corruption made it all the more sorely needed. Many Chinese of middle age or older felt that society was changing for the worse, while many young people, seeing a future of empty prospects, retreated into apathy and despair. No one could have guessed the eventual outcome, but by late 1988 and early 1989 Chinese in all walks of life, of many political and cultural persuasions, believed that something bad was going on, and worse was to come. The documents in this section provide a sampling of the range of discussion, and the depths of malaise about the plight of China and the Chinese as the first decade of reform began to look like the last. Some authors focus on the economic dislocations unleashed by reform; some treat the emergence of socioeconomic ills; others address the needs and prospects for political reform; still others examine culture, both high and low, as the culprit or potential savior. Taken together, these writings present a cross-section of the dreams and fears of urban Chinese—workers, cadres, intellectuals, students—on the eve of the popular movement.

The Balance Sheet on Economic Reform:
Growth, Crisis, and Socioeconomic Ills

Ten years of economic reforms had wrought phenomenal changes in both rural and urban China.[1] Rural areas had taken the lead in the reforms, beginning the process in 1978. In the early stage, running roughly from 1978 to 1984, reform policies focused on market liberalization, producer price increases, and reorganized management of collective farms. By the end of that period, virtually all of rural China had returned to household-managed farming on contracts from the collective farms. A flourishing private trade in agricultural products had developed alongside the centrally controlled state commercial network, and the average state purchasing prices of major food and fiber crops had risen by 50 percent or more.

The successes of this early phase made possible a second phase, initiated in 1984. Farmers were encouraged to orient their production toward urban and even foreign markets. Rural industries experienced mushrooming growth, helped along by generous credit, tax and other incentives, and by investments and technical assistance from urban and international industries subcontracting to the rural enterprises. Manufacturing, transport, construction, and service enterprises sprang up. Together, these developments transformed the economic and social face of rural China.

Urban reforms only began in earnest in the fall of 1984. Decentralization gradually freed state-owned enterprises from central state controls over profits and planning. The reorientation of firms toward market signals was attempted, largely through freeing them to buy inputs and sell output at market prices once

---

[1]Information in this section is based on a more detailed discussion of the issues and evidence in Kathleen Hartford, "The Political Economy Behind Beijing Spring," in *The Chinese People's Movement: Perspectives on Spring 1989*, ed. Tony Saich (Armonk, NY: M. E. Sharpe, 1990), pp. 50–82.

they fulfilled their quotas at state-fixed prices. This, termed the "two-track" price system, was created in 1985. The industrial reforms offered more incentives to both workers and managers for productivity, efficiency, and entrepreneurial, profit- and income-maximizing behaviors. Some pilot reforms introduced, for the first time since the 1950s, insecurity of job tenure for state-sector workers: a "labor contract system," introduced in 1986, for newly hired workers, and lay-offs of large portions of the labor force in some industrial cities. Documents 13 and 15 provide several examples of these methods of "breaking the iron rice bowl" of state employees and pose some of the questions raised by the policies. By 1987, industrial reforms had also brought in a "management responsibility system," contracting state enterprises out for three to five years under (supposedly) competitive bidding, making enterprises more responsible for their own profits and losses.

Competition from both cooperative and private enterprises was expected to spur efficiency in state-owned enterprises. Some highly successful privately owned enterprises burst upon the local, national, and even international scene. The best known of these was the high-tech Stone Company, begun by young entrepreneurs who left their secure state jobs to try the private route and rapidly built a multinational company doing business in Asia and Europe. Stone Company, along with a number of much smaller private enterprises, was to provide considerable material assistance to the popular movement.

Finally, the reforms generally encouraged expansion of China's international trade and of foreign investment in China. Both imports and exports zoomed upward after 1978. By 1988, foreign trade accounted for approximately one-tenth of the national income, and far more than that in the booming coastal provinces. Foreign investment was first attracted through "special economic zones" (SEZs) where foreign capital was released from controls imposed elsewhere in China. Investment in joint ventures outside the SEZs began to take off by 1986.[2]

Probably none of those launching the economic reforms initially dared to hope for the degree of success achieved in the 1980s. World Bank data rank China as the third fastest growing economy in the world from 1980 to 1987, nearly matching the performance of South Korea during its period of takeoff from the mid-1960s to the mid-1970s. From 1978 to 1988, the country's GNP rose by 150 percent.[3] The new prosperity was shared by city and countryside.

---

[2]Hong Kong capital accounted for about 40 percent of the total foreign investments, and coastal areas, particularly Guangdong, received the lion's share of the foreign capital input. Guangdong alone raked in 60 percent of the foreign investment funds. *Nanfang ribao* (Southern daily), March 6, 1989, trans. in Joint Publications Research Service (hereafter JPRS), *China Report*, 89-034, April 18, 1989, p. 27.

[3]World Bank, *World Development Report 1988* (New York: Oxford University Press, 1988); State Statistical Bureau, comp., *Zhongguo tongji nianjian 1989* (China statistical yearbook 1989) (Beijing: Statistical Publishers, 1989), p. 21. Hereafter cited as *TJNJ 1989*.

Privately owned motorcycles, automobiles, and trucks appeared in growing numbers. Refrigerators, color televisions, and a wide array of light consumer goods appeared in department stores and markets. High-rise apartment buildings spread through the cities and into the surrounding fields, while sparkling new two- and even three-story houses began to spring up in prosperous rural areas.

Yet by 1988, China's economic situation was painful indeed. Central government tax revenues had essentially stagnated since 1985, while its deficits grew. The foreign debt doubled from 1984 to 1988, totaling U.S. $40 billion in the latter year. Every year after 1985, imports outstripped exports, and although the country had good foreign exchange reserves, they could not be maintained indefinitely.[4] Much of the problem stemmed from the erosion of central government controls due to decentralization: local retention of significant amounts of foreign exchange undercut the central government's ability to control imports and short-term borrowings of foreign funds, while local profit retentions made tax evasion both endemic and enormous.[5]

The demands on the state exchequer, meanwhile, were growing. Transportation, energy, and agricultural infrastructure all desperately needed injections of capital (Doc. 14). Ensuring cheap urban food supplies and propping up faltering state industries cost the government more and more. Total central state subsidies to loss-making state enterprises and for retail (mostly food) prices increased sevenfold from 1978 to 1988; by 1988 they accounted for about a third of total state budgetary expenditures.[6]

Inflation, climbing since the early 1980s, took off skyward in 1988. In comparison with the hyperinflation suffered by some Latin American countries, China's double-digit inflation rate was negligible; to a population accustomed to three decades of stable prices, it was terrifying. In the summer of 1988, rumblings of new and dramatic price reforms set off widespread panic buying.[7] As Document 9 describes, the panic purchases ballooned well beyond foodstuffs; citizens rushed into banks to withdraw their life savings, spending them on any consumer good in sight as a hedge against inflation.

Economic boom times had produced some glaring differences in a country long accustomed to praising equality. The coastal provinces pulled rapidly ahead

---

[4]On deficit size, see *Far Eastern Economic Review*, April 6, 1989, p. 78. The trade balances reported for 1985–88 fluctuated but were consistently negative. *TJNJ 1989*, p. 21.

[5]Beijing Domestic Service, March 21, 1989, in Foreign Broadcast Information Service (hereafter FBIS), *Daily Report: China*, March 22, 1989.

[6]*Nan-pei chi yueh-k'an* (The perspectives), Hong Kong, February 18, 1990, pp. 37-40; and *Jingji ribao* (Economic daily), September 2, 1989, p. 2, translated in *Inside China Mainland* (April 1990): 12; (November 1989): 3–4, respectively. These estimates omit the additional, and often sizable, subsidies provided by provincial, municipal, and local governments.

[7]In May 1988, the government ended subsidies on pork, vegetables, eggs, and sugar, "causing price rises of 30 to 60 per cent overnight." Anita Chan, "The Challenge to the Social Fabric," *The Pacific Review* 2, 2 (April 1989): 121; *Asia 1989 Yearbook* (Hong Kong: Far Eastern Economic Review, 1989), p. 105.

of other regions. As Document 14 explains, that widening gap was felt to result from inequitable preferences accorded coastal areas.[8] The inability to keep up with coastal regions' growth, or even to grow at all, aroused bitterness in the inland areas among citizens and officials alike.

Poverty emerged as a serious social problem. In 1988, nearly one-third of rural China may have been living below the poverty (i.e., subsistence) line.[9] Rural poverty was nothing new to China, but for the first time in thirty years, it could move. By late 1988, an estimated fifty million "transients" clogged China's cities, and the numbers increased dramatically in 1989.[10] Meanwhile, urban poverty, virtually unknown since the 1950s, emerged rapidly; by 1988, as many as one-fifth of the *officially* urban population (excluding rural migrants) were below the poverty line.[11]

Inflation affected more than these. Over a third of urban households suffered a drop in real income in 1988; many more probably kept ahead of inflation only by working more hours at second and even third jobs. Unemployment and employment insecurity caused worry and privation for many urban residents.

The contrast with the apparent luxury enjoyed by the newly prosperous rankled. The greatest animus was reserved for those who had profited from the cornucopia of opportunities for corruption created by the reforms, and particularly from *guandao* (profiteering by party and state officials) as the source of huge riches for a few and huge losses for the rest of the country. Public resentment against such corruption by officials both high and low mounted steadily during the reform era, reaching a high pitch in 1988 and early 1989.

The two-track price system gave rise to unprecedented opportunities for corruption. Local authorities or enterprises who controlled the allocation of (low) fixed-price goods indulged in rounds of resales at ever higher prices. The introduction of management contracts in industry opened a new arena for corruption. Although such contracts were supposed to be subject to open bidding, some individuals bribed local authorities to secure them. Documents 12 and 13 provide some vivid examples of these corrupt dealings.

---

[8]The shift to lump-sum payments from provinces to Beijing introduced after 1984 left increasing funds in the hands of provincial and local authorities and enterprises in the faster-growing coastal areas, which meant further acceleration of their growth as they reinvested. Guangdong benefited more than other coastal areas, paying only about one-seventh the tax rate of Jiangsu Province, and only about one-ninth the rate of Shanghai Municipality. *Zhongguo qingnian yuebao* (China youth monthly) (June 1989), trans. in *Inside China Mainland* (November 1989): 5.

[9]Two Chinese scholars made an estimate of 244 million. *Pai Shing Yueh-k'an* (Commoners semimonthly), no. 210, February 1, 1990, pp. 21–22, trans. in *Inside China Mainland* (April 1990): 20–21.

[10]For an example of huge influxes into Hainan Island, see Guangzhou Guangdong Provincial Service, March 3, 1989, in FBIS, *Daily Report: China*, March 6, 1989, p. 57; Anita Chan, "The Reality behind the Cokes," *New Age Monthly* (October 1989): 14.

[11]*Pai Shing*, no. 210, February 1, 1990, p. 21.

Foreign trade and investment contracts with foreign businesses also offered rich pickings. The *Wall Street Journal* reported that it had become "almost standard practice to offer kickbacks."[12] The adult offspring of the very highest-ranking cadres were widely reputed to be the ranking "fixers" who, for rather hefty considerations, would circumvent bureaucratic procedures and other obstacles to get contracts signed. Deng Xiaoping's oldest son and two sons of Zhao Ziyang were all rumored to be up to their ears in corrupt deals, as were the adult offspring of innumerable provincial- and municipal-level officials. Some stories were undoubtedly true, some not. Politically, what mattered was that the Chinese-on-the-street was ready to believe all of them. Economically, what mattered was that far too many of the stories about corruption *were* true. Reform had become a trough from which the privileged could drink their fill at the expense of others. As Document 12 points out, lesser mortals all too often tended to emulate them on a smaller scale.

In the face of burgeoning economic problems, the country's leaders displayed anything but inspiring statesmanship. Initiatives on supposedly bold new price reforms were made repeatedly and then repeatedly withdrawn when each touched off worse inflation than the last. Finally, by fall 1988, the party leadership decided to put price reform on indefinite hold and announced a strict austerity program. But while that program contracted credit, employment, and incomes, inflation and corruption continued to flourish.

Underlying this impasse were two fundamental political quandaries. First, the top party leadership, including not only those occupying formal positions of power in the Politburo but also their mentors and sponsors, the "retired" elders, were deadlocked on economic reform. Deng Xiaoping had managed to patch together a reform coalition in the late 1970s, when the economy was doing so badly that something drastically different obviously had to be done about it. After all, as Deng had maintained in the early 1960s, it mattered not whether the cat was black or white; if it caught mice, it was a good cat. By the late 1980s, however, the reform cat's reputation as a mouser was tarnished. The more ardent reformers among the leadership took this to indicate that bolder reform was needed; the conservatives, that reform had failed and retrenchment was in order. As Document 10 shows, those observing this clash from the sidelines very much feared that a conservative backlash would roll the reforms back to the status quo ante. The deadlock among the leadership persisted right up until the eruption of the popular movement in April 1989. A Central Committee plenum slated for February 1989 was postponed and still had not been held by the time of Hu Yaobang's death on April 15—a strong indication of the leaders' inability to reach a consensus on any of the major economic policy issues.

Second, even those relatively lackluster policy decisions that the center made in September 1988 simply could not be enforced. Having relaxed controls over

---

[12]*Wall Street Journal*, July 20, 1989, p. A10.

localities and enterprises, Beijing found it virtually impossible to reassert them. Its inability to do so attested to its loss of both power and authority, and ultimately, to the increasing weakness of a political system that had failed to keep pace with the changes in the economic arena.

The Arrested Progress of Political Reform

The two main means of control over ordinary citizens during the Maoist era were the work unit (*danwei*) and political campaigns. The work unit controlled not only wages and bonuses, but also access to housing, education, medical benefits, consumer goods, certain foodstuffs, travel permits, and even marriage and divorce. Work units thus could manipulate such resources to extract compliance from their members under normal circumstances.

In extraordinary circumstances, and especially when certain central leaders (Mao usually figuring prominently among them) wanted to achieve results rapidly or break through bureaucratic obstacles, the campaign method was trotted out. The height of the Cultural Revolution in 1966–68 was the most extreme of such campaigns, but numerous campaigns large and small punctuated the period from 1949 to 1978. The modus operandi in a campaign was to identify a target for attack, usually some "class enemy," and then to mobilize all units to find representatives of this enemy in their midst and subject them to group denunciation and criticism, forcing them to confess and sometimes turning them over for imprisonment, labor reform, or execution. Few dared refuse to participate in the campaigns, for to do so was to risk being branded as the enemy as well.

In the immediate post-Mao era, the Chinese people's manifest revulsion over the arbitrary and disruptive campaigns of the late Maoist era led the ascendant reformist leadership under Deng Xiaoping to forswear campaigns entirely. Henceforth the party-state's coercive attentions would be administered through regular legal-bureaucratic channels. In the several years after the consolidation of the reform coalition's hold on power in 1978, as many as three million of those victimized in previous campaigns, as far back as the anti-Rightist campaign of the late 1950s, were rehabilitated.[13] Hu Yaobang's leading role in the rehabilitation process before ascending to the CCP general secretaryship was one major reason for his popularity among many cadres and intellectuals.

At the same time that campaigns declined as a means of control, the effectiveness of the work unit began to decline as well, as the resources under its control shrank while the employment, goods, and opportunities outside the life-long work unit channels expanded dramatically. The work unit still had considerable power, for good or ill, over its members, but its monopoly was broken.

It is in this context that one must view the progress of political reform in the

---

[13]Hui Duanmu, "China's Decade of Enlightenment," unpublished manuscript by Beijing intellectuals, written after the crackdown, 1989.

post-Mao era. The party-state voluntarily renounced its most effective means of coercive control and launched economic reforms undermining its principal means of remunerative control. Meanwhile, its proof-is-in-the-economic-pudding approach to its own legitimation spelled abandonment of the old means of normative control, the enforcement of ideological orthodoxy.

The removal of the political detritus of the Maoist era did not, however, proceed in linear fashion. Nor did the reconstruction of the political order on the basis of democracy, legality, and various other "modern" political virtues, embraced rhetorically by the party reformers. Invariably, moves in the direction of political reform failed to satisfy the reform constituency, while provoking backlash from party conservatives. The dance between reform and reaction was an unceasing one from the landmark Third Plenum of the Eleventh Central Committee (December 1978) until the outbreak of the popular movement in spring 1989.

On the reform side, several key meetings introduced the agenda for political reform:

1. The Third Plenum of the Eleventh Central Committee, in December 1978, stripped the remaining Maoists of power. It repudiated the use of class-struggle methods in mass campaigns and, by making "socialist modernization" the central thrust of the party's work in the new era, in effect repudiated the Maoist approach of "[ideological] politics in command."

2. At an enlarged Politburo meeting in August 1980, Deng outlined his proposals for political reform, singling out for elimination "bureaucratism, the excessive concentration of power, patriarchism, life-long tenure in official posts, and abuse of privilege . . . , [and] also alluded to the need to develop a high degree of democracy."[14]

3. The Sixth Plenum of the Eleventh Central Committee in June 1981 adopted a resolution that, in addition to passing a largely negative verdict on Mao's contributions after the mid-1950s, issued a call to "seek truth from facts" and to "emancipate our thinking," thus spelling the lifting of rigid ideological controls over permissible ideas and policies.

4. At the Thirteenth Party Congress (October–November 1987), Zhao Ziyang's work report called for a series of reforms in the political structure, including limiting the role and power of the party within state organs and increasing the independence of enterprise managers from party committees.[15]

There were strong limitations on political reform, however. It was clear almost from the outset that Deng Xiaoping himself had a bottom line. A "theoretical conference" of leading intellectuals in 1979, shortly after the Third Plenum,

---

[14]Tony Saich, "Reforming the Political Structure," in *Reforming the Revolution: China in Transition*, ed. Robert Benewick and Paul Wingrove (Houndsmills and London: Macmillan Education, 1988), p. 28.

[15]Ibid., p. 30.

tested the new ideological waters so boldly that Deng, in his closing address to the conference, was moved to raise for the first time the "Four Cardinal Principles" later enshrined in the state constitution.[16] These principles established the socialist economic system, the "dictatorship of the proletariat," the leading role of the CCP, and the primacy of Marxism–Leninism–Mao Zedong Thought as nonnegotiable underpinnings of the Chinese political order.

Second, even those political reforms that Deng personally promoted experienced heavy going, both in policy-making forums and in the implementation process. A case in point is Deng's August 1980 proposals, many of which were rejected by the Twelfth Party Congress in September 1982. Not until the Thirteenth Party Congress in 1987 was there a clear brief for reform of the political structure—and by then, proposals from the reform constituency, primarily intellectuals, had progressed far beyond the level of 1980. Both the progress and the limitations in political reform contributed to the political climate on the eve of the 1989 popular movement.

Reforms of the administrative apparatus and administrative methods of the party-state, seen as crucial to the success of the economic modernization program, were dear to Deng's bureaucratic heart. Ministries were revamped; central commissions to coordinate the work of several ministries were formed. The State Council and individual ministries set up think tanks to help generate and test new policy proposals. Younger, professionally and technically trained cadres were recruited into responsible party, state, and army posts. The average age of central and provincial-level leaders fell considerably. Older cadres were eased into retirement with more or less twisting of arms. At the central level, the Twelfth Party Congress in 1982 approved the formation of a Central Advisory Commission that would organize the talents and experience of superannuated leaders who agreed to retire, leaving them a regularized and legitimized advisory function while—theoretically—removing them from decision making. Similar advisory commissions were formed at lower levels of the hierarchy to entice lower-level cadres into retirement. But senior cadres at the central level proved reluctant to step down; major headway was not made until a party conference in fall of 1985, at which one hundred senior cadres collectively resigned.[17] Deng Xiaoping himself resigned most of his posts, eventually retaining only his chairmanship of the party's Military Affairs Commission. Also in 1985, a party-initiated restructuring of the military eliminated half the senior officer corps in one stroke.[18]

Legal reform was more easily put on paper. The country adopted a host of economic laws, a new penal code, a new civil code, and laws and regulations

---

[16]Interview with Su Shaozhi, July 1989.

[17]John Gardner, "The Politics of Transition," in *Reforming the Revolution*, ed. Benewick and Wingrove, p. 23.

[18]Saich, "Reforming the Political Structure," p. 45.

establishing an institutional infrastructure for the legal system. A new, fourth state constitution was adopted in December 1982.[19] Yet despite hoopla about the reinstatement of "socialist legality" and construction of a modern legal system, there were far too many indications that the laws were worth only the paper they were printed on.

First of all, law and legality were not ends in themselves but the handmaidens of economic development.[20] The principle of *étatisme*—the state's primacy over lesser legal entities—while somewhat muted, is itself codified. Valid economic contracts, for example, may be abrogated if they conflict with the "state plan," even when the plan postdates the contracts in question.[21]

Second, as the leading Chinese legal scholar Yu Haocheng observed, no amount of codification or constitutional "guarantees" prevented abuses of citizens' rights so long as the legal authorities acted outside the law. Regulations enacted in the 1980s stipulated that the police could make no arrests without a procurator's approval; instead of "arresting," therefore, they "detained" people. Administrative sentencing to labor reform without trial remained legal, but even once their labor reform terms expired, prisoners were being kept "without legal basis."[22] And, whatever the law, some were less answerable to it than others, as Document 12 makes clear. Investigative officials are often the hierarchical subordinates of some of those whom they are charged with investigating, and they pursue cases of wrongdoing by superiors or their associates at considerable personal risk. At all levels, judicial authorities often found their hands tied when it came to enforcing court decisions unless they had the active support of their party and governmental (nonjudicial) superiors.[23]

Calls for improved legal protection of individual rights mounted in the late 1980s. By late 1988 and early 1989, some also began to clamor for constitutional revision (see Doc. 10). Some wanted more explicit constitutional guarantees of individual freedoms (including property rights); others saw constitutional revision as the avenue for redefining the role of the Communist party within the state system, and for curbing the power of arbitrary government *or* party action. In this respect, the agitation for legal and constitutional reform increasingly converged with the thrust of expanded popular political participation.

The post-Mao regime promised the separation of party and governmental functions from an early date. Elections and regular meetings of representative assemblies were one of the first steps taken in this direction. Elections for county

---

[19]Yves Dolais, "Tendances récentes du droit en Chine" (Recent trends in Chinese law), *Revue Tiers-monde*, no. 108 (October–December 1986): 868.

[20]Ibid., p. 867.

[21]David Zweig et al., "Law, Contracts, and Economic Modernization in China," *Stanford Journal of International Law* 23, 2 (1987): 327–28.

[22]*Wen hui bao*, January 14, 1989, in JPRS, *China Report*, May 3, 1989, p. 7.

[23]See Zweig et al., "Law, Contracts, and Economic Modernization," p. 353n, for a local-level example.

people's congresses were held in 1980 (the first in thirteen years), 1984, and 1987. Delegates to the congresses were directly elected, as were those to congresses at subcounty levels. Although party authorities still approved the nominations lists, there was some competition in the elections, with candidates exceeding the number of posts by one-third to one-half.[24] Nominally such congresses were to be the supreme organs of power at each level of government, selecting the chief members of the executive, passing major legislation, and selecting (at county and municipal levels) delegates to the National People's Congress. In practice, the congresses met infrequently, had too many members and far too many inexperienced or illiterate members to transact business carefully, and generally meekly rubber-stamped nominations and legislation decided in advance by party authorities.

The charge of rubber-stamping was applied as well to the two national-level "representative" bodies, the National People's Congress (NPC) and the Chinese People's Political Consultative Congress (CPPCC). The CPPCC is an advisory body that represents, far more than the NPC, the range of variation in the Chinese population.[25] The NPC, like the congresses at lower levels, is supposed to be the supreme governmental body but meets only once a year for about two weeks. Between plenary sessions, the NPC's Standing Committee, with a membership of approximately two hundred, is empowered to adopt legislation and supervise the work of the government (i.e., the State Council).[26]

The plenary sessions of the NPC and the CPPCC in spring 1988 featured lively debates, outspoken delegates, and some refreshingly open press coverage of both. Delegates publicly aired their dissatisfaction with a wide range of trends, legitimate and illegitimate. Some revealed that, contrary to official assurances from the center, IOUs given to peasants in lieu of payment for fall 1987 deliveries had not been redeemed, and enormous sums were still outstanding. Delegates from interior provinces complained of losing out under the policies favoring coastal areas. Numerous denunciations of *guandao* (profiteering by party and state officials) were made, illustrated with specific examples. Inflation was sharply attacked.

Perhaps this bad publicity prompted the center's attempt to keep the lid on at the March 1989 sessions. Two of the more liberal press organs, including the Shanghai-based *Shijie jingji daobao* (World economic herald), were denied press credentials for the sessions. Some Hong Kong journalists were also excluded. Delegates were "requested" not to hold independent press conferences or to voice their complaints too volubly. "Stability and unity" were the watchwords of

---

[24]Robert Benewick, "Political Participation," in *Reforming the Revolution*, ed. Benewick and Wingrove, p. 59.

[25]Certain constituencies—urbanites, intellectuals, and CCP members in particular—are greatly overrepresented in both bodies.

[26]Saich, "Reforming the Political Structure," p. 40.

the day. And yet, although the debates (or press reports on them) were less rambunctious than in the preceding year, debates there were. Li Peng, presenting a government work report heavily emphasizing the country's economic problems and the leadership's responsibility for the "errors" in 1988 that worsened those problems, came in for a grilling by delegates. The usual complaints from various different constituencies emerged. Some Hong Kong delegates and one courageous delegate elected by Qinghua University in Beijing raised human rights concerns. Of special interest, some delegates began pressing for the NPC and its Standing Committee to fulfill in earnest their constitutionally decreed watchdog function.[27] Wan Li, chairman of the Standing Committee, underwent heavy criticism for the organ's failure to perform that function, and he even voiced a *mea culpa* in a speech before the full body. Still, he raised a thorny question: "How should the NPC give full play to its supervisory role under the unified leadership of the party [according to the language of the constitution]? . . . I have not yet solved this question."[28] Perhaps he and others already had begun to realize that the NPC's "supervisory role under the unified leadership of the party" was nothing but a particularly tortured oxymoron.

Participation and debate outside such officially sanctioned forums, and beyond the officially sanctioned ideological bounds, persisted throughout the post-Mao era despite repeated suppression. The most public debates came in the form of "movements," periods when discussion rose to a high pitch, bold political proposals were presented in big-character posters and unofficial publications, and protest marches, demonstrations, and petitions were organized. The first major movement of the post-Mao era was of course the Democracy Wall Movement of late 1978 and early 1979, centered in Beijing. In its early phase, the movement assisted Deng's rise to power, but by early 1979 democracy activists began to propose an end to the party's political monopoly, and Deng saw to their muzzling. Some of the movement's leaders were sentenced without trial to labor reform camps; the leading activist, Wei Jingsheng, was tried for purportedly giving military information to a foreigner. He was sentenced to fifteen years in prison, thus becoming China's most famous political prisoner in the post-Mao era. When in early 1989 leading intellectuals began to agitate for recognition of human rights, several petitions addressed to Deng Xiaoping, the NPC, and other bodies were organized asking for the release of Wei Jingsheng and other political prisoners (see Doc. 6).

After a lull in the early 1980s, democratic activism increased again, usually centering almost exclusively among intellectuals and university communities. In 1985, the fiftieth anniversaries of the Japanese seizure of East Hebei and Chahar

---

[27]FBIS, *Daily Report: China*, from March 22 to April 6, 1989, carries translations of numerous reports on specific debates and complaints.

[28]Beijing Domestic Service, April 1, 1989, in FBIS, *Daily Report: China*, April 3, 1989, p. 29.

and of the subsequent December 9 Movement sparked student demonstrations, whereupon some of those who had been ringleaders in the original December 9 demonstrations appealed to students to "study hard to save the country"—the very appeal made to them by Guomindang authorities in 1935. Some of the protesters, however, believed that "saving the country" necessitated greater democracy, and certainly the honoring of existing constitutional guarantees of personal and political freedoms.[29] In late 1986, attempts by authorities in Hefei, Anhui Province, to prevent students from running for local office touched off protest marches. These rapidly spread to other cities; in Shanghai, some fifty thousand students hit the streets. Eventually the movement reached Beijing, where students demonstrated on January 1 in Tiananmen Square in defiance of a government ban. Some called for instituting a multiparty system, but most of the movement's participants backed the more limited political reform that they saw Deng as promoting.[30] In late 1988, an incident at a Hehai University dance sparked ostensibly anti-African marches and protests in Nanjing and other cities. To what extent the avowed purposes of these protests were merely smokescreens for venting more general dissatisfaction it is impossible to ascertain, but apparently some of those involved cared more about inflation, lack of job prospects, official corruption, and the stagnation of reforms than they did about the alleged state favoritism toward foreign students.[31] China's minority nationalities also grew restive over their own grievances. Uighur students in Beijing protested atomic testing in Xinjiang. In Tibet, the suppression of demonstrations after the death of the Panchen Lama touched off rioting, which led to the imposition of martial law.

The authorities met dissent and democratic agitation with varying degrees of sternness. After suppression of the Democracy Wall Movement, the guarantee of the public's right to post big-character posters was removed from the constitution. In 1983, at the insistence of conservatives angered by the erosion of orthodox Marxism's hold on intellectual life, the party launched an anti–"spiritual pollution" campaign, conducted through bureaucratic action and a propaganda drive aimed at eradicating the polluting influence of foreign bourgeois ideas that had slipped in through the open door. Some prominent intellectuals were victimized by this campaign.[32] The chill inflicted on academic and intellectual life was palpable; many feared that another witch hunt was imminent. The campaign was called to a halt within a year when it became clear that it was having a deleterious impact on economic reforms and on Westerners' willingness to do busi-

---

[29]For background on student unrest, see FBIS, *Daily Report: China*, December 13, 1985, pp. W1–W3.

[30]Robin Munro, "Political Reform, Student Demonstrations and the Conservative Backlash," in *Reforming the Revolution*, ed. Benewick and Wingrove, pp. 71–72.

[31]Based on conversations in Nanjing, January 1989.

[32]Hui Duanmu, "China's Decade of Enlightenment," p. 17.

ness.[33] In the end, Hu Yaobang is said to have been the critical factor, persuading Deng that the campaign was counterproductive.

Hu himself fell victim to the next major wave of conservative reaction, for having resisted demands to suppress the student movement of 1986–87. Accused of fostering "bourgeois liberalization" by his leniency, Hu was forced to resign from his post as the party's general secretary, to be replaced by Zhao Ziyang. Several prominent party intellectuals also became targets of the backlash: Fang Lizhi, then vice-president of the Chinese University of Science and Technology in Hefei, in which position he supported the student protesters; Liu Binyan, China's leading and boldest journalist; and Wang Ruowang, another outspoken writer. All three were booted out of the party.[34] Those who had spearheaded the 1986–87 demonstrations were sentenced to prison or labor reform.

Thus, by 1988 there was no dearth of evidence on the risks run by those pressing for political reform. Yet calls for reform persisted and once more grew bold. They were given a boost in 1988 by the relative leniency of officialdom toward maverick publications, by the officially sponsored debate over a controversial television series, by the changes in Eastern Europe and the Soviet Union, and by the furor over a new political "theory" purporting to offer a route out of China's developmental impasse.

Currents of Political Change

By late 1988 the discussion of political issues was open, intense, and widespread. Numerous conferences on the subject of reform were held, their proceedings widely reported. More private and unreserved discussion went on at a number of "salons" (*shalong*) organized for the exploration of political ideas, most notable among these the "New Enlightenment Salon" organized in late January 1989. Other discussion groups were organized throughout educated circles, some of private citizens, some of highly placed cadres, mostly in their thirties and forties.[35] Western visitors to China in late 1988 and early 1989 reported that the range and openness of views expressed by Chinese friends and colleagues were astounding.

The official press, while still controlled by the CCP's Propaganda Department, enjoyed relatively relaxed constraints. Newspapers like *Nongmin ribao*

---

[33]Maurice Meisner, *Mao's China and After* (New York: Free Press, 1986), p. 489n.

[34]Munro, "Political Reform," p. 74.

[35]Hartford interview with Su Shaozhi, July 1989; Chen Xitong, "Report to NPC on Quelling the Counter-Revolutionary Rebellion," in *Beijing Spring 1989: Confrontation and Conflict, The Basic Documents*, ed. Michel Oksenberg, Lawrence R. Sullivan, and Marc Lambert (Armonk, NY: M. E. Sharpe, 1990); Jiang Zhifeng, *Countdown to Tiananmen: The View at the Top* (San Francisco: Democratic Books and Pacific News Services, 1990).

(Peasants' daily), *Gongren ribao* (Workers' daily), and *Zhongguo qingnian bao* (China youth daily) featured remarkably outspoken reports on problems and issues of concern to their readership. More intellectually oriented publications like *Xin guancha* (New observer) and the Shanghai-based *Shijie jingji daobao* (World economic herald) attracted numerous readers with their bold reportage and commentaries by leading thinkers on reform. Some of those thinkers, not content with the forum afforded by official publications, founded a new publication called *Xin qimeng* (New enlightenment).[36] To get around the regulations on periodical publications, they issued groups of articles as a series of books. Other book series (some bona fide monographs, some journals in disguise) popped up. Many of these explored Western political and economic theories and institutions in detail.

Among the official press, the *World Economic Herald* took perhaps the greatest risks, publishing inter alia a controversial article from the Theoretical Discussion Meeting on the Ten Years of Reform sponsored by the Central Committee in December 1988. At that conference, although the CCP's Propaganda Department tried to keep discussion within bounds, the iconoclastic Marxist theoretician Su Shaozhi raised sharp criticisms of the anti–bourgeois liberalization campaign and the punishments inflicted on certain individuals. When Su's conference paper was omitted from the proceedings, the *World Economic Herald* decided to run it, albeit with some of the more inflammatory passages omitted. The publication nevertheless enraged Hu Qili, the Politburo's leading member for propaganda affairs. Because of this and similar publications, the Propaganda Department was said to have listed a number of intellectuals for official repudiation, including Su, political scientist Yan Jiaqi, jurist Yu Haocheng, Wang Ruoshui (a former deputy editor of *Renmin ribao* [People's daily] fired during the anti–spiritual pollution campaign), and the economist Yu Guangyuan. Apparently an instruction by Deng Xiaoping forestalled this move, but this only further encouraged intellectual critics in the belief that freedom of speech and debate might expand.[37]

Political debate in China has for centuries clothed itself in controversies over ostensibly nonpolitical, or at least noncontemporary, subjects, and political debate in the People's Republic has followed this pattern. Such apparently academic controversies permit the oblique statement of potentially risky views under a rhetorical cloak of rich metaphors for contemporary political issues. Just such an opportunity arose out of *He shang* (River elegy), a six-part television series aired throughout China twice during 1988 (Doc. 5). The series excoriated China's traditional culture (represented by the Yellow River) for holding the

---

[36]Four issues of *Xin qimeng* were published between October 1988 and April 1989.

[37]*Chiu-shi nien-tai* (The nineties), no. 230, March 1, 1989, pp. 53–55, in FBIS, *Daily Report: China*, March 2, 1989, pp. 15–16; Hartford interview with Su Shaozhi, July 1989.

country back in the modern era, orienting it inward and to the past while the West and Japan moved outward and into the future. Only by rejecting and sloughing off that traditional culture and taking on the modern world (i.e., Western) culture, represented by the "blue ocean," would China be able to take its place in the world of the late twentieth century. Among educated Chinese, the series was an overnight success; some considered it the single most important cultural event in the PRC's history. But it provoked a storm of criticism and debate, egged on by the disapproval expressed by conservative officials such as Wang Zhen. In the fall of 1988, newspapers and journals throughout China carried articles about the series, while universities provided copies of the script and commentaries to students and faculty for small-group political study. Running through much of the commentary, as through the series itself, was a strong thread of political analysis. In the guise of assessing traditional culture, Chinese of all political persuasions could publicly air their views on the place of "authority" and "stability" (pro) or "feudal despotism" (con) in the political system, as well as deliberate the relative merits of reform or wholesale rejection of Chinese culture—including political culture.[38]

The debate begun over *River Elegy* glissaded, in late 1988, into a controversy over the "theory" of "Neo-authoritarianism," first floated by some of Zhao Ziyang's bright young brain trusts and then picked up by some more conservative proponents. As initially conceived, Neo-authoritarianism was supposedly based on the experiences of Taiwan, Singapore, and South Korea and on the ideas of the American political scientist Samuel Huntington, but exponents often got both the facts and the ideas wrong. The basic proposition was that authoritarian leadership (or an authoritarian leader) was necessary to facilitate rapid economic modernization and to maintain political stability during that process; democratization could only come after the economic and social transformations into modernity had been achieved. Premature democratization invited instability and anarchy and would impede economic development.[39] The ostensible purpose of Neo-authoritarianism was to provide an appropriately Asian "modernizing" political "theory" that could counter the growing clamor for Western-style political reform and democratization. Many observers suspected, however, that the real purpose as first conceived by Zhao was to provide a justification for buttressing his own power within the political system.

Although the first calls for Neo-authoritarianism alarmed reform elements, including many of Zhao's own supporters, the publicity given the theory ironically generated a golden opportunity for advocates of democratic reform to air

---

[38]See *China Information* 4, 3 (Winter 1989–90): 28–55. For a small sampling of commentary translated into English, see *Inside China Mainland* (January 1989): 1–10. More extensive commentary may be found in articles translated in FBIS, *Daily Report: China* throughout the fall of 1989. Leslie Swartz provided details on the small-group study sessions.

[39]See Oksenberg et al., eds., *Beijing Spring*, docs. 7–13.

their own critiques of the existing system and present detailed proposals for reform. While some of the debate remained at a theoretical level, for example, in analyzing the relationship between economic and political modernization or in establishing the need for a reliable system rather than a virtuous ruler, much of the discussion got quite concrete. Among the major political reform ideas voiced during this debate were the principles basic to democratic governance (parliamentarianism, majority rule, minority rights, observance of legal procedures in selecting and replacing leaders), the rights of citizens (equality before the law, the right of the public to be informed, the right to supervise leaders, the right to "know, discuss, and participate in state affairs"—that is, freedom of speech, assembly, association, and the press), and the nature of modern policy making ("scientific," "democratic," and "transparent") (see docs. 1, 2, and 3).[40] The debate also permitted counterattacks assailing autocracy as the root of both political *and* economic ills in China, for intensifying the arbitrariness of power that had helped generate the current economic crisis.

The unfolding of dramatic political changes in Eastern Europe and the Soviet Union lent added force to the Chinese demands for reform. For the first half of the 1980s, because of the bold economic initiatives taken under Deng, China could pride itself on being in the forefront on socialist reforms. Even as the reforms got stuck from 1985 on, it could still claim to have gone further than any of its sister systems. But by 1989, the rapid pace of political change elsewhere was obviously leaving China far behind, at a time when the economic reforms were headed nowhere but backward or into disaster (or both). Meanwhile, Poland's government had acceded to "round table" discussions during which the Polish Communist party yielded ground to the Solidarity organization on economic policy, citizens' rights, and the structure of the political system. By April 1989, the Jaruzelski government agreed to free elections permitting Solidarity and other opposition parties to contest over a third of the seats in the lower house of the parliament, and all seats in the upper house. In Hungary, the tiny dissident movement had grown apace since the thirtieth anniversary of the 1956 revolution. Janos Kadar, the Hungarian Socialist Workers' party general secretary since the Soviet invasion of that year, was forced to resign in spring 1988. The Hungarian Socialist Workers' party began to crumble from within, while opposition pressures mounted from without. A new law early in 1989 guaranteeing freedom of association cleared the way for concerted and open organization by the existing dissident groups and a number of new ones. In the Soviet Union, Mikhail Gorbachev had introduced political reforms culminating in elections for the new Congress of People's Deputies, which was to enjoy real legislative

---

[40]Numerous articles for and against Neo-authoritarianism may be found translated in FBIS during late 1988 and early 1989, right up to the outbreak of the popular movement in April. For a representative sampling of articles against, see various articles in FBIS, *Daily Report: China*, March 29, 1989, pp. 39–42.

powers. In late March 1989, elections to that body resulted in resounding defeats of many prominent CPSU officials, including some who had been running for uncontested seats.[41]

Reports on such developments reached urban China through Voice of America and BBC broadcasts, articles in scholarly publications, and news stories in the national and local press. The contrast between the pace of political reform in Eastern Europe and the USSR and the lack of movement in China was lost on no one, and interest was heightened by Gorbachev's projected visit in May 1989. The revival of reform in the Soviet Union, Poland, and Hungary helped foster the belief that political change was not only possible, but inevitable. This was the paradoxical benefit of falling behind in the march of change: instead of leading the way into the unknown, China could now follow the path charted by others into a more certain future (Doc. 7).

The analogy with Eastern Europe and the Soviet Union added another string to the bow of critics of the CCP monopoly on power. The tradition of "feudal autocracy" was not alone responsible for China's developmental difficulties; as in its sister socialist systems, Stalinism had been grafted onto the traditional autocracy and borne poisonous fruit (Doc. 1). This "existing socialism" bore only superficial resemblance to the socialism envisioned by Karl Marx; it was a travesty rather than a Sinification of socialism that had been achieved. Zhao Ziyang's formulation of "the initial stage of socialism," introduced at the Thirteenth Party Congress, had acknowledged this to some extent, but what Zhao envisioned in the political realm was to allow more backseat driving but with the CCP still in the driver's seat. Crusading political reformers went much further. Smashing Stalinism meant not only "freedoms" but also pluralism, organized opposition, and—though few dared state this logical corollary outright—a multiparty system (see docs. 1 and 7).[42]

Currents of Reaction

As the pressures for political reform grew, so did the intensity of conservative reaction. The CCP conservatives could seize on numerous signals that continued leniency toward dissent, ideological and social laxity, and the open door to the West threatened to erode the underpinnings of China's political and social order.

Certainly there is every indication that, by the late 1980s, the prestige and

---

[41]On the rapidly evolving developments in Eastern Europe and the Soviet Union, see Bernard Gwertzman and Michael T. Kaufman, eds., *The Collapse of Communism* (New York: Times Books, 1990), and the chronology provided in Karen Dawisha, *Eastern Europe, Gorbachev and Reform: The Great Challenge*, 2d ed. (Cambridge: Cambridge University Press, 1990), esp. pp. 284–85.

[42]Zhao himself rejected the notion of a multiparty system. *Zhongguo tongxunshe* (China news service), March 2, 1989, in FBIS, *Daily Report: China*, March 2, 1989, p. 17.

legitimacy restored to the party by the early success of reforms had begun to decline precipitously. A 1987 nationwide poll provides a glimpse of the general climate of opinion. Although slightly over half the respondents claimed to be proud they "belong to a socialist country," 62 percent had a negative image of the CCP—as did 69 percent of the cadres! Fewer than 60 percent of party members claimed pride in party membership.[43]

While the future of the party's leading role in the body politic was a matter of worry for conservatives, changes in the society and culture intensified their sense of urgency about remedying the situation. All around them they could see the old spartan-socialist ethos evaporating, particularly among those under forty. The mode of dress, aspirations, uses of leisure time, and moral principles (or lack of them) of younger Chinese departed dramatically from those of their elders. For many, the new wealthy entrepreneurs had become role models, the roles consisting largely of conspicuous consumption. Virtually everything Western carried a cachet, and young Chinese came increasingly into contact with things Western as foreign investment, economic and cultural exchanges, and tourism brought a large influx of Westerners to even the remotest parts of the country. Exhibitions of avant-garde art, the popularity of rock music and Chinese rock stars, the runaway sales of martial-arts novels and other works judged dissolute or pornographic, and the prevalence of serious theater and fictional works exploring the alienation and sterility of life in contemporary China offended conservative sensibilities.

Many Chinese, both young and old, saw indications of cultural and moral bankruptcy. As economic and social structures shifted without a solid center emerging, all the old certainties vanished without replacement. At all levels of the society, in all endeavors, Chinese increasingly operated in a "moral vacuum" (docs. 5 and 13), which the repeated calls for establishing some abstract "socialist spiritual civilization" seemed only to accentuate. Money became the new currency of status, power, and self-esteem. For the conservatives, the vigor of the attacks against *River Elegy* came not merely from the sense that the culture was in trouble (a sense shared by many reformers, including the creators of the television series), but from the belief that it was the new rather than the old elements on the contemporary scene that accounted for the depth of the moral crisis.

If official corruption excited popular disapprobation, criminal activity among the masses exacerbated the worries of conservative leaders. As private employment and market opportunities flourished, so too did illegal currency dealings, drug trade, prostitution, and violent crime. In 1988, the incidence of serious crime rose alarmingly; robbery cases increased by 43 percent, and "serious larceny," by 64 percent. In the same year, fifty thousand were arrested for prostitution, in a country that ten years previously could boast of having none. The rise

---

[43]*Pai Shing*, March 16, 1989, no. 188, pp. 9–10, trans. in *Inside China Mainland* (May 1989): 2–4.

in crime was particularly pronounced in those areas modernizing most rapidly: "cities, coastal areas, and along communications lines."[44] Conservatives tended to blame "aliens" for the upsurge. One source claimed that transients committed about half the crimes in coastal and urban areas; another blamed "foreign decadent ideas and culture" for much of the increase.[45]

In late 1988 and early 1989, encouraged by the rollback on economic reforms represented by the austerity program, party conservatives began more determinedly to counter the pressures for political reform. The public statements deploring *River Elegy* and the numerous articles favoring Neo-authoritarianism were not the only instances of this counterattack. Some reform proponents found the climate at the Theoretical Discussion Meeting on the Ten Years of Reform a chilling indication of the resurgence of the CCP Propaganda Department's reassertion of ideological controls; to these people, Su Shaozhi's forthright statements were the exception rather than the rule, and the conference was on balance a defeat for academic freedom. Their pessimism was amply confirmed by the suppression of New Enlightenment Publishers. *Zhongguo qingnian bao* (China youth daily) and *Zhongguo qingnian* (China youth) were censured for taking too "radical" an approach over the impending anniversary of the May Fourth Movement (Doc. 1). The government also issued a circular forbidding the publication of journals in book form. The Beijing CCP vice-secretary criticized the New Enlightenment Salon, accusing its founders of planning to start a new political party, a serious and potentially dangerous charge in the PRC.[46]

Many in the party establishment considered 1989 an especially delicate year. In a culture that attributed great significance to anniversaries, three highly loaded anniversaries would coincide in the same year: the fortieth anniversary of the establishment of the People's Republic, the seventieth anniversary of the May Fourth Movement, and the two hundredth anniversary of the French Revolution. The latter two were particularly rich in possibilities for recollecting, under the umbrella of officially sanctioned observances, the gap between the modern, Western, democratic values represented in the historical event and the contemporary Chinese reality. This point was not lost on either proponents or opponents of reform. Both sides had begun preparing for a symbolic showdown. Probably none anticipated the speed and magnitude of the transition from symbolism to reality.

---

[44]Xinhua, March 29, 1989, in FBIS, *Daily Report: China*, March 29, 1989, pp. 15, 24; *Zhongguo tongxunshe*, March 29, 1989, in FBIS, *Daily Report: China*, March 30, 1989, p. 25.
   [45]Xinhua, March 29, 1989, in FBIS, *Daily Report: China*, March 29, 1989, p. 24; Hefei Anhui Provincial Service, February 27, 1989, in FBIS, *Daily Report: China*, March 10, 1989, p. 34.
   [46]Interview with Su Shaozhi, July 1989, and with an intellectual in Beijing who must remain anonymous, January 1989; *South China Morning Post*, March 23, 1989, p. 1, in FBIS, *Daily Report: China*, March 23, 1989, p. 53.

Out of Nowhere: Genesis of the Student Movement

Students, meanwhile, had been fairly though not totally quiescent. Most educated Chinese, students included, tended to characterize the current college and secondary-school generation as apathetic and apolitical. In describing the college generation, both students and their elders often referred to two "factions," in a play on words on the old pre-1949 distinction between orthodox "Marxist" (*mapai*) and "Trotskyite" (*tuopai*) factions. The new *mapai* were those who spent all their time playing mah-jongg; the new *tuopai*, those who devoted their energies to studying for the TOEFL (Test of English as a Foreign Language), hoping for an opportunity to go abroad. The former tended to view the future as pretty hopeless and saw no possibility of academic effort offering a chance for a better life. The latter saw their best hope in getting out of China, at least for a long spell of study, and often permanently.

And yet a few hardy souls not only kept a political flame alive on campus, but planned to fan it as soon as the opportunity presented itself. Surrounded by a sea of at best cowed and at worst crassly self-centered peers, they organized a core of activists and began analyzing China's situation and the possibilities of acting upon it. The best known of these, at Beijing University, became the leadership core for the April student demonstrations. They had begun their activities well in advance, particularly in preparation for nonofficially sanctioned activities around the May Fourth anniversary. Some of them had been through the movements of 1985 or 1986, recognized the reasons for the lack of continuity in the student protest movements, and hoped to remedy these through careful education and advance planning. Wang Dan, a history major, organized democracy salons at the university that featured sometimes relatively unknown speakers, sometimes more famous dissidents like Li Shuxian, the wife of astrophysicist Fang Lizhi. Shen Tong and a handful of other students formed a group that engaged in a comprehensive analysis of the economic, political, and social forces for change in China and the exploitable opportunities for coalescing them, utilizing a network of contacts throughout urban China.[47] Wang Dan also wrote some bold analyses on reform that appeared in the campus publication *New May Fourth* (docs. 7 and 8).

Most, however, refrained from political discussion and activity except, perhaps, in very private surroundings. The authorities took every possible step to keep them that way. For the most part, until the storm of emotion evoked by the death of Hu Yaobang, students, like most of their fellow Chinese, remained quiet. But in the setting of late 1980s' China, this was the quiet not of contentment, but of despair. Reform, which had promised so much, had unleashed

---

[47]Based partly on presentation by Shen Tong at Harvard University in April 1990. The activities of Wang Dan's salon were more public and better known.

economic crisis, moral corruption, and political standoff. No one knew what would work; some thought they knew nothing would work. As one young intellectual remarked in early 1989 when queried about the chances that political reform could solve the economic reform problems, "Nothing but a revolution will fix this place." He could not have known how many would soon agree with him.

DOCUMENTS FOR SUMMER 1988–SPRING 1989

Descendants of the Dragon
In the remote Orient there is a river
called the Yangzi River
In the remote Orient there is a river
called the Yellow River

Though we've never seen the beauty of the Yangzi
we often dream of it at night
Though we've never heard the roaring of the Yellow
it's roaring in our hearts

In the remote Orient there is a dragon
whose name is China
In the remote Orient there is a group of people
who are descendants of the dragon

With black eyes, black hair, and yellow skin they are
descendants of the dragon grown up. . . .
—Hou Dejian[1]

---

[1]This song was a popular hit first in Taiwan. The author/performer Hou Dejian later moved to the mainland, where he became a leading rock star. His lyrics express great respect for the ancestors of China and pride in being their descendants. In this sense, the lyrics contrast with the cultural iconoclasm of works such as *River Elegy. Descendants of the Dragon* was sung on the square throughout the demonstrations. Hou himself was one of four leading figures who declared a protest hunger strike on June 2 (see Doc. 178).

1

What Will the Year 1989 Tell Us?

SU SHAOZHI ET AL.

Source: *Zhongguo qingnian* (China youth) (January 1989): 2–3.

To hundreds of thousands of Chinese, especially to those Chinese youth who are determined to plunge themselves into the reforms, 1989 has a special meaning: this is a year of great historical anniversaries. This year, we will commemorate the fortieth anniversary of the founding of the People's Republic of China, the seventieth anniversary of the May Fourth Movement, and the bicentennial of the French Revolution.[1] Seemingly there is no direct connection among these three anniversaries. One is the anniversary of the birth of New China; one, of the beginning of the New Culture Movement; and one, of the rise of the bourgeois revolution in Europe. They nevertheless have a common theme, namely, denouncing feudal despotism and carrying forward the spirit of democracy and science. The birth of a new China indicates that the principle of the people's democratic republic has been formally affirmed in China; and it puts an end to China's humiliation in modern times as a semicolonial and semifeudal society. The May Fourth Movement sounded a clarion call to struggle against feudal despotism in modern China when a group of advanced intellectuals began to recognize the miserable status of the Chinese nation and of the Chinese individual. The French Revolution achieved one of the greatest victories in the most inexorable struggle against

---

[1]The author of this document, Su Shaozhi, was director of the Institute of Marxism–Leninism–Mao Zedong Thought in Beijing until demoted in the conservative backlash after the suppression of the 1986–87 democracy demonstrations. He continued as a researcher in that institute until leaving China after the 1989 crackdown began. His attempts to modernize Marxist thinking for contemporary Chinese conditions became well known. At the nationwide symposium on the ten years of reform, held in December 1988, he delivered a speech so remarkable for its frank discussion of shortcomings in the system that it was censored before publication in *World Economic Herald*. (For text of this speech, see Su Shaozhi, "Speech at the Theoretical Discussion Meeting Marking the Tenth Anniversary of the Third Plenary Session of the Eleventh CPC Central Committee," December 26, 1989, in *Beijing Spring*, ed. Oksenberg et al., Doc. 14.) Su and some of his associates were engaged in a series of comparative studies of socialist systems before the 1989 popular movement began, and he himself had traveled to Eastern Europe for research on this topic. The references to the common problems and experiences of "existing socialism" (a term commonly used to refer to the socialist systems as they actually operate rather than as theoretical constructs) undoubtedly reflect his conversations with East Europeans grappling with these issues as well as his own observations.

feudal despotism in the history of mankind. The "Declaration of the Rights of Man" showed that humanitarianism and the spirit of reason had replaced medieval religiosity and the spirit of despotism as the leading forces in society and history.

May Fourth is a holiday for young people. Seventy years ago, "Mr. Science" and "Mr. Democracy" were the banner and slogans of *New Youth* magazine.[2] Seventy years later, *China Youth* still finds itself constantly revealing things as depressing as those described in the trilogy *Family, Spring, and Autumn.*[3] Indeed, feudal despotism all along has exerted an influence on our society. The immense contrast between the ideals of the May Fourth Movement and the reality of China today especially merits reflection and vigilance by contemporary Chinese youth.

No Chinese of conscience can fail to recognize the fact that democracy and science in China today are extremely incomplete. On the difficult road to democracy and science in China, feudal despotism has always been the number one enemy. The "ghost" of this old system, of this old society, and of this old ethic is frequently to be found wandering about today, and by constantly changing its appearance, it continues to exert its influence on our society. Feudal despotism is by no means just a rotten remnant. It is a potentially powerful force and ideological pattern. Today, feudal despotism is manifested on three different levels. First, it is old moral teachings and ethical norms, such as the superstitious activities, the cardinal guides, and the constant virtues[4] specified in the feudal ethical code that persist in the Chinese countryside and in backward areas. Second, it is an old political-ideological pattern and cultural despotism, such as the suppression of criticism and retaliation against opponents by "giving someone tight shoes to wear," "declaring the forbidden zones," and "coming down with the big stick on someone." Third, it is manifested as something institutionalized and normalized, such as the monopolistic ownership structure and the system of administrative control and manipulation of factories. These are so deeply rooted that they have obstructed the progress of Messrs. "Democracy" and "Science." If feudal despotism is not toppled, there is no hope for democracy and science in China.

One cannot help asking one question: Why, after several decades of struggle

---

[2]This magazine, started by Chen Duxiu, later one of the founding members and head of the Chinese Communist party, was very influential in introducing younger Chinese intellectuals to a wide range of ideas on modernizing Chinese culture. Chen Duxiu popularized the idea of "Mr. Science" and "Mr. Democracy" as the key to solving China's problems and reviving it culturally.

[3]This trilogy by Ba Jin, perhaps the most famous of twentieth-century Chinese novels, describes the oppressive weight of the traditional Chinese family system for Chinese youth.

[4]The three cardinal guides are ruler guides subject; father guides son; husband guides wife. The five constant virtues are benevolence, righteousness, propriety, wisdom, and fidelity.

against imperialism and feudalism, and after decades of building up socialism, is feudal despotism still so deeply ingrained and incorrigibly obstinate? It is no coincidence that the Soviet Union and Eastern European countries are probing into the same question. It has forced us to seek, in the origins, characteristics, and structures of existing socialism, an understanding of its essential problems.

First of all, contrary to what Marx and other authors of classical works [of Marxism] generally predicted, existing socialist society is not a real "post-capitalist society" but a society born of "precapitalist society" (serfdom, feudal, or semicolonial society). Thus this society, in its economic, political, cultural, ethical, and many other aspects, is unavoidably stamped with the brand of the old system. It also necessarily lacks some of the progressive elements of contemporary and modern capitalism. For example, it lacks the deep influence of the [European] Renaissance, Enlightenment, or Reformation. It lacks elements of the modern political economy, such as economic liberalism; and it lacks the idea of checks and balances, general elections, and parliamentarianism.

Second, the reason why feudal despotism is particularly tenacious and powerful in existing socialism is that the Stalinist model and the special measures used by Communists in the era of revolutionary war provided certain conditions and convenience for the existence and growth of feudal despotism. On the one hand, Stalinism and feudal despotism can be traced to the same origins: They are mutually reinforcing in their patterns of thought and behavior, and they have produced the same structure and content. On the other hand, once the [concepts of] "an all-encompassing unity,"[5] iron discipline, and unitary leadership adopted by the revolutionaries in the harsh environment of armed struggle became solidified, dogmatized, and deified and came into conflict with the requirements of peaceful construction, [such] virtues become defects and strong points become weak points. The old practices become increasingly a tool for protecting feudal despotism.

Third, many parts of the economic and political systems of existing socialism are unfavorable to the development of democracy and science but sometimes are conducive to the expansion of feudal despotism. For example, in conditions where party and government are combined, where government and enterprises are combined, the planned economy becomes the "controlled economy"; distribution according to work becomes distribution according to power; state ownership becomes the economic basis for worship of the state. Moreover, under the pretext of "centralization" and "unity," the principle of checks and balances of

---

[5]The term *da yitong* embraced the notion of an empire ruled by one emperor, and the idea that the basis of autocratic control was continued under communism, making it feudalistic. The term was again popularized by Jin Guantao in his analysis of the feudal system. Jin was the editor of a book series entitled *Toward the Future*, and a major participant in *River Elegy*, the television film series produced in 1988 that examined how China has remained a feudal despotic regime for two thousand years (Doc. 5). For further comment on Jin, see note 1 to Document 76.

modern political systems has been denied. The noble standard of the supremacy of the law has been blasphemed and mocked by the talk of "Both the law and the party are supreme." In many areas and government institutions, the centralization of unchecked power has made the bad old peremptory and corrupt practices die hard.

The reforms have provided a new . . . opportunity to eliminate feudal despotism and to expand democracy and the scientific spirit. At this crucial historical moment, a new generation of youth should have more consciousness of hardship, crisis, struggle, and revolutionary transformation in order to make democracy and science benefit our nation.

Precisely because the old system and old ideology have obstructed the development of democracy and science, the socialist countries have all launched, without prior consultation, a new historical movement called "the reform." Today [this has come to mean] not only agricultural reform, but also urban and industrial reform. It is a reform not only of the economic system, but also of the political system; a reform not only of the forms of the system, but also of its ideology; a reform not only of domestic policy, but also of foreign policy. The reform is a revolution and reconstruction in all aspects.

Here we should particularly point to the necessity and importance of creating a market economy as the goal pursued in economic reform and political pluralism as the necessary direction of development for political reform. Experience proves that only the mechanism of market competition can thoroughly eradicate . . . "eating in the canteen like everyone else—egalitarianism," "the sluggard mentality," and low efficiency. Only the competitive mechanism can shatter the worship of power and the narrow-mindedness bred in the mode of production of the small-scale peasant economy. It has also been proven . . . that a modern society based on the rule of law can be effectively built only in a pluralistic political situation. Political pluralism is the only sound strategy for checking the excessive power of the governing party and preventing official corruption. Of course, creating a market economy and political pluralism is not . . . without cost or pain. Their actual realization is a long, tortuous, difficult process. Chinese youth today should have the courage to bear the historical responsibility and be prepared to pay the cost. This is the best way to commemorate the seventieth anniversary of the May Fourth Movement.

The open door and reform in China should be conducted under the banner of democracy and science and should not be stamped with any other narrowly defined nationalist or ideological colors. Otherwise, there will be no true modernization.

Democracy and science are closely linked. The great leaps in the world of science usually accompany enlightenment and growth of the democratic spirit, while backwardness or stagnation of scientific research is usually the result of political sabotage or intervention. The history of the socialist system proves that, without democracy, there is no scientific progress; without democracy, there is no real modernization. Modernization is by no means merely economic modernization or "four modernizations."[6] It should also be political modernization and the modernization of people.

Democracy and science recognize no distinctions by region, race, nationality, or class. Their only opposites are dictatorship and ignorance. We should . . . learn and make use of any practice or concept that conforms to modern democracy and science, regardless of its origin. We should reject and deny any practice or concept that runs counter to modern democracy and science, no matter what sacred "halo" graces it. Only thus is there hope for China; only thus is there hope for socialism.

Mr. Lu Xun [1881–1936] once said, "It actually doesn't matter whether there is any hope. This is like a path. As a matter of fact, there was no path before, but once many people have walked there, a path is made." If thousands upon thousands of young people consciously choose to stand under the banner of democracy and science, the future of reform will be very bright.

---

[6]The four modernizations, first proposed as goals of a rapid development program in 1975, became the banner of the reform decade. They refer to modernization of agriculture, industry, science and technology, and national defense. In 1978, democratic activists called for a fifth modernization: democracy.

2

The Safe Passage of the Reform
of the Political System

CAO SIYUAN[1]

Source: *Shijie jingji daobao* (World economic herald) (Shanghai), November 21, 1988, pp. 9–11.

. . . Whether or not the proletariat should take the route of violent revolution or of parliamentarianism to seize power is a question that has been debated for over one hundred years and should really be judged by history. If you ask, however, after the proletariat and the laboring people have seized the polity and the socialist undertaking has continued to advance, whether or not they should take the route of violent revolution or of peaceful reform, I believe that the vast majority of people would answer without hesitation: take the route of peaceful reform. This is a truth that goes without saying for the Chinese people, who paid a bloody price in the ten years of turmoil in the Cultural Revolution and of full-scale civil war. To achieve this truth, however, one cannot rely solely on good will. We must soberly analyze and strive to avoid two possible causes of turmoil. One is . . . rebellion by the people. The other is . . . governmental crackdown on the unarmed masses.

Certainly the government is a public servant of the masses of the people, and they have the right to remove their public servants and change the government. If there are no legal channels for changing the government, contradictions will build up for a time and then erupt, making violent actions unavoidable. In circumstances where a socialist parliamentary democracy is really established, the citizens have the legal right to change the government through the parliamentary route, that is, through the resolutions of their representative bodies. At the same time, no citizen has any right to use violence to

---

[1]Cao Siyuan was director of the Institute of Social Development of the Stone Company and in charge of the Bankruptcy Law Drafting Group. The Stone Company, "created in 1984 by several technicians in the Chinese Academy of Sciences, who were willing to give up their iron rice bowls, . . . is mainly engaged in research, development, production, and promotion of the use of microelectronic products." By the spring of 1989, the Stone Company had set up branches in more than one hundred areas of China (and a branch in Hong Kong), and had invested in four joint ventures. The company's goal "is to become the Chinese IBM." See Li Jia, "The Path to Success for the Stone Company," *Gaige* (Reform) (February 1988). The Stone Company was in the forefront of providing electronic equipment and loudspeakers to the students in Tiananmen Square.

overthrow a government elected by the majority of the citizens and their representatives. In other words, if only our National People's Congress would finally shed the elegant name of "rubber stamp" and really exercise the power of installing or removing a government according to the socialist parliamentary democratic system, it would provide a peaceful means of changing the government. Then we could fundamentally avoid rebellion by the common people and its destructive consequences. The implication of the socialist parliamentary route is the nonviolent route.

Another implication is . . . that the government must not use violence against the masses who have not used violence. Our society is in an era of grand transformation, and inevitably various adjustments of benefits and consequent contradictions and conflicts will emerge between the government and the people and among the different [social] strata. . . . We must do careful organization of reform and sensible and vigorous propaganda and education to solve these contradictions and conflicts. To protect social and economic order, the government sometimes has to impose somewhat coercive standard restraints on . . . citizens. But these coercive restraints may only be set through legislative procedures and implemented within the limits of the law. Only those who violate the laws can be punished according to the law. The government absolutely may not use coercion against or arrest citizens who have different viewpoints or different interests and demands in the political and economic system reform. Comrade Mao Zedong once relied on his incomparable personal authority and also used the method of military control on a large scale, but still he could not clean up the mess of the Cultural Revolution's turmoil. We must bear in mind this historical lesson. Were any government at any level rashly to use violence against the citizenry, the damage done to social stability would be simply incalculable.

3

Seminar: The Cultural Crisis and the Way Out of It

Source: *Qunyan* (Voice of the masses) (March 1989): 4–9.

Editor's note: On December 30, 1988, *Qunyan's* editorial bureau held a seminar on "The Cultural Crisis and the Way Out of It." The vice-chairman of the Central Committee of the Democratic Alliance, Tao Dayong, presided. Those participating included (according to the stroke order of their first names): Liu Zaifu, institute head and researcher in the Literature Institute of the Chinese Academy of Social Sciences (CASS); Li Zehou, researcher in the Philosophy Institute of CASS; Ren Jiyu, head of the Beijing Library; Su Wei, associate researcher in the Literature Institute of CASS; He Xin, associate researcher in the Literature Institute of CASS;[1] Jin Kemu, professor, Beijing University; Ji Xianlin, professor, Beijing University; Zhong Jingwen, professor, Beijing Normal University; and Yang Tao, researcher in the Literature Institute of CASS. . . .

He Xin: I feel that, in some respects, the political, economic, and cultural situation in contemporary China is a repetition of the history of a hundred years ago. Many problems that we are encountering today replicate the problems that the Chinese faced in the late Qing and the early Republican periods. . . .

Su Wei: Recently I have been shocked at some of the discussions. Among intellectuals of the "Elite Group,"[2] some have proposed the theories of so-called Neo-authoritarianism and enlightened autocracy, which in essence are theories of "good emperorism."[3] Some argue that society is too chaotic, while norms and order are collapsing. We need a dictator to take control; only if a new, good emperor appears can we "clean up the mess." Some are even "calling for dictatorship," and not in jest. These people have said these things in public as

---

[1]For a biographical account of He Xin and an essay he wrote in April 1989 analyzing the sources of popular protest and possible solutions, see He Xin, "A Word of Advice to the Politburo," text by He Xin, trans. Geremie Barmé, *The Australian Journal of Chinese Affairs*, no. 23 (January 1990): 49–76. As the excerpts of the discussion here suggest, He Xin, although advocating a measure of political and cultural liberalization, tends to favor centralized economic controls and clearly draws the line against certain kinds of cultural exploration.

[2]"Elite group" (*jingying*) refers to the highly educated individuals affiliated with the various "think tanks" established by Zhao Ziyang. Several of these were associated with Neo-authoritarianism.

[3]For documentation on Neo-authoritarianism, see Oksenberg et al., eds., *Beijing Spring*, docs. 7–13.

spokesmen for the intellectuals. This is a new hot topic deriving directly from the controversy over *River Elegy* [Doc. 5]. Some say in a self-satisfied manner that this is "reaching the same goal by different routes."

I consider that there are two major causes of the present "cultural crisis." One is that the Cultural Revolution destroyed the system of values. The other is the open door and reform after that [period of] destruction. The world is on the level of a large pool of water. China is, in turn, like a well. Ideological obstacles were the original walls around the well. Placed in the vast spiritual and material ocean of the world and of humankind, the water inside and outside the walls of the well will necessarily come to the same level. When we say that "reform is irreversible," it is based on this assessment. . . .

Li Zehou: Mainly the crisis is not cultural, but . . . social. Aside from economic problems, there are also problems of social order and ecological problems, including water shortages, pollution, misuse of chemical fertilizers, the decline in the fertility of the soil, loss of control over population growth, and so forth.[4] Not only are these present-day crises, but there is also turmoil hidden in the future. . . .

Su Wei: . . . I want to emphasize one point. No matter how acute the problems that our nation and culture face, no matter how grave the crisis is, I am always a pacifist. I believe that any attempt to use violence to solve China's problems, in the name of any cause whatsoever, is doomed to failure.

He Xin: My concrete suggestions are as follows:

1. To maintain social stability, the economy must be strictly controlled.

2. Politically, we must implement and expand the existing democracy and strengthen the legal system.

3. In thought and in culture, we need more opening and enlivening. They should not be tightened up because of the economic tightening. History shows that an economic slump does not necessarily mean a slump in culture and thought. Various viewpoints and lively discussions may facilitate the search for a new route.

For intellectuals, I also have two suggestions: first of all, intellectuals must have a sense of responsibility. They should not only dare to speak out about state affairs, but also responsibly express their true thoughts. In the present situation, any agitation is utterly inappropriate. Second, it is a form of agitation to advocate nihilism in culture and values. Responsible intellectuals should look out for and resist such agitation. . . .

Jin Kemu: The way out can be summarized in only two sentences. The cultural crisis today consists of the increasing illiteracy and the beleaguerment of teachers and doctors. The way out is to reduce illiteracy and to provide for universal education. Actually, it can be put into one sentence: modernization is impossible in a culture of illiteracy.

---

[4]For a detailed analysis of China's serious environmental and population problems, see Oksenberg et al., eds., *Beijing Spring*, Doc. 4.

Li Zehou: Intellectuals must not expect to bestow favors, but I am also against violence. Viewing it historically, violence cannot solve the fundamental problems. I hope that we can reform gradually and peacefully, but this type of reform, too, needs intellectuals to promote, strive for, and struggle for it. We should raise a cry of warning, and not only in the cultural arena. We should say something on behalf of intellectuals and participate in political debate. . . .

4

A Perspective on the Problems of China's Intellectuals: Lack of Freedom Stifled Chinese Scientific Genius?

ZHANG WEIGUO

Source: *Shijie jingji daobao* (World economic herald), September 12, 1988, pp. 28–29.

Our correspondent Zhang Weiguo reports from Beidaihe:

The first "Academic Symposium on the Problems of Intellectuals" since the establishment of the PRC was held the other day, jointly sponsored by this paper, by the newly established *Xin xuefan* (New study models), and by *Guangming ribao* (Guangming daily) and *China Youth*. Over sixty representatives from throughout the country attended the conference, presenting nearly thirty papers. . . .

4. The key to intellectuals' participation is the establishment of an independent character.

Intellectuals' [political] participation has been a hot issue in recent years. Some people consider that Chinese intellectuals participate more than their counterparts in other nations. In Chinese chess, the close connection between the general and the scholar-official vividly reflects this relationship. When we look throughout history, we find that [the Chinese] intellectuals' character was always appended to the person of the emperor. Under such circumstances, if [the emperor] did not like [their] participation, it led to the burning of books and execution of scholars. This was [essentially what happened in] the anti-Rightist campaign of 1957.[1] If intellectuals lack an independent character,

---

[1]Deng Xiaoping played a leading role in the suppression of intellectuals during this campaign.

their participation is meaningless. An independent character usually indicates a self-consciousness of the mission and nature of one's own class (stratum). In ontological terms, it is a self-demand without externally induced motives. Self-judgment yields a sense of social responsibility in the patterns of behavior. China has always been a unitary state of imperial authority, and there has been no independent character to speak of. Thus, while we emphasize the creation of intellectuals' independent character, we should also establish the independent character of entrepreneurs, politicians, and other strata.

Precisely because Chinese intellectuals have participated too intensely while lacking an independent character, they have developed an uncommon awareness of suffering. Such awareness often leads intellectuals to play the role of spokesperson for the public. This has constrained [them] from making unremitting efforts to explore the essence of the natural world. Western culture, as represented by Greek culture, originated in the impulse to explore the essence of nature and led to a search for a system of pure knowledge outside the human world. Thus, it has created a kind of authority beyond the human world and established the independent character of intellectuals. This is exactly what Chinese intellectuals most lack.

Some posit that the intellectuals' participation as individuals in society, whether in ancient times or today, in China or the outside world, has taken five forms:

1. Scholar-officials, traditionally the road of Chinese intellectuals, who lacked a cultural system independent [of the state].

2. Scholarly intellectuals administering government—as in Roosevelt's New Deal brain trust.

3. Reformers outside the power structure—England's Fabian Society made great contributions, by not entering officialdom in order to preserve their independence, [having an impact through] osmosis by making endless proposals to the government.

4. Those holding views at variance with the government's—we see quite a few of these in the Soviet Union and Eastern Europe—"An independent critical voice is a priceless treasure for any society."

5. Intellectual revolutionaries and people who pay no attention to (or are even divorced from) politics. At present some people are hotly and wholeheartedly discussing, "Why hasn't China produced modern science?" "Why couldn't China produce capitalism?" and such scientifically unanswerable questions. This is an effete escape into "intellectual games." Even though they can use this to give vent to their dissatisfaction with the present situation, how much is it likely to push history forward?! . . .

"Our country is so backward we don't need democracy."
—Xiao Zi, ed., "New Sayings," courtesy of HFKS

5

River Elegy, a Television Documentary

SU XIAOKANG AND WANG LUXIANG

Summer 1988

Source: Translation of *He shang* (River elegy) by Frederick Wakeman, University of California, Berkeley, 1989. Reprinted with permission from The New York Review of Books. Copyright © 1989 Nyrev, Inc.

Su Xiaokang's introductory remarks (excerpts): There is no more ancient conversational topic than the Huang He [Yellow River]. But any discussion of the [Yellow River] must take place in the context of the modern age, of the perplexities, contradictions, and difficulties of today. It must relate itself closely to the practical concerns of the people. The need to search for a "catalyst" is particularly acute in a political-commentary type of television documentary that runs a great risk of becoming boring and preachy. And nothing works better as a "catalyst" than direct references to issues of the utmost public concern. Accordingly, our discourse . . . is sprinkled liberally with references to important current events that we all know about, that are on everybody's lips, and that are socially sensitive. Examples include river rafting, dragon and deity worship, the circumstances of intellectuals, prices and the market, the student movement, democratization, and "cultural fever." In a fundamental sense, answers can be found to all these most practical of issues in the most deep-seated "cultural roots" of this nation. . . .

Yellow soil, yellow water, a yellow-skinned people. Can all this be merely coincidental? The ancient yellow people of the Orient were once feared by the West ("yellow peril"). Napoleon said a long time ago, "Do not wake up the sleeping giant." By the time the Orient woke up, however, it had lost to the West.

From Lantian Man to Confucius,[1] it seems that we can ask one other question: of all cultures, why did the Chinese people pick the Confucian culture?

The Confucian culture no doubt is a big part of the rich heritage of the civilizations of the world. Not only did it give rise to countless geniuses and heroes, but it also nurtured the yellow Chinese race into the largest spatial and temporal entity in the history of all mankind. It created a psychology that craved harmony and stability and stressed rational order and human relations. But it was also an isolated and conservative psychology. Today the Confucian

---

[1]Lantian, Yunnan Province, is the site of prehistoric skeletons.

culture has decayed to such an extent that it is beyond salvage. Is this really a good thing or a bad thing for the Chinese people?

Some people say that Confucian teaching should be destroyed and that we should Westernize wholesale. Others say the only way out for China is to adapt Western learning to serve Chinese purposes. Yet others argue that we must bring about the third flourishing of the Confucian civilization. In recent years, Chinese soul-searching has touched upon the most profound of issues—selecting a culture. This is true whether we are talking about intellectuals pondering the Confucian destiny and discussing cultural strategic matters or about the solemn memorial ceremonies for Confucius in Qufu [in Shandong Province, Confucius's birthplace].

We cannot change the color of our skin any more than we can change the color of the [Yellow River]. Yet we must rebuild the culture and psychology of the Chinese people. It will be an extremely daunting and complex piece of systems engineering in cultural psychology.

In the twentieth century, faced with the great gamble of reform, with what sort of courage, insight, and introspectiveness should we equip ourselves?

This was what originally prompted us to make *River Elegy*.

Following are excerpts from the script of *River Elegy*:

. . . So the Chinese civilization is not all that unique and special. Its long course was exactly the death throes of the entire ancient world. The challenge facing Asia was the challenge posed by Europe to all mankind.

This is precisely why the very ancientness of their civilization made the burden of history on the Chinese even more burdensome psychologically. When the Yellow River civilization finally declined, like those of Egypt and India, the spirit of the Chinese nation was particularly mournful and bitter.

A massive Oriental country that once left Marco Polo awestruck. An enormous nation that conjured up visions of "yellow peril" in the heads of fearful European monarchs. The sleeping giant that once prompted the peerless Napoleon to warn the West about waking it up. Why did it decay to such an extent that it allowed itself to be trampled upon? And when we finally weathered the crisis of national subjugation and genocide, why do we now suddenly feel that we are very powerful?

There is also this psychological block in our national feelings. We tend to dismiss our humiliations in the past one hundred years as a mere blot on an otherwise glorious history. Since 1840, there has been no lack of people who seek to cover up China's weaknesses and backwardness in modern times with the greatness and splendor of the past.

After suffering through a century of painful reality, we seem to be in constant need of a strong dose of long-lasting tranquilizing medicine. Every time [our archaeologists] make an earth-shaking archaeological find, we feel a little consoled.

Yet the civilization has declined after all.

The richness of our history, the longevity of our civilization—both belong to yesteryear after all.

Our archaeological discoveries may yet yield more treasures. Our cultural relics may turn out to be even more exquisite. Our civilization may go back even further in history. But doesn't all that suggest that our ancestors are laughing at their descendants? Doesn't it make us even more regretful, remorseful, and ashamed still?

There is a story about the director of an auto plant who stood at the rostrum of Tiananmen and counted the cars passing by on Chang'an Street. When he counted to one hundred, he had seen only three domestic cars, the other ninety-seven being imports.

This story is reminiscent of the dense smoke rising from the opium being burned by Lin Zexu in 1840 or the wave of boycotts against Japanese goods in the 1930s.

Yet history and reality laugh at us mercilessly.

Our pride and our sorrow often are one and the same thing. . . . This ancient idol [the dragon], both awesome and fearsome, embodies many of our ancestors' nightmares. How can we let it express our present sorrow and nostalgia too?

Dragon worship seems to prove that deep down inside, we are still emotionally strongly attached to the land where the Yellow River mothered our ancient civilization, and that we are still lingering in the shadow of the history of our forefathers. Our soul seems to be living in a dream. The time has come for us to wake up totally.

. . . Nor should we beat our breasts and stamp our feet over the loss of a football game. Winning Olympic gold medals does not prove that we are a world power. Our thousand-year-old dream of empire came to an end back in the days of Kangxi the Great [Qing dynasty emperor, 1661–1722]. Today the most important thing is that we no longer continue to deceive ourselves.

Our civilization has declined, but we need not grieve over that. All great riverine civilizations in the world have declined, without any exception. According to the calculations of Toynbee, the British historian, there have been a total of twenty-one civilizations in human history, fourteen of which have become extinct and six of which are in decline. Only the civilization of the ancient Greeks developed into an industrial civilization and swept across the entire world like a tidal wave. We should bravely face up to history.

Many a time history had proven that the source of cultural decline is not an external blow, but the degeneration of its internal mechanisms. Toynbee said that the most an external enemy can do to a society that has committed suicide but is not yet dead is to deliver the final blow.

In the course of millennia, the Yellow River civilization has suffered many conquests and the accompanying upheaval. But it was never destroyed. Its tremendous ability to assimilate other cultures we have always admired. Today, as the twentieth century draws to an end, our old civilization can no longer stand up to foreign cultural assaults even though they are accompanied by gunboats and iron heels no more.

It has aged.

It needs to be supplemented by new cultural factors.

Oh, descendants of the dragon. The Yellow River has given us whatever it can give us. The Yellow River cannot give birth again to the civilization our forefathers created. What we need to create is a brand-new civilization, one that would not flow from the river again. The residues of the old civilization have built up in the blood vessels of our nation, much like the mud that has silted up the Yellow River. What is needed is a good scrubbing by a flood peak. The flood has come. It is industrial civilization. It is calling us!

. . . The tidal wave from the West was totally different from the nomadic cultures of the past that cascaded onto the plain from the Mongolian Plateau like a flood only to disappear quickly without a trace. What came across the sea was a new culture, something that could not be assimilated by the ancient Chinese agricultural civilization. Hence the twin crisis of the nation and its culture dying out at the same time.

To save the nation from extinction, it was imperative that we keep foreign invaders out. Checking cultural decline, on the other hand, required us to open up to the outside world and embrace a new dawn of science and democracy. National salvation and modernization alternately dominated China's abnormal history over the past one hundred years, interacting with each other in myriad complex ways, their relationship so interwoven as to be inseparable. For that the Chinese paid a heavy price.

With their ancient and decrepit agricultural civilization, our forefathers never thought of anything other than defending themselves with a wasteful and useless wall. When at sea, it did not occur to them to trade and compete. This cultural atrophy was then sapping our entire nation's vitality and creativity. Never again can we afford to miss any opportunity offered us by destiny.

We have become much smarter these days.

China once turned down history's offer, but we will never again refuse a chance to make choices.

Fate is not the same as fatalism, and we will never again put ourselves at its mercy.

We have seen that the Yellow River must flow into the sea in the end after traveling eastward for ten thousand li.

Never again should we turn down the sea's invitation.

. . . What sort of powerful force was able to hold such a large country so firmly together for more than two thousand years? The riddle of this "great unity" has caused Chinese and foreign scholars to rack their brains in amazement.

Marx characterized as "a sack of potatoes" social structures founded on feudal natural economies. Though they are in one bag, they are all separate from each other. In ancient China, peasants engaged in small-scale agriculture were as close and numerous as stars on a summer night, or like a plate of loose sand. It was the Confucian intellectuals who functioned to hold the society together, and who believed in unity; they effectively organized the scattered small peasants into a society.

This distinctive social structure made China flourish greatly even though within this marvel of great unity, and beneath the glowing exterior of this overly ripe civilization in which absolute adulation of the emperor, of sages, of the old, and of ancestral memorial tablets were entwined, the core of this social structure was slowly rotting. This situation very much resembled the present situation in which the Yellow River dikes are silently being hollowed out by mole crickets, ants, and field mice. The corps of bureaucrats organized by the Confucianists had an irresistible tendency to corrode, power itself becoming a corrosive agent. Hence, once a dynasty reached its peak, collapse lay just ahead.

When an old dynasty collapsed, however, a new dynasty rapidly replaced it; the social structure was restored to its original form, and it continued to move along to the next collapse. The same is true of the Yellow River dikes, which collapse only to be restored and then wait until the next collapse. Why do we always get caught up in this never-ending fate?

This mysterious superstable structure dominated us for two thousand years. Today, the emperor's throne in the Forbidden City has long since become a historical artifact, and the huge Confucian network of bureaucrats has dissipated like smoke. Nevertheless, the specter of the great unity seems to linger in the good earth of China. The nightmare of social shocks makes people remember it anew. Nor is it possible to ignore the damage that is still being done to our "four modernizations" by bureaucratism, the idea that prerogative and privilege go with position, and even some corruption as well. These persistent ancient social disorders are somewhat like the silt that the Yellow River carries every year, which clogs the lower reaches of the watercourse, gradually building up to a crisis.

When manmade disasters occur one after another, such as the great fire in the forests of the Xing'an Range [Heilongjiang Province], problems with the air in Chongqing [Sichuan], train collisions, and a hepatitis epidemic in Shanghai, isn't the feeble social mechanism issuing us yet another veiled warning?

Possibly, in just the way that people are deeply apprehensive about the steady increase in the height of the dikes, can permanent superstability make people apprehensive? Is it possible that the enlightenment that history has given us has been too little?

. . . History is the realities of the past; however, we feel even more that history is an unending dialogue between the past and the present. In the course of this dialogue, we can produce a very profound sense of sorrow that is beneficial for contemporary people. The inspiration that history provides for the Chinese people is that China should avoid destructive upheavals in the transformation of its society. Compromise and creation should take the place of upheavals. When an old thing crumbles, new elements grow. I think that consciousness about the sorrow of the Yellow River and consciousness about the sorrow of China are good things. A consciousness of crisis is, in itself, an expression of historical consciousness that enables all the people to summarize the past from the heights of history. I believe that if in the course of self-questioning of history, the Chinese people are able genuinely to understand history, and absorb the experiences of history, and make them into historical wisdom, the coming twenty-first century will be a new starting point for the Chinese in becoming flourishing and prosperous.

. . . The historical victory of this continental civilization could be contained neither by the lamentations of [the poet] Qu Yuan nor by the earth-shaking resistance of the tyrant king of Chu. . . .

The eternally restless azure waves of the Pacific Ocean have always secretly beckoned this ancient people reposing on the continent, and occasionally it aroused their excitement, leading their ships all the way to the Persian Gulf and the Arabian Peninsula. But the attraction of the blue ocean was much weaker than that of the yellow soil.

The mystery of the tremendous cohesiveness of this yellow civilization stems from the singular position of respect gradually attained by the Confucian civilization in this land.

The whole body of Confucian thought expressed the standards and ideals of life in a continental civilization. Its flourishing in Oriental feudal society was clearly rather rational; nevertheless, the unity of undiversified ideology weakened the plural development of the elements of a maritime civilization that enriched medieval life. It was like several trickles from a spring on the hard loess of continental civilization, immediately disappearing without a trace. . . .

. . . The tragic fate of Yan Fu as well as of numerous other great ideological pioneers such as Kang Youwei, Liang Qichao, and Zhang Taiyan seems to demonstrate that even after the finest Chinese had taken part in revolution for a time, in the end, they were unable to get away from returning to the Confucianists.

Even right up until the great discussions during the "Chinese cultural craze" of the 1980s people were still continuing the debate that has gone on for one hundred years without being resolved about the superiority of Chinese and Western cultures. Both the "complete Westernization" faction's illusions, and the "third flowering of Confucian civilization" faction's wishful thinking seem to be a going over of old ground. No wonder that some young scholars sigh with feeling and say: Tremendous cultural assets became a tremendous cultural burden; a tremendous feeling of cultural superiority became a tremendous feeling of cultural blame, which can only be said to be a major psychological obstacle to China's modernization.

The difficulty in changing methods lies, perhaps, in our constant apprehensions about whether "Chinese will still be Chinese." It seems we do not realize that during the past two hundred or three hundred years in the West, Western Europeans at least had no apprehensions about whether following literary and cultural revival, religious reform, or the Enlightenment would turn them into something other than Italians, Germans, or Frenchmen. Only in China is this the greatest taboo.

Possibly this is a critical point and a weak point in the yellow civilization!

Two thousand years ago, the philosopher Zhuangzi provided us with a parable: When the waters rose greatly one autumn day, the river god in the Yellow River found that he was very great; unexpectedly, it had become impossible to distinguish oxen from horses on both banks, so great was the distance. He floated down the river to his heart's content, when suddenly he saw the open sea about which he was ignorant. The ruler of the sea, Beihainuo, told him that he would not talk about the sea like a frog at the bottom of a well, because he only knew about his own tiny area and had no way of imagining how vast the sea was. But now, my river god, you have finally left the confined river, and you can see the vastness of the open sea. You know your limits, and you have entered a higher realm.

This is a symbol. It does not refer to ancient China but seems to be a forecast of today.

It has been only a century since the spirit of the ancient Yellow River really did see clearly the face of the great sea and realized the vastness and the power of the sea. The long sigh that it emitted when it faced the sea echoes today across more than one hundred years of history.

This plot of earth-colored land cannot teach us what is a true scientific spirit.

The devastating Yellow River cannot teach us what is true democratic awareness.

Sole reliance on this plot of yellow earth and this Yellow River that cannot nurture the ever-swelling population and cannot give birth to a new culture is futile. It no longer has the nutrition and the energy it once had.

Possibly Confucian culture had some perfect ancient "talismans," but during the past several thousand years, it never created a national spirit of enterprise, a national legal system, or a mechanism for renewing the culture. On the contrary, it became degenerate and shaped a fearful suicide mechanism that constantly devastated its own quintessential qualities, killed its own internal vitality, and stifled a spirit of adventure in generation after generation of the nation. Even though it possessed rare qualities, today it is difficult to avoid destroying the good with the bad.

History provides testimony that modernization undertaken according to the governing style of a continental culture, though it may incorporate certain new achievements in science and technology, or even put satellites in the sky and be able to explode atomic bombs, basically cannot give an entire people a powerful cultural vitality.

Only when the sky-blue ocean wind finally turns into rain and remoistens this arid yellow land will this astounding vitality that starts up only in the joyous days of the lunar new year be able to make the vast loess plateau regain a new lease on life. . . .

. . . Bao Zunxin (assistant research fellow, Chinese Academy of Social Sciences, and editor of *Cultural Philosophy Collection* and *Study of the History of Chinese Philosophy*). China's traditional culture was founded on a small-scale agricultural natural economy in which everything was politicized. This politicization has to be done away with, traditional views changed, and a democratic awareness and democratic spirit among the people established. The dominant feature of the traditional culture was the application of [Confucian] ethics to everything, or, in other words, "ethical centralism." This value principle must be done away with, and self-initiative must be established. It is a democratic spirit and a scientific spirit that our nation lacks most. Without these two spirits, China's modernization is unthinkable. A nation's distinguishing characteristics cannot be resolved solely through an expansion of tradition or a return to tradition, but rather through an opening to the outside world. It is in a clash between Chinese and foreign culture that our nation can make historic innovation and historic choices in the modernization process. Otherwise, though the Yellow River may be made to hurry to the sea, the turbid yellow color of the water in the Yellow River cannot be changed. After all, the sea is the sea and the Yellow River remains the Yellow River. Only destruction of the traditional cultural structure, and building a culture that meets needs for the building of socialism, offer a way out for our Chinese culture.

China's history never created a Chinese middle class to produce victories in science and democracy, nor did China's culture nurture a civic sense. On the contrary, it inculcated a scholar-official–subject mentality. This scholar-official–subject mentality could produce only obedient subjects resigned to oppression, and desperadoes who risked danger out of desperation. Nevertheless, history created an extremely distinctive group for China, the intellectuals.

They had no common economic interests or independent political advocacy; they were servants of others for several thousand years.

Nor could they become a solid social entity able to use steel-like economic strength as armament in criticizing the old society.

Their literary and artistic talents could be subverted; their will could be misrepresented; their souls could be emasculated; their backs could be bent; and their bodies could be destroyed.

However, they held in their hands the weapons for wiping out ignorance and superstition.

It was they who could carry on a dialogue with the maritime civilization.

It was they who could sprinkle the sky-blue, sweet, spring water of science and democracy on the yellow soil!

6

Open Letter to the Standing Committee of the National People's Congress and the Party Central Committee Calling for a General Pardon of Political Prisoners

THIRTY-THREE CHINESE INTELLECTUALS[1]

February 16, 1989

Source: Courtesy of HKFS.

We are deeply concerned upon hearing of the open letter to Chairman Deng Xiaoping by Mr. Fang Lizhi on January 6, 1989.[2]

We believe that, on the occasions of the fortieth anniversary of the founding of the People's Republic and the seventieth anniversary of the May Fourth Movement, a general pardon of political prisoners, particularly the release of political prisoners like Wei Jingsheng, will create a harmonious atmosphere

---

[1]The thirty-three signatories were Bei Dao (poet and playwright), Shao Yanxiang (poet and writer), Niu Han (writer), Lao Mu (editor), Wu Zuguang (playwright), Li Tuo (literary critic), Xie Bingxin (writer), Zong Pu (writer), Zhang Jie (writer), Wu Zuxiang (professor of Chinese literature), Tang Yijie (professor of Chinese philosophy), Yue Daiyun (professor of literature), Zhang Dainian (professor of Chinese philosophy), Huang Zipeng, Chen Pingyuan, Yan Wenjing, Liu Dong, Feng Yida (writer), Xiao Qian (writer), Su Xiaokang (writer), Jin Guantao (theorist), Liu Qingfeng (theorist), Li Zehou (research fellow in philosophy), Pang Pu (professor of Chinese philosophy), Zhu Wei, Wang Yan, Bao Zunxin (associate researcher, CASS Institute of Modern History), Tian Zhuangzhuang (movie director), Wang Ke, Gao Gao (research fellow), Su Shaozhi (former director of the CASS Institute of Marxism–Leninism–Mao Zedong Thought), Wang Ruoshui (theorist in philosophy), and Chen Jun (artist).

[2]The title given Deng refers to his chairmanship of the Central Military Commission. Note that the Fang Lizhi letter was addressed to Deng, since the action requested by Fang could not have been taken without Deng's approval, even though his only formal post would not give him the legal authority to take such action or to veto it. The letter reproduced here, being addressed to the NPC Standing Committee, is aimed at a body that has the constitutional authority (though no real power) to issue a general pardon; but it is also addressed to the CCP Central Committee, which has no constitutional authority (but does have the real power) to issue such a pardon. It was generally known that Deng Xiaoping was not disposed to grant a pardon to Wei Jingsheng, a leading democracy activist sentenced to fifteen years in prison after the Democracy Wall Movement of 1979 was suppressed; probably no signatory to this or other similar petitions expected any pardon to be granted him. See text of Fang Lizhi's January 6, 1989, letter to Deng in Oksenberg et al., eds., *Beijing Spring*, Doc. 16.

favorable to the reform. It will also conform to the widespread trend of increasing respect for human rights in the world today.

"News from the radio: No news today."
—*New Sayings*

7

The Star of Hope Rises in Eastern Europe

WANG DAN

March 4, 1989

Source: Courtesy of Robin Munro.

Thirty-three years ago, various developments, namely the secret report to the Communist party of the Soviet Union by Nikita Khrushchev, the Polish and Hungarian incidents, and the "Hundred Flowers" Movement in China, all at once created hope for the international Communist movement, which was then on the verge of darkness. Regrettably, there followed a prolonged period of military autocratic rule. Today, what is happening in Eastern Europe excites us once again—the freshness of the spring of 1956 permeates the air.

On February 10, [1989,] the Socialist Workers' party of Hungary held its plenary session. In its communiqué, the 1956 Nagy Affair was recognized as a "genuine people's uprising." The same congress affirmed the multiparty system and pluralism within the political system. In Hungary, many parties announced they had been formed or had resumed their activities. The nonparty members of the parliament even formed an "outside party faction." What should be noted is that these developments have taken place with the approval of the [ruling] party and in reaction to an appeal by the people.

In Poland, roundtable meetings entered a stage of concrete negotiations. Opposition organizations like Solidarity and the Writers' Union were legalized, and they organized mass demonstrations. On February 10, Polish Prime Minister Jaruzelski indicated in a speech that the United Polish Workers' party would "give up its monopoly of political power."

In Czechoslovakia, although the authorities have been cautious and somewhat indecisive, the activities of the masses have been frequent and forceful. Recently, over one thousand cultural workers petitioned the prime minister to demand the release of students arrested in the Prague demonstrations in mid-January. What is happening in Eastern Europe should inspire us in two ways. First, dictatorship by one party, or a similar ruling system known by a different name, should be abandoned. The implementation of democratic politics is the major trend in socialist development. It is obvious that the refusal to reform the political system thoroughly in an attempt to protect vested interests is running against the tide of the day. Second, the very promising developments in Poland, Hungary, and Czechoslovakia must be attributed to the ceaseless efforts of the opposition forces inside the party and within the population. Once again, this forcefully testifies to the fact that democracy is not given but must be fought for by the people from below. In the process, the educated elite must act as the avant garde and play a leading role.

We feel that the road taken by the Eastern European nations of Poland, Hungary, and Czechoslovakia is the only way socialist countries can be saved from serious crisis. Let us be straightforward: Only if China steers itself step by step in the near future onto the road of development like the Eastern European countries can a highly democratic, developed country be successfully established.

8

On Freedom of Speech for the Opposition Faction

WANG DAN

No date

Source: Courtesy of Robin Munro.

Although freedom of speech is contained in the [PRC state] constitution as an important principle, it has long been blatantly and arbitrarily violated. This is clearly manifest in the illegal and violent suppression of opposition voices by the political authorities. Such suppression reveals the following formula: Truth = the world view of the proletariat = Marxism = the world view of the party = the announcements of the party's leading institutions = the highest leader. Since such an argument obviously makes no sense, there is no need to elaborate.

Restrictions on the freedom of speech of the opposition probably reflect the following justifications:

1. The ruling party or the authorities represent the interests of the people and hold the truth.

2. The absurd views of the opposition faction will lead to undesirable consequences in society. As the leader of the people's thoughts, the party should restrict the spread of those ideas.

3. The development of the opposition faction will disrupt the stability, unity, and normal order of political development.

The following counters the first argument:

a. Truth is neither absolute nor singular. Certainly, the proletariat may grasp the truth. Yet, the capitalist class or the minority can also grasp the truth. This is the meaning of the phrase: "Everyone is equal before the truth." Even if the views of the opposition are obviously flawed, it cannot be said with certainty that there exists no element of truth in their ideas. No truth ought to be suffocated or weakened by monopolistic means.

b. Anyone who really grasps the truth will not suppress opposition views. On the contrary, the spreading of fallacious thinking should lead to a wider recognition of the truth. This is because all truths arise out of conflicts among various fallacies. If there were no confrontation between fallacies, truths would lose their basis of formulation. It can be seen that the suppression of opposition voices is a sign of weakness and lack of confidence. And it definitely obstructs the spreading of the truth.

c. The people's interests are diverse. All social strata harbor their own special interests. The ruling party that purports to represent the interests of the people cannot represent the interests of everyone. At most, it represents only the majority of the people. No citizen can be deprived of his legitimate interests. They should be expressed through permitted channels.

Who can be certain that the view of the opposition may not represent the interests of some part of the people? Under such circumstances of uncertainty, the suppression of opposition views would be the suppression of people's demand to satisfy their own interests.

d. No party is made up of identical members. As a mass political organization, it certainly contains people of different sorts, including those who intend to use power to distort the truth and to fool the masses in order to satisfy their greed and ambition. If there exist no outside voices to criticize and supervise, those hungry for ambition will fearlessly pursue the path of distorting the truth. Even if there is an internal checking mechanism within the party, it may be controlled by them and thus becomes ineffective. In reality, China is governed monopolistically by one party, and it is not possible to develop an effective supervisory mechanism within the governing party. That is to say, the suppression of opposition views will provide fertile ground for the bad elements who have infiltrated the party. What causes the greatest damage to a governing party usually comes first from its own corruption and darkness. It is especially true in a time of peace. . . .

e. It is permissible to criticize the truth. In fact, truth does not just refer to grand macro theories or behavioral principles. Truth includes statements that are "nonsense" like "When man has eaten enough, he will not be hungry." As far as such truths as these are concerned, I could say anywhere that man can still be hungry even if he has eaten enough, and I would not be punished or restricted. At most I would be treated as an idiot and ignored. Why is that so? Obviously because this kind of opposition view is too absurd; therefore, if the views of the opposition generate confusion in thought, it is definitely because certain aspects of those views are not acceptable. Thus, two questions arise. First, truth may be in the hands of the minority. Second, absurd views are not punished, but fallacious views that have a certain value are punished with restrictions. This is another unfairness. [Such] unfairness arises out of a decision made by arbitrary force. And how can things that have to be bolstered by arbitrary force be regarded as truth?

The following is said to counter the second argument:

a. [Let's assume] that we recognize that the government and the ruling party have the responsibility to punish deviance and unhealthy ideas, and to practice so-called political leadership. When opposition views are suppressed and not allowed to be propagated, such views must be harbored secretly and unknown to anyone. The consequence is that the meaning of deviant thought, let alone punishment, is unclear to anyone. In this case, the opposition views are not allowed free propagation and are, therefore, not punished in time. Later this might have a negative effect on society. . . . We can see that the suppression of opposition views is at the same time the condoning of the fallacious thinking contained in opposition views.

b. The government rules as a representative of the citizens' will. It should be based on mutual trust between the government and its citizens. The fear that opposition views may create undesirable consequences obviously shows a mistrust and contempt of the citizens' capacity to judge. Any government that does not subscribe to the idea that "the people's eyes are clear and bright" will attempt to suppress the views of the opposition.

c. No matter how fallacious are the views of the opposition, they should be allowed to propagate them freely. . . . Whether or not they are fallacious is now only judged by censorship authorities. [But] the value judgment on a theory or belief is naturally varied, and there is no one single representative [of truth]. As a result, the judgment of censorship authorities cannot represent the judgment of the majority of people. It is obvious, therefore, that only when ideas are allowed to circulate freely will it be possible to identify whether they are correct or not.

d. . . . Freedom of speech is a holy and inviolable human right. Marx himself once likened the freedom to associate, publish, and assemble (certainly the freedom of speech is included) to "soil, air, light, and space." This is a very apt analogy because it shows concretely that views opposed to the existing system should be allowed to circulate freely, just as vandals, idiots, or the mentally ill should also enjoy air, soil, and light.

e. If the views of the opposition create extremely undesirable consequences, the government can wield the power vested in it by the people to reprimand and punish. But there definitely should not be any prior restraint or limitation.

The following is said to counter the third argument: The functioning of a political structure involves a lot of contradictions, and only when these contradictions are mutually checked can the structure operate properly. On the contrary, if one contradiction is backed up by violence to prevail over another contradiction, this will produce an imbalance in the structure and create turmoil in society. For forty years we have suppressed opposition views and struck at dissenting forces, and yet we have not established any stable and unified political scene. On the contrary, we had ten years of turmoil. It can thus be seen that only when opposition views are allowed to circulate freely, and opposition parties and opposition within the party are allowed to exist, will democratic politics be guaranteed. Only then will the normal order of the political life of society be properly maintained. The suppression of the freedom of speech is the real cause of social turmoil.

We do not support absolute freedom of speech. This is impossible, for there always exist internal restraints in any development. But we object to all restraints coming from the outside, especially those imposed on us by violent means.

In the present new enlightenment movement in China, the educated elite must first be concerned with freedom of speech and must have the courage to level criticisms at injustices—including the decisions and behavior of political parties and the government. This is because intellectuals can influence social changes only through their ideas and speeches. If the freedom of speech is lost, there is no way for intellectuals to promote the process of democratization, and we shall not be able to maintain an independent, critical attitude. We shall be mere adjuncts to the party and the government. [In that way,] our fate will not improve compared with what we had over the past forty years.

9

The Summer of the Year of the Dragon—1988: Panic Buying

JI HONGMIN AND JU MEIPING

Source: *Zhongguo qingnian* (China youth) (November 1988):24–27.

. . . Just as the summer of 1988 began, thrifty Chinese suddenly rushed to banks large and small. . . . They wanted to withdraw their savings deposits post haste.

This wind first blew in Central and South China, then in North and East China. Thereafter it swept cities and towns throughout the country. Long lines formed in front of the [urban] banks. . . .

What are people panic buying? At first, it was top-grade consumer durables: refrigerators . . . washing machines . . . electric fans. . . . Whether it's imported or not, famous brand or not, no matter. They don't stop to consider whether the quality is good or bad. Anyway there's a warranty. . . .

Initially people still did some calculations, buying the things whose prices were going to rise. Tobacco's going up, get several cartons; alcohol's going up, get ten bottles. There are still matches, toilet paper, cotton cloth, woolen cloth. Later, it seems, they calculated little, buying everything because there's no guarantee that the price of anything won't rise. . . .

What is wrong with the Chinese people's currency [*renminbi*]? When consumers indiscriminately throw their money into the market, this question keeps emerging in their minds. . . .

10

Where Is the Way Out for the Chinese Reform?—A Dialogue between Yan Jiaqi and Wen Yuankai

GAO YU

Source: *Hainan fazhan bao* (Hainan development daily), February 3, 1989, pp. 2.7–2.12 (excerpts).

Late last year, the scholars Wen Yuankai and Yan Jiaqi conducted a splendid dialogue at the "Conference on Entrepreneurial Culture" in Beijing.[1]

Yan: In the conference speech you just gave, you said the chariot of reform in China has gotten stuck in the mud. This is a metaphor indicating reform has encountered serious difficulties. However, the Chinese reform is not doomed to fail. Everyone now feels that there is no way out, and no one knows what to do. This in turn has become the main problem in China.

Wen: . . . The Chinese reform now faces three options. The first option is for

---

[1]At the time of this dialogue, Yan Jiaqi was China's leading political scientist, based at the Chinese Academy of Social Sciences; Wen Yuankai was a professor at China Science and Technology University and deputy director of the Education Commission for Anhui Province. Both were well known as liberal political thinkers and spokesmen.

[the reform] to stay where it is. But if reform stops, it will get mired even deeper in the mud. The second option, which seems at present to be underway, is to "turn back the wheel," attempting to pull it out of the mud and to search anew for a way out. Of course, recentralization and tightening up are necessary, but a danger lies therein: "After working hard for a decade, we go back to the prereform situation overnight." We have already seen that Poland and Czechoslovakia [did this]. That is terrible. What I am trying to explore right now is a third option. Is it possible to go forward to get out of the crisis, out of the mud? We should not turn "deepening the reform" into an empty slogan. I worry that the present readjustments, "bringing the economic environment under control and rectifying the economic order," may wash away entirely the "deepening of the reform."

Yan: Where is the crisis? Much confusion has appeared in the process of reform, and there is seemingly no solution. The morale of the Chinese people is very important. Disappointment with reform will lead to certain kinds of regression or stagnation, which, if they reach a [critical] point, will necessarily lead to calls for new reforms. [But] if this period [of regression/stagnation] is prolonged for five years, or ten years, it will be seriously damaging to China. From the history of the Soviet Union, we can see that Khrushchev was an important reformer. Tito had recognized the maladies of the socialist system even earlier than Khrushchev, but it was Khrushchev who really touched the maladies of the socialist system in the Soviet Union. The Khrushchev reforms got stuck in the mud. Only after almost twenty years of stagnation under Brezhnev did the Soviet Union once more step onto the route to Gorbachev's reforms. Gorbachev's reforms are actually a renewal of reform after a long period of stagnation, summarizing the experiences and lessons of the failures of Khrushchev's reform. I hope that when the reform in China faces difficulties, it will not be followed by a long Brezhnev-type period of stagnation. . . .

If China actually stagnates for five or ten years, it will create new problems, in the end making China even more backward. Then, China would have to begin reform anew, and new Gorbachev-type leaders would have to appear. . . .

I hope all of today's Chinese leaders can hold firm in their confidence in reform. They should not look for the route to retreat, but continue the reform in order to overcome the difficulties in it. The main problem now is how to find a way out. . . .

Our newspaper propaganda always says that "This should be done," and "We hope for this to be done." Such propaganda lacks a sense of the legal system. It won't work. Anyone who violates the law should be punished according to law. . . .

China lacks the idea of legality, first of all, because the constitution has no authority. I believe that political reform and economic reform are equally important. From now on, the primary problem of China's political reform is to prepare a constitutional revision in the 1990s. The greatest rule in China should be the constitution, and thereafter various kinds of laws, decrees, administrative regulations, and local regulations, including regulations protecting fair competition in the economy.

At present the stipulations of the constitution and political reality are two different things. The constitution stipulates that the National People's Congress is the highest organ of power, but everyone knows that in reality it is not. . . . If the constitution is treated in this way, then traffic violations and taxi drivers fleecing passengers are only small matters. Indifference to the supreme authority of the constitution led to tragedies like Liu Shaoqi's death in the Cultural Revolution. Therefore, the first rule in China is that we must establish the supreme authority of the constitution, not some other new authority. . . .

Now I feel that a type of "crisis" exists: Some people who have been against the reform all along are watching [the situation] . . . worsen and regard China's difficulties as an opportunity for them to gain power. They are getting ready to "clean up the mess," to push China into a long period of stagnation or regression. We must watch out for such people, who regard a disaster for China as their hope.

Wen: Right. At this moment, as the Chinese reform faces many difficulties and the reform is mired in mud, we must still make a strong appeal to the public. China's reform has made great achievements that are universally acknowledged. The reform has brought about great progress in China.

Yan: Although there is so much confusion, the Chinese still support the party and the government in pushing the reform ahead.

Wen: We should do more to make people throughout the country recall which people have made efforts to promote China's reform.

Yan: And remember who has done nothing and is waiting for the reform to fail.

Wen: They want to take reprisals.

Yan: We must watch out for such people, who take advantage of the turmoil . . . in China to stop the reform. The news media should speak out frankly and point out the main problems.

Wen: We should pay attention to studying a type of mentality found in traditional Chinese culture: Historically, the critics standing on the sidelines found fault with others. They "rectify" the men of action who have made mistakes. If you do ten things right but make one mistake, they will totally deny your merits based on this one mistake. Those who have never made any contribution, have never been enterprising, are always right. . . .

Yan: I quite agree with you. Worries about the confusion in reform relate to this. China must not permit a Brezhnev-type long-term stagnation.

Wen: Right! Right! [This] would be even more serious than the failures of reform.

Yan: That "stagnation is even more serious than failure" is a good theme. If we have twenty years of a Brezhnev-type stagnation, China's modernization will be delayed by fifty years, or perhaps even longer.

11

The Crisis in Moral Values Is a Crisis in Human Values: We Must Establish Behavioral Ethics Suited to a Commodity Economy

Source: *Shijie jingji daobao* (World economic herald), October 3, 1988, trans. in *Inside China Mainland* (March 1989): 10–11. Some corrections made to translation.

Over the past several years we have regularly applauded the overturning and the collapse of the traditional morality. However, we do not seem to have taken into account that while the old system has been overturned and the new system has not yet been established, the psychological attitude and behavior of the people, after turning their backs on the traditional morality and leaving it behind, have not developed in the direction that is most appropriate for constructing the rational order that is required by a commodity economy. . . .

"Slogans Without Substance"

Crisis No. 1: The outlook in which there is no order and there are no rules. . . . (1) With the gradual development of a commodity economy, the old morality, which had Confucian ethics as its main pillar, has been basically eliminated. (2) The Communist morality and the socialist morality which have been introduced and propagandized by the party and the government since the founding of the nation are actually mere slogans without substance. (3) Except for a few criminal laws that have been enacted by legislation, in society generally there is no consensus on matters of morality.

Crisis No. 2: Just as there is no concept of right and wrong, there is no moral psychology based on the feeling of shame.

Crisis No. 3: There is almost nothing left of critical evaluation based on moral concepts or supervision of behavior through public opinion. . . .

Crisis No. 4: The reduction and the distortion of moral education. The classes in moral education recently established in the schools have produced very meager results. At home, because the education provided for young people by the head of the household tends, whether deliberately or inadvertently, to be stern and overbearing, such an approach, though conducive to a vigorous upbringing, can hardly avoid planting latent hostility in the hearts of the younger generation. This develops into a mutual animosity, making it hard for the different generations to live in peace. This is a great calamity.

"Lawlessness" Makes "Tough Guys"

The crisis in moral values is a crisis in human values. Building modernization requires a kind of person who is diligent and always pressing forward, who is tolerant and good, healthy, and rich in spiritual creativity. The development of this kind of character needs to be encouraged. On the other hand, the kind of hardened "roughneck" who will stop at nothing, who is willing to inflict injury on others for his own benefit, who is an opportunist always "on the make," and who is opposed to science and to culture—this is the type of character that has become the model for universal imitation because under conditions of lawlessness it has much greater "competitive strength" in the "struggle for survival."

. . .

To resolve the present crisis of morality in China, it is necessary to carry out a general program of "straightening out and tightening up." (1) Deepen the reforms. Through developing a commodity economy and a system of regulation and supervision of the exercise of power under a system that has been made democratic, we can establish the basis for blocking off the sources of corruption. (2) We must establish a just and rational system for the distribution of profits. We must make readjustments in the direction of rewards and penalties in our society. (3) We must strengthen the legislation of morality. (4) We must revise the strategy of cultural development in such a way as to put primary emphasis on creativity and secondary emphasis on criticism. (5) We must develop a number of different kinds of movements to encourage morality.

12

An Inquiry into the Phenomenon of "Profiteering Officials"

Source: *Gongren ribao* (Worker's daily), August 24, 1988, p. 1, excerpted and trans. in *Inside China Mainland* (February 1989): 3–5. Some corrections made to translation.

. . . On the Chinese market, rules governing commodity economics have been implemented in a twisted, crooked fashion. Bureaucrats turn into powerful businessmen. . . . In referring to those officials engaged in buying goods at a discount and reselling them at a profit, the public uses the straightforward term "profiteering officials." All kinds of "companies" and "centers" have ties to the government at all different levels; some are operated half by the public, half by officials; some merely give the appearance of being publicly run, while others have no masses in their "solidarity with the masses" whatsoever. Behind these businesses, political involvement stands in either deep or shallow support. In inquiring into the "official profiteering" phenomenon, we cannot help but return to the source of the situation—bureaucratic commerce.

Two Big Booms

. . . In 1985, the total number of companies or "centers" of all kinds stood at about 320,000. Of these, most were "briefcase" factories, which employed few people, had no investors, no equipment, practically no land, and relied on swindling and speculation for profits. This was called the first "hot business" period in ten years.

After that, there was a year and a half of adjustment; in 1986 there were still 170,000 companies and "centers."

From 1987 to June 1988, the number of companies increased to 400,000! . . . [T]he majority of these companies are bureaucratically controlled. More than 700 companies are operated under the authority of various offices in the State Council alone. . . .

These bureaucratically controlled companies operate in the cycle of consumption like an endless series of buckles, tightly connecting together all the points of circulation in the market. . . . The pulses of many businesses are already controlled by bureaucratic commerce, and business is coming to depend on profiteering officials for survival. . . .

Bureaucratic commerce extends maliciously into the sphere of circulation in a limitless way, agitating prices. In the present market, "slips" (contract forms) are priceless. . . . In a hotel in a certain large city, this episode involving a transaction by a profiteering official took place: a profiteer of political standing came in carrying a delivery "slip" for 50 tons of steel products, added 100 yuan to the original price per ton and sold the piece of paper to another profiteer, leaving the hotel with 5,000 yuan in "profit." The second profiteer sold the delivery sheet to a third profiteer, after hiking the price another 150 yuan per ton, and in this way the same delivery contract was transferred five times, and the original price went from 700 yuan to 1,500 yuan per ton without ever leaving the hotel.

Instances of transactions like this are found everywhere. The mixing of public office and commerce has become like an extra chapter in the "Records of Activities among the Bureaucrats." The merchant officials of old China, while especially feudal and "compradoristic," were not only unable to rescue ancient China from backwardness, poverty, and foreign aggression, but even contributed directly to a destructive abyss of economic collapse.

Who can believe that modern merchant officials will be able to carry China's economy forward and provide hope and strategy for the future?

. . . The powerful presence of officials in the marketplace has led to a "voo-doo" economy and a warping of market standards.

An official's approval report can pass off contaminated water as fuel, and swagger into the country with it; that's what began happening a few years ago. With no more than a purchase order slip and a phone call, officials can make the prices of marketable goods fly around. . . .

. . . Officially operated companies now have an almost divine power in business. Whatever they want, they get, and whatever is scarce can be had, at a price. . . . A certain profiteer conditionally supplies 5,000 kilowatt hours of electrical power to a factory; later, he asks the factory to give him certain hard-to-find consumer commodities. If he gets "no" for an answer, then the 5,000 kilowatt hours of power immediately become negotiable. What factory owner would dare to refuse?

. . . Among the entire country's 360,000 companies at the end of 1987, 250,000 of them are prospering as a result of the purchase and resale of goods in the sphere of circulation by profiteering officials.

The situation has progressed to the point that the market maxim has gone from "more channels, fewer links" to "more links, fewer channels,"[1] the tricks of exchange have become increasingly complex, and the methods of exchange have become more secret and unfathomable, with hundreds, thousands, and millions never reaching the coffers of the national treasury, and instead going into the private pockets . . . of profiteering officials. . . .

These luxury- and power-worshipping officials have tended to monopolize prices, materials, and the market step by step. . . . The market has developed into a producer of substandard products, and moreover, the bureaucrat business-men have used all their power to push the market's distortion to its furthest limit. This . . . has brought about a period of mock prosperity, and when the market collapses in the future, the cause of the ruin will be buried by the lack of order and market chaos.

Failure of Supervision

. . . In a northwestern city, there was a sensational news story about the investigation of an administrative organ by a judicial branch. A certain large company operated by the city government incurred a loss of several million yuan and went into extreme debt. Creditors from all over the nation swept into the city and filed charges against the company. After the city lost the case, the company casually plucked the money out of the city's treasury reserves and paid off its creditors.

---

[1]"Channels" refers to channels of circulation other than the state-controlled one; "links," to the network of personal connections based on bureaucratic position and access to controlled materials.

Later, a city leader who gave written authorization for the establishment of this company tried, with the stroke of a pen, to persuade the functional sections conducting the investigation not to check into the matter too carefully. The neglect of this official's duties nearly led to another lawsuit. Since this year, the number of cases involving economic crime have increased dramatically, but the rate of cases solved remains comparatively low. . . . In the face of power, the heads of investigative departments are often broken. "You have the authority to check on me, I have the power to interfere in your work." . . . Under the restrictions placed on those who supervise, "supervision" is being supervised; thus has the performance of our country's legal line of defense ended in tragedy. The abuse of power inevitably requires greater power to shelter behind. The special background of power in which profiteering officials operate can only lead to greater chaos in the nation's system of checks and balances and the destruction of the legal system.

Polarization of Wealth

In the Gospel of Matthew, it says: "To those who already have, more shall be given. From those who have not, even what they have not will be taken away." This phrase is called the "Matthew Effect" in central theory. In the unbridled competition in the market, the expansion of "trading officials" and the sensitivity of the market are bringing about an "ever-more" cycle, in which the peculiar "Matthew Effect" can be seen throughout. Those in subordinate positions will follow the example set by their superiors, and if the State Council can switch nameplates on administrative departments, bureaus, districts, and offices with company names, and then go out and "deal," why can't provinces, regions, cities, and counties follow suit? As a result, "dealing" has become the rage. . . .

As a result of the gluttony, collusion, sales commissions, bribery, and extortion derived from this activity, all kinds of extravagant forms of corruption and greed are in operation, with officials making no attempts at all to hide their dealings, and unafraid to hear of them.

. . .

Some say the phenomenon of bureaucratic commerce is a mere side effect, and that the pains it brings into society are an inevitable cost of undergoing a period of getting on the right track. But if we must pay the type of social price described here, then what sort of world will we be left with after the pains stop?

13

The "Two-Track" Phenomenon: Investigation and Consideration of the Simultaneous Existence of Old and New Systems

Source: *Liaowang zhoukan* (Outlook weekly), no. 37, September 12, 1988, pp. 10–12, excerpted and trans. in *Inside China Mainland* (January 1989): 21–22. Some corrections made to translation.

. . .

In the bustling shop of the No. 2 Cotton Mill in Tianjin, within the same factory team, using the same set of machines, are two different types of workers: fixed laborers and contract laborers. The former were assigned to the factory by the state; the latter come from the labor market. The former are assigned their jobs for life; the latter, once their contract is up, can look for another occupation. The two groups have different systems of wages and labor insurance. . . .

In the searing furnace that is Capital Steel Company's steel rolling mill, wire rods and steel threads wriggle out of the milling machine like snakes of fire. In a production site unchanged from ten years earlier there now exist two types of production: that under the auspices of state planning and that outside of it. Raw materials for state-planned production are supplied at prices fixed by the government. Those for production outside of state quotas are secured from companies supplying them at market prices, which are far higher. Naturally, rolled steel is sold at two different prices: wire rods are priced at 700 yuan within the plan, at 1,400 yuan on the market. This is the "two-track" system of plan management, on the one hand, and goods and materials management and production material pricing, on the other. Of last year's total national steel output of 43.85 million metric tons, 22.8 million or 52 percent was allotted at plan-fixed prices, while the remaining 48 percent was sold at prices determined according to market conditions.

Moonlighting Universal

The rate of attendance at Tianjin's Red Flag Chemical Plant workshop is 94 percent. This is not considered low. However, 40 percent of the shop's workers have second jobs: running street stalls, repairing bicycles, pedaling pedicabs, cutting hair, etc. . . . Their behavior is also "two-track." Two workers named Gao used their time after work to establish a "ten-thousand-yuan business." Due to disruptions they caused in the factory's production, the two were fired by the factory. People began talking: "At work you're poor, after work you're rich. If you're fired then you can open a "ten-thousand-yuan business.". . . According to statistics of the ministries concerned, of the total income of workers in Tianjin, 51 percent is derived from basic wages; the other 49 percent comes from the "other track."

Engineers also work on "two tracks." From Monday through Saturday they work hard at their jobs. At dusk on Saturday, they take a small van operated by a rural transport company into the countryside, where they operate "Sunday engineering firms." In the Langfang district, the number of "Sunday engineers" brought in from Beijing and Tianjin is around four thousand.

. . . The "two-track" phenomenon is everywhere:

The system of selecting cadres follows "two tracks." One is the traditional method of appointment, the other, inviting applications for the vacant positions.

The enrollment of undergraduate and graduate students takes "two tracks": students sent by the state have their costs borne by the state, while all others must depend on their own funds or those of their unit.

The purchase of agricultural and sideline products follows "two tracks": one of plan-determined prices and one of market prices. Identical food products, under two different purchasing systems, have different prices.

. . .

"Two tracks" is merely a term we've become used to. One should really say "two rules": that is, two sets of rules for the same situation.

Old and New Overlap

. . . In such a vast and complex country, with a low productivity level and limited powers of endurance on the part of society, it is impossible to reach our goal in one fell swoop. We must adopt a "step-by-step" approach. This means that old and new systems will exist side by side with the elimination of the old gradually making way for the new. . . .

An expert studying "structural dissipation theory" believes that in changing from one traditional system to a mixture of old and new, a wide range of societal structures are moving from order to disorder. . . . Up until now, the not fully eradicated old system and the virtually virgin new system have both had negative social impact, and this . . . is the root cause of many major problems now emerging. If one word can be used to describe the abuse of the two-track system, the word is chaos. . . .

The two tracks engender frictions and conflicts. Market prices for production materials far exceed prices fixed by planning. Producers look for any way they can to reduce production of goods for plan quotas and increase production for orders outside planning. . . . Some producers take products ordered by planners and sell them on the market for much higher prices. Thus, they are unable to honor their contracts with state planning departments. According to information from the National Statistics Bureau, the contract fulfillment rate for steel and coal for the first quarter of this year was 91.2 percent and 89 percent respectively.

The market track harms fulfillment of state plans, while the planning system hinders full utilization of market potential.... As the government has control over all fixed-price raw materials, factory managers find any way they can to "get to the mayor" rather than "get to the market."

Money, Power, and Crime

The frictions and conflicts of the two-track system are all around us.... One legal expert, speaking to reporters, made this analogy: If our roadways were governed by two separate sets of traffic rules, accidents would be unavoidable. Similarly, in a two-track (or two-rule) system, "collisions are inevitable."

Under the two-track system, the malicious link between authority and the market leads to illegal activity. For the past three years at the Tianjin Bureau of Goods and Materials, every year has seen county-level cadres led away in handcuffs. More than ten county-level department cadres have been jailed. The benefits to be had from the difference in prices between the two tracks is a temptation that turns someone with authority into a seller of commodities. A case of bribery in the city of Shiyan in Hubei County paints a picture of the exchange of money with authority: "I used my money to buy his power and then used his power to make myself more money." These business operators who rely on privilege to take advantage of price differences are a poisonous fungus that has grown out of the two-track system....

The lacunae and the loopholes of the two-track system have weakened society's ability to control disparity.... Furthermore, management in this transition period is a much more complex and difficult task compared to the past.... Because the norms of management are unclear, it is difficult to judge the line between right and wrong, to the point that some obvious lawbreakers have gotten off scot-free. One industrial manager complained: "If people take advantage of price differences between here and abroad to smuggle, at least it can be countered by customs; when it's done domestically with the two-track system, there's no way to stop it!"

The chaotic effect of the two-track system on society has caused people to lose their judgment. Often, they are plagued with internal contradictions: the factory head, when buying raw materials, looks to the "old track," hoping to secure what he needs at fixed prices. When he is selling finished products he seeks out the "new track" and market prices; the worker wishes to retain the "iron rice bowl" guarantee of his regular job yet also wants to put effort toward his moonlighting work to obtain the "golden doll" (personal profits). Housewives scurry between state-run stores and the farmers' market, lured to the former by its better buys, then drawn to the latter because of the quality and variety it offers....

A gap has opened up between the old norms and concepts, which have yet to be eradicated, and the new ones, which have yet really to take hold. It has become difficult to judge standards of right and wrong. People have lost their judgment: what's "worth it" has taken on a different meaning to different people. Among these different levels of people dissatisfaction and conflict are rife.

The myriad abuses of the system have led people to cry out, "Create the conditions for ending the two-track system!"...

14

Uneasiness over Inequitable Distribution

TANG MINGFENG

Source: *Zhongguo qingnian* (China youth) (June 1988).

The problem of equity has never been so acute as in China today. Everyone knows that the present economic reform is aimed at breaking away from the inequitable principle of egalitarian distribution; and to encourage some people, some areas, and some sectors to get rich first, so as to achieve the goal of promoting social productivity. Up to this day, however, because we have neglected the impact of preproduction distribution on equity, and the negative influence of postproduction distribution on efficiency, not only has egalitarianism not been eliminated, but the old pattern of irrational distribution of benefits has not been changed. In many respects, this has considerably aggravated the inequitable distribution of benefits and caused new social contradictions. Today, not only are ordinary citizens complaining about inequitable social distribution when they look at the "upstart" ten-thousand-yuan households,[1] but also many entrepreneurs, and even some local government officials and leaders in [various] sectors, also feel that various kinds of social distribution are inequitable.

---

[1]The "ten-thousand-yuan households" first appeared in the countryside under the rural reforms of the early 1980s. For a time they were widely publicized as evidence of the success of the reforms, and to motivate others to emulate their efforts. Later, widespread animosity against such households (stemming partly from envy, and partly from resentment against the favoritism that got many of them their opportunities in the first place or magnified their benefits thereafter), caused the government to tone down the publicity on the new rich. By then, such windfall gains had also begun accruing to some urban entrepreneurs.

1. Inequity in Distribution of Benefits among Regions

Different regions contribute revenues to central finances, receive fixed subsidies, or enjoy tax breaks in an extremely disproportionate manner. Let us look at the following statistics:

In 1987 the fixed fiscal quota of revenue paid to the central government [i.e., the proportion of provincial revenues that had to be handed over to the central government] from Guangdong Province was 8.6 percent; . . . from Jiangsu Province, it was 59 percent; . . . from Shanghai Municipality, it was 76 percent.

In 1988 when they began conducting the local finance responsibility contracts,[2] it made the existing pattern of inequitable fiscal distribution even more entrenched. In these few years, Guangdong's economic strength and fiscal revenues have doubled and redoubled, but the "fixed quota" of one billion yuan that it hands over [to the central government] hasn't changed. Guangdong's provincial governor Ye Xuanping has candidly said that Guangdong's relatively rapid development during these several years has mainly depended on the center's policy preferences.[3] This sort of policy preference has directly brought about an enormous rise in the consumption level of the residents of the preferred areas, to the point that the gap with other areas' standard of living has rapidly widened. . . . From 1979 to 1986, the GNP of the two provinces of Guangdong and Fujian increased by an annual average of 10.99 percent and 10.66 percent respectively, higher than the national average of 8.8 percent during the same period.

Not only have the provinces of Guangdong and Fujian benefited from preferential policies; the open-door policy[4] has strengthened the vigor of the coastal areas, increasing greatly their share of the gross state investment in fixed assets.

---

[2]These contracts bound administrative entities to pay a fixed amount of revenues to the central government and permitted them to retain the rest and use it as they wished. This was partly an attempt to make central revenue more predictable (the central government had encountered difficulty in collecting taxes owed to it by local governments and enterprises) as well as to decentralize investment and finances as part of the overall program of reform.

[3]Guangdong benefited more rapidly from the reforms than any other province or province-level municipality. There are numerous reasons for this success, including its proximity to Hong Kong and its attractiveness to foreign investors. (For a comprehensive study, see Ezra Vogel, *One Step Ahead in China: Guangdong under Reform* [Cambridge: Harvard University Press, 1989].) However, because Guangdong was also seen as a test case for the reforms, in typical fashion for the CCP-style generation of policy "models," it was given numerous and incalculable boosts by preferential treatment. Its preferential treatment was, some suspect, linked with the fact that the chief reformist leader, Premier and later Party General Secretary Zhao Ziyang, had put in some twenty years in posts in Guangdong.

[4]The "open-door policy" refers in general to the policy of encouraging foreign investment and foreign trade, and in particular to the types of inducements used to promote them: special breaks for foreign and joint ventures in certain "special economic zones," and retention by local entities of some foreign exchange.

In 1982, these proportions . . . broke down for China's three major regions, east, central, and west—as 50.65 percent, 27.81 percent, and 14.61 percent, respectively. By 1987 they had changed to 56.12 percent, 25.57 percent, and 14.22 percent. Not only has the unfairness of the distribution of benefits among regions seriously affected the regional balance of development; it has also caused similarly amazing regional disparities in people's standards of living. In 1978, the consumption levels of the inhabitants of the . . . east, central, and west [regions] were 192 yuan, 164 yuan, and 147 yuan, respectively. By 1986 these had changed to 514 yuan, 418 yuan, and 368 yuan.[5]

2. Inequity in Sectoral Distribution of Benefits

Inequity in distribution of benefits is mainly manifested in state investment policies for different sectors. Or irrational price relations have harmed the interests of certain sectors. Here we can select two main sectors as examples.

The railway industry. Outside of China, railways are an industry with priority for state investment, without which the West would not have developed modern industry so rapidly. But in China, the railways are used as a resource for accumulating capital. For instance, the state has for a long time applied a policy of low transportation fees and high tax rates in the railway system. On the one hand, the railway sector hands over 85 percent of its profits to the state in the form of a tax, retaining only 15 percent, and aside from using this for welfare expenditures[6] and bonuses, it has virtually no capacity for self-transformation and self-development. On the other hand, the railway sector has to make do with superannuated equipment. Thirty percent of the locomotives and cars in the entire [system] have had their period of service extended, and as much as 15,000 kilometers of track are in disrepair. In particular, the rails on the busiest main lines are seriously damaged by [metal] fatigue, and the safety threat to trains increases daily. The development of railway transportation is lagging far behind social and economic development and has already become an emergent weak link in the development of the national economy and society.

Based on reports from the railway administration, in the forty years of national construction, the indices of railway transport prices and materials prices have always been out of step, with the gap growing steadily wider. . . .

---

[5]Obviously, the regional percentage breakdowns do not add up to 100. The source provides no explanation for this. Regarding the income figures, the reader should note that although there were probably increases in average real incomes in all three regions; the numbers given here probably are for nominal not real increases. Because of shortcomings in the statistical reporting system, it is impossible to adjust these accurately to reflect the real figures. However, inflation had so cut into the value of the currency that the 1986 figures should probably be divided by at least two, to estimate the real incomes.

[6]These refer to pension funds, health insurance, employee housing, and a wide range of other nonwage benefits.

The depression of rail transport prices has made [the railway's] purchasing power . . . fall enormously, severely limiting railway development. . . .

Natural gas and petrochemical sector. In 1981, the state, in order to transform a state of affairs in which investment and returns in the petroleum industry were getting out of balance, . . . applied crude oil responsibility contracts for the petroleum industry. It . . . achieved fairly rapid development. Beginning in 1981, however, the national average cost of oil extraction rose from thirty yuan per ton to around eighty yuan per ton.[7] Yet the price of one hundred yuan per ton of crude oil set in 1971 did not increase until 1987. Thus, the enterprises producing crude oil basically transferred the profits they created to the downstream crude-oil processors. . . .The natural gas and petrochemical sectors' responsibility system then produced similar labor productivity but a wide disparity in funds, profit, and tax rates. This sort of inequity greatly weakened the crude-oil industry and its development has lagged; moreover, this could retard the development of the entire national economy.

3. Inequity in Distribution of Benefits among Enterprises

The inequity in sectoral distribution of benefits will necessarily be reflected in the enterprises in different sectors and cause inequity of their respective employees' incomes. For example, at the same time that labor productivity was enormously increasing in the state coal-mining sector, the average wage of its employees, among the forty sectors under the control of the State Council, fell from fourth place in 1984 to eleventh place in 1987. . . .The income level of employees of industries in sectors where the commodity market is broad and the prices have been decontrolled generally is higher than in enterprises belonging to sectors still primarily under command planning.

With the progress of reform and opening, China's ownership system has been changing; because the state has been applying different economic policies to enterprises under different ownership systems, it has also caused relatively large disparities of employee incomes in enterprises under different types of ownership.

. . . In 1987, the average wage-income[8] of Chinese employees working in foreign-owned enterprises was 2,826 yuan; in Chinese-foreign joint ventures . . . it was 2,406 yuan; in state-owned enterprises, because of limits imposed by the state policy of taxing bonuses . . . it was 1,546 yuan. Collective enterprises, especially the township and [rural] town enterprises, have independent accounting and are responsible for their own profits and losses. Generally speaking, their

---

[7]One major reason for this was the exhaustion of the most productive of the oilfields, such as Daqing, and the need to prospect for and open new fields that were more expensive to exploit (including offshore oilfields).

[8]This constitutes a recognition that some enterprises' employees receive in-kind income and subsidies that also contribute to their standard of living, but which are extremely difficult to quantify accurately.

employees' average wage level is a not very high 1,207 yuan. But policies in various places are different; the levels of [collective-enterprise] employees' wage-incomes are greatly unequal. Shanghai's is 1,623 yuan, exceeding the average wage of state-managed enterprises' employees. In Beijing it is 1,536 yuan; in Zhejiang it is 1,356 yuan; in Jiangxi and Henan it is only 974 yuan. . . .

. . . Enterprises in the same sector, the same region, and under the same type of ownership, the profitability of capital, labor productivity, and the levels of income from wages are all far from identical due to differences in the level of their original equipment, differences in how much money the state releases, and even in the proportional weight of inputs within the plan [i.e., supplied at low fixed prices] and the level of profit retention.

4. Inequity in Distribution of Benefits to Labor

As to the problem of distribution of individual labor incomes, a current popular saying goes: Those who teach earn less than sweet-potato vendors, and those who work on missiles earn less than tea-egg vendors. Leaving aside famous actors, singing stars, labor contractors, and "individual households"[9] (because there is no way to get statistics on the true incomes of these people), according to a statistical survey done . . . in Beijing, the average wage level in the sectors with a high concentration of intellectuals is lower than the average wage level in the sectors with a high concentration of manual laborers.[10]

. . . Everyone knows that equitable distribution, for individuals, is distribution according to work, that is, conducting a rational distribution according to the amount of exchangeable commodity value the labor creates. But for a variety of reasons, there is no way to conduct this sort of rational distribution,[11] and the sort of labor enthusiasm that relies mainly on stimulation by increasing bonuses is bound to be unsustainable. . . .

. . . [Thus,] to raise economic efficiency, we must reform the past "one big pot" type of income distribution system; but if we overlook the importance of equitable distribution, not only will we be unable to raise economic efficiency successfully; to the contrary, it will bring confusion to economic life and an inflation of aggregate demand. This requires that in our reform and economic work from now on, we handle skillfully the relation between equity and efficiency, so as to guarantee the healthy development of economic reform and the task of construction.

---

[9]This refers to those running family businesses.

[10]"Intellectual" in China is commonly used to refer to all who work primarily with their minds rather than with their hands—i.e., white-collar workers.

[11]This sounds like a mild statement, but one should note that "distribution according to work" was one of only two criteria distinguishing the reformed Chinese economy as socialist. It was also used to legitimize those inequalities that did emerge under the reforms as right and proper.

15

Pastoral or Pitfall: A Report about the Problem of Unemployment in China

XIAO BINGCHEN AND SHI YUNFENG

Source: *Baogao wenxue* (Reportage) (April 1989): 2, 4.

An upsurge of unemployment is coming from heaven! . . . Thirty-odd years ago, we were happy and excited at giving every urban citizen an "iron rice bowl,"[1] but now we have to use our own hands to smash some people's iron rice bowls.

—In 1987, within one year the state-operated enterprises in Hubei Province discharged fourteen thousand permanent state employees.

—By mid-summer 1988, there were already thirty thousand persons receiving unemployment benefits in Shanghai.

—In Zhuzhou [Hunan], the reform has forced forty thousand "excess workers" out of their jobs . . .

According to the most recent news, issued . . . by the state's . . . Xinhua News Agency, by the end of August 1988, nationwide at least three hundred thousand permanent state employees had been removed from their jobs. They have become the first group of people openly unemployed in new China. . . .

What is left are many puzzling questions.

—Isn't it true that unemployment only belongs to capitalism? Why is there also unemployment in a socialist country?

—Aren't we the masters of the country? Why smash the rice bowls of the masters?

—Aren't the directors of the factories public servants? On what grounds can they dismiss workers?

—For more than thirty years, didn't people have a comfortable life with the

---

[1]The "iron rice bowl" (*tie fanwan*) refers to guaranteed employment for state-sector workers. Most of these reside in the cities, and full or nearly full urban employment (urban collectively owned enterprises did not guarantee lifetime employment) was made possible in part by the household registration system and the strict controls on rural-urban migration that were imposed at the end of the 1950s. Thereafter, almost no one not born in a city could acquire permission for permanent urban residence. State enterprises might on occasion hire temporary contract workers, but these generally were brought in from the countryside and were expected to return to their collectives when their term expired. Without official urban registration or permission for an urban sojourn, one could not obtain grain ration tickets, which, until the reform era, meant that one was unable to buy food in urban markets or restaurants.

"iron rice bowl"? Why is it now necessary to break their "rice bowl"? . . .

During the four years between 1984 and 1987, the trade unions in large, middle, and small cities in China . . . conducted large-scale surveys among the workers. Fifty-six percent of the workers surveyed believed that the status of the Chinese workers as the masters of the country had declined. The interests of the workers are hurt.

II

April 15–April 27: The Movement Begins

Hu Yaobang's Death Sparks Mass Demonstrations

Lawrence R. Sullivan

*Gai si de mei si
bu gai si de que si le*

The one died who should not have died.
Those who should have died live.
— Slogan from photo

This period begins with Hu Yaobang's sudden death on April 15, 1989. It ends with the strident April 26 *People's Daily* editorial that, inspired by Deng Xiaoping, provoked the largest demonstrations since 1949 in Beijing on the next day. In the interim, violence erupted in Xi'an, Changsha, and Beijing, where students sparred with the government over issues ranging from arrangements for Hu's funeral to the future of economic and political reform in China. Students and the government grew increasingly polarized during the period, with the prodemocracy movement declaring itself "patriotic" and potentially autonomous, on the one hand, and government hardliners labeling the demonstrations as counterrevolutionary "turmoil" (*dongluan*), on the other.

Three interrelated developments, reflected in the following documents, shaped the rapid turn of events in this period. First was the popular reaction to Hu Yaobang's death. Students and the general population alike were shocked by Hu's unexpected demise, which they quickly interpreted as another blow to proreform political forces in the party. Second was the opportunity afforded to students by the official mourning for Hu to express their growing alienation from China's political and social system. From the very first demonstrations following Hu's death, Tiananmen Square became an arena where students made specific demands on the leadership for both "campus democracy" and reform of the entire political system. Third was the unprecedented response to the student demonstrations from Beijing's population and even some party members. Student parades in the capital in late 1986 had elicited virtually no popular support as government criticism of the students evidently swayed the population.[1] Spring 1989, in contrast, would witness an outpouring of political backing from the "common people" (*laobaixing*), with even some rank-and-file party members joining the protests.

The Death of the "Soul of China"[2]

Hu Yaobang was probably more popular among students in death than he had ever been in life as CCP general secretary. During the 1986 demonstrations, students had derided Hu, as well as Deng Xiaoping, with sarcastic political chants.[3] Yet students basically understood that Hu had been the main person responsible for the greater intellectual and cultural freedoms instituted in China since 1983.[4] One reason Chinese students took considerable personal risk in organizing public demonstrations after Hu's death was, in fact, a feeling of guilt that the previous student-led movement in 1986 had effectively ended Hu's career. Beijing's *laobaixing* also felt deeply indebted to Hu for having

---

[1] Demonstrations viewed by this author in Beijing in late December 1986 were met with apathy or outright hostility by the city's population, who openly complained of the students' excessive "privileges." The most vocal critics of students in 1986—the city's taxi drivers—became some of their most avid supporters three years later.

[2] This phrase—*Zhongguo zhi hun*—was inscribed on pictures of Hu Yaobang placed on the Monument to the People's Heroes by students in Tiananmen Square.

[3] Students in Shanghai had chanted *Hu Daobang*, a homophonic play on his real name that roughly translates as "Hu destroys China," with *dao* meaning to destroy and *bang* an old classical term for China. *Deng Xiaoping wan shui* was also chanted as a slight distortion of *Deng Xiaoping wan sui*. The latter means "Long live Deng," while the former derisively translates as "Ten thousand taxes under Deng."

[4] Hu had pushed political and intellectual liberalization against conservative opposition and protected intellectuals during the 1987 anti–bourgeois liberalization campaign even after his dismissal as general secretary. Students considered Zhao Ziyang primarily a supporter of economic reforms who did not necessarily embrace political liberalization. Many of Zhao's supporters had, in fact, supported "Neo-authoritarianism," while Deng Xiaoping was believed to be the behind-the-scenes manipulator who, despite advocating political reform in the early 1980s, had shifted his support to the conservatives by purging Hu Yaobang in 1987. The fact that students in mid-April criticized "corruption" in Zhao's family may explain why conservative leaders, particularly Li Peng, initially tolerated the demonstrations in hopes of bringing down the general secretary. Ruan Ming, *Hu Yaobang yu wo* (Hu Yaobang and I), trans. in *CCP Research Newsletter* (forthcoming), and Oksenberg et al., eds., *Beijing Spring*, docs. 7–13.

personally supported the establishment of the first "private vendors" (*getihu*) in Beijing when he overrode objections to such economic reforms by the capital's notoriously conservative political leadership in 1985.[5] There was also great disappointment over the dashed hopes of a possible political comeback for Hu, something students and intellectuals had yearned for ever since his dismissal in early 1987. Along with the political pressure that party conservatives had recently exerted on Deng Xiaoping to depose General Secretary Zhao Ziyang, Hu's death darkened the already bleak prospects for further liberalization in China.

Following the announcement of Hu's death late on April 15, students were initially unsure how to respond. The last student-led demonstrations in Beijing not only had met with public apathy, but also had led to the arrest of student leaders in both Beijing and Shanghai. Some still remained in jail. After hearing of Hu's demise, graduate students at several scientific institutes urged a march on Tiananmen. But the more conservative Communist Youth League (CYL) wanted to restrict student actions to participation in the official mourning activities without making any political statements.[6] Reflecting their long-standing discontent with "loyal" CYL leaders, students nevertheless organized several small marches over the next few days. New student leaders also emerged to press for a "dialogue" (*duihua*) with the government on the basis of the first of several "demands" issued on April 18. These included a call for a formal reevaluation of Hu Yaobang's political career and of the notoriously illiberal anti–spiritual pollution and anti–bourgeois liberalization campaigns.[7] Students were also irate over the Beijing city government's sudden promulgation of the "Ten-Point Regulations" outlawing demonstrations, which they claimed violated the state constitution's allocation of such authority solely to the National People's Congress. Finally, Beijing's people expressed their heartfelt feelings by visiting Hu's home in an unprecedented display of respect for a leader they considered to be honest and frugal.[8]

---

[5]Beijing First Party Secretary and arch conservative Li Ximing reportedly reassured Deng throughout the conflict that he was "fully prepared" to handle the situation. (Interview, Beijing CCP member, 1990.) Hu's support for the *getihu* may explain why so many private vendors took part in the demonstrations, despite the fact that, unlike intellectuals and others, they have prospered economically in recent years.

[6]Steven Chang, lecture, Fairbank Center for East Asian Research, Harvard University (hereafter FCEAR), July 5, 1989. Police blocked an attempted demonstration on April 5 to mark the anniversary of the 1976 "April 5 Incident" in Beijing. Many of the early student organizers were older graduate students in their twenties and even thirties.

[7]These demands are repeated almost verbatim in Document 22, below.

[8]*Beijing ribao* (Beijing daily) strengthened this image of Hu by publishing several articles describing the ex–general secretary's meager financial holdings—reportedly only 1,000 yuan (4.7 yuan to the dollar)—which contrasted greatly with the personal enrichment of other leaders and their families. Even though Zhou Enlai had been revered, Beijing people dared not visit his house after the premier's death in 1976 because of his status as a leader far removed from the common people. Interview, Beijing resident, 1990.

Student actions were quickly supported by prominent intellectuals. Ever since Hu's 1987 dismissal, Su Shaozhi, Fang Lizhi, and others had pressured the government on issues of human rights and political liberalization.[9] Describing Hu as the "symbol of Chinese democratization," two hundred intellectuals now called for a "speed up [in] the process of democratization and the reform of the political system," including "freedom of speech, press, and publication." The same group also tapped popular distress over the social disruptions caused by the reforms by demanding that the leadership "eliminate widespread corruption in the party and government . . . and solve the increasingly grave problems of social inequality" (Doc. 20).

Despite their overall commitment to the reforms, intellectuals shared the general public's widespread feeling that relatively few people in the government had personally benefited from the new policies, among whom Hu Yaobang had been a notable exception. Almost everyone confronted unprecedented inflation and higher taxes, growing unemployment for workers, and bureaucratic extortions (a practice that targeted the new "private vendors," in particular). But officials and their offspring at all levels (from the center down to the smallest township) had managed to use their political position and connections to make an economic killing. It verged on a national scandal when the freewheeling sons of Zhao Ziyang were reportedly involved in business schemes assisted by their father. But the public found it especially galling that the families of conservative leaders, such as Chen Yun, exploited the opportunities afforded by the reforms and then relied on the restrictive practices of the party-controlled press to cover up their activities.[10] The focus of most complaints was economic; but it was the tightly controlled political system that was believed to lead both proreform and conservative leaders to "shirk their personal responsibility" behind a continuing facade of empty rhetoric (Doc. 20).

The Students Take the Lead

The government's initial refusal to respond to student demands for a "dialogue" reinforced this image of bureaucratic arrogance experienced daily by citizens

---

[9]See, for example, Su Shaozhi's remarkable speech at the December 1988 Theoretical Discussion Meeting Marking the Tenth Anniversary of the Third Plenary Session of the Eleventh Central Committee, Fang Lizhi's Letter to Deng Xiaoping in January 1989, and an Open Letter to the Party and Government Leaders by Thirty-three Intellectuals in February, 1989, in Oksenberg et al., eds., *Beijing Spring*, Doc. 14.

[10]One of Chen Yun's sons was purportedly involved in a highly profitable Beijing restaurant at the very time that his father opposed private economic activity. Zhao Ziyang reportedly intervened with the Bank of China to secure loans for one son's venture selling color television sets. For a description of the bureaucratic "squeeze" on *getihu* and their resulting active role in the demonstrations in Chongqing, Sichuan, see Anita Chan and Jonathan Unger, "Voices from the Protest Movement: Chongqing, Sichuan," in *The Australian Journal of Chinese Affairs*, no. 24 (July 1990): 261–63.

without high-level connections. Despite the increased presence of undercover police on university campuses since the 1986–87 demonstrations, the government was clearly unprepared for the student movement. On April 18 student demonstrators skilled in "struggle techniques" (*douzheng yishu*) gathered outside the leadership compound in Zhongnanhai and apparently wanted to storm the gate, though cooler heads ultimately prevailed. Two days later, on April 20, military police beat student petitioners under the cover of darkness. The violence was both gratuitous and indiscriminate: One young student had his "two legs . . . beaten into a mixture of flesh and blood," while a nearby private vendor "was kicked viciously in the back . . . and could hardly stand up." Police violence was also directed at women as "several girl students were beaten into tears" (Doc. 16). Previous leaders, such as Zhou Enlai, would have probably defused the crisis at this early stage, many Chinese subsequently argued, with adroit political maneuvers and persuasive oratory.[11] But in April 1989, the government deepened the conflict by unleashing club-wielding police against young college students.

The demonstrators' response to government intimidation was generally mild. The students' widely publicized "seven demands" issued one day after the April 20 conflagration merely called for "punish[ing] severely the assailants" and demanded an "apology" (Doc. 22). Unlike such countries as South Korea where open-pitched battles between students and police were commonplace in the 1980s, Chinese students did not take to the streets to exact immediate retribution. Instead, they focused mostly on the situation at the universities. Their primary goal was to "strive for campus democracy" by "impeaching" the student leadership of the government-controlled student unions, which had failed to protest the police violence against students (Doc. 21). Organized down to the level of academic departments and often connected to the Communist Youth League, these institutions, students believed, bred political "yes-men." This made the promise of a future "socialist democracy" in China an unlikely possibility under CCP tutelage. The students argued that if true democracy was to be realized in China, it had to begin on campus where student-run democracy "salons" had been prohibited. Although students favored reform of the entire political system, they were primarily concerned at this point with achieving "autonomy" of their elected student organizations and winning the freedom to publish their own newspapers outside direct CCP control.

In this sense, students were initially committed to making universities models of democracy. With comprehensive democratization in China several decades away, many students hoped, perhaps naïvely, to win a measure of self-government by holding free elections for student leaders. This would further undermine the CYL, which had already lost substantial influence throughout the 1980s.[12] The authority

---

[11]This was one reason students later displayed pictures of Zhou Enlai with purported "quotations" from the late premier expressing disapproval of Li Peng, his adopted son, for disregarding his public duty to "serve the people." Interview, Beijing resident, 1989.

[12]Interview, Beijing University students, 1990.

of party secretaries on campuses had also diminished considerably as more academically qualified presidents had recently taken over management of the universities. They had not only allowed students greater individual freedom in lifestyle, but had also protected the universities from CCP-run political campaigns, such as the 1987 attack on bourgeois liberalization, which many students at Beijing area universities considered a "joke."[13] Intellectually, students were now free to pursue highly popular Western ideas, such as Karl Popper's theory of the "open society" and Nietzsche's philosophy of individuality.[14] Chinese campuses had also recently experienced a much greater air of personal freedom, as previously unknown habits of heavy drinking, late parties, premarital sex, and adulation of rock singers—from America's Michael Jackson to China's Cui Jian—spread among the student body. While older teachers complained of poor student discipline in comparison to the traditional model, students called for radical changes in curriculum, textbooks, and faculty. The fact that students won unprecedented concessions from university authorities may have emboldened them to take the next step and challenge the state.

Yet the Chinese students who ultimately took to the streets in Beijing were generally apolitical. After the experience of the Cultural Revolution in which students had become pawns in high-level political struggles, the level of political apathy on campus was high. Although students were strongly attracted to the ideals of Western democracy and individual liberty,[15] as long as a relatively free atmosphere prevailed on campus, they seemed inclined to remain politically quiescent. The relatively poor turnout for the demonstrations in late 1986 in Beijing provides evidence of this. The death of Hu Yaobang and the continuing pressure on Zhao Ziyang, however, threatened the tenuous political balance that had preserved a modicum of individual freedom for students, artists, and other intellectuals. The animosity of conservative party leaders toward Western culture and general intellectual freedom was abundantly clear from their recent denunciations of Chinese avant-garde culture, such as *He shang* and the prize-winning film *Hong gaoliang* (Red sorghum).[16] Cultural and ideological retrenchment had, in fact, already occurred prior to Hu's death in government education policy, where changes formulated in December 1988 aimed at restricting study abroad to more politically reliable students and to countries other than the

---

[13]Ibid. The campaign's major targets were writers and a few intellectuals.

[14]Nietzsche's selected works and Karl Popper's *The Open Society and Its Enemies* had both been recently translated in China and were favorites among organizers of the salons, such as Shen Tong.

[15]The fear of becoming tools in a high-level political struggle led most students to shun advice on strategy and tactics from Zhao Ziyang's supporters in the central government. Interview, Wu'er Kaixi, FCEAR, Summer 1989.

[16]Conservative leader Wang Zhen condemned *Red Sorghum* for its unflattering descriptions of China's backwardness and portrayal of peasants resisting the Japanese during the Ani-Japanese War without CCP leadership. Interview, Beijing intellectual, 1989.

United States. With Hu's demise, the linkage between high-level political developments and a student's personal and intellectual life was now abundantly clear.

The Debate over Strategy

This student concern with preventing a regression to cultural and intellectual conservatism shaped the initial student strategy of moderation. The students generally employed rhetoric that had often appeared in the official media to press for their demands, at least up until the beginning of the hunger strike on May 13 (See part IV). The goal was not to overthrow the system—which most students believed to be impossible anyway—but to push the leadership to resist the conservatives and continue with reform. Despite government violence on April 20, students reiterated their commitment to "nonviolence." Any "call for overthrowing the government" or "knocking down a few leaders" was also condemned (Doc. 24). Most students presented themselves as loyal remonstrators who revered the "national emblem," quoted from Lenin, and simply called on leaders to live up to the standard of a "people's government" (docs. 16, 38). The students' constant singing of the *Internationale*—which continued up through the crackdown—and the unfurling of unit and even Communist Youth League flags during parades were all intended to associate "patriotic" student demands with legitimate institutions and national symbols.[17]

Not all student and emerging popular groups supported such moderate tactics, however. Appeals for more militancy were already expressed in the April 15–27 period. While some voiced anti-CCP slogans, other individuals attacked China's "bureaucratic class" as hopelessly corrupt (docs. 17, 25). Students and intellectuals were fools, the authors of the first document claimed, if they believed China's "autocratic" regime was going to respond to a few street demonstrations. Chinese students were, instead, encouraged to "establish an armed organization" modeled on South Korean youth, and to use "revolutionary violence to fight the violent regime."[18] But such demands would never capture the Beijing Spring Movement even during the midst of the violent army crackdown.

Overall, the students remained committed to moderation even as government intransigence continued up through Hu Yaobang's April 22 funeral. Although some students described the government as having given "tacit consent to the student movement," the government refused to accede to student demands to allow the hearse bearing Hu's body to drive through the large crowd gathered in

---

[17]Students on the square also sang patriotic songs written to commemorate soldiers who had fought in China's war against Vietnam. Ironically, it may have been veterans of that war who carried out the massacre on June 3–4. See part VI.

[18]Chinese awareness of the violent tactics by South Korean students may have reflected the heavy coverage of these demonstrations on China Central TV over the past few years.

the square for a final farewell (Doc. 24).[19] Three student representatives demonstrated their fundamental loyalty to the state by kneeling on the steps of the Great Hall of the People to present their petition containing student demands. Yet they were conspicuously neglected by high state officials who insisted this was an inappropriate moment for such political actions. In the view of some Chinese, even an autocratic emperor would have sent an emissary to receive the petition; but the " 'people's' government has totally ignored the demands of the people" (Doc. 25).[20] Some student leaders, such as Wu'er Kaixi, even opposed this "feudal method of kneeling down" as excessively obsequious and demeaning. Already basic fissures were developing among students over tactics and political demands that would intensify throughout the upcoming period. Yet popular support for the students grew as the government's intransigence unwittingly galvanized Beijing citizens behind the students. Unlike 1986, the city's population responded to student actions as widely disseminated pictures of the kneeling students and numerous wall posters and handbills denounced the government's bureaucratic arrogance in terms the average person evidently found painfully familiar (Doc. 26).

Violence in Xi'an

The clash between government and students over honoring Hu Yaobang turned much more violent in Xi'an, the capital of Shaanxi Province. After two days of sporadic confrontations, students and city residents attempting to lay floral wreaths near the city's central square were assaulted by police in a manner reminiscent of the April 5, 1976, suppression of Beijing residents mourning Zhou Enlai in Tiananmen. The crowds in Xi'an then responded with bricks and stones which provoked an even tougher government reaction, including deployment of the notorious "antiriot police" (*fangbao jingcha*) (Doc. 27).[21] These events evidently convinced the central leadership in Beijing to issue the

---

[19]Deng apparently wanted to placate a public incensed over rumors that Hu Yaobang had suffered his heart attack during a high-level party meeting. Strict protocol did not require such an elaborate ceremony for an ex–general secretary. The obviously cold reaction of Hu Yaobang's widow to expressions of condolence by Deng Xiaoping, shown on national TV, reinforced the population's tendency to blame the conservative old guard for mistreating Hu. Interview, Beijing resident, 1989.

[20]Students claimed they had been promised a personal reception by Li Peng. This was subsequently denied by Beijing Mayor Chen Xitong, who blamed lower-level officials for irresponsibly making such promises. Students strengthened traditional allusions by writing their seven demands on a replica of the long paper scrolls presented by petitioners to emperors. Oksenberg et al., eds., *Beijing Spring*, Doc. 1; and Scott Simmie and Bob Nixon, *Tiananmen Square: An Eyewitness Account of the Chinese People's Passionate Quest for Democracy* (Seattle: University of Washington Press, 1989), p. 28.

[21]This unit was formed in the mid-1980s to deal with the increasingly volatile situation in cities created by inflation and the influx of the large population of itinerant workers. Some Chinese claim the force was staffed with "criminal" elements as an alternative

tough April 26 *People's Daily* editorial (discussed below).

Xi'an protesters, meanwhile, demanded that authorities investigate police brutality. As street demonstrations in the city declined until mid-May, students concentrated on inaugurating a formal investigation of both the police and the Shaanxi governor (who had personally ordered the attack on demonstrators) to be conducted by a special tribunal composed of Supreme Court judges and the procuracy from the national government. The Shaanxi government's violent reaction to the demonstrations was just an extreme example of abusive police power in a system lacking legal constraints.[22] Students also accused the Shaanxi government of resorting to *agent provocateurs* to provoke violence even as officials claimed to support social "stability."[23] But rather than taking the struggle back to the streets, Xi'an students tried to challenge government action through legal channels. Like their predecessors in the 1978–79 Democracy Wall demonstrations and the earlier 1919 May Fourth Movement, China's current generation of students advocated an independent judiciary and rule of law, which even CCP media had promoted throughout the mid-1980s, as necessary checks on absolutist political authority (see part I).

Cracks in the CCP

Back in Beijing, the question quickly arose: "Where will the student movement go?" If it was allowed to "die halfway," then, some young teachers advised the students, "China [will] remain the same" (Doc. 28). For some CCP members, largely at universities, the only answer was to withdraw from the party.[24] The CCP, they claimed, "has gradually deteriorated under the conservatism, narrow-mindedness, and stupidity of its peasant-like characteristics" so that internal "party reform" (*dangnei gaige*) was now considered hopeless. Although once a "progressive force," the CCP, they declared, "cannot represent the interests of the people." These members

---

to prison. Violence also occurred in Changsha, Hunan, purportedly in the form of unprecedented robberies of stores. *Renmin ribao* (People's daily), May 14, 1989, in *Jieyan ling fabu zhiqian* (Before the promulgation of martial law), comp. Propaganda Section, Beijing Party Committee (Beijing: Economic Daily Publishers, 1989), and interview, Beijing resident, 1990.

[22]Joseph Esherick has described the April 22 events in Xi'an as a "classic police riot" accompanied by sporadic brick throwing and arson by what appeared to be unemployed youth. "Xi'an Spring," *The Australian Journal of Chinese Affairs*, no. 24 (July 1990): 215. For a comprehensive examination of the abuse of police powers in China, see Amnesty International, *China: Torture and Ill-Treatment in China* (1987).

[23]Xi'an students argued that the brick throwers were government-hired *provocateurs*. Although this was not independently verified, Beijing police admitted after June 4 that they had used such tactics, at least in Beijing. Interview, Beijing CCP member, 1990.

[24]Although guaranteed by the party constitution, party members cannot, in practice, voluntarily resign from the CCP. Higher-level party authorities must instead agree to dismiss a member so as to preserve the image that the organization is superior to the individual. Ibid.

then boldly announced the formation of an opposition political organization modeled on Polish Solidarity (Doc. 29). With a promise to "struggle relentlessly against the ruling party," this newly established "Society to Promote the Chinese Democratic Movement" would give expression to group-based interests that the CCP had blocked since 1949.[25] The prodemocracy movement, it was promised, would not only fundamentally alter China's political institutions but transform the basic character of the system from an authoritarian to a representational mode of politics.

Public resignations by CCP members also occurred in other cities such as Shenyang and Shanghai, though the attempted establishment of opposition parties during the entire Beijing Spring was uncommon.[26] For party members to declare support for the students was also still relatively rare. But it carried symbolic significance as the willingness of CCP members to break with organizational discipline indicated the depth of the students' appeal within the very organs of the dictatorship of the proletariat.[27] Student demands on CCP leaders also became more radical and personal as other elite groups jumped on the movement's bandwagon. After initially advising students against demonstrating, senior professors now backed up student calls for a "dialogue" with the government (Doc. 37). Previously quiescent newspaper reporters also began to show support by insisting on accurate coverage of the movement, and even by joining demonstrations.[28] Some students originally reluctant to join the protests were even encouraged by their parents (also CCP members) to march "for freedom and democracy" (Doc. 35).[29]

---

[25]Throughout the history of the PRC, party propaganda has tried to deny the political validity of group interests distinct from the party, particularly among workers. This has been done by consistently portraying workers as devoted to the CCP and national development without regard for their own wages or safety. In addition to the more well-known Daqing oil workers, there was the "March 8th Women Work Team Operating on Live Wires," a group idealized in the early 1960s for working under hazardous conditions. Since June 4, 1989, similar themes have reappeared in the government's promotion of "selfless" coal miners who purportedly "give no thought to their lives," an obvious effort to prevent Chinese workers from following their Soviet counterparts in striking over wage and safety issues. Xinhua, January 22, 1990.

[26]An exception was the China Democratic Political Party, formed in Dalian, Liaoning Province. Liaoning Provincial Service, June 13, 1989, in FBIS, *Daily Report: China*, June 14, 1989, p. 67.

[27]Students in the party history department at Beijing's People's University were also in the vanguard of the protest. Prof. Lee Feigon, personal communication.

[28]Some journalists participated in the April 21–22 demonstrations, but it was not until after Hu Qili gave tacit support to "objective" coverage of the events in late April that the media took a more active role, mainly in mid-May in Beijing and other cities. Anne Gunn, "Tell the World About Us: The Student Movement in Shenyang, 1989," *The Australian Journal of Chinese Affairs*, no. 24 (July 1990): 248.

[29]At an institution in a city other than Beijing, however, some reticent students were evidently pressured and even coerced into participating in the demonstrations by their classmates. Interview, Chinese student, 1989.

The substance of student demands shifted dramatically after April 22 to reflect this growing support from key groups. Even as students lamented their "humiliation" at Hu's funeral, they now shifted their major concerns to bringing about fundamental changes in the political system, including the resignation of Li Peng (docs. 30, 32). Real institutional constraints, they argued, needed to be imposed on the CCP, especially by a free press and an independent judiciary. In a country where "the same mistakes are made time and again," dramatic institutional changes were necessary to free China from control by a geriatric leadership that, it was argued, prevented the country from entering the modern political world (Doc. 39). The unchanging political structure in which decision-making authority was still "concentrate[d] in the hands of the leader" provided the means for old conservative leaders to block further reforms by transferring authority to compliant clients like Li Peng (Doc. 41). Without general "political liberalization," the vast corruption and bureaucratic bungling that has cost the country considerable wealth since 1949 would continue unabated, leaving China far behind its rapidly developing neighbors like Taiwan and South Korea.[30] Contrary to the self-congratulatory praise pouring out of government propaganda organs, China was not in the vanguard of development. It was, instead, mired in a "Stalinist political system" more characteristic of a feudal "monarchical autocracy" than the dynamic societies of East Asia (Doc. 41). Incremental policy making championed by CCP leaders and embodied in the slogan of "feeling stones to cross the river" (*mozhe shitou guohe*) was also considered a dead end in the political realm. Only radical system changes, it was now argued, could solve the country's enormous problems (Doc. 39).[31] Unless China adopted fundamental social contract principles and eliminated once and for all the profound anti-intellectualism that has influenced CCP policies for decades, the government would remain unaccountable and the country would continue to stagnate (Doc. 42).

The People Join In

The fundamental difference between 1986 and 1989 was the response of Beijing's *laobaixing* to the student demonstrations. The political apathy

---

[30]Liu Binyan estimates investment losses in China since 1949 at 400 billion yuan. Liu Binyan, *China's Crisis, China's Hope* (Cambridge: Harvard University Press, 1990), p. 64; also, He Bochuan, *Shanao shang de Zhongguo* (China in the valley) (Xi'an: Shaanxi People's Publishing House, 1988). This book revealed enormous bureaucratic corruption and was widely read by top leaders before being banned.

[31]Chinese students and proreform advocates in the CCP supported political reform as a necessary precursor to economic modernization, the strategy employed by Mikhail Gorbachev in the Soviet Union. Without democratization, some Chinese reformers have argued, the country will continue with such irrational economic policies as building enormously costly infrastructural projects, such as the Pudong development zone in Shanghai, which party cadres favor to expand their local power base and political influence. Interview, CCP member, 1990.

displayed in Beijing in 1986 had led some Chinese intellectuals, such as Wen Yuankai, to argue that "China's civilization was too decrepit and decayed" to produce people capable of responding to the challenges of the modern era.[32] The Chinese people were "asleep" and politically "numb" (*mamu*)—a view that not only informed *He shang*, but had also been promulgated during the 1919 May Fourth Movement. But contrary to such pessimistic judgments, the urban population in 1989 would not bow under political and then military threats. The effects of economic reform, interaction with Western and recently modernized Asian nations, greater internal mobility, and a relatively relaxed social and political atmosphere had all forged a social cohesion antithetical to the Leninist structure and Maoist paternalism still defended by CCP conservatives. Chinese society was no longer an atomized "loose sheet of sand" incapable of generating its own political will and organization. The recent establishment of labor unions and other citizen groups throughout the late 1980s indicated that an embryonic "civil society" was emerging to challenge the CCP's autocratic political structure and rigid ideology.[33]

The population's receptiveness to the prodemocracy movement was evident from the beginning, though it would take the April 26 editorial and the subsequent student hunger strike to bring out vast numbers of citizens. Immediately after the April 20 violence outside Zhongnanhai, some workers voiced open support for the students by condemning the government leaders as "murderers."[34] Imploring the police to "come and stand on the people's side," the union also called on Zhao Ziyang and Deng Xiaoping to reveal their own and their family's expenditures of public funds on frivolous activities. Workers also raised such serious issues as China's foreign debt and the impending negotiations with Taiwan (docs. 18, 19). This emerging popular discourse undoubtedly threatened

---

[32]Speech by Wen Yuankai, a professor at China Science and Technology University in Hefei, Anhui, and a member of one of Zhao Ziyang's "think tanks," recorded in the late 1980s. This image of a "decaying" China was reinforced by the growing problems of environmental pollution and agricultural deterioration outlined by CASS researchers.

[33]Liu Binyan dates the emergence of "civil society" in China to the April 5, 1976, movement. Throughout the 1980s, there was a rising level of labor organization and militancy in China, with assaults on factory managers becoming more frequent. The willingness of workers, such as Beijing bus drivers, to join the students in spring 1989 may have reflected their discontent over the government's recent decision to hold back on annual pay increases. Liu, *China's Crisis*, p. 49; Lawrence R. Sullivan, "The Emergence of Civil Society in China, Spring 1989," in *The Chinese People's Movement*, ed. Saich, pp. 126–44; and Wang Shaoguang. "Analyzing the Role of Chinese Workers in the Protest Movement of 1989," in *China: The Crisis of 1989: Origins and Implications*, ed. Roger V. DesForges et al., Special Studies no. 159 (Buffalo: Council on International Studies and Programs, State University of New York, 1990), 2:245.

[34]This accusation of "murder" stemmed from the death of a woman student hit by a trolley-bus while being pursued by the police even though she had not participated in the April 20 demonstration. Michael Fathers and Andrew Higgins, *Tiananmen: The Rape of Peking* (London: The Independent, 1989), p. 40.

the CCP's political and ideological monopoly as workers and other popular groups exhibited a basic grasp of the nation's problems that is readily apparent in the documents reproduced throughout this volume.

Following Hu Yaobang's funeral, more and more workers joined other key groups in coalescing behind the students' demands. Although still unwilling to participate in demonstrations, workers combined continuing vocal support with promises to raise money and provide equipment to aid in the students' cause.[35] Yet workers were also concerned that the students were focusing too heavily on narrow partisan issues, such as more money for education (Doc. 34). Concerned over the gap between educated and noneducated, workers appealed to the students to avoid the condescension toward the common people that has traditionally split Chinese society and limited the challenges to CCP dictatorship from below.

The Impact of the *People's Daily* Editorial

Despite public sympathy for the students, popular enthusiasm for further demonstrations seemed to be waning until the *People's Daily* published the provocative April 26 editorial (Doc. 43). This critical document was based on a talk given by Deng Xiaoping a day earlier, evidently in response to briefings on the situation in Beijing and Xi'an by Beijing Mayor Chen Xitong and the capital's first party secretary, Li Ximing. It is believed that the actual text of the editorial was written by Xu Weicheng, a vice-mayor of Beijing and an old protégé of the Gang of Four who had launched frenzied attacks in *Beijing ribao* (Beijing daily) against intellectuals during the 1987 anti–bourgeois liberalization campaign.[36] Cultural Revolution rhetoric not seen for years appeared in the editorial's title— "We Must Firmly Oppose Turmoil" (also translated as "It Is Necessary to Take a Clear-cut Stand against Turmoil")—and throughout the text in such key terms as

---

[35]Workers' initial unwillingness to take part in demonstrations reflected their fear of losing coveted jobs and the fact that many were offered extra pay to stay away from the student parades. Students were also warned that any attempt to involve workers constituted prima facie evidence of a "counterrevolutionary conspiracy." Long-standing mutual suspicions between the two classes also made unified action difficult throughout the spring movement. Giving money to students became a major way for *laobaixing* to support the movement without taking the risk of joining parades.

[36]Xu had also been a member of the left-wing "rebel faction" (*zaofanpai*) during the Cultural Revolution. Hu Qili and Li Peng also reportedly had a hand in crafting the editorial. A senior official at *People's Daily* tried to replace key Cultural Revolution rhetoric, such as "turmoil," with less provocative language. He was overruled by higher leaders, however, and later purged from his post. Zhao Ziyang reportedly approved the text while visiting North Korea, but he may have signed off on a less inflammatory version than the final one. See He Xin, "A Word of Advice to the Politburo," n. 51, and Wu Guoguang, "From Head to Tongue: The Formulation of *People's Daily* Editorials," lecture, East Asian Institute, Columbia University, October 4, 1990. Wu worked at the paper in the mid-1980s.

"beating, smashing, looting, and burning" (*da, za, qiang, shao*), and "a small group" (*yi xiaocuo*). Students were also compared with Red Guards as the editorial accused them of "going to factories, rural areas, and schools to establish ties (*chuan-lian*)." Mimicking Mao Zedong's political style, Deng Xiaoping and the conservative leadership thus polarized the situation by presenting students, workers, and prodemocracy party members with a Hobson's choice: either declare loyalty to the current CCP leadership or be labeled anti-CCP and "counterrevolutionary."

If the intent of the editorial was to cow the students and their popular supporters, the effect was just the opposite.[37] Although Li Ximing would later claim that the editorial "stabilized" the situation, April 27 witnessed the largest demonstration to date.[38] Beijing's common people not only joined the demonstrations but also took the lead in intervening to prevent police from blocking the advance of student-led parades. Students also impressed the city's population by maintaining strict discipline within their ranks, avoiding any violent conflicts (as had occurred in Xi'an), which the government could then exploit by accusing them of "beating, smashing, and looting." Challenging the editorial's claim of a "planned conspiracy" against CCP rule, students now shouted such slogans as "Support the CCP" and unfurled banners with proreform quotations from Deng Xiaoping. "All we want is an honest government . . . and a speeding up of reform," Beijing Normal University students claimed in defense against the editorial (Doc. 44). But even as students moderated their political attacks on the leadership, the huge turnout on April 27 and the willingness of many common people to become directly involved in confronting police authority indicated the depth of resentment the students had tapped. Although fears of the use of military force by the government increased as the first PLA units moved into Beijing immediately after the editorial's publication, public defiance of the CCP and Deng Xiaoping's authority grew.[39] Journalists, too, expressed outrage by accusing the Beijing Party Committee of precipitating the "present crisis," while even an adviser to the conservative leadership derided the April 26 editorial as "stupid" (Doc. 45).[40] What had begun as a purely student action was now rapidly developing into a confrontation between Chinese civil society and the state.

---

[37]Some foreign eyewitnesses in Beijing suggested, in contrast, that the editorial and other provocative government acts were actually intended to intensify the crisis so that conservative leaders could use the demonstrations, which initially targeted Zhao Ziyang, to purge the general secretary and his supporters. See part VI.

[38]For Li's speech, see Oksenberg et al., eds., *Beijing Spring*, Doc. 45.

[39]Jiang Zhifeng, *Wangpai chujin de Zhongnanhai qiaoju* (The last card of the Zhongnanhai bridge game) (San Francisco: Pacific News Services, 1990), pp. 95–97. A survey of more than seven hundred Beijing residents by Chinese social science students indicated, however, that 60 percent of the people polled still opposed the students, though this number would drop considerably after the hunger strike. Shi Tianjian, Columbia University, personal communication.

[40]He Xin, "A Word of Advice to the Politburo," p. 72.

"Li Peng, Come Out!"
—Poster at Beijing University

16

Under the National Emblem
of the People's Republic

A Group of Witnesses of the April 20 Murder Case

April 20, 1989

Source: *ORSI*, p. 13.

We can never forget the Tiananmen Square Incident of April 5, 1976. Today a similar episode is again taking place in front of Zhongnanhai, the heart of the People's Republic, under the solemn national emblem. We shall never forget this day of April 20, 1989, when a government used state machinery in a fascist crackdown on the students and city residents who were participating in mourning the death of Mr. Hu Yaobang and presenting a peaceful petition.

Recently, tens of thousands of people spontaneously carried out activities in Tiananmen Square mourning the death of Hu Yaobang. . . . On the evening of April 19, these mourning activities reached a climax when the Monument to the People's Heroes was overwhelmed by a sea of people and floral wreaths. Students from ten colleges and universities in Beijing and people from all over the country, numbering about two hundred thousand, had gathered in Tiananmen Square. . . . At about ten o'clock that evening, some students and people held high the floral wreath and the elegiac couplet of "Eternal repose to Yaobang" and marched together toward the Xinhua Gate [in front of Zhongnanhai] to make a petition. At 12:00 midnight, students from the colleges and universities in the capital sat down quietly in front of the gate and collectively made seven suggestions to the government, hoping the government leaders would have a dialogue with the students. . . .

However, policemen patrolling Xinhua Gate soon drove most of the students and masses to Chang'an Boulevard. . . . In the meantime, government leaders time and again delayed giving a response to student demands. Students sitting in front of the gate had to wait patiently, while the national anthem and *Internationale* were sung loudly and the slogans of "Long live the republic," "Long live democracy," and "Long live freedom" rang out continuously. The students reorganized their groups, and hand-in-hand they sat down in a quiet and orderly fashion. No radical actions were taken.

At 3:00 the next [morning], bloodshed occurred when the police attacked the students.

They attacked the students and people on the east and west sides of Xinhua Gate and on Chang'an Boulevard. Large numbers of military policemen suddenly appeared and rushed the petitioning students and people who were sitting there peacefully, defenseless, and without any preparation. The policemen shouted "beat them to death" and "beat them fatally." Belts with steel heads were their weapons and big leather boots their instruments of torture in their abuse of power. The peaceful, petitioning people were severely beaten, and those who did not scatter quickly stumbled and were attacked by several policemen.

Scene 1: Seven or eight policemen chased a Wuhan college student to the corner of the Great Hall of the People. They trampled on him, beat him with their belts, and kicked him with leather boots. This student was immediately paralyzed on the ground, begged for mercy in tears, and said, "Uncle, Uncle . . . "

Scene 2: In the inner street near the Bank of China, more than ten military policemen chased a young man of fifteen or sixteen years old whose legs were beaten into a mixture of flesh and blood.

Scene 3: A group of policemen caught up with a male student and one woman student riding on a bicycle. They surrounded the woman student and attempted to use violence. Then the boy shouted, "If you want to beat people, just beat me." Afterward this student was never seen to stand up again . . . .

Scene 4: One private vendor who sold cakes was surrounded by seven military policemen. He was kicked viciously in the back more than twenty times and could hardly stand up.

The bloody violence spread widely, extending to Liubukou in the west, Beijing Railway Station in the north [*sic*], and Heping Gate in the south . . . .

By 5:00 A.M., many people were lying on the ground, moaning and groaning . . . .

Scene 6: Police forcibly took away the film in the camera of a Hong Kong reporter.

Scene 7: Policemen beat students, who were sitting in an orderly fashion . . . by tearing their hair, and by kicking and choking them. Three or four policemen pulled a student into a trolley bus and kept beating him. Ten women students bravely participating in the sit-in were brutally beaten by the brutish policemen. They knocked off their shoes, pulled their hair, and tore their clothes. Several girl students were beaten into tears. . . .

Scene [8]: The head of the secret police . . . directed this beating on the spot, and he grinned hideously with satisfaction.

The national emblem on the Xinhua Gate was still shining amidst the shouts of the beasts and the cries of the victims. How solemnly "great"! The beasts trampled on peace and brutally destroyed knowledge. Again, how solemnly "great"!

At this moment, flashing across our minds was a dimly audible but vigorous and desolate echo: "People's Republic! People's Republic . . . "

Proposals: [attached] by Federation of the Student Movement of Beijing University.

Students of all the colleges and universities in Beijing [should] jointly boycott classes to protest the violence and demand punishment for the prime culprits.

Publish an open telegram to the whole country. We will not resume classes until achieving our goals.

17

A Short Comment on the Slogan "Down with the Communist Party"

A MARXIST DISCIPLE

After April 30, 1989

Source: *ORSD,* 1:56.

China Central TV has reiterated that the slogan "Down with the Communist party" was heard during the April 20 incident. Whether this slogan was shouted, and whether it was shouted by the students, is not my concern. What's worth looking into is the meaning of the slogan itself.

When Sun Yat-sen founded the Nationalist party . . . it undoubtedly was a leader of current [political] trends and, therefore, was well received by the people. Even some founders of the CCP, such as Li Dazhao, Mao Zedong, and Zhou Enlai, joined the Nationalist party for some time. The slogan "Down with the Nationalist party" was surely a counterrevolutionary slogan then. But with the passing of time and degeneration of the Nationalist party, things changed. During the Great Revolutionary and Anti-Japanese War and the Liberation War periods, the Nationalist party became a political force that tried to oppose the historical trend. It aimed at establishing a one-party dictatorship and one-man autocracy in China. The people thus responded with the slogans "Down with the Nationalist reactionaries" and "Overthrow the feudal regime of the Chiang [Kai-shek] family." Such slogans were undoubtedly the common will of the progressive forces and [constituted] a correct historical judgment on the situation.

The process through which the Nationalist party developed from a revolutionary position to a counterrevolutionary one proves a general Marxist viewpoint—any political party, organization, or leader who doesn't represent the interests of the people will be deserted by history.

The time now is the 1980s and the People's Republic is middle-aged. We feel confused when we suddenly wake up and find ourselves within the international community. We begin to wonder: Just what has the Communist party brought to us in the last forty years? The living standard has certainly improved. But what's behind this phenomenon? We have read the "Contemporary Bureaucratic List" and "A Worker's Letter to the Students" (see Doc. 56 for a similar description). And we have an idea about the peasants' present situation. We ourselves have experienced . . . cheating and being bled. Thus we come to the following conclusion: "Prosperity" is merely superficial and inflated. We are building our pagoda on sand!

What does the slogan "Down with the Communist party" indicate? We suggest the following to [the CCP] since the present government still claims it represents the people's interests: (1) We ought to determine who shouted the slogan and if the slogan really exists. (2) Ignore [the slogan] if it was shouted by our enemy. "No matter how strong the northwest wind, it's unable to destroy the magnificent Kunlun mountain; no matter how thick the clouds, they are unable to block out the shining sun!"[1] No matter how widespread rumors, the one billion people can judge them fairly.

18

Letter to People of the Entire City

BEIJING WORKERS' AUTONOMOUS UNION

April 20, 1989

Source: *ORSD*, 1:27.

The situation for people throughout the country has now become intolerable. After a long period of bureaucratic dictatorial government, inflation is out of control, and the people's living standards have slipped. To cover up their extravagance, the small group of ruling officials have issued a large number of various types of government and treasury bonds. They are thereby squeezing every

---

[1]A poem by Mao Zedong.

penny out of the people. We appeal to people from all walks of life to come together to fight for truth and the future of China.

Police brothers, soldier brothers: Please come and stand on the people's side. Come and stand for the truth. Do not serve as tools of the people's enemies. You too are being oppressed and suppressed. The people will never forget the crimes of those murderers involved in the "April 5 Incident" [1976][1] and the "April 20 Bloodshed" [1989].

19

Ten Questions

BEIJING WORKERS' AUTONOMOUS UNION

April 20, 1989

Source: *ORSD*, 1:27.

Will the party [Central] Committee please answer the following questions:

1. How much did Deng Xiaoping's son place in his bet on horse racing in Hong Kong? What was the source of his money?

2. Mr. and Mrs. Zhao Ziyang play golf every weekend. Have they paid the fees? Who paid for their expenses?

3. How does the [Central] Committee evaluate the earlier reforms? Premier Li Peng admitted during the Chinese New Year gathering that some mistakes had been made in the reform movement. What are these mistakes? What exactly is the real situation?

4. The [Central] Committee has proposed a list of actions to control inflation and prices. However, in reality inflation continues. The people's living standards have declined. How do you explain that?

5. Beginning next year, China has to pay back its foreign loans. How much does each citizen have to pay for these debts? Will this affect the basic living standards of citizens? Please answer.

6. Deng Xiaoping once suggested raising the status of intellectuals from the "ninth rank" to the "top rank." What is the position of "top rank"? Is it the landlord or the landlord's father? Please answer.

---

[1]"April 5" refers to the popular protest that erupted in Tiananmen Square in 1976 following the death of Zhou Enlai, and in support of Deng Xiaoping. A nationwide repression with many arrests followed.

7. How many houses and villas do the party's top officials have all over the country? What are their expenditures? Can this be publicized? Please answer.

8. Publicize the private incomes and expenditures of the top officials in the party.

9. How will the [Communist] party respond to the three preconditions for opening peace talks suggested by the Taiwan government?

10. Will the party explain the concept and meaning of the following terms: (a) party; (b) revolution; (c) reaction.

Would the party please publish its answers to the above ten questions in the newspapers as soon as possible?

"The life tenure system is abolished but the hereditary system is installed."

—*New Sayings*, courtesy of HFKS

20

Open Letter to the Party Central Committee, Standing Committee of the National People's Congress, and State Council

TWO HUNDRED INTELLECTUALS

April 21–25, 1989

Source: *Tiananmen 1989*, pp. 328–29.

To the Chinese Communist Party Central Committee, Standing Committee of the National People's Congress, and State Council:

Mr. Hu Yaobang is the symbol of Chinese democratization, the model of an honest and upright government official, the true friend of the people, and the promoter of social progress. He resolutely opposed conservative ideas and regression, and he actively pushed forward the reform and the opening of China. He enjoyed high esteem among the masses. We hereby wish to express our profound grief at Mr. Hu Yaobang's death.

In the past few days, students from colleges and universities in Beijing have been mourning Mr. Hu Yaobang's death in various ways. . . . The news media should provide fully objective and fair coverage of the students' mourning activities and their demands for democracy.

As we understand it, the main demands of the students . . . are:

1. Carry out Hu Yaobang's behest to speed up the process of democratization and reform of the political system.

2. Adopt practical and effective measures to eliminate the widespread corruption in the party and government institutions at various levels and to solve the increasingly grave problems of social inequality.

3. Actually solve the problems of ineffectiveness, incompetence, and inefficiency that exist at various levels of government. Implement the target-responsibility system [that will decentralize decision-making powers] from the central government to the various local governments. No one should shirk their personal responsibility under the pretext of "collective responsibility."

4. Realize freedom of speech, press, and publication as granted in the [state] constitution and assure that the mass media play a supervisory role.

We believe that the above demands are positive and constructive. . . . The actual realization of the above goals is also a necessary precondition for achieving stability and unity over a long period of time. Thus, we suggest that the party and state leaders earnestly listen to the wishes and demands of the students and hold a dialogue with them on the basis of full equality. The leaders should draw an historical lesson from the Tiananmen Square Incident of 1976. They must not ignore the demands of the students. . . .

21

Impeach the Existing Students' Union and Strive for Campus Democracy

RATIONAL AND ARDENT YOUTH OF CLASS OF 1988,
DEPARTMENT OF MATHEMATICS, BEIJING UNIVERSITY

Undated

Source: *ORSD*, 1:11.

We are students at Beijing University. We have the ability and power to exercise our democratic rights. The existing student union did not lead the vast majority of the students in the petition movement as an autonomous organization of our students. The members of the student union kept silent after the students were severely beaten, and some of them even sold out their classmates. We therefore demand an impeachment of the existing student union and establishment of a new one that can effectively lead our students and represent our interests and demands.

1. A meeting of all the students of the university will be held at 2:00 P.M. on April 24 on the May Fourth Drill Ground, to take a vote of no-confidence. If more than half of the students cast no-confidence votes, the existing student union will be impeached.

2. Following that vote, the students of the whole university will directly elect a new student union. Efforts will be made to elect a chairman, vice-chairman, and heads of the various sections of the student union through secret ballot. . . . This will be a free, competitive, and fair election.

3. The student union of the university leads the student unions of the departments in the university. Departmental student unions will also be elected directly by the students. We will not recognize members of the student union nominated by university authorities. Neither the chairman, vice-chairman, nor heads of the sections of the student union of the whole university is allowed to serve concurrently as a chairman of the student union of the department.

4. The university authorities must unconditionally recognize the university and department student unions directly elected by the students.

5. The student union shall hold an election on April 22 each year to be organized by an election committee composed of two representatives from each department of the university. . . . This committee will immediately dissolve after the election is over. No one is allowed to hold the chairmanship of the student union for more than two terms. . . .

7. The student union must publicize its bylaws, and any violator of them will be immediately impeached. If the whole body of the student union violates the bylaws, then the whole student union will be impeached and a new student union will be elected. . . .

8. If more than half of the chairmen, vice-chairmen, and section heads resign or are impeached, the student union should stop functioning. Their functions will then be performed by a temporary student union composed of the rest of the union members and new representatives elected by the student unions of the departments in the university until the next general election.

9. The university radio station should be managed by the student union.

The student movement has touched every student. But without support from the workers' movement, the student movement will only be [accused of] "making trouble by a handful of people with ulterior motives." Thus we make the following suggestions . . . .

1. Among the "seven demands" [Doc. 22], choose the ones that can be easily accepted by the government as the goals for the present demonstration, so as to achieve a substantial victory and to win the people's understanding and support.

2. We must establish broad connections with the people. We therefore suggest organizing speech-making groups to [go among] the people and help them learn the truth so that workers will hold a strike to support us.[1]

---

[1]Students acted on this proposal, giving effective speeches on Beijing street corners.

3. Call on all college and university students to unite and boycott classes indefinitely. We will not end [the boycott] until we reach our goal.

22

A Peaceful Petition of Seven Demands

BEIJING UNIVERSITY STUDENTS' PREPARATORY COMMITTEE

April 21, 1989

Source: *ORSI*, p. 12.

1. Reevaluate Comrade Hu Yaobang's rights and wrongs, achievements and errors. Affirm Hu's views favoring "democracy, freedom, loosening [of controls], and harmony."

2. Severely punish the assailants who beat up the students and masses. Demand compensation and an apology to the victims from those responsible.

3. Promulgate the press law as soon as possible to allow the publication of private newspapers and assure freedom of the press.

4. Demand that state leaders publicly reveal . . . their own and their children's sources of income and property. Investigate and deal with official profiteering and publicize details of the investigation.

5. Demand that relevant state leaders make formal self-criticisms to the people of the whole country for mistakes in education policy, and seek out those responsible. Demand a big increase in the education budget and improve the treatment of teachers.

6. Reevaluate the [1987] "anti–bourgeois liberalization" campaign, and rehabilitate those citizens who were incorrectly denounced.

7. Strongly demand fair and faithful news coverage of this patriotic democracy movement.

23

Students of Beijing Colleges and Universities and People of All Walks of Life

TEMPORARY ACTION COMMITTEE OF BEIJING COLLEGES
AND UNIVERSITIES

April 21, 1989

Source: *ORSI*, p.12.

To mourn the death of Comrade Hu Yaobang, support his proposals for democratization, and protest the fascist violent actions by policemen in the bloody "April 20" incident, the students of Beijing University, Beijing University of Political Science and Law, Qinghua University, Beijing Science and Technology University, Beijing Normal University, Nankai University [Tianjin], Chinese People's University, and the Chinese Academy of Sciences have organized a march of tens of thousands of students toward Tiananmen Square to present a peaceful petition. Our actions have gained strong support from Beijing residents. We thank you! The people of the whole country thank you!

If the government ignores our seven demands [Doc. 22], we will call on the workers, peasants, intellectuals, private businessmen, service workers, and the workers in government institutions to support us . . . .

Victory to the people! Victory to democracy!

"I want to give you my hope, I want to help make you free."
—Cui Jian[1]

---

[1]Cui Jian is a popular Chinese rock star whose songs were played on the square throughout the demonstrations. This phrase comes from his song *Yi wu suo you* (Nothing to my name).

24

Questions and Answers about the Student Movement

ANONYMOUS

Late April 1989

Source: Printed handbill, courtesy of HKFS.

Q: What is the purpose of this student movement?

A: We do not aim to oppose the government led by the Communist party, nor do we aim to knock down a few leaders. We want to use nonviolence to pressure the present government in order to achieve the goal of establishing a truly democratic government. Only in so doing can we fundamentally wipe out all kinds of corrupt practices and push social progress forward. This student movement is different from the [1919] "May Fourth Movement." It is neither right nor realistic to call for overthrowing the government. The situation we are facing now is that present-day China lacks a healthy democracy, and the government is not equipped with a mechanism for self-renewal. We therefore need a driving force from outside the government to push it to carry out the reform of the system from top to bottom. . . .

Q: Are you worried that someone may take advantage of the student movement?

A: There is no such problem as taking advantage of, or being taken advantage of. Although the student movement may cause some temporary factional struggles [among CCP leaders], from a long-run perspective its objective effect will ultimately be to promote the process of democratization. . . . The government's tacit consent to the student movement and the pressures on the government exerted by the student movement have already pushed forward the process of democratization. . . . What we are concerned with is [this] process, not changes in [party] leadership. We will not stop trying to pursue democracy because of certain leadership changes.

Q: What are the goals of this student movement?

A: This student movement should achieve two goals. One is to establish a national higher education student union that can lead and coordinate the students' democracy movement all over the country. Establishing such a union in Beijing is the first step toward achieving this goal . . . . The other goal is to gain support from people of all walks of life in society, using the method of boycotting classes and doing public opinion and propaganda work, so as to pressure the government into having an open dialogue with the students on the "seven demands." All the students' activities at this moment should be focused on achieving these two goals.

25

After the Peaceful Petition . . .

Anonymous

Late April 1989

Source: *ORSI*, p. 18.

The "people's" government has completely ignored the people's demands. This is a crime against the people and a crime against history. The government cannot be pardoned.

In China neither a reformist nor conservative group exists, but only a feudal, bureaucratic regime with different faces. The Chinese people have already lost confidence in the government. Our knowledge has become a tool of the bureaucratic class for promoting their personal interests. Our [university] study is for the benefit of the bureaucrats. The bureaucratic, autocratic regime has deceived one generation after another of intellectuals into making sacrifices for the bureaucrats in the name of "saving the country."

During many years of hardships and difficulties, the blood of the people has been shed all over China. What is there to be happy about in a country under autocracy? Should we hail the bureaucrats even more for having enhanced their personal interests? No!

We should print large numbers of pamphlets (every student act consciously!) and copy many handbills by hand. We should go among the residents. At the same time, we should establish an armed organization, following the example of the ardent South Korean youth in using revolutionary violence to fight against the violent regime. (Just think of the May Fourth Movement that burned the "Mansion of the Zhao Family.")[1] We should go to the streets in and outside of Beijing and make public speeches! We are living in a dark, autocratic society. What is the use of our study? Let's devote our youthful vigor and our blood to scoring a victory for democracy in the republic!!!

---

[1]The reference here is to the violent action taken against Republican government officials during the May Fourth Movement by students irate over China's agreement to sign the Versailles Treaty, which transferred sovereignty over parts of Shandong Province from Germany to Japan.

26

The Whole Story of the "April 22 Incident"

ANONYMOUS

Late April 1989

Source: *ORSI*, p. 15.

To carry out Mr. Hu Yaobang's behests—to accelerate the process of democratization in China, oppose . . . autocracy, dictatorship, corruption, and official profiteering in the party and government, so as to invigorate education and rescue our China—about one hundred thousand college and university students in the capital marched toward Tiananmen Square for a gathering on the early morning of April 22 to mourn the death of Hu Yaobang and to present a petition for the people.

To prevent the "April 20" bloody incident [Doc. 16] from recurring, students from colleges and universities in the capital jointly organized an "Autonomous Student Union" to lead and coordinate this demonstration.

At 10:00 P.M. on April 21, groups of marchers departed from Beijing Normal University.

At 3:00 A.M. on April 22, groups of marchers entered Tiananmen Square and sat on the ground in good order.

At 10:00 A.M., the memorial ceremony for Hu Yaobang began inside the Great Hall of the People. With the funeral dirge emanating from the Great Hall, all the students stood in silent mourning . . . [and] began to sing the *Internationale*.

At 11:30 A.M., the leaders began to walk out of the Great Hall and the students shouted "Dialogue, dialogue, we demand a dialogue!" and "Li Peng, come out!" When student representatives went to discuss the matter, the people working in the Great Hall promised to pass on the message to Li Peng.

At 12:30 P.M., . . . representatives from Beijing Normal University told the students that the government would make a response to the students at 12:45.

At 1:30 P.M., there was no sign of Li Peng. At this moment, three student representatives knelt down below the national emblem to present a petition, holding high the petition letter.

At 2:00 P.M., Li Peng still did not appear. The students realized that they had been fooled and tearfully shouted: "Stand up, representatives." Many students even began to cry loudly, for this tragic country, for the people living under bureaucratic rule, and for the fact that the title of the people's prime minister was given to such a faithless and incompetent man. . . . Angry students began to push forward and military police quickly rushed toward them. One student from the physics department of Beijing Normal University was beaten on the head and was unconscious for more than ten minutes. . . . But soon the students calmed down. Someone shouted: "Don't push forward anymore. We have the national emblem in front of us. Forty years ago the Chinese people won her and we cannot commit crimes against her." So the students retreated. To avoid conflicts with the military police, the students began an orderly withdrawal.

The students petitioned for the people, but they were severely beaten by the police. The newspapers and radios have made false reports about the "April 20" incident to deceive the people. Today the prime minister of the country again deceived the students. The state has finally resorted to violence and lied in order to maintain their rule over the people. We young students are very worried and angry, but we know all the more that we must change this incompetent and shameful way of ruling. We are determined to keep making our petitions and are ready to undergo the most severe trials. . . .

"A few leaders cannot stop the progress of history."
—Placard carried by Sichuan medical students.

27

Who Is the Ruffian? Who Is Provoking the Turmoil? True Facts of the April 22 Xincheng Square Tragedy in Xi'an

STUDENTS AND FACULTY MEMBERS OF UNIVERSITIES
AND COLLEGES IN THE XI'AN REGION

April 26, 1989

Source: Big-character poster, Xi'an, courtesy of Robin Munro.

Comrade Hu Yaobang has left us. Chinese with a good conscience are reflecting on his life, which was honest, above-board, unselfish, and fearless. They are also thinking about how to carry on Hu Yaobang's legacy and to push ahead with reform and democracy in China. A majority of the city residents, college students, and teachers in Xi'an, together with the people of the whole country, have mourned over the passing away of Comrade Hu Yaobang.

On April 22, college students and Xi'an residents gathered on Xincheng

Square, which is situated in front of the Shaanxi provincial government building, where they held floral wreathes with mourning couplets to express their sorrow for Comrade Hu Yaobang.

At 12:00 noon, Xincheng Square was full of students and residents. At this time, four thousand armed policemen formed a wall in front of the provincial government building and blocked the east and west gates of the provincial government courtyard.

At about 1:00 P.M., twenty or thirty people went to the gate of the west side of the courtyard, holding a floral wreath, and asked the armed police (*wujing*) guards to give them permission to take the floral wreaths into the building. The police refused and pushed them outside the gate. The same group went back, holding the wreath, supported by the voices of the masses around them. They approached the police guards until the two sides collided. At this point, some armed police kicked and beat the masses while people holding the wreaths were pushed out of the gate. A few among the crowd then started to throw stones and bricks at the policemen. More than ten armed policemen guarding the gate beat the masses with leather belts. People started to flee. The armed policemen then returned to the courtyard gate, and the masses again approached it. At this point, two trucks from inside the courtyard were driven to block the gate on the west side. The policemen near the gate now retreated into the courtyard. Some people from the crowd then set fire to the canvas covers on the trucks, but the fire was small. A few armed police pulled the cloth covers off the trucks and let them burn on the ground. Then a few people from the crowd threw stones and bricks at the armed police inside the courtyard. The armed police inside the yard started to gather in a line to rush the square and beat people with leather belts. The crowd then withdrew. But as soon as the policemen retreated, the crowd started to push forward again. This situation occurred three times and produced a tense atmosphere on the square.

At about 2:00 P.M., a group of demonstrators from Northwest University and Xi'an Transportation University arrived at the square in succession. They paraded around the square in good order, gathered in the center of the square, and then went to the east gate of the [provincial government] compound. During the students' demonstration, confrontations between the crowd and armed police stopped. There was now temporary tranquility on the square.

At about 2:30 P.M., there was an announcement by the Xi'an municipal government over loudspeakers at the top of the provincial government building. Then, speeches were repeatedly broadcast by the deputy party secretary of [Xi'an] Northwest University and the president of Xi'an Transportation University, asking the students to leave the square. At about 3:00 P.M., there was a disturbance at the west-side gate. Someone had set fire to the gatehouse. The armed police inside the compound were very close to the site. They neither stopped the person nor extinguished the fire. After that, a fire truck arrived and quickly put out the small fire. However, the firemen did not leave.[1] They pointed their high-pressure hoses at the crowd and knocked some students and bystanders to the ground. The people started to counterattack, and the back-and-forth confrontations started again. The two trucks that had been used to block the gate but had been removed during the fighting of the fire now returned. The trucks had already been set afire. Why did they use these same trucks that easily catch fire to block the outraged people? According to an "inside source" (*neibu renshi*), the point was to let the crowd set fire to the trucks! So, immediately somebody set fire to the trucks, and black smoke poured into the square.

From about 3:30 P.M., the loudspeaker started to broadcast the speeches by directors of the student unions of Northwest University and Xi'an Transportation University, which repeatedly claimed that the provincial government had accepted the students' requests and asked the students to leave the square. Having seen that the situation on the square had become tense, teachers from various universities persuaded the students to go back. Given these conditions, some students started to leave the square. But there were still quite a few who stayed on.

After 4:00 P.M., once the provincial governor—Hou Zongbin—went to the command center inside the provincial government building, beatings of the crowd by the police increased dramatically. Many antiriot police wearing helmets and carrying shields rushed out of the west gate. They assaulted the people with electric truncheons and leather belts and threw stones and bricks at unarmed people. Many students and city residents were bloodied by the beatings. It was too cruel to watch. Comrades from the provincial court and the procuracy, which are located in the courtyard on the west side, shouted at the policemen from the windows to stop the beatings. But even they were cursed by the armed police. The people on the square started to throw stones and bricks at the police. As the police attacked, the people withdrew. The policemen dared not stop among the outraged crowd.

Soon, after they withdrew, the crowd pushed forward again and rushed at them. Such a situation occurred four or five times. Some people were arrested and brought inside the provincial courtyard where they were badly beaten. Others working in the building witnessed police beating the arrested and defenseless people with leather belts and electric truncheons. [The police] did not even bother to ask them questions. They also stomped on their bodies with their big leather boots, immediately knocking them out. Some cadres working for the provincial government tried to stop the beatings but were cursed by the police, who looked ready to kill [literally, "beat them with red eyes"].

At 5:00 P.M., quite a few people who had been beaten tried to escape from the square. But more and more people were returning home from work and, unaware of events, gravitating toward the square. The policemen continued cruelly to beat

---

[1]"Firemen" (*xiaofang jingcha*) are under the direct authority of the Public Security Bureau.

the people in front of the crowd, arousing their anger and provoking them to counterattack.

The confrontation between the two sides increased in intensity from 6:30 P.M. onward, and there was great chaos on the square. The police were unable to control the situation. Some trucks and ancillary buildings inside the compound were set afire.

At about 8:00 P.M., the armed police started to surround the whole square. They indiscriminately beat people with electric truncheons, leather belts, and bricks, and then arrested them. People tried to escape toward the east, west, and south. During the ensuing chaos, the Tiantian garment store was robbed.

According to eyewitnesses, however, the true facts of the robbery of the Tiantian garment store were these. Policemen chased after some people to the intersection of Xihua gate. Blocked by the crowd, they didn't know where to go and thus fled into the garment store, which was still open for business, to hide. There they were badly beaten by the police and arrested for robbery. The policemen appeared on the scene almost from the very beginning. On the one hand, the [party-controlled] press reported that eighteen robbers were caught on the spot; on the other hand, it said that the garment store was emptied out by the robbers. This obvious contradiction exposes some secrets that cannot be told to the public.

The above is a general description of events on Xincheng Square on April 22. According to information provided by somebody familiar with internal affairs, during the tragedy eleven people were beaten to death, and a few hundred were injured.[2] A public bus was blocked by the crowd. The driver, who disembarked to figure out how to traverse the square, was also beaten to death on the spot by the police. Plainclothes police were also injured by uniformed police. However, [the government's] newspaper claimed that nobody was killed.

Prior to the April 22 tragedy, the Central Committee had issued explicit orders that stated: Don't stop the masses from carrying on mourning activities. Don't intensify the problem and provoke incidents. But some people in the Shaanxi provincial government and its police bureau publicly opposed the spirit of the Central Committee's order and deliberately provoked and enlarged the incident, and thus caused the [most] astonishing bloody tragedy since the founding of the People's Republic of China and seriously changed the image of the party and the government in the minds of the people.

It is true that some bad people were intent on exacerbating the situation by using this opportunity to create chaos. But the chaotic situation resulted from the fact that the policemen beat innocent people without reason. What makes people even angrier is that those arrested by the police—irrespective of guilt or innocence—became targets for the police to practice their techniques of beating with

---

[2]Xi'an students subsequently interviewed by Robin Munro in Beijing admitted that the reports of deaths among demonstrators were fabricated for "propaganda purposes." They testified, however, to the authenticity of the rest of the account contained here.

fists and legs. People apprehended should have been sent to the judicial departments to await trial since their alleged criminal actions had been stopped, and
they were incapable of counterattacking while in police custody. But some policemen beat anyone they managed to grab, even beating some to death.

The law of the [People's] Republic has been seriously undermined by law
enforcement officials. Their police insignia and badges have been covered with
blood and dirt that cannot be washed away.

At present, the instigators of the April 22 tragedy, taking the opportunity to
use their propaganda machine, are cheating both their superiors and the people
by claiming that the bloody cruelty performed by them was actually a case of a
"small handful" [of people] engaging in "beating, looting, smashing, and burning."[3] This was done to cover their own criminal actions and to cheat the people
of the entire country and the Central Committee. However, the fire cannot be
covered by paper. The crime that those people have committed was witnessed by
more than one hundred thousand people in Xi'an. Many pictures verifying that
policemen acted in a brutal fashion are also in the hands of the masses. These
powerful evidentiary materials will surely clarify the truth for the public.

[We] Xi'an residents will not allow the city's fame to be besmirched by hands
covered with the people's blood. And we will not tolerate the fact that the
creators of this tragedy continue to carry on bad deeds. Because of this unprecedented tragedy we demand:

1. A special negotiation group should be established by the Central Committee, the NPC, the State Council, and the Supreme People's Court. This group
should immediately clarify the truth behind the April 22 tragedy (the Shaanxi
provincial government and its relevant departments are not allowed to join this
[investigatory] group, for they are the defendants).

2. [We] demand that according to the results of this investigation, the NPC
appoint [representatives] from the Supreme People's Court to serve on a special
court in which the Supreme People's Procurators will bring a public suit [against
the Shaanxi provincial government], and thus bring the April 22 tragedy to trial.

3. The instigators and commander [i.e., the provincial governor, Hou Zong-
bin] responsible for the April 22 tragedy should be sued in accordance with the
criminal law [of the PRC].[4] Those [police] who beat people should be punished,
and those who treated the people's lives as weeds should be executed so as to
mitigate the people's aroused anger.

4. The result of this trial should be reported and broadcast to the whole
country by *People's Daily*, the Central People's Broadcast Service, and China
Central TV, to clarify the truth.

---

[3]These Cultural Revolution–era terms appeared prominently in the April 26 *People's
Daily* editorial.

[4]After the June 4 crackdown, Hou Zongbin was instead promoted to provincial party
secretary of Henan.

Social stability and unity of the Xi'an region depend on whether the Central Committee is going to investigate and resolve this case. We Xi'an city residents are waiting to see what will happen.

28

Where Will the Student Movement Go?
Letter to the Patriotic Students

INDEPENDENT YOUNG TEACHERS' UNION
OF BEIJING NORMAL UNIVERSITY

April 22, 1989

Source: *ORSI*, p.7.

Dear students:

When today's China needs you most, you have again stood up selflessly and fearlessly. The facts have fully demonstrated that your actions have won the gradual understanding and support from people of all social strata. Now where will the student movement go? There are two possibilities. One is to die halfway and leave China the same. The other is to push the movement forward to develop in depth until a major step is made toward democratization in China. The people long for the second possibility to come true.

What to do? The most urgent thing to do now is to organize propaganda work, and to formulate programs followed by strong actions.

Organization. Only organized force has strength, and only strong organization can achieve victories. No one should scramble for fame and profit.... You should be united and unified [and] publicly elect some students from the most influential universities in Beijing or the entire country as your leaders. It would be extremely lamentable if the student movement failed because of internal strife. Beware of student scabs.

Propaganda. Only widespread propaganda work can win the understanding and support from people of all social strata, prevent the people from deception by officials, and prompt the workers, peasants, businessmen, and soldiers to take concrete actions to support us.

Programs. They are the banner and symbol of coherence. Our short-term programs should be to wipe out corrupt officials and establish a clean, honest, multiparty coalition government.

Our ultimate goal is to establish a truly democratic, free, and prosperous People's Republic.

Our strategy must be one of perpetual struggle. We can only gradually achieve our programs. Our strongest method is to boycott classes.

You must learn how to utilize all social forces that can be won over. You must build strongholds among every social stratum. When all this is done, victory is inevitable.

A movement needs truly brave, strong men and democracy fighters who are not afraid of shedding their blood or sacrificing their lives. This is the most crucial factor.

29

A Proposal for Quitting the Communist Party and Preparing to a Establish a "Society to Promote the Chinese Democratic Movement"

SOME PARTY MEMBER TEACHERS AT PEOPLE'S UNIVERSITY

Mid-April 1989

Source: Big-character poster, *ORSD*, 1:63.

To all patriotic Chinese intellectuals:

The corrupt and incompetent high-level officials of the ruling CCP trample on the people, view democracy as heresy, ignore the reasonable demands proposed by patriotic youth, use the intellectuals, and adopt a hostile attitude toward them. Hence, we propose that all intellectuals gather together, withdraw collectively and successively in groups from the CCP (to which we have made great contributions), and reestablish an organization that represents the interests of the people, that is, a "Society to Promote the Chinese Democratic Movement" [abbreviated as] MCH (Mincuhui).

A. The Necessity to Quit the Party

1. When the CCP overthrew the last government, it was a progressive force, but it has gradually deteriorated under the conservatism, narrow-mindedness, and stupidity of its petty peasant-like characteristics.

2. Before gaining power [the CCP] allied with intellectuals; but after its success, intellectuals became the target for defending its dictatorship. All previous anti-Rightist movements were basically aimed at suppressing intellectuals.

Even in the period of respect, intellectuals were used but not valued by the CCP.

3. The CCP has no sincerity in carrying out policies to meet the widespread call for improving the conditions of teachers and increasing expenditures on education. One reason is that putting value on education has not proven to be an asset (to the leaders) in the power struggles (within the party).

4. Intellectuals can no longer protect either their own interests or the people's through any Communist-controlled organization. Besides, the reputation of the CCP has been ruined both in and outside of the country. Intellectuals would only taint their bright image by getting involved in [the party].

B. The Means and Procedure of Quitting the Party

A group of celebrities numbering from several tens to more than a few hundred in the fields of education, theory (*lilunjie*), and the arts have taken the lead in quitting [the party] and will hold a press conference in Beijing the day after applying for withdrawal in accordance with the party constitution, [which requires members] to state publicly the reasons for quitting.

In addition, all intellectuals should in groups successively issue statements of withdrawal. If collective withdrawal by celebrities is not possible, they could liaise with the young and middle-aged teachers and graduate students at Beijing University, People's University, Qinghua University, the Chinese Academy of Social Sciences, and the Chinese Academy of Sciences to lead the withdrawal.

C. Preparation for Establishing the Mincuhui

Since the CCP cannot represent the interests of the people and because the various democratic parties are agents of the CCP, the intellectuals have no choice but to set up their own organization or political party to represent the people. It can be named the "Society to Promote the Chinese Democratic Movement." In the early stage, procedures for joining [this organization] could be simplified so as to recruit as many members as possible, including political personnel from other democratic parties. The MCH should set as its objectives promoting political democratization, freedom of the press, independence in the administration of justice, punishment of corrupt bureaucrats, and improvement in education.

D. The Struggle for the Legalization of the Mincuhui

At present the CCP will surely not agree to the establishment of the MCH. It will take thousands of intellectuals to join the society to make it an objective reality and then to struggle relentlessly against the ruling party, just as Polish Solidarity did, until the legalization of the MCH is realized. China's modern history of democratic movements proves that without the organization and support of a party, the Chinese people and students were scattered like sand and were eventually more suppressed by the government. The most urgent duty of the intellectuals at the moment is to form a party organization to counteract the CCP. . . . Let us take action now.

> "Your freedom belongs to heaven and earth.
> Your courage belongs to you alone."
>   —Cui Jian, *Bu zai yanshi* (No more disguises) (song)

30

Our Humiliation Must Be Wiped Out!

A GRADUATE STUDENT IN THE LAW DEPARTMENT WHO WAS
HUMILIATED INTO TEARS FOR THE FIRST TIME SINCE
BECOMING AN ADULT

April 23, 1989

Source: *ORSI*, p. 16.

After the memorial meeting of Hu Yaobang was over yesterday afternoon, tens of thousands of college and university students who had been sitting silently for seven to eight hours unanimously demanded that the government hold a dialogue with the students. But up to the time when the gate of the Great Hall of the People was closed and all the people inside had left, Li Peng had not come out to meet the students. The students felt totally disappointed at this moment. Then came the episode that made everybody stare, tongue-tied: three student representatives knelt down on the doorsteps of the Great Hall of the People. One of them was holding high the student's petition letter. About ten government officials standing in front of the Great Hall totally disregarded them, however, and the policemen lining up were fully prepared to attack the defenseless students. More than twenty minutes passed, and three student representatives were still kneeling on the doorsteps. Yet no government official came to accept the petition letter. By now all the students felt humiliated and indignant. Some choked with sobs.

   The national emblem on the front gate of the Great Hall of the People must have now seen how the "masters" of the "republic" were petitioning like slaves, and how the dignified emperor-like officials were treating them with indifference! The Monument to the People's Heroes over its shoulder could have seen clearly how "a generation of God's favored ones" had lowered their status and had been extremely humiliated, and how those government officials had become utterly devoid of human nature and conscience!

This is not our republic!

We are humiliated, but we should not be desperate. We should march forward. We will finally make masters into the [true] masters, and [public] servants into the [true] servants.

To wipe out our humiliation, we should now:

1. Hold a general boycott of classes and publicize an open telegram to the whole nation;

2. Demand that Li Peng step down;

3. Demand a reelection of the representatives to the NPC so that they may become the real representatives of popular opinion, not those so-called senators (yiyuan) who are dependent on the pleasure of the government.

(I have another suggestion: Next time, the student representatives should not make such a self-humiliating petition because we now know that we are facing cold-blooded animals who are not even worth a straw.)

31

Maximum Program and Minimum Program

TEMPORARY UNION OF BEIJING STUDENTS

April 23, 1989

Source: *ORSI*, p. 12.

Maximum program: Fully and effectively push forward the reform of the political system, guarantee the citizens' rights and freedoms granted in the constitution, and guarantee a smooth process of economic reform.

Minimum program: Urge the government to hold a dialogue with the students, clarify the true facts of the "April 20" incident, issue an apology to the students, and faithfully report the student movement.

32

Letter to All Compatriots

BEIJING UNIVERSITY STUDENTS

April 23, 1989

Source: *ORSI*, p. 4.

We are from different families all over the country. After twenty-one years of hard study, we were admitted to enter the university through very tough competition. We cherish our opportunity to study. We are deeply aware that it was not easy for our parents to raise us.

However, we have seen the reality in China with our own eyes: Taking graft has become a common practice and corruption is widespread; prices are rising arbitrarily and official profiteering is everywhere; education is facing a crisis and public morals are declining.

Taking the risk of being punished, dismissed, beaten, and even imprisoned, we are marching from Zhongguan Village [the university district in the northwest of the city] to Tiananmen Square, a distant of more than thirty li. Sometimes in cold wind, sometimes under the burning sun, sometimes in storms, and always under the threat of the police, we march, mourn, sit-in, and boycott classes. We are tired, weak, hungry, and thirsty. We support the reform and do not oppose the government. Like everyone else, we have been born and raised by our parents. All we have is the minimum conscience possessed by any Chinese. We love our parents, our compatriots, and our motherland. We are duty-bound not to turn back, and we are willing to make sacrifices. . . .

33

Declaration of Ph.D. Students at People's University of China

PH.D. STUDENTS AT PEOPLE'S UNIVERSITY

April 23, 1989

Source: Wall poster, courtesy of HKFS.

1. Fully support the "seven demands" put forward by higher education students in Beijing.

2. From now on, all Ph.D. students will boycott classes.

3. "The mistakes caused by a collective decision under the collective leadership" (Li Peng's words) should be followed by "collective resignation" to show the [leaders'] sincerity in assuming "collective responsibility."

4. Demand that those leaders over seventy-five years old in the party, government, and army step down.

5. Oppose violence and protect human rights. The military should not intervene in state affairs.

34

A Beijing Worker's Open Letter to the Students

A WORKER IN BEIJING

April 23, 1989

Source: *ORSI*, p. 10.

Your just action has stirred the feelings of our workers and the whole society. You have spoken words from our heart. Your grief and anxiety for the country are exactly ours. The rise and fall of a nation is the responsibility of each individual.

For various reasons, we, the working class, still cannot go out onto the streets to shout slogans and carry out an overall strike like you students. However, our hearts are linked, our views are the same. We firmly support the seven reasonable requests you have made. In fighting for the truth, death is nothing to fear.

Although we cannot join your march, we can support you spiritually and with material help. In that case, you don't have to fight on your own. If you need capital, we will raise the money. If you need equipment, we will provide it. The working class is generous, and, what's more, because your just and reasonable actions serve the nation and the safety of the people, you should gain the citizens' wide support.

Finally, here is a list of suggestions for reference:

1. Because the news media have twisted the facts and hidden the truth from the ignorant people, I suggest that you engage in widespread propaganda efforts, including printing pamphlets and organizing lobbying groups, to insure that all citizens learn the truth.

2. After boycotting classes, you should take part in such activities as marches, petitioning, and demonstrations to pressure [the government].

3. Allow more higher [education] institutions to join the marches, and invite more celebrities and famous personages in various places who support the student movement to give public speeches, so as to gain influence and win wide sympathy and support.

4. Hold on to the end, continue until we reach our goals, and stick to the spirit of success or death. . . .

The future is bright, but the road is winding. The first light of the morning has emerged. Struggle now, comrades. Let us cry: Long live democracy, equality, and freedom!

35
Dad and Mom Support You!

REPORTER OF A UNIVERSITY JOURNAL

Late April 1989

Source: *ORSI*, p. 19.

A woman student from the department of psychology of Beijing University reportedly left campus for home on Saturday. Once she arrived at her family's home, both of her straight-speaking parents rebuked her. They said that the students are now enduring hunger and the coldness of night to march for democracy and freedom and to demonstrate against corrupt officials. . . .They asked their daughter just what she could do at home. Moreover, on the morning of the next day, [her] parents forced her to return to the university. When leaving, her mother encouraged her by saying that if she were beaten or put in jail, both parents would renounce their party membership immediately.

Thank you, our respectable parents. Thank you, true Communist party members.

In addition, a neighbor of this student who before Liberation had participated in a student movement at Beida . . . also expressed support. He said, "We Beijing University people who are now in our fifties and sixties took part in the student movement at that time. . . .We had no regard for our lives and we were duty-bound not to turn back. Now your movement this time is also a just one. I support you!" These are the people, the real people. They support us. Old Beijing University people support us!

36
Voice of the News Reporters

REPORTERS OF *GUANGMING DAILY* AND *PEOPLE'S DAILY*

End of April 1989

Source: *Xinwen daobao* (News herald), a student-published newspaper.

1. I am a reporter working for *Guangming Daily,* whose editors and reporters firmly support the students of Beijing University and other colleges and universities.

I graduated from Beijing University, as did many other comrades working at *Guangming Daily.* We have always been proud of being Beijing University alumni. We feel as if we've been raped by the authorities and the Propaganda Department of the party's Central Committee.

We have witnessed everything that took place in front of Xinhua Gate and at other places. One day, when freedom of the press is won, we will publicize our stories. We will never forget how our students shed their blood.

2. It's not that we news reporters lack a conscience, but that we are not the real masters of the newspapers. The vast majority of news reporters at *People's Daily* firmly support the students. . . .

From April 21 to 22, about one hundred journalists stood side by side with the students. Many reporters wrote eyewitness accounts for this newspaper, but none was published. Journalists are intellectuals who also have a conscience, but we have no power. We can only keep silent, but we will never write false stories against our conscience.

Salute to the students!

37

Our Views

PROFESSORS IN THE PHYSICS AND MATHEMATICS DEPARTMENTS,
BEIJING NORMAL UNIVERSITY

April 24, 1989

Source: Handbill, courtesy of HKFS.

. . . As older intellectuals experienced in all kinds of hardships and difficulties, we are deeply shocked by the ignorance of the central leadership regarding the students' petitioning in Tiananmen Square on April 22. Facing ten thousand young students who have undergone the spring coldness at midnight and who have sat in Tiananmen Square, hungry and thirsty, for as long as fifteen hours, and facing the student representatives kneeling down to present the petition letter and make sincere appeals in tears, the party and state leaders remained indifferent and unmoved. This indeed cannot be tolerated, and we feel indignant.

Thus, as senior teachers who have taught for thirty or forty years, we make the following urgent appeals:

1. Party and state leaders should immediately hold a dialogue with the students, listen to their opinions with an open mind, and truly accept their reasonable suggestions and demands, thus preventing the situation from getting worse.

2. Firmly defend the sanctity of the legal system and cease all violence against the students. The legal rights of the students must be protected, and their personal security must be guaranteed. Illegal behavior, such as beating and suppressing the students, must be dealt with according to the law.

3. Promote the building of political democracy, which is the irresistible tide of history in our times. The future of China lies in reform. The basic way to escape the present difficulties is through political democratization. Life tenure of leaders must be completely abolished, and the disguised hereditary system and all feudal privileges must be eliminated. The citizens' basic civil rights—freedom of speech, the press, publication, and the right to vote and stand for election—must be protected. Only political democratization can effectively eliminate corrupt practices. Efforts opposing political democratization under the pretext of "not being suitable to China's conditions" enjoy no popular support and are extremely harmful.

4. Take practical measures to advance education. The treatment of teachers should be improved, knowledge valued, talented people esteemed, and great efforts made to reverse the critical situation in education.

38

Lenin Is Crying in the Nether Regions

ANONYMOUS

April 24, 1989

Source: *ORSI,* p. 19.

In repudiating Kautsky and others' views about "general democracy" and "pure democracy" in 1919, Lenin pointed out that in the capitalist countries, the exploiting class controlled 90 percent of the best buildings [in which to hold] conferences, and the newspapers and printing houses, while the urban workers, peasants, and seasonal workers were kept away from democracy by the inviolable ownership rights and power organs of the capitalist countries. Lenin further argued that bourgeois democracy was only democracy and freedom as enjoyed by the rich, and was thus a fake . . . .

China claims that now classes have been eliminated and no exploiter remains. But in reality, "democracy" in China is in the hands of a few people, or even one man (even many fewer than a few exploiters). One word from one man can make the national newspapers and publications stand facts on their heads and confuse right and wrong. Except for a few [leaders], 1.1 billion Chinese people (including the late party general secretary, Hu Yaobang) have lost their freedom of assembly and association. Democracy and freedom have been seriously trampled on, and the people's legal rights have been severely violated. The ideas of Lenin have been defiled, and Lenin is crying in the nether regions.

39

Letter to Compatriots

5321 STUDENTS' UNION

April 25, 1989

Source: *ORSI*, p. 9.

Compatriots:

No ardent Chinese will forget that day seventy years ago [the 1919 May Fourth Movement]. Today China has again arrived at the brink of a crisis, when taking graft and corruption is common, public morals are declining, and official profiteering is widespread. Are Chinese with a conscience and a sense of justice still to be deceived by the "news" that tells no truth?

It is right under this circumstance that the 5321 Student Union be organized.

Our aims:

Unite the people of all walks of life and raise questions for serious consideration and discussion so as to create a democratic atmosphere of popular participation.

Questions:

1. Reflecting upon history, we want to know why the same mistakes are made time and again. Why have all kinds of corruption emerged? Why is official profiteering so widespread? What are its essential causes?

2. What is the direction of the reform? Is it possible to carry out the reform with a strategy of "feeling stones to cross the river"? Where lies the way out for China?

3. How can institutional guarantees be established so that no mistakes, or fewer mistakes, will be made in the future, and mistakes can be corrected quickly?

4. What should we do from now until May 4? What is the direction of the student movement? Are the strategies and decisions of the students correct and sophisticated? Are the goals of the student movement realistic?

5. How can we win the support of the vast majority of workers and peasants?

6. Can we have a democracy without a legal system to protect it? Is the existing legal system a real one? Is it a people's legal system?

Let those who create the wealth get rich first!

40

Our Proposals

A GROUP OF MARXISTS

April 25, 1989

Source: *ORSD*, 1:62.

We are student [party] members and, at the same time, comrades who took to the streets with all students waving their arms, crying for democracy and science. Every one of our upright members with a party spirit is deeply grieved and disgusted with corruption, official profiteering, and a press that refrains from telling the truth. . . .

We propose to:

1. Avoid direct personal attacks and [allow] freedom of speech, and operate within the confines of the constitution.

2. Stage student strikes but without abandoning the schools, and open democratic discussions on the future of China based on the platform of the (students') autonomous associations.

3. [Encourage] every party member to think seriously [about the present situation] and make the right choice. No action based solely on self-preservation is acceptable.

41

Defects of the Stalinist Political System

XXX OF BEIJING NORMAL UNIVERSITY

April 25, 1989

Source: Big-character poster, in *ORSD*, 1:55.

The fundamental defect of socialist countries is that the political structure makes officials, not the people, into masters. . . .The leader enjoys life-long tenure of office and becomes an autocrat who even possesses the power to appoint his successor. Such a practice violates the basic principle of a republic. It is the characteristic of monarchical autocracy. That is why socialist countries are, in general, republics in name but monarchies in reality. China is no exception in this respect. Our socialism in the past was, in reality, feudalistic socialism, which can also be called socialism on the Stalinist model. (Stalin was a typical tyrant whose regime was a proletarian, or socialist, monarchy. Mao Zedong was of the same genre.)

The defects of this political structure can be summarized as follows:
1. Concentration of power in the hands of the leader.
2. Life-long tenure in office.
3. Appointment of the successor by the leader.
4. Lack of separation between party and government.
5. Rule by men instead of by law.
6. High-ranking cadres engaged in gaining privileges.

Keeping in mind our understanding of the Stalinist political structure, the most imminent task facing China today is to carry on speedily and resolutely with political reform.

Some notes scribbled on this big-character poster by readers:
—The text is incomplete. I hope the author can copy out the full text once again, or publish it in the form of a leaflet.
—Tear down the portrait of Stalin [exhibited annually on May Day] in Tiananmen Square.
—Struggle for the independence of the press.

42

The True Meaning of Freedom, Law, and Democracy

BEIJING UNIVERSITY

April 25, 1989

Source: Courtesy of HKFS.

There is one universal and eternal truth: Men are created equal. Therefore, no one can enjoy privileges that others cannot. Everyone's rights are equal. That is to say, [in theory] everyone has the right to do whatever he or she wants to do. This is freedom and it is an inviolable right.

It is obvious, however, that there is a contradiction hidden here. If everyone fully enjoyed power and did whatever one liked, then people would be caught up in endless conflicts; or they would be unable to achieve anything that goes beyond their own abilities. This does not conform with the human being's goal of pursuing a better life. To solve this contradiction, therefore, people have made a set of laws through joint discussion. These laws are aimed at solving the contradictions among human beings. To enhance the sanctity of the laws, everyone has voluntarily given up a certain part of his or her rights and freedom. That is to say, everyone still has the right to do whatever one pleases, but one's rights must not violate the law.

Here two points must be emphasized: First, it is for the purpose of achieving the goal of having a better life that everyone has voluntarily given up a certain part of their rights. This is the sole reason. Second, the laws are made by the people through joint discussion, and no one, and no single group, has the power to make laws. Laws imposed on the people are illegitimate and unjust.

After we have laws, we must have law enforcers to whom the people have relinquished a certain part of their power. Because these law enforcers have the power that others have given them and control the state machinery for law enforcement, they must be trusted by the people. People must prevent them from abusing their power to do things against the will of the people. How can we make sure that the law enforcers are trusted by the people? There are only two ways:

1. Law enforcers must be directly elected by the people.

2. They must be under the supervision of the people. If they betray the people and trample on the laws, people must remove them from power. These two are the [basic] elements of democracy [and] sacred and supreme rights.

Thus, the power holders are those trusted by the people. The people have transferred some of their rights to them in order to allow them to serve the people better. It is clear that the power holders are the servants of the people.

Freedom, law, and democracy are nothing mysterious, nor are they unattainable goals. Originally, they accompanied human beings as they formed societies. Only with the evolution of society did law enforcers frequently begin to utilize religion and superstition to deprive the people of their power while deifying themselves. Maybe it is a tragedy of history that people have been moaning and groaning under the [rule of] divine right for several thousand years. But it is also historically inevitable. Nevertheless, history will inevitably return to its original starting point. Now people have again realized the truth that "men are born equal." When other countries in the world are relying on this historical inevitability to modernize quickly, it is time that our poor and backward country with its two thousand years of feudal dynasties begin to open a new chapter in the [country's historical] annals.

We should never forget:

"People are their own masters!"

"Power belongs to the great people."

43

It Is Necessary to Take a Clear-Cut Stand against Turmoil

EDITORIAL, RENMIN RIBAO (PEOPLE'S DAILY)

April 26, 1989

Source: Beijing Domestic Service, April 25, 1989, in FBIS, *Daily Report: China,* April 25, 1989, pp. 23–24.

In their activities to mourn the death of Comrade Hu Yaobang, Communists, workers, peasants, intellectuals, cadres, members of the People's Liberation Army, and young students have expressed their grief in various ways. They have also expressed their determination to turn grief into strength to make contributions in realizing the four modernizations and invigorating the Chinese nation.

Some abnormal phenomena have also occurred during the mourning activities. Taking advantage of the situation, an extremely small number of people spread rumors, attacked party and state leaders by name, and instigated the masses to break into Xinhua Gate at Zhongnanhai, where the Central Committee and the State Council are located. Some people even shouted such reactionary slogans as "Down with the Communist Party." In Xi'an and Changsha, there have been serious incidents in which some lawbreakers carried out beating, smashing, looting, and burning.

Taking into consideration the feelings of grief suffered by the masses, the party and government have adopted an attitude of tolerance and restraint toward some improper words uttered and actions carried out by the young students when they were emotionally agitated. On April 22, before the memorial meeting was held, some students had already shown up at Tiananmen Square, but they were not asked to leave, as they normally would have been. Instead, they were asked to observe discipline and join in the mourning of Comrade Hu Yaobang. The students on the square were themselves able consciously to maintain order. [Beijing Xinhua Domestic Service in Chinese at 1400 GMT on April 25, reporting on the April 26 *Renmin ribao* editorial, deletes this sentence.] Owing to the joint efforts by all concerned, it was possible for the memorial meeting to proceed in a solemn and respectful manner.

After the memorial meeting, however, an extremely small number of people with ulterior purposes continued to take advantage of the young students' feelings of grief for Comrade Hu Yaobang to spread all kinds of rumors to poison and confuse people's minds. Using both big- and small-character posters, they vilified, hurled invectives at, and attacked party and state leaders. Blatantly violating the constitution, they called for opposition to the leadership by the Communist party and the socialist system. In some of the institutions of higher learning, illegal organizations were formed to seize power from the student unions. In some cases, they even forcibly took over the broadcasting systems on the campuses. In some institutions of higher learning, they instigated the students and teachers to go on strike and even went to the extent of forcibly preventing students from going to classes, usurped the name of the workers' organizations to distribute reactionary handbills, and established ties everywhere in an attempt to create even more serious incidents.

These facts prove that what this extremely small number of people did was not to join in the activities to mourn Comrade Hu Yaobang or to advance the course of socialist democracy in China. Neither were they out to give vent to their grievances. Flaunting the banner of democracy, they undermined democracy and the legal system. Their purpose was to sow dissension among the people, plunge the whole country into chaos, and sabotage the political situation of stability and unity. This is a planned conspiracy and a turmoil. Its essence is, once and for all, to negate the leadership of the CCP and the socialist system. This is a serious political struggle confronting the whole party and the people of all nationalities throughout the country.

If we are tolerant or conniving with this turmoil and let it go unchecked, a seriously chaotic state will appear. Then, the reform and opening up; the improvement of the economic environment and the rectification of the economic order, construction, and development; the control over prices; the improvement of our living standards; the drive to oppose corruption; and the development of democracy and the legal system expected by the people throughout the country, including the young students, will all become empty hopes. Even the tremendous achievements scored in the reform during the past decade may be completely lost, and the great aspiration of the revitalization of China cherished by the whole nation will be hard to realize. A China with very good prospects and a very bright future will become a chaotic and unstable China without any future.

The whole party and the people nationwide should fully understand the seriousness of this struggle, unite to take a clear-cut stand to oppose the turmoil, and firmly preserve the hard-earned situation of political stability and unity, the constitution, socialist democracy, and the legal system. Under no circumstances should the establishment of any illegal organizations be allowed. It is imperative firmly to stop any acts that use any excuse to infringe upon the rights and interests of legitimate organizations of students. Those who have deliberately fabricated rumors and framed others should be investigated to determine their criminal liabilities according to the law. Bans should be placed on unlawful parades and demonstrations and such acts as going to factories, rural areas, and schools to establish ties. Beating, smashing, looting, and burning should be punished according to the law. It is necessary to protect the just rights of students to study in class. The broad masses of students sincerely hope that corruption will be eliminated and democracy will be promoted. These, too, are the demands of the party and the government. These demands can only be realized by strengthening the efforts for improvement and rectification, vigorously pushing forward the reform, and making perfect our socialist democracy and our legal system under the party leadership.

All comrades in the party and the people throughout the country must soberly recognize the fact that our country will have no peaceful days if this turmoil is not checked resolutely. This struggle concerns the success or failure of the re-form and opening up, the program of the four modernizations, and the future of our state and nation. Party organizations of the CCP at all levels, the broad masses of members of the Communist party and the Communist Youth League, all democratic parties and patriotic democratic personages, and the people around the country should make a clear distinction between right and wrong, take positive action, and struggle to firmly and quickly stop the turmoil.

"Numerous 'a handful's still amount to 'a handful.' "
—*New Sayings*, Courtesy of HKFS

44
Denounce the [April 26 Editorial of the] *People's Daily*

PEOPLE OF BEIJING NORMAL UNIVERSITY

End of April 1989

Source: Transcript from a [Student] Broadcasting Station of Beijing Normal University, courtesy of HKFS.

We are very angry after reading the *People's Daily* editorial. The government leaders are so decrepit and muddleheaded that they simply cannot be tolerated. Any honest Chinese with a conscience cannot fail seriously to repudiate the slander and libel made by the Central People's Radio.

We have already heard the editorial of *People's Daily* broadcast in full text by Central People's Radio. It calls for taking a clear-cut position against the so-called turmoil. We understand the efforts of the party and government to maintain a stable environment of unity. But the government has libeled our movement with a threatening tone. All students of Beijing Normal University hereby solemnly declare that, up to this moment, all our activities have not gone beyond the limits set by the laws. A movement of ten thousand students is not the activity of "a handful" or "a small group" of people. Moreover, we have not been manipulated from behind the scenes by someone. We can fully represent our own wishes. We have not shouted slogans of "Down with the Communist Party." Nor do we have any intention to "overthrow the socialist system." All we want is an honest government, a wiping out of corruption, and a speeding up of reform. People who know the truth support us. The government's use of military force will not suppress the students but will have the opposite effect. We young students have the courage to struggle for the truth. We strongly demand that the government have a peaceful dialogue with us and stop accusing the students of creating "turmoil." They should not regard the just student movement as the same thing as the acts of "beating, smashing, and looting" that occurred in Changsha.

Finally, we strongly protest the erroneous judgment on the nature of the student movement made by the editorial. We must carry the just student movement through to the end under the banner of freedom and democracy.

"Support the Communist Party and Socialism."
—Banner, April 27 march

45

The Beijing Party Committee and Beijing Municipal Government Must Tell the People the Truth about the "Request for a Battle Assignment"

SOME JOURNALISTS WORKING IN NEWS UNITS IN BEIJING

Late April 1989

Source: Printed handbill, courtesy of HKFS.

On April 24, when briefing the members of the Politburo of the party Central Committee about the development of the student movement, the Beijing

Party Committee initially "requested a battle assignment" and asked permission to stand at the first front to "fight back," which directly led to Deng Xiaoping's April 25 speech and the April 26 editorial of the *People's Daily* [Doc. 43]. The Beijing Party Committee has the inescapable responsibility for the unprecedented present crisis of the Chinese. Thus, we journalists working in the news media in Beijing strongly demand that the Beijing Party Committee tell the people the truth about its "request for a battle assignment" [*qing zhan*].

1. The news media should publicize the analyses and reports about the student movement made by the Beijing Party Committee; the stories about the whole process during which the Beijing Party Committee made the "request for a battle assignment" and requested authorization from the party Central Committee to "fight back"; the full texts of Li Ximing's and Chen Xitong's speeches at the April [25] meeting; and the concrete measures of "fighting back" directed to the districts, counties, and bureaus . . . by the Beijing Party Committee.

2. Stories should also be publicized about the whole process of how the Beijing Party Committee and the municipal government formulated and then implemented measures cutting the supply of water, food, and donations to the students, and measures forbidding Beijing residents to meet with and observe the students.

3. The Beijing Party Committee and municipal government must publicly reveal their erroneous views and their grave responsibility during the student movement.

4. [We] demand that Li Ximing and Chen Xitong immediately hold a direct dialogue with representatives from the Beijing news media to discuss actual implementation of the chief-editor responsibility system, abolition of news censorship, and other urgent issues.[1]

"Support the Four Cardinal Principles"
—Slogan, April 27 march, in *56 Days*

---

[1]Mayor Chen Xitong did, in fact, conduct a dialogue with students in early May in which he was queried about his personal salary and smoking of expensive imported cigarettes. Chen's admission that "We have made some mistakes" was generally well-received by student representatives. Interview, Beijing CCP member, summer 1990.

III

April 28–May 12
The Conflict Escalates as the
Students Defend Their Patriotism

Suzanne Ogden

Aiguo wuzui.
Patriotism is no crime.
—Photograph of placard

Less than a week after Hu Yaobang's memorial service on April 22, *People's Daily* published an editorial, "It Is Necessary to Take a Clear-Cut Stand against Turmoil" (Doc. 43). This editorial set the direction and tone for the ensuing two weeks. It signaled the government's concern with the direction of a nascent student-led movement, and a decision to build a case for quashing it. It was during this period that the students grew frustrated with "dialogue" with the government, beginning with the April 29 "dialogue" with the State Council spokesman, Yuan Mu. Students organized into an independent association to counter the officially sponsored and controlled student association. Leaders of the student movement slowly began to emerge. Campus commemorations of the seventieth anniversary of the May Fourth Movement, which the students and intellectuals had planned long before the death of Hu Yaobang, were scuttled in favor of demonstrations in Tiananmen Square to gain the attention of the international press, now gathering in Beijing for the Asian Development Bank's Board of Governors meeting and Mikhail Gorbachev's May 15 visit. The presence of the international press affected the students' strategy for achieving their objectives and became a factor in the decision of China's domestic press to report the student movement more objectively. The period ended on May 12 with a tactical escalation by the students: a hunger strike aimed at increasing pressure on the government to accede to the demand for a "dialogue."

For those hoping for greater democracy in China, this was an important transitional period: The students reorganized, the press grew emboldened, the government floundered and changed course, the conservative party leaders sought out the "black hand" behind the student movement, ordinary citizens came out to support the students, and the students began to criticize openly both the Communist party and specific party leaders. By the end of this period, both sides had grown increasingly rigid and unyielding. Behind it all, a furious internal power struggle raged within the top leadership of the government. Students and citizens alike could only speculate as to what was happening behind the leadership's closed doors, and what it might mean for achieving their objectives. The documents in this section address these aforementioned events and themes.

**Beijing Students Reorganize: Establishment of the
Autonomous Student Union of Colleges and Universities in Beijing**

The student movement was on the verge of disintegration prior to the publication of the April 26 *People's Daily* editorial. Many potential student leaders hesitated to step forward and take on the responsibility—and risk—of leadership. In the leadership vacuum, the student movement had also failed to make collective decisions. A meeting scheduled earlier between high-level party officials and eighteen Qinghua University student representatives on April 26 had fallen through as school officials and informal student leaders battled over the right to choose their representatives. The result was that no representatives were chosen. Further, mutual suspicion and animosity plagued the student movement: News filtered down that at Beijing University, the newly created unofficial student union's preparatory group had barely begun functioning when it expelled two of its leaders, calling one a "spy" for school authorities, and alleging that the other was "not capable enough." The unofficial student union at People's University experienced similar suspicion and division.[1] The government would later point to this failure to attend the meeting as a sign of student duplicity. The government's choice of Qinghua itself invites examination: Some have asserted that Qinghua had a "meek" student body compared to Beijing University. Student activists may have believed that Qinghua students simply could not represent the entire movement.

Students rejected the formal leadership of the officially recognized Students' Federation, a leadership easily manipulated by the Communist party. The Students' Federation fell under the control of the CCP Central Committee and Communist Youth League. In an effort to establish a student organization independent of the party, students involved in the democracy movement on April 26 formed the Autonomous Student Union of Colleges and Universities in Beijing

---

[1]Tammy Tam, "Division Threatens Students," *Hong Kong Standard*, April 26, 1989, p. 6, in FBIS, *Daily Report: China*, April 26, 1989, p. 20.

(ASUCUB). Its members were elected by the respective student bodies of most of the universities and colleges in Beijing participating in the democracy movement. The establishment of a nonofficial, autonomous organization moved the students into dangerous territory, particularly in light of the April 26 editorial's warning. Individual dissent is risky enough in China. Setting up *an organization* for dissent exposes its leaders to having the full force of the law against "counterrevolutionary" activities thrown against them. The repercussions of leading organized dissent were already well known: Leaders of the 1986 student-led movement had, minimally, lost the opportunity to be assigned a good job by the state upon graduation. Many were jailed and had not yet been released three years later. In 1989, therefore, only those willing to risk everything for a political cause would come forth for leadership. Inevitably, this meant that the more radical, more daring students would, at each crucial juncture, control the course of the student movement and move it onto ever more precarious ground.

Under ASUCUB's leadership, the students became better organized and were able to formulate objectives, tactics, and strategies. But, the creation of ASUCUB did not end the fragmentation of the student movement, in part because even ASUCUB itself lacked strong leaders and organization (docs. 47, 62), and in part because neither the students nor their leaders were ever entirely clear about their objectives (Doc. 60). Moreover, since many colleges and universities that had elected their own "autonomous student unions" refused to go along with the decisions made by the umbrella ASUCUB organization, the creation of ASUCUB may at times even have augmented problems within the student movement (Doc. 68).

Unfortunately, the students' demand for official CCP recognition of ASUCUB as the legitimate student organization itself became a major new issue. Not only did it thereby add to the complexity of the student-led movement's objectives; it was also at the center of the student-government political confrontation (docs. 53, 62, 70, 71). Workers emboldened by the students' daring themselves began to establish autonomous unions. Had the government recognized the students' right to self-representation, almost certainly workers would have demanded that their own autonomous trade unions, run by freely elected workers' representatives, be recognized. And for the CCP leadership, well aware of the consequences of Solidarity for Poland's Communist leadership, the prospect of independent trade unions in China assumed nightmarish proportions. Thus, the students' insistence on official recognition of ASUCUB provoked the government's conservative leadership into an even more rigid position.

Criticism of the Communist Party and Its Leaders

Throughout the spring democratic movement, students adopted the vocabulary and policies of the CCP as their own: The students, no less than the CCP, were against corruption and supported reform. As a result, both sides were really saying the same thing. The difference was that the students could say they supported the *announced* policies of the CCP but could at the same time point out the CCP's failure to carry out these policies. By the end of April, however, students had to defend their movement as "patriotic" and supportive of party objectives for reform (docs. 44, 53).

Their defensiveness on this score was prompted by the April 26 *People's Daily* editorial accusing "an extremely small number of people with ulterior purposes" of calling for "opposition to the leadership by the Communist party and the socialist system" (Doc. 43). By denouncing the students for creating "turmoil" and plotting to destabilize the political situation, the editorial actually refired a not-quite-organized and flagging student movement. The charge that "an extremely small handful of people" were conspiring to overthrow the CCP, and that the autonomous student unions in the colleges and universities were "illegal organizations," shifted the focus of the movement. Up to this point, students had focused on demands to reassess Hu Yaobang and official corruption. The new official labeling of the movement indicated the government was laying the rhetorical groundwork for arrests of students as "counterrevolutionaries," hence criminals.

The use of Cultural Revolution–style tactics and verbiage to condemn their movement infuriated the students, who now took up as their major cause the demand that the government retract the April 26 editorial and reassess the student movement as "patriotic." Sensitive to the students' anger, Zhao Ziyang tried to calm them down in his speeches of May 3 and 4.[2] Li Peng also gave a conciliatory speech, but neither leader was able to assuage the students' anger.

The students compared the April 1989 "patriotic" movement with the Cultural Revolution, the April 1976 Tiananmen demonstrations, and the December 1986 student movement. They argued that the Cultural Revolution was violence orchestrated from the top down, a manipulation of the population in service of a power struggle at the top. The most important difference, they contended, was that their current movement was "democratic," whereas the Cultural Revolution was not.[3] Furthermore, the April 5, 1976, Tiananmen demonstrations (an outpouring of popular grief over the death of Zhou Enlai, thinly masking criticism and defiance of the "Gang of Four") were originally denounced as counterrevolutionary but later termed "patriotic." The students believed the same would happen to their spring 1989 movement. As for the December 1986 movement, the students were concerned that the 1989 movement not end the same way:

---

[2]For texts of Zhao's speeches, see Oksenberg et al., eds., *Beijing Spring*, docs. 28, 29, and 31.

[3]Anonymous, "Ten Differences Between the Present Patriotic Movement and the Cultural Revolution," big-character poster at People's University, Beijing, April 28, 1989, in *ORSD*, 1:67.

With a mere issuance of the stern party document Number One on January 1, 1987, that movement had died and student leaders had been arrested.[4] To prevent such an eventuality, the students of the April 1989 movement set up their own "think tanks," informal study groups on the square, to establish a guiding theory for the movement, and encouraged students to be prepared to sacrifice themselves for the cause of democracy.

While the party leaders were attempting to cast doubt on the legitimacy of the student protests, students began to raise their own questions about the terms of loyalty to the party. For some demonstrators, support for the party was conditional: They supported the CCP's "correct" policies but not its "incorrect" policies (Doc. 62). One document refined the concept of "support" by comparing the relative importance of Chinese culture and citizenship versus CCP membership and its implied obligations. As one disillusioned CCP member wrote, "The CCP and our motherland are not one concept. The people's love [for China is greater than their love for] the party, [whose purpose] is to serve the country." The object of this critique, as of the protests in this phase, was not "the party" as such, but rather "the central administration of the party."[5] Implicitly, the objective of the protests was not to overthrow the party, but to challenge the ineffective policies and corruption of the central party leaders. Perhaps more importantly, the claim to being "patriotic" gave the students an alternative standard of legitimacy independent of the CCP. That is, the students claimed a legitimate right as "patriots" to criticize the CCP for failing to serve the country well. Indeed, to avoid criticizing the CCP for its failures would be unpatriotic.

Serious criticism of the party and a one-party system mounted during this period.[6] One document referred to socialism in China as "a dynasty of personal dictatorship" and blamed Deng for not stepping down so the party could in fact be reformed (Doc. 57). Other documents pointed to nepotism, the "vast net of connections," and China's "feudal culture" as the foundations upon which corruption in the CCP had been built (Doc. 56). From this point on, these themes became central to the student and mass protest.

The Government Recharts Its Course

One might argue that the government's stern warnings to the demonstrators grew out of genuine concern at the prospect of escalation and geographic spread of the movement. Rioting and looting had accompanied demonstrations in Xi'an and Changsha. Some eyewitnesses, however, have asserted that Xi'an's violence was

---

[4]Revolutionary in the Department of Foreign Languages of Beijing Normal University, "Hail the Democracy Fighters," wall poster or leaflet, late April 1989, courtesy of HKFS.

[5]CCP member, "A Statement of My Position," April 30, 1989, big-character poster, Beijing Normal University, in *ORSD*, 1:67.

[6]Nonrevolutionary at Beijing Normal University, big-character poster and/or leaflet, May 2, 1989, in *ORSD*, 1:53.

provoked by the government, in that first the demonstrators were beaten by police, and *then* the demonstrators threw rocks and bricks. This line of argument, that the government actually provoked dissent, has been used to analyze many of the events of the spring of 1989; but it is hard to prove just whose actions were responsible for subsequent violence, and it does little to advance the argument that the government did not view the demonstrations as a threat.[7]

Some Chinese who participated in the movement insist, moreover, that the student leaders had taken the decision to march on April 27 several days before the *People's Daily* editorial appeared. In anticipation of even larger demonstrations in the capital, the government may have feared that Beijing's crowds would suddenly turn violent. As it turned out, rather than meekly bowing to the government's implicit threats, the students decided to demonstrate again on April 27. They were more committed than ever to fighting for their goals against a government seemingly unable either to satisfy them or to halt their activities.

The government had forewarned the students that under a two-year-old directive (supplemented by newly passed regulations), no demonstrations were legal without prior authorization from the Public Security Bureau. Moreover, the authorities on April 26 had ordered factory managers to prevent their workers from striking in support of the students.

Yet, although the students were still poorly organized, they were joined on their march by workers, government and party cadres (Doc. 64), their teachers (Doc. 50), and the residents of Beijing, making it the largest demonstration to date. The students felt exhilarated by their new sense of power.

Remarkably, despite the government's ominous warnings, its expressed intransigence—there would be no reassessment of Hu Yaobang as the students had demanded—and the movement of large numbers of troops to Beijing, the government did not carry out its threats to crack down on the demonstration.[8] It was apparently at this point that the regime had to reconsider its tactics. Students remained defiant and had elicited a great outpouring of popular support. An internal power struggle had deadlocked the Standing Committee of the Politburo, making it impossible for it to reach a decision on *anything*. And the seventieth anniversary of the May Fourth Movement—a movement that began in 1919 as student demonstrations at Beijing University—loomed large with promises of further huge demonstrations under the intense scrutiny of the

---

[7]For documents that suggest there were, in fact, significant reasons for the government to be concerned, see Doc. 27 on the violence in Xi'an; and Doc. 44 on the violence in Changsha.

[8]Some Chinese have argued that the government had, in fact, stationed soldiers and armed police in Tiananmen Square, and that they planned to surround the students in the square and use violence against them; but the students *bypassed* Tiananmen Square in their march. This argument would suggest that it was the students' clever strategy, not the government's decision, that avoided a confrontation.

international media's cameras. Clearly, the government feared that still larger numbers of workers, clerks, cadres, teachers, and other major groups might join with the students against the government in order to press for their own demands. Nonetheless, the earlier tactics of roughing up protesters and threatening them had failed.[9] In chaos, the government tried desperately to cope with the delegates from the Board of Governors of the Asian Development Bank, the international press, and the upcoming Gorbachev visit as if nothing were wrong.

The Awakening of Conscience and Growing Popular Support

The students' refusal to be intimidated by the party's threats led to an awakening of conscience on the part of many citizens. The student protesters contended that the people's docility and their indifference to government policy permitted the government to exploit them.[10] The students argued that the people had permitted themselves to be led blindly, and that they should take more responsibility for themselves and their country, perhaps even to the point of overthrowing the government.[11] Convincing the people, as well as the more reluctant students (Doc. 54), to take a stand was a major objective of the students' "propagandizing" efforts.

The students' own refusal to be cowed by the authorities spurred others to think that they might successfully defy the CCP, that it was neither omnipotent nor unified enough to quash them. "People power," modeled on the Philippine people's successful overthrow of the entrenched regime of Ferdinand Marcos, began to demonstrate its effectiveness against the CCP government.

Some ordinary citizens grew incensed by the government's tactics of blaming the student movement for creating "turmoil," for suggesting that the students' protests were criminal in intent. A leaflet at People's University (Doc. 46) retorted by blaming the government for China's turmoil through its refusal to respond to the students' demands. The newspaper *Xinwen daobao* (News herald), created and published by the students on Tiananmen Square during the spring 1989 demonstrations, offered a particularly trenchant analysis of the upheaval in hundreds of millions of Chinese lives caused by the party's method of governing through *People's Daily* editorials. The newspaper listed the "historical achievements" of the *People's Daily* in creating turmoil from 1966 to 1976:

---

[9]Evidence from the students' perspective that the government had, in fact, compromised is in Doc. 68.

[10]Student party member from People's University, "Choice Between the Conscience and Party Loyalty: Open Letter to the Party Members," big-character poster at People's University, April 28, 1989, in *ORSD*, 1:59; and Nonrevolutionary at Beijing Normal University, "Also on One-Party Dictatorship," big-character poster and/or leaflet, May 2, 1989, in *ORSD*, 1:53.

[11]Girl student of the history department of Beijing Normal University, "My Sorrow," poster and/or handbill, May 2, 1989, in *ORSD*, 1:72.

"Almost all the large-scale turmoil and bloodshed started with the *People's Daily* sounding a bugle call to stir up the people" (Doc. 73). He Xin, an associate research fellow at the Chinese Academy of Social Sciences, wrote in an "internal report" to senior government leaders: "For the center to have used yet again an editorial in the *People's Daily* [on April 26] to mobilize people and issue instructions was stupid—according to my information, this move was highly unpopular even among the staff of the *People's Daily* itself."[12]

Press Freedom Strengthened

Press freedom actually grew during this period, even as student protesters continued to demand it (Doc. 50). In late April, the CCP Propaganda Department continued to prevent the media from printing the most "radical" student slogans and demands, pressing them rather to emphasize the importance of "unity and stability."[13] But in a dramatic turnaround, journalists from *Workers' Daily*, *China Youth Daily*, and *Science and Technology Daily* requested their editors to permit "truthful" reporting of the students' activities.[14] Indeed, some members of the press decided to "speak the truth" about them and even joined in the demonstrations (Doc. 45). Journalists had long been pushing for greater freedom; but student demands for more objective press reports on the student movement as one of the conditions for ending their boycott of university classes emboldened many members of the press to take action.

Hu Jiwei, a renowned journalist who had recently edited an important book about democracy for China, argued in an article on May 8 in the *World Economic Herald* that China's constitutionally guaranteed freedom of the press was a prerequisite for political stability (Doc. 69). His ability to write about democracy both before and during this particular period of student demonstrations suggests a press that was, at least at the edges, not completely under the thumb of the party.[15] Indeed, the fact that Hu Jiwei was able to publish this article after Qin Benli, the editor of *World Economic Herald*, had been dismissed on April 27 for trying to publish an article by well-known Chinese intellectuals advocating a posthumous

---

[12]He Xin, "A Word of Advice to the Politburo," p. 72.

[13]Willy Wo-Lap Lam, "Media 'To Truthfully Report,' " *South China Morning Post*, Hong Kong, April 26, 1989, in FBIS, *Daily Report: China*, April 26, 1989, p. 21.

[14]Ibid., pp. 10–11.

[15]By 1987, 1,574 newspapers, 5,248 magazines, and 446 publishing houses had sprung up in China. The proliferation of so many outlets for ideas made it difficult for the party even to know what was being published, much less control it. Efforts to consolidate publishing by shutting down some newspapers and magazines in 1987 did not go far in making inroads on a more vibrant press. See Suzanne Ogden, *China's Unresolved Issues: Politics, Development, and Culture* (Englewood Cliffs, NJ: Prentice-Hall, 1989), pp. 168–69.

rehabilitation of Hu Yaobang and support for the students' demands,[16] showed the maverick media's continued willingness to test the limits. As long as the liberal fringes of the press could get away with such articles, it enlarged the more conventional media's room for maneuver as well.

More important, as events unfolded with such rapidity during this period, the Central Party Propaganda Department's usual mechanisms for control of the press lapsed. Control techniques had been rigid: Ordinarily, the propaganda authorities would meet weekly with Central Committee leaders to decide on press guidelines for the week's news coverage. They would then set out those guidelines in sessions with the newspapers' senior editors, who in turn passed on the guidelines to their subordinate editors. Probably because the Central Committee was preoccupied with infighting, however, press directives ceased to be issued, leaving the media free to decide for themselves how to cover the student-led demonstrations.

A crucial shift occurred at the end of April. Hu Qili, the Politburo member in charge of propaganda, had allegedly told the newspapers not to report on the university students' class boycotts. On April 28, however, Hu Qili (no doubt at the urging of Zhao Ziyang) gambled on which way the internal power struggle would go: Apparently believing the forces favoring Zhao would win out, he told newspaper editors they could truthfully report what was happening.[17]

The media, however, were definitely receiving mixed signals. The April 27 firing of Qin Benli may have angered the press enough to cause it eventually to join in the prodemocracy demonstrations (Doc. 59), but not until some time had elapsed. Qin's firing, the reorganization of *World Economic Herald* to put it more firmly under the Shanghai Communist party's control, and rumored warnings to two other newspapers to curb their reporting on the student demonstrations left the press suspicious of directives and in a quandary as to whether to show greater boldness.[18] Indeed, although the press covered much more about the demonstrations after Zhao Ziyang's speech to the Asian Development Bank meeting, it remained hesitant. On May 10, a few days before the hunger strike, the students took a bike trip to all the major press organizations, including *People's Daily*, as a method of mobilizing both the press and the people to become more involved in the democracy movement. Until the hunger strike began on May 13, the press, unleashed but fearful, trod wearily. But with the hunger strike, it lunged from the delicate fringes into the heretofore uncharted sea of press freedom.

---

[16]For excerpts from the banned April 24 edition of the *World Economic Herald,* see Oksenberg et al., eds., *Beijing Spring,* Doc. 1.

[17]Hu must have taken this action without the approval of the entire Politburo; for when he was later expelled from the Politburo along with Zhao, his directive to the *People's Daily* on April 28 was cited as one of his major "mistakes."

[18]Simmie and Nixon, *Tiananmen Square,* p. 72.

The International Media Arrive

The international media, which felt perfectly free to report the demonstrations as they saw them, by their example added to the pressure on Chinese editors and reporters to present a more truthful account of the demonstrations. Members of the international media arrived to cover the meeting of the Asian Development Bank's Board of Governors on May 4, and to prepare for Mikhail Gorbachev's visit for the Sino-Soviet summit scheduled for May 15. It was during this period that the extensive coverage offered by the increased presence of the international media began to affect the students' presentation of themselves on what they by then realized was an international stage. International media coverage also affected the Chinese media's coverage of events and augmented the knowledge the Chinese themselves had about the demonstrations through the feedback loop offered by the Voice of America and the British Broadcasting Company (Doc. 53). The broadcasts from the VOA and BBC about events in Tiananmen Square and the student-led movement would in turn be broadcast at full volume in the square and on street corners. Demonstrators also distributed leaflets offering verbatim broadcasts or summaries.

Xerox machines, computers, telephones, and fax machines became the weapons of the democracy movement. Students and their supporters in major state-run organizations used these weapons to communicate information about the movement both within China and abroad. With the help of their compatriots in the United States, Western Europe, Canada, Australia, and Hong Kong, they set up an extraordinary international network that they would soon tap for financial and moral support. On the eve of the hunger strike, the availability of even this level of technology to the Chinese was able to revolutionize the approach of China's democratic activists to achieving their goals.

Anticorruption as a Unifying Theme

Curtailing corruption was the one issue on which all could agree—students, intellectuals, workers, ordinary citizens, and the government itself. Countless documents spoke of the nepotism and patronage that create "a web of connections." Some attributed this syndrome to the lingering influence of feudal culture on China (Doc. 56). Others spoke of "state ownership" as in fact ownership by a small number of people who exploited the people and made profits through their abuse of power—all in the name of "the state."[19]

The elimination of corruption was a demand long before the events of 1989; and the government had over the years launched repeated campaigns to ferret out corruption. Yet in spite of these efforts, corruption flourished in ever more fertile conditions. Corrupt individuals fed on the nexus between the demands of a

---

[19]Nonrevolutionary at Beijing Normal University, "Also on One-party Dictatorship," big-character poster and/or leaflet, May 2, 1989, in *ORSD*, 1:53.

semifree market and those of a socialist state-run market; on the proliferation of companies that handled the sale of state-produced goods; on the availability of foreign currency; and on the vulnerability of foreign businessmen eager to make investments in China (who often would pay bribes to facilitate business). The corrupt party and state officials who controlled opportunities, access, and resources profited the most.

The government was not blind to corruption. Even the April 26 editorial endorsed the demands made by "the broad masses of students" who "sincerely" wanted corruption to be eliminated and democracy promoted. Heretofore, the party had claimed that capitalism and foreigners were responsible for corruption in China. By this point there was no refuting the CCP's own culpability. Still, the authorities seemingly lacked the will or power effectively to eliminate the corruption that hurt ordinary citizens. The question was, once the demonstrations drove home just how angry Chinese in all walks of life were about corruption, would the regime take measures any more effective than before? We already know that in the period subsequent to June 4, 1989, the government applied only a few cosmetic measures to control corruption.

Corruption seems to be an intractable issue for most developing economies. But the PRC leaders, whose families ranged from ankle-deep to neck-deep immersion in corruption, had proven conspicuously unable to address this problem with much effect at all. Thus, even the palpable threat of the spring 1989 demonstrations to the CCP's very existence did not lead to a major campaign against corruption. Even had it done so, without changing the basic *system* so as to allow a free press and a law-based society, such a campaign would undoubtedly have floundered.

Retrospective

As this period drew to a close with the students' decision to breathe life into a flagging movement by organizing a hunger strike, two perhaps imponderable questions were left unanswered.

First, what would have happened had the student movement been better organized, with a united and strong leadership able to agree on goals and methods? This period (April 28–May 12), which followed in the wake of Hu Yaobang's funeral, opened with the students still calling for better treatment of intellectuals and a reevaluation of Hu's career; but by the end of it, Hu was but a vague memory. In a matter of some two weeks, demands had moved on to include:

1. Retraction of the April 26 editorial.

2. CCP recognition of ASUCUB as the legal representative of the university students (docs. 53, 62, 71); and recognition of the democracy walls and freedom forums on campuses by university authorities as legitimate forms of expression (Doc. 71).

3. A government dialogue with the students. Since the April 29 "dialogue"

(with State Council spokesman Yuan Mu representing the government) had only served to infuriate the students (Doc. 55), ASUCUB demanded another dialogue carefully circumscribed by preconditions (Doc. 60). When the government refused to meet these preconditions, ASUCUB denounced it as "rigid and uncompromising" (Doc. 81). The government's rigidity, as encapsulated in the statement by the vice-minister of the State Education Commission, He Dongchang, was, one could argue, a catalyst to the hunger strike that began on May 13. In his statement, made after the May 4 demonstrations, when the students ended their boycott, and after they had returned to classes on May 6, He Dongchang stated that there would be no retraction of the April 26 editorial's accusation that the students had caused "turmoil"; student leaders would not be pardoned; the "black hand" behind the student movement would be found; and the "four cardinal principles" could not be discarded.

4. The party [should tolerate] a free press, eliminate corruption, and establish the constitution as the basis of the legal order and governmental legitimacy (docs. 56, 69).

The students' tactics also changed rapidly: They began with demonstrations, petitions to officials, and class boycotts (Doc. 53). Later they abandoned class boycotts not only because of Zhao's speeches on May 3 and 4, and Li Peng's May 5 speech, but also because the class boycotts seemingly had no impact on anyone outside the university campuses (Doc. 66). Instead, they pursued other methods for "democracy on campus" (docs. 67, 72), propaganda work among Beijing's citizens by publishing student-written newspapers, and peaceful petition and demonstrations (one of the tactics to attract more demonstrators) (Doc. 53).

When the democracy movement had begun, conservative forces within the CCP leadership first tried to implicate Fang Lizhi, China's well-known astrophysicist and dissident, as the "black hand" behind the movement. Later, these leaders tried to implicate Zhao Ziyang and his supporters as the black hand. But it was not just the government that wondered whether the student movement was being manipulated by a black hand. As one individual involved in the demonstrations wrote in a big-character poster: Why "Down with Li Peng!" and "Support Zhao Ziyang!" (Doc. 58)? This individual suggested that there were pro-Zhao factional forces within the government, as well as some older intellectuals, who were manipulating the student movement to their own ends. Not all, in short, were in accord as to who was the real enemy in the government.

With the students unclear as to who was on whose side—who was the enemy, who was the friend—it was difficult for them to predict how any one action, any one statement, might help or harm their supporters within the government. As events in the subsequent periods make clear, they did indeed miscalculate. In the end, they bear some responsibility for undermining the power of the leaders who most favored them, notably Zhao Ziyang and those aligned with him.

Finally, the shifting profile of the student-led demonstrations contributed to changes in methods and objectives. The influx of students from the provinces, who eventually supplanted the exhausted Beijing students on the square, itself brought a shift in the values, objectives, and methods of the student-led movement. And so did the growing support of the workers—who, except for anticorruption, had quite different bones to pick with the CCP leadership. Although worker support for the movement remained negligible during the period from April 28 to May 12, students already had to consider how—or whether—to accommodate the particular demands of workers in exchange for their support.

It would be unfair to suggest that such a hastily organized movement ought to have been better organized. Further, the students' ability to regroup rapidly, to try new tactics and set new objectives, perhaps should be interpreted as flexibility and a strength. Still, the movement's lack of organization, leadership, and "theory" was a fact, and it influenced its decisions and undercut its effectiveness. ASUCUB itself admitted to inadequate "theoretical guidance" and "theoretical preparation," to a lack of strong leaders and thinkers, and to loose organization (docs. 47 and 68). Although the workers had many objectives that differed from the students', they implored the students to get better "theory." Others argued that the lack of knowledge about the theory or practice of democracy left the movement without clear objectives (Doc. 57). Still others suggested it was the ASUCUB leadership that lacked familiarity with democracy, whereas the rest of the students, accustomed to being commanded, were ignorant of their responsibility to supervise the work of ASUCUB. As a result, some believed ASUCUB gradually cut itself off from the students and became a machine simply issuing orders in an authoritarian manner (Doc. 68).

But a more persuasive argument would be that the students' real problem was not that they were uninformed about democracy, but that they didn't know at which point to cut into the issue of how to establish democracy in China. They were aware of the many facets of democracy, and that democracy can take many different forms; but they were not sure which aspects of democracy were the most vital *first steps* for the PRC, nor how the composite picture of democracy should look. Document 57 hints at some of the dilemmas of establishing democracy, even though the writer seems oblivious to the problems: The precondition for freedom of press is abolition of personal dictatorship; the precondition for freedom of speech is an institutional guarantee of a multiparty system and real power for the National People's Congress. But it has happened elsewhere (e.g., in Latin America and even in Taiwan) that a "free press," or at least a daring dissident press, has managed to cut away at an already troubled and flagging dictatorship.

Finally, had the demonstrations ended on May 12, rather than shifting into high gear with the beginning of the students' hunger strike, there would have been no pretext for declaring martial law, much less a military crackdown; but one is left to wonder whether there would have been a repression such as that witnessed after June 4 anyway. Would the greater openness and objectivity achieved by the press prior to the hunger strike have been reversed? Would those work units whose members had participated in the demonstrations have continued to demand greater openness, less interference by the CCP, and an end to corruption after returning to work? With hindsight, it appears that even had all demonstrations ceased after the April 26 editorial, repression of some sort was probably inevitable.[20] The students and other demonstrators were well aware of this. It had been the pattern after all previous movements. This time, the demonstrators were trying a different strategy—to get a commitment from the regime *before* ending the movement that such repression would not follow. They failed in their objective. In part this was because the "conservative" faction in the CCP had learned in 1987 that the removal of a key figure, Hu Yaobang, was not enough to change the CCP's political orientation toward reform. In 1989, this faction wanted to condemn the entire student-led movement as "counterrevolutionary" so as to justify the complete condemnation of the political orientation and reform program of the preceding ten years. What one witnessed in the period from April 28 to May 12 was the conservative leaders' eventual ability to take advantage of a divided and poorly led movement to pursue this objective.

---

[20]In the last effort at attempted repression, the anti–bourgeois liberalization campaign in 1987, Zhao Ziyang was, however, able to stop the repression. So nothing is truly "inevitable" in Chinese politics.

It is better to get divorced
Than to be a concubine of the other party;
Democratic parties, become independent
While it is still not too late to speak for the people.
—Wall poster

46

Who Are the Manufacturers of "Turmoil"?

LEAFLET AT PEOPLE'S UNIVERSITY

April 28, 1989

Source: Courtesy of Robin Munro.

The great patriotic student movement has been labeled as "turmoil." The students are referred to as manufacturers of "turmoil." In fact, anyone with brains can discover that this is an attempt at deceiving oneself and others . . . .[T]he corrupt and incompetent government is the real manufacturer of this large-scale patriotic "turmoil."

The students' peaceful movement to petition would not be a bad thing to an open-minded government. Yet from the very beginning, our government adopted a very nonchalant attitude [toward the students]. Our government did not respond until the movement was widespread. And their response was to utilize all the tools under their control—radio, newspaper, and TV—to point an accusing finger at the students and to label their actions "turmoil." Thus began "turmoil."

We were all children during the "Great Cultural Revolution." We do not remember much of it, nor do we know much. Yet those writers sought out by the officials as their mouthpiece during the Cultural Revolution remember their "Cultural Revolution" terms, such as "a small handful," "with ulterior motives," "a conspiracy long concocted." [These terms] sound so fearful and yet so funny. They are the ones who are trying to take China back to the days of the Cultural

Revolution. Let us students and the masses tell you that this truly "small hand-ful" with "ulterior motives" shall never allow your "long-concocted conspiracy" to come true!

Stability and unity are conducive to development. Yet do not forget that a docile population gives certain people a great opportunity to exploit the masses. Therefore, we must not continue to be so tame. We must first eliminate the termites of reforms and the parasites of development. . . .

Of course, leaders of the country cannot be made available on demand, and it is not necessary "for the leaders to appear whenever the masses want it." But please inform us: what, then, are the conditions for the leaders to meet the people? More than a hundred thousand university students are asking to meet the leaders. . . . Is this not a sufficient condition?

"We seek nothing but a prosperous and strong China!"
—Placard, from photo

"Support the Communist Party and Socialism!"
—Banner slogan, April 27 march, in *56 Days*

47

Statement of the Autonomous Student Union of Colleges and Universities of Beijing

AUTONOMOUS STUDENT UNION OF COLLEGES AND UNIVERSITIES IN BEIJING

Late April 1989

Source: Courtesy of HKFS.

At the urging of the vast majority of the college and university students in Beijing and after a preliminary informal discussion, the representatives from various universities in the student movement organized a temporary student union of Beijing on April 23 at a meeting in Yuan Ming Garden.[1] This was a temporary liaison organization, later renamed the Autonomous Student Union of Colleges and Universities in Beijing. It remains a loose organization that collects

---

[1]This is the old Summer Palace located near Qinghua University.

and synthesizes information from various universities and coordinates student activities. Looking back on the past few days, we think we made two major mistakes: First we made a mistake because of our miscalculation of the situation in the early morning of April 27. This dampened the enthusiasm of the students and damaged the reputation of the autonomous student union in some universities.[2] We hereby express our deepest regret. The second mistake was our failure to make an immediate response to the government's promise of "having a dialogue."[3] We failed to live up to the expectation of the people and of the students. Moreover, there is a third aspect: Our organization lacks theoretical depth, as it lacks great thinkers like Li Dazhao;[4] its propaganda work is not very effective; and its organizational structure is too loose.

"Oppose bureaucracy, corruption, and privileges!"
—Banner, April 27 march, in *56 days*

48

Letter to the Students

A WORKER

April 28, 1989

Source: Courtesy of Robin Munro.

Dear students:
    Your actions have been going on for quite a few days. You must fight for the wide support of workers, peasants, soldiers, and private vendors. But how to gain their support? First of all, do not [over]emphasize the treatment of intellectuals and the higher-education budget; do not be impractical in your cry for democracy, for this would affect the relationship between the students and the workers and peasants and is harmful to unification.
    [You should] tell the workers, peasants, and soldiers that "public ownership"

---

[2]This probably refers to the poor organization of student marches on the morning of April 27, following the April 26 *People's Daily* editorial.
    [3]Qinghua University students evidently failed to appear for a government-approved dialogue scheduled for April 25. According to the government's announcement, the students "could not agree on who should represent them." Xinhua Press Agency, "Student, Government Meeting Not Held," in FBIS, *Daily Report: China*, April 25, 1989, p. 23.
    [4]One of the CCP's still revered founding fathers.

has actually become "ownership by a small group [within] the bourgeoisie." The wealth earned by workers and peasants is spent extravagantly by this small group of aristocrats. They call us "masters of the country," but these "masters" live in jammed apartments generation after generation. However, those self-proclaimed "civil servants" own many luxury sedans and have police car sirens clearing the road for them. Comrades, [if] they hoist the flag of maintaining stability and unity to stop us, then what are the causes of instability and disunity? Can we just turn a blind eye on their theft of the national treasury? Where does their money come from? From our sweat and blood. They do not care for the welfare of the nation. They ride in luxury sedans and play golf, which costs several hundred yuan. No wonder people say, "The GNP is their income." That makes them no different from feudal rulers.

We should not rely on only one or two wise leaders. We need to establish a perfect democratic political system, with freedom of the press, an independent judicial system, and people's representatives elected by the people. . . . People's representatives are [now] appointed by [members of the] bourgeoisie. How can they represent the people, or reflect their concerns?

Dear students, remember the student movement two years ago? A small group of people took the press as a tool to cheat the people, and they provoked dissent between the students and the workers and peasants by saying, "To educate a university student, the nation has to spend over ten thousand yuan, which is provided by workers and peasants; however, the students do not treasure [it]." Actually, the truth is that the [wealth] built by the sweat and blood of the workers and peasants and millions of us comrades was all spent extravagantly by this small group of people. They are the biggest capitalists in the country, and they let the people suffer from disasters, such as inflation. . . . The student movement and the interests of the workers' and the peasants' are identical.

"Stabilize Prices!"
—Banner, April 27 march, in *56 Days*

49

Letter from Young Teachers of Beijing Normal University

YOUNG TEACHERS OF BEIJING NORMAL UNIVERSITY

April 28, 1989

Source: Handbill, courtesy of HKFS.

. . . Since the publication of the *People's Daily* editorial of April 26 [Doc. 43], we have felt heavy-hearted. We are shocked by and feel sorry for the central authorities in their judgment of the student democracy movement. At this very moment, we as teachers most fear the shedding of student blood and shaking student morale. On April 27, we joined in the demonstration. We heard about and witnessed the students' bravery. We were deeply moved by their spirit of struggle. We are also moved by the support shown by residents in the capital for the students. The sounds of "thank you" and "the people support you"[1] have rung in our ears ever since. We are your teachers, bearing the heavy task of passing on knowledge to you. We clearly recognize the importance of this task, but the cruel and ruthless political struggles carried out since the founding of the [People's] Republic have made us lose almost all our courage. Confronted with reality, we have concentrated on hard work and endured all kinds of hardships so as to lay a foundation for the revitalization of the Chinese nation. We thought this was a remote possibility until the glorious day of April 27, when we suddenly discovered your strength. We have heard your voices and personally felt your intense enthusiasm and passion. You are the elite of the Chinese nation. . . . We will always feel happy for having had students like you. That is true. Right at that moment, the question of life and death was distilled in our minds: to live for China and to die for China. Long live the students! . . .

Since that day, we have . . . come to realize that we are still young and that the blood of youth still flows in our hearts. Under the trammels of multiple layers of bureaucratic regulations and customs, we were almost dead. Thank you for awakening us. We must firmly oppose the yoke, the oppression, and the dictatorship. We must strive hard for China. When we were walking with you in the demonstration [and heard] the solemn and stirring cries for "freedom, democracy" and "The Chinese nation must be revitalized," our feelings

---

[1]Such vocal public support did not exist before April 27.

ran high. We were also disturbed, afraid you might lose your passion. . . . We hereby appeal to those elders who are working in the same positions as we are to stand up. We have a deeper, more accurate, and more passionate sense of the reality. How can you just stand on the sidewalks, waving flags and shouting battle cries? What are you afraid of? What should you be afraid of? The young students are not afraid of death. Are you willing to see them shed blood for you? Three million soldiers belong to the people, not to a handful of persons. We want stability, but we want socialist stability, not feudal stability.

. . . We also wonder, what on earth is in this for you students? You have nothing to gain personally. All you want is the vitalization of China. As young teachers we are willing to stand along with you forever, because your goals are noble . . . .

"News should tell the truth!"
—Banner, April 27 march, in *56 days*

50

Freedom of the Press Becomes the Major Issue

BEIJING UNIVERSITY TEACHERS

April 29, 1989

Source: Handbill or poster, in *ORSD*, 1:16.

The reports in all the state's major newspapers, on radio, and on TV have blocked and distorted the truth about or slandered the student movement. The *Science and Technology Daily* and the *World Economic Herald*[1] are being severely punished because they dared to tell the truth. More and more, people throughout the country are expressing their opinions in the form of big-character posters. As ordinary people know very little about the inside operation of state machinery, it escapes their supervision. All these things demonstrate that freedom of the press, the basic element of a democratic society, still lacks a foothold in China. A lack of freedom of the press means that the independent existence of individuals is not recognized. It means deprivation of a basic human right—the

---

[1]Shanghai's *World Economic Herald* was silenced as a "liberal" newspaper after April.

right of speech. A lack of freedom of the press means one man has the say and only one flower blossoms; that a few people try to keep the majority of the people silent; and that there is no open and effective supervision of the ruling party and government. Even if they make mistakes that lead to serious consequences, they can easily get away under false pretenses. How can we talk about "opposing official profiteering" and "opposing corruption" when there is no supervision by the people? . . . Without freedom of the press, there is no way to mobilize the entire nation's people into actively thinking and bringing into full play the wisdom of the majority. Thus, to create a vivid and vigorous political culture is impossible. Comrade Xiaoping once pointed out that the greatest threat to a political party results from not listening to the people. So, if the party wants to hear the voice of the people, it must first open channels through which the people may voice their opinions.

Since our party takes communism as its goal and regards the liberation of all mankind as its duty, then why can't it . . . learn strong points from others and let the public freely speak . . . ? Can't our people be trusted? Is it true that only the Communist party is fully justified in speaking while everyone else is just rebelling, using TV and radio to hurl abuses, and using newspapers to publish pornographic novels? Marx once fiercely condemned the news censorship in the Prussian Empire: "You (the censorship organ in the Prussian Empire) do not demand that roses and violets send out the same fragrance, so why do you demand that the richest thing in the world—[the human] spirit—exist in only one form?" Since our Communist party takes Marxism as its guiding ideology, it should first of all learn from Marx's breadth of vision. Otherwise, it is simply blaspheming his spirit.

We adamantly demand that freedom of the press be placed at the top of the list of issues in a dialogue with the government, and that the government bring about freedom of the press.

There is no need to fear the voice of the people. . . . Our state is the people's state, where every ordinary citizen should have the power to speak for its benefit. Only with their participation can China really become revitalized.

"Our respect to the *World Economic Herald* and Mr. Qin Benli!"

—Banner, May 4, in *56 days*

51

A Talk with Two [White-Collar] Workers

REVOLUTIONARY FROM THE FOREIGN LANGUAGES
DEPARTMENT, BEIJING NORMAL UNIVERSITY

April 29, 1989

Source: Handbill or poster, in *ORSD*, 1:35.

I do not have much understanding of the student movement and did not join the April 20 and 22 demonstrations and sit-ins. Yet now I cannot make myself calm down, as subsequent developments have awakened me. . . . I was one of the participants in the big demonstration on April 27. As for what happened later, I do not need to repeat it here. In this article, I want to reveal a dialogue I had with two workers at noon today, along with the hopes and desires of the citizens in the patriotic movement.

The two workers came from two different units, and both of them had graduated from universities. One of them had resigned from the government's "blessed" post and works in two cafeterias. The other one is a researcher at a research institute. Our main topic was aptly expressed by one of the workers: "The student movement has gained the support of citizens and workers." He also revealed the fact that after the April 26 *People's Daily* editorial, they were asked by their unit to offer their views and opinions. The workers, however, asked many unanswerable questions and expressed many grievances and complaints, such as the unequal distribution [of income], long working hours, poor social welfare, lack of protection for the rights of workers to receive continuing education, and other impossibilities. That fellow—the low-ranking official of the party—listened to all the complaints and then exclaimed: "Not just you, but we too have a lot of dissatisfaction." (Notice the sarcastic remark.)

Another worker told me that he went to a meat store to buy some ribs. The clerk said: "Ribs are reserved for the university students." The customers in the shop heard this and agreed. "Yes, ribs are reserved for the students. They need it for good health." This worker also requested that the students go to various units and ask for donations, and they will get what they want. The workers are waiting for you. . . .

Fellow students. Your actions have been recognized by society. People are hoping this movement will be carried on. Don't stop halfway as people will then be disappointed. The students will lose even more. The government has already lost the will of the people. If students lose a drop of blood in this fight, workers in the city will unite together and protest against the government and even go on strike. . . .

"Dialogue on the basis of equality!"
—Slogan, in *56 days*

52

True Story of the So-Called Dialogue

ANONYMOUS

After April 29, 1989

Source: Courtesy of HKFS.

The so-called dialogue between the government and students that the people saw on television is actually a two-man comic show performed by the government's representatives.[1]

First, the majority of the "student representatives" to the dialogue were representatives of the officially appointed student union, not representatives jointly elected by the vast majority of the students participating in the student movement.

Second, during the course of the dialogue, the students were clearly in an unequal position. They could only ask questions, not repudiate the answers, because after they asked the questions, or even when they were asking the questions, their microphones were grabbed away. This was not a dialogue, but a news conference by the government. Also, many cuts were made in the TV coverage, thus deleting many sharp questions.

Third, the government spokesman often talked evasively about the nature of the student movement. His answers and the so-called conclusions are always said to be targeted at "a handful of bad people." This student movement, however, is a completely spontaneous patriotic democracy movement, and there is no such thing as "a handful of bad people" manipulating and taking advantage of the student movement. Besides, based on the behavior of the so-called few individuals for making conclusions about the general situation, the conclusion must

---

[1]For the full text of the April 29 dialogue between students and Yuan Mu, see Oksenberg et al., eds., *Beijing Spring*, Doc. 27.

necessarily be quite absurd and completely illogical. The vast majority of students and people are deeply dissatisfied with the content of this so-called dialogue. We strongly demand that the government make a correct judgment on this student movement in conformity with the will of the people.

In view of all this, the vast majority of the students strongly protest against and do not recognize this so-called dialogue.

> "Don't Postpone the Dialogue!"
> "It's Not Turmoil!"
> —Slogans, in *56 Days*

53

The Current Situation and Our Task

GENG FU

Late April 1989

Source: Handbill and/or poster, in *ORSD*, 1:85.

From any perspective, the "April 27" peaceful demonstration is successful. It signifies that the patriotic democracy movement that started on April 15 with peaceful petitioning students from the colleges and universities in Beijing has entered a new stage.

This success, however, far from proves that the basic demands of ASUCUB and the students are satisfied. This can be seen from the "April 29" dialogue jointly sponsored by the government and the "Students Federation." As of today, the government has refused to have a dialogue with the so-called illegal organization—"ASUCUB"—and has refused to recognize its legal status and that of its subordinate student autonomous unions (preparatory committees) in various colleges and universities. At the same time, a few diehards lurking in the government are trying to avoid a direct dialogue and are waiting at ease for the students to become exhausted. . . . They are trying to split the students' organizations and drive a wedge between the students and their organizations . . . .

At this crucial moment, where will the patriotic democracy movement go? What are our tasks? . . . In a certain sense, the establishment of the legal status of ASUCUB is a substantial victory for this democracy movement. The current struggle should be carried out around this core goal. It is consistent with the goals of supporting an honest and clean Communist party and maintaining the democratic leadership of the government.

The possibility of . . . achieving the above goal [is evidenced by] the fact that this democracy movement has already spread to or simultaneously happened in China's major cities. This has shocked the people . . . and touched the vast number of cadres and Communist party members, the minor democratic parties, and people in the news media. It has also won [international] sympathy, understanding, and support. . . . A handful of diehards in the government have lacked the means to suppress the large-scale patriotic petitioning of students during demonstrations and marches. Moreover, [they] have wrongly estimated the situation and the people's strength. Their insistence on maintaining the wrong judgment of the movement, their irresponsible and high-handed policy, the deceptive propaganda, and the distorted reports by the news media have allowed the vast number of students and city residents who know the truth to perceive the true features of a handful of antidemocratic diehards. . . . As for seeking legal weapons to protect the personal safety of the patriotic student leaders and the [continued] existence of the student organization, ASUCUB and its subordinate student organizations will make unremitting efforts to gain legal status and have a dialogue on the basis of equality.

The concrete tasks facing the patriotic democracy movement at present are:

First, solicit votes of no-confidence for the official municipal "Student Federation" in several dozen colleges and universities in the city so as to negate and remove its leadership authority over the student unions and graduate student unions in various colleges and universities. This "Student Federation" has already ceased to exist except in name; and it was passively sabotaging the movement.

Second, perfect all kinds of concrete preparations for a dialogue with the government; in particular, help to elect the true students' representatives to participate in the dialogue with the government. Moreover, strengthen the contacts and coordination with the student organizations in the colleges and universities in other major cities, provide mutual support and encouragement, and make preparation for establishing a unified, legal, national students' autonomous organization when the time is right.

Finally, carry out additional propaganda work among the city residents, exposing the tactics of deception and schemes by a handful of diehards who have lurked in the government. Help the people of all strata fully understand the nature of the student democracy movement, which is patriotic and supportive of the party, to win their sympathy and support for the struggle and achieve a legal status for the student organizations.

The methods of the patriotic democracy movement at the moment should be mainly those of propaganda, including speeches, big-character posters, wall papers, broadcasts, handbills, and theatrical performances. We should publish newspapers if conditions permit. The most important and powerful means available to the democracy movement are large-scale peaceful petition and demonstration, but we must exercise these means appropriately and with restraint. Boycotting classes can only be a supplementary means, particularly in view of the fact that the pressure produced through boycotting classes is limited in a country like ours, which underestimates the importance of education. Hence, a decision universally to resume classes at an appropriate time is wise. We should lose no time in constructing campus democracy and in establishing student organizations, but we should not be diverted from the main direction of the movement. We should strictly prevent internal strife and factional struggles for power and profits. Under the preconditions and principles of purity and representativeness, the students' autonomous organizations and their main leadership should maintain continuity and stability.

Once the autonomous student organizations achieve legal status, we should immediately shift the focus of our work to promoting reform of the political system and helping the ruling party build democratic leadership. We should try to establish and strengthen cooperation and alliance with leaders possessing a modernizing consciousness, and with cadres and some CCP members, to help the ruling party and government overcome the malpractices of weakness and corruption. We should clearly distinguish among all kinds of elements in the party and government, isolating a handful of antipeople and antidemocracy diehards and punishing corrupt officials; establish and strengthen contacts with the minor democratic parties; do propaganda and explanation well so as to win sympathy, support, and cooperation; and win support and help from the journalists. Our goal represents the fundamental interests of the overwhelming majority of the people: to work hard toward establishing a highly democratic, prosperous, powerful, and modernized socialist country. Our goal must be achieved! Our goal will certainly be achieved!

Long live democracy!

54

Confession of an Ugly Soul

A RESURRECTED UGLY CHINESE

Late April 1989

Source: Leaflet circulated at Beijing Normal University, in *ORSD*, 1:70.

. . . Yesterday, I fell down. As I faced walls of soldiers in green uniforms and heard their fierce and malicious threats, I was frightened out of my wits. I could not look up. Although I bravely participated in the April 22 demonstration and I sincerely cried out for democracy on campus, I collapsed in the face of such power and intimidation and the strongly worded editorial in the *People's Daily*. With my weak body and dirty soul, I kowtowed at the foot of the fierce and cruel devil. I suddenly changed from a freedom fighter to a coward who just wanted to drag out an ignoble existence. I sold my soul in exchange for temporary safety. I sold my value as a human being for an empty body. My God, I want to tear apart my dark mind! Please use my tears of confession to clean away my mind's dirt!

Surely I walked bravely at the front during the April 22 demonstration. Who could have known that every action of mine was aimed at enlisting praise and reward from others? To gain honor and benefit, I pretended not to fear death. In front of the solemn Great Hall of the People, I shouted and cried out in righteous indignation when our student representatives kneeled down under the national emblem and students clashed with the police. When the military police began to beat us with fists, belts, and boots, however, I sneaked away from the "front" to the "rear area." During the demonstration, when my classmates were singing the battle songs and marching hand in hand, I sneaked from the side to the middle of the demonstration groups because I was afraid of the fists of the military police. I let my classmates beside me form a wall of protection for me. When the people in the streets sent us a box of flavored ice bars, I bravely made a grab at the box for fear I would not get one. When we went out to raise funds, I held onto the donation box for dear life for fear that others might steal the public funds. My friends, when I recall this, I simply dare not believe that this extremely ugly Chinese intellectual was me![1] In normal times, I pretended to be easygoing and

---

[1]The term "ugly Chinese" is a reference to the book by Taiwan author Bo Yang, *Choulou de Zhongguo ren* (The ugly Chinese), published in 1988. Bo sharply criticized Chinese culture and portrayed Chinese people as cowards. In the People's Republic, some Chinese praised the book as accurate; but conservative government leaders such as Wang Zhen, who defended Chinese culture, found it offensive.

generous, to be selfless and fearless like a noble saint. But when the critical moment came, I turned out to be a pitiful creature who cravenly clung to life instead of braving death. It is by no means an exaggeration to say that I was a coward, a selfish, mean, and shameless person. I really implore some brave individuals to shoot me!

On the morning of April 27, all the classmates around me had written their wills, swearing to sacrifice their lives and shed their hot blood for victory of the democracy movement. Only I was sitting alone, with a disdainful and taunting smile. In my mind I was scolding them as "Foolish B" (*Sha B*)[2] as if their demonstration had nothing to do with me. When they were blocked at the gate of the university and pressured by university authorities, I instead felt somewhat satisfied. As I watched one truckful after another of policemen come onto the streets and heard continuous stern warnings over the radio, my weak heart surrendered to their power. I tried to persuade my classmates that they did not understand the complexities of things, as if I were the only hero who understood the times. I said that whoever did not listen to the advice of the old people would suffer in the future; that the tools of the Communist party dictatorship were not maintained for nothing. I used this kind of slave mentality to shake morale and intoxicate myself with self-satisfaction. Yet what I feared was "death." Time was passing quickly, and all my classmates had gone to the battleground, leaving my lonely soul wandering in the quiet dormitory. But my conscience gave me no peace. At this moment, I began to fear I had died and felt the condemnation by my conscience for fearing death. Thereupon my numb mind began to function. . . .

Gradually, from the examples of my classmates, I discovered my ugly features. Suddenly my black heart died and I recovered a revived red heart. I have come to believe that a man's life is not merely the existence of flesh and blood. What is more important is a firm belief in life, a noble mind, and the wisdom and courage to make sacrifices for justice. It is more worthwhile to die a martyr's death than to lead a life devoid of meaning. To strive for justice is the greatest happiness in life. One who drags out an ignoble existence with no sense of justice and against one's conscience will inevitably be cast aside by the people. Only now do I understand why we say that the meaning of one's life lies not in what one gets, but in what one contributes.

We young college students must uphold the cardinal principle of righteousness and be prepared to lay down our lives for the just cause. This student movement will not only push forward democratization and liberal reform in China, but will also expose ugly souls (like mine) of the Chinese under sunshine, so as to re-create a new Chinese soul!

---

[2]Calling them "*Sha B*," with "*B*" written in English, is inspired by Lu Xun's character Xiaobi, in his *Story of Ah Q*. Xiaobi is a foolish figure who argues with Ah Q over silly things. *Shabi* is also a strong Chinese curse word.

55

Is It a Dialogue or an Admonitory Talk?
On the "Dialogue" of April 29

GRADUATE STUDENTS OF BEIJING NORMAL UNIVERSITY

April 30, 1989

Source: Mimeograph, in *Tiananmen 1989*, p. 344.

In response to the strong demands by hundreds of thousands of colleges students in Beijing and the students' hard struggle that took the form of boycotting classes and demonstrations, the government finally agreed to a dialogue with the students. The authorities bypassed the Autonomous Student Union, however, which truly represents the just demands of the vast number of the students, by directly naming some so-called student representatives and pretending to conduct a serious dialogue with the students on the afternoon of April 29.[1]

Let's not discuss the fact that the "student representatives" [those students who were officially appointed, not elected by the students themselves] cannot represent the young and progressive students who are actively participating in this movement. Merely look at the attitudes of the leading comrade [Yuan Mu, the official spokesman for the State Council] in this dialogue, and you will know that the authorities have no sincerity whatsoever in fundamentally solving the problems. Aware that the big accusation of "creating turmoil" against the students dished out in the April 26 editorial of *People's Daily* had not crushed the students, and that the charges of being antiparty and antisocialist had not intimidated them either, this leading comrade changed his tactics of deception. He called a few college students to a dialogue. It was meant to turn big problems into small problems and small problems into no problems at all. Even at a dialogue on this level, whenever any substantive question arose, the leading comrade still tried to stall the students in every possible way and acted in a perfunctory manner. He often gave lengthy comments on certain unimportant and small details in order to stall for time. Because of the poor quality of the students, some inconsistencies or flaws frequently appeared in the students' questions. Whenever this happened, several leaders present at the dialogue would courageously forge ahead and vie with each other in attacking the students. They seized upon one point and ignored the overall picture. What is more outrageous is that the leading comrade treated the young students striving for

---

[1]The complete translation of the April 29 "dialogue" appears in Oksenberg et al., eds., *Beijing Spring*, Doc. 27.

democratic reform . . . as hotheaded little children. He put on the manner of a lord and said, "You are still young and easily carried away by your emotions." "You weren't even born when the Cultural Revolution broke out," and "I treat you as if you are my children." During the three hours of the so-called dialogue, the talk of the government leaders took up more than 90 percent of the time. We cannot help asking: Was it an equal "dialogue" or an admonitory talk by a father to his son?

The leading comrade participating in the dialogue proved himself to be a battle-tested veteran in official circles. By making empty gestures, he avoided substantive questions. While talking cheerfully and easily, he disarmed the so-called students' representatives. But we sternly warn those "lords of public servants" who believed that they prevailed: Don't try to play petty tricks any more. The eyes of the students are discerning. We hope the government leaders recognize, for the sake of the whole country, that this great patriotic student movement is the continuation of the "May Fourth" Movement seventy years ago. It cannot be mentioned in the same breath with the Red Guards in the ten years of the Cultural Revolution, during which the people were ordered about and fooled around with by one man. The government leaders should stop any kind of mudslinging and attack against the progressive young students. They should quickly abandon their lordly manner and conduct a true discussion about the students' demands with the real students' representatives on the basis of equality. . . .

56

Dead Fish and Broken Net—Some Thoughts on "The Family Links of Contemporary Chinese Bureaucrats": The Curse of a Slave in the Department of Education

April 30, 1989

Source: Wall poster, in *ORSD*, 1:57–58.

Facing this extensive network of connections, I dare not believe that it is made up of relatives, in-laws, fathers, and sons. I groped for reasons to justify this network of connections, such as, "If a father is a hero, then his son will be a brave man"; or "The family of a general gives birth to brave sons"; or "There are no cowardly soldiers under the command of a strong general." The examples of the sons and brothers of the "Eight Banners" [the notoriously weak military units of the Manchus in the late Qing dynasty] will, however, refute the above arguments one by one. I myself won't say more, as the late Premier Zhou Enlai long ago made this point.

Perhaps due to the fact that I was born into an old cadre's family, I could only see small busy spiders cautiously weaving together smooth and slick networks of connections piece by piece. Having lived on catching fish, it is unimaginable to me that our respected "proletarian revolutionaries, outstanding Communist fighters, and brilliant senior leaders of the Chinese Communist party" are also capable of skillfully weaving such networks; and that they are also consciously or unconsciously weaving their own "omnipotent networks." Our party is covered by the networks of these spiders. The eyesight of our party is failing, and its ears are clogged with disease. The party's mouth is becoming dulled and its strength wasted within. The best and brightest cannot enter the party, yet riffraff swarm into it. Increasingly the party is falling under the control of those "sham Communists." The "spiders" in the party can only enhance their connections by weaving networks. The idea of communism, the duty of the proletariat, the cause of socialism, and the process of democratization seem to be fairy tales for them. They merely function as the disguise and bait to attract more wealth for themselves. I no longer believe in great men or supernatural beings. All past propaganda was beautiful lies and deceptive words.

Perhaps I must recognize that many revolutionary predecessors have made significant contributions. They performed deeds of valor in the revolutionary wars and the wars for democracy. But during the peaceful period of reconstruction, many of them lost the firm party spirit they displayed during the wars. They lost the makings of selfless revolutionaries and sought out their own self-interest. They wanted no longer to be public servants who bore hardships, but rather to be lords and masters over the people. They wanted privileges, glory, splendor, wealth, and rank. Pity, what a pity!

The weaving of China's super network of connections is due not only to the . . . degeneracy of the "spiders" themselves, but also to their being deeply nurtured by the old culture and psychology. From a historical perspective, we could say they are puppets manipulated by history in a dance on the vast land of China. . . . Although they appear very cocky, they cannot escape being manipulated by old habits and longstanding practices. During their revolutionary youth, they were attracted by the powerful magnetic force of justice. They were called upon by truth, which was like the sun shining with boundless radiance, and they made great contributions to the people. In peaceful and quiet times, however, the feudal bureaucratic consciousness that was soundly sleeping in their innermost soul and the flickering feudal genetic factors became active. . . . They began to poison the people and grew increasingly harmful.

Maybe someone who doubts this will ask whether the Chinese proletariat cannot possess a thorough revolutionary will. . . . After it has achieved victory, can't the proletariat accept proposals for democracy and freedom? Can't it continue to work hard to progress from the realm of necessity to the realm of freedom? We can see now that the proletarian party in China lacks the promise that Marx had described. For historical reasons, the Chinese proletariat inevitably was congenitally deficient: Their number was small, relatively young, and at a low level of cultural development and education. Those who propagated Marxism and Leninism were also congenitally deficient. Many leaders of the proletarian revolution were not born into proletarian families. In a certain sense, their revolutionary spirit was not determined by their own will. Only at the most critical moment of national survival and because of the unity of the interests of the workers, peasants, students, businessmen, and soldiers did the Chinese proletariat get pushed onto the stage of history. . . . Once it achieved revolutionary victory, deficiencies generated its poor qualities, which gradually began to surface. Forty years after the founding of the People's Republic, the struggles against feudalism continue uninterrupted, but the feudal roots are still functioning. . . . As one grows older, the feudal spirits grow more powerful. Mao himself had vividly displayed such a feeling of "longing for the past." . . . These are the products of the time in China: wear feudal robes while criticizing feudal socks; prohibit hereditary official titles while tolerating positions and benefits to be granted to one's wife and son; eliminate the existence of an emperor, but permit only one man to have the say; prohibit the existence of a gentry and clan system while tolerating the matching of social and economic status in marriage; prohibit people from running wild while disregarding the sanctity of the constitution. Enough! Enough! The advocacy of the concepts of "freedom of assembly and speech as the legal rights of the citizens" exists on paper, but not in society. If a true report is read in the newspapers, it is legal; but if it is heard in the streets, it is illegal. The government represents the constitution and the constitution defends the government. The government has disregarded popular opinion. Party law is beyond the law of the state. This is the result of Marxism being transplanted into China!

China's network of connections, official profiteering, and family relations may well be regarded as one marvelous natural world wonder. We cannot expect surviving feudal remnants to break this network and promote the process of democratization. They have AIDS [*aizibing*].[1] The real driving force is the youth who do not take feudalism as a tonic! . . .

---

[1]Here the author is taking the conservatives' accusation that Westerners are a threat to China because they purportedly carry AIDS (portrayed in a recent movie, *Aizibing huanzhe* [AIDS patients], produced by the Beijing Youth Film Studio), and turning it against these very leaders by suggesting that they suffer from a degenerative political disease. The Chinese pronunciation for *aizibing* can also mean "the loving capitalism disease."

57

Raise the Flag of Rationality

A PROFESSIONAL REVOLUTIONARY AT BEIJING NORMAL UNIVERSITY

April 30, 1989

Source: Wall poster or handbill, in *ORSD*, 1:73.

. . . The tragedy of Hu Yaobang is the tragedy of the Chinese people. Such tragedies appear throughout the entire history of the Chinese nation.

Looking back, suddenly I was shocked, saddened, and, quite simply, in despair. Personal dictatorship started with the first emperor of the Qin dynasty [221–207 B.C.]. Despotic dynasties continued thereafter. Chinese history subsequently followed this logic: One after another, a peasant war would overthrow a corrupt dynasty, only to choose a new dictatorial and despotic dynasty. The Chinese nation has been caught in a dead-end cycle of periodic shocks. Our great motherland has thus been tortured by periodic disasters, thereby periodically sacrificing society's productive forces. . . .

At the time that some countries in the West began their development along the capitalist road, ancient China still floundered in the dynastic cycles of feudalism. When the Chinese empire grew intoxicated with self-satisfaction about its power and influence as "the heavenly dynasty and upper state," the guns of the Western powers began to bombard the door of China. At that time, some progressive Chinese awoke. They began to realize that China could no longer flounder amidst the rise and fall of dynasties. The bourgeois revolutionaries headed by Sun Yat-sen launched the Revolution of 1911 to overthrow the corrupt Qing dynasty.

As the feudal forces were too strong for the bourgeois forces, however, the "dead-end cycle" remained unbroken. Yuan Shikai's efforts to restore the imperial system sounded the death knell of the bourgeois republic. Traditional warlord politics reappeared in China. When Chiang Kai-shek wiped out the separatist warlord regimes and superficially unified the country, it was clear that he established not a bourgeois republic, but rather, a new despotic system in a semicolonial country.

Isn't the socialist system established after the overthrow of the Chiang Kai-shek regime in a revolution led by the Communist party a dynasty of personal dictatorship? We all know that in our country the party exercises its leadership over everything. Everything serves political objectives. In reality it is the party chairman[1] or party secretaries who direct everything. The People's Congress is

---

[1]Deng Xiaoping eliminated the position of party chairman in the early 1980s. The most powerful position in the party now is that of general secretary.

nothing but a decoration, a flower vase, a rubber-stamp, a fig leaf. Under such despotic rule cloaked by Marxism-Leninism, even the chairman of the state [Liu Shaoqi] and other outstanding leaders were persecuted or murdered: the cult of personality and personal worship spread everywhere like a pestilence. The constitution of the republic was trampled upon, and only the words of one man had the power of law.

What is the situation after the Third Plenum of the Eleventh Party Congress [December 1978]? Have we left the peculiar dynastic cycle?

Deng Xiaoping put forward proposals to reform the political system, but he lacks the wisdom and courage of George Washington, who refused to continue to hold the office of the presidency, so as to establish a good democratic tradition. So the Chinese political system has remained the same. The chairman of the Central Military Affairs Commission became the one to pull strings behind the scenes.[2] Deng Xiaoping acts as if he is holding court from behind a screen. He somewhat resembles the Empress Dowager [Ci Xi]. . . .

The democracy fighters during the Renaissance upheld the banner of rationality. It was this banner that added a new page to the annals of civilization.

What is rationality? Rationality is the fusion of impulses and enthusiasm with knowledge. The great thinker [Sir Francis] Bacon once said, "Knowledge is power." I believe that the melding together of knowledge and enthusiasm will produce an immeasurable force of rationality. These days I am very saddened to see that the students in the democracy movement at Beijing Normal University have impulses and enthusiasm but lack knowledge, the knowledge of democracy. Because of this, the movement lacks the guidance of knowledge. Inadequate knowledge leads to a lack of confidence, and a lack of confidence undermines courage. For this reason, it is difficult to organize the movement.

We must be equipped with knowledge of democracy. Otherwise we are likely to collapse into a state of blindness. Democracy primarily means that the political system needs a rational mechanism of checks and balances over political power. . . .

Among the seven demands put forward by the students of Beijing University, one is for "freedom of the press"; but they forget that a precondition for realizing freedom of the press is the abolition of personal dictatorship. Why do the journalists in the United States dare to expose the illegal activities of the president and his officials? If there were no checks and balances on the president by Congress, if there were no supervision of the ruling party by the opposition party, how would the journalists dare to do so?

There is one provision of freedom of speech in the Chinese constitution, but it lacks the necessary institutional guarantee. The People's Congress is a rubber-stamp, and other political parties dare say nothing.

---

[2]Deng Xiaoping resigned as chairman of the Central Military Commission in November 1989.

To carry out the democracy movement, we need to have a correct direction. Our slogans must . . . grasp the essential issues. Thus, I suggest the following slogans:

1. Revise the constitution and abolish the one-party dictatorship!
2. Open competition in elections by all the political parties!
3. Implement a parliamentary system and abolish dictatorship!
4. Allow freedom of the press and enact a press law!
5. Separate the party from enterprises and abolish privileges!

58

Suspicious! Suspicious!

ANONYMOUS

Late April 1989

Source: Big-character poster at Beijing University, in *ORSD*, 1:74.

What are the purposes of our actions this time? They are to strive for democracy, to punish those engaged in official profiteering, and to overthrow the autocratic system. What is very suspicious, however, is the sort of slogan put forth at this point by the Chinese University of Political Science and Law: "Knock down Li Peng and support Zhao Ziyang"—?!

Anyone with brains may investigate the political context out of which this slogan has appeared. They will see how a handful of intellectual scabs shamefully betrayed the solemn goals of democracy and freedom by becoming tools in the power struggle of the autocratic and conservative forces represented by XXX and XXX;[1] and by becoming part-time politicians who maintained a subtle connection with the "party of the crown princes."

How strange that, when it is the [CCP] Central Committee that really has decisive power in handling the issue of evaluating Comrade Hu Yaobang and democracy, we follow the others in raising our arms and shouting for the premier of the State Council to come out to answer; yet why don't we ask the party general secretary to do the same? We indeed need to think it over. Why on earth should we have a strong aversion to Li Peng . . . ? Those students who have shouted, "Li Peng, step down!" please think about why you demand this. Is it merely because the central authorities sent no one to talk with

---

[1] XXX and XXX probably refer to Deng Xiaoping and Yang Shangkun.

the students? Or is it simply because someone irresponsibly said that Li Peng would come out to answer the students? I do not intend to argue in favor of those bureaucrats who have disregarded the students. I cried for the students' representatives who kneeled down [on the steps of the Great Hall of the People]. . . . But I wonder if someone has an ulterior motive in suggesting that the premier of the State Council, not the party general secretary, should come out to answer the students. . . .

Please go to society and ask the people, both those who want to consolidate the economy and those who know about internal conditions, how they evaluate current Chinese leaders. The measures of Li Peng to regulate the economic environment and rectify the economic order have already achieved some initial success. Besides, he advocates wiping out official profiteering; but heavy pressures have made his proposal ineffective. His policies have won support from a vast number of cadres, workers, and peasants. At the moment, when we can't confirm political inside stories or think of a better candidate, we should not . . . irresponsibly demand the removal of one leader.

It is said that the previous student movements were always taken advantage of by someone. . . . The student movement may generate extremely destructive forces and cause a political struggle that will make our economic reconstruction stagnate for several years, ten years, or even longer. Our economic takeoff might lose out because of it. We should clearly set our goals. If we are for democracy, then we strive for democracy; if we oppose official profiteering, then we protest against it. We need not get involved in the politics whose inner machinations we cannot know. Just think how Hu Yaobang was forced to step down last time. Just imagine whether someone else will be forced to step down after this student movement. How will history judge this person? . . .

It will be sad, outrageous, and unbearable if the enthusiasm and devotion of the young people, their sincere enthusiasm and devotion, is taken advantage of by someone with ulterior motives. . . . Be aware not to become a tool of political factional struggle!

(Do not believe any groundless rumors. You may not believe this big-character poster of mine either; but everyone should use his own brain to think about it.)

59

Statement of Our Views on the Shanghai Party Committee's "Decision" to Reorganize the *World Economic Herald*

EDITORIAL BOARD

May 1, 1989

Source: Editorial Board, *World Economic Herald* (Shanghai), May 1, 1989, *Xinwen daobao* (News herald), May 12, 1989, reproduced in *Tiananmen 1989*, pp. 306–8.

. . . 2. Our Attitudes and Demands

1. In view of all the facts, we believe that the Shanghai Party Committee has reached a conspicuously unjust verdict and has thereby damaged the image of the party and state. This has led to adverse consequences both inside and outside Shanghai. The reasons are as follows:

a. The main leader of the Shanghai Party Committee disregarded the facts and dealt with the problem in an oversimplified and crude way.

b. Unfair treatment of a party comrade, particular an old comrade who worked diligently and conscientiously for the party, has negatively affected a large number of party comrades.

c. [The decision reflects a] disregard of the responsibility system of the chief editor. Comrade Yuan Mu, the spokesman of the State Council, clearly pointed out in his "dialogue" with the students' representatives on April 29 that "There is no news censorship in our country. In the journalists' work and reports, we have implemented the chief-editor responsibility system." Thus, in view of the *World Economic Herald* incident, if the wrong decision is not corrected, it will necessarily affect the whole nation's news media.

2. We still believe that the "Urgent Report"[1] presented to the Shanghai Municipal Party Committee on April 25 is correct. Since people both in China and overseas know that the original version of this issue of the *World Economic Herald* was banned, and since several hundred copies of this version have already been distributed, we suggest avoiding contradictions . . . by publishing the original banned version as well. Moreover, the contents of the discussion and speeches in the original version are accurate and true. . . .

---

[1]The "Urgent Report" was presented by the Editorial Board of the *World Economic Herald*.

3. The personnel in our *World Economic Herald* office are now in a very difficult situation and cannot work normally.

. . . Thus we make the following demands to the Shanghai Municipal Party Committee:

a. Immediately annul the erroneous decision to suspend Comrade Qin Benli from his position as chief editor.

b. Strictly follow the law to handle this matter and respect the fundamental rights of the news agencies. Withdraw the "reorganization" group now in charge of the work in the *World Economic Herald* and let the personnel in the *World Economic Herald* return to normal work.

We hope the Shanghai Party Committee and people from all walks of life will correctly judge our attitudes and demands.

60

Petition of University Student Representatives in Beijing

REPRESENTATIVES OF BEIJING'S UNIVERSITY STUDENTS

May 2, 1989

Source: Petition, in *ORSD*, 2:99.

To the Standing Committee of the National People's Congress, State Council, and Party Central Committee:

After the "April 27 Demonstration" by the students and people, the government expressed the wish, through the news media, to have a dialogue with the students. We wholeheartedly welcome this gesture. To ensure that a substantive dialogue is carried out soon, we, as the elected representatives of the students, . . . make the following demands to the government and [CCP] Central Committee:

1. A dialogue between the two sides should be based on complete equality and sincerity. . . . Both sides should have an equal opportunity to speak and ask questions.

2. The student representatives . . . should be openly elected by the majority of college students (particularly by those who participated in this April patriotic democracy movement). In the meantime, we believe that due to the fact that the official student unions and graduate student unions in the colleges and universities did not provide correct leadership or a good organizational role, we will not

agree to allow them to appoint the students' representatives; nor will we recognize any student representatives privately invited solely by the government and not approved by the majority of the students.[1]

3. We propose that the student representatives be elected in the following way:

In view of the fact that in Beijing the Autonomous Student Union of Colleges and Universities, which emerged out of many autonomous student organizations, has been continuously playing a leadership and organizational role and has been recognized by most of the students, we believe that it should be in charge of organization work. A certain number of representatives will be elected by the students in each university in Beijing proportionate to the size of its student body, and it will in turn form a student dialogue delegation. After full discussion and consultation among the students, several students will be elected [from among all the universities' dialogue delegations] to act as the general spokesmen for the student delegations. Other representatives have the right to attend the dialogue and listen. They can also add some points to the speeches made by the students as well as raise questions about the speeches made by the government.

4. Representatives to the dialogue from the government should be at or above the level of member of the Standing Committee of the [CCP] Central Committee, vice-chairman of the Standing Committee of the National People's Congress, or vice-premier of the State Council, that is, those individuals who understand affairs of state and possess decision-making power.

5. During the dialogue, nongovernmental persons or groups invited by either side should be allowed to attend the dialogue and listen. Neither side should refuse or block this under any pretext. Invited representatives do not have the right to speak during the dialogue but may comment on the dialogue afterward.

6. The spokesmen from both sides must have equal rights and opportunities to speak. A time limit must be set for the presentations by the spokesmen of both sides. Each question may take no more than three minutes, and each response is limited to ten to fifteen minutes. The spokesmen are allowed to ask many questions during the process of questions and answers.

7. Spot coverage and reports about the dialogue by both Chinese and foreign reporters must be allowed. In the meantime, China Central TV, and the Central People's Radio Broadcasting Station, should provide nationwide live coverage of the dialogue. Those participating in the dialogue have the right to videotape, record, and take notes on the spot. No group or individual is allowed to interfere or obstruct this process under any pretext.

8. The dialogue should be conducted alternatively in places separately chosen by the government and the students. Dates will be determined by both sides.

---

[1]The first dialogue involving State Council spokesman Yuan Mu and other officials was almost exclusively with student representatives from government-controlled student unions.

9. The government representatives in the dialogue process should try to answer as many questions as possible and immediately begin to address those problems that are solvable. If some problems cannot in fact be resolved immediately, both sides may agree to have another dialogue within a set period of time. Neither side should unreasonably refuse to do so.

10. To guarantee the legal validity of the results of the dialogue, both sides participating in the dialogue must issue a joint statement, which must also be verified by the signatures of both sides.

11. The personal political safety of the representatives from both sides in the dialogue must be guaranteed.

12. After each round of dialogue, the results must be reported faithfully in the major state newspapers and over the radio. Public announcements must be made to inform the people of the results and to state the time, place, and agenda of the next round of dialogue.

Concerning the aforementioned demands:

1. To ensure that a dialogue will be conducted soon, we hope to receive an answer to the aforementioned demands before 12:00 noon on May 3. The concrete reasons for specific answers to our concrete demands should be written into the document.

2. If we do not receive an answer before 12:00 noon on May 3, we reserve the right to continue demonstration marches on May 4.

3. We suggest that the first round of the dialogue be conducted at 8:30 A.M. on May 4. Beijing University could be the location for the dialogue.

4. A copy of this petition letter will be presented to the Political Consultative Conference of the People's Republic of China.

61

Choice Between [Personal] Conscience and Party Spirit: An Open Letter to Party Members

PARTY MEMBER, PEOPLE'S UNIVERSITY

May 3, 1989

Source: Big-character poster at People's University, in *ORSD*, 1:59.

Party comrades:

As seen from the analysis in the *People's Daily* and the party members' general assembly, which conveyed the spirit of the Central Committee, its hardline attitude is obvious:

[According to] Deng Xiaoping, "In Beijing, only sixty thousand students have taken part in the class boycott. One hundred thousand are still inactive. We have three million troops. What should we fear?"

The government is likely to use force to suppress this democratic movement. It is very probable that the march and demonstration to be held tomorrow will lead to another bloody tragedy.

There are only two choices to make. We either act as conscientious Chinese, conscientious party members, and struggle for democracy and prosperity in China; or we answer the call of the party so as to secure our future by complying enthusiastically with the demands of the party central. Which should we choose?

62

Letter to the University Students of the Whole Country

SOME GRADUATE STUDENTS FROM THE CHINESE ACADEMY OF SOCIAL SCIENCES

May 3, 1989

Source: Mimeograph, in *Tiananmen 1989*, p. 348.

1. In recent days, continuous internal strife has appeared in several universities in the capital and elsewhere. Without a doubt, this constitutes a serious threat to the current democracy movement. We hope the students will be vigilant and immediately desist from internal strife.

Those students who participated in the so-called April 29 dialogue conducted by the authorities are, after all, our comrades-in-arms. Any attack on them will only exacerbate the split and ultimately lead to the aborting of this very promising movement. Undoubtedly, this is a result that no Chinese citizen with a sense of justice is willing to see.

2. We should oppose the tendency of seeking personal publicity. The freedom fighters for the people should rid themselves of the ugly features of the Chinese and become united in common struggle. A democratic consciousness must first be implemented throughout the democracy movement. This would provide the basic guarantee for the victory of this mighty movement.

3. This movement is a citizens' movement to defend the constitution, with the college students as the main force and with people of all social strata partici-

pating. The highest aim of this movement is to defend the sacredness of the constitution.

4. The goals of this movement are to eradicate corruption, severely punish those engaged in official profiteering, perfect the legal system, and promote the process of democratic politics in China.

5. The preconditions for the students to resume classes are:

a. That the authorities recognize the Autonomous Student Union of Colleges and Universities in Beijing as the true and legal representative of college students. Only this organization may participate in any form of dialogue.

b. That the specific laws and regulations concerning the freedom of the press, publication, assembly, association, and demonstration be published in the *People's Daily.* . . .

63

China's Patriotic Democracy Movement and the Cultural Revolution

DEPARTMENT OF THEORY AND INFORMATION
DISSEMINATION COMMITTEE, BEIJING UNIVERSITY

May 3, 1989

Source: Appeared in *ORSD*, 1:66. This translation is by Nicki Croghan, P. K. Chen, and M. Zhang and was published in *Radical America* 22, 4 (July–August 1989): 16–17.

On April 26, 1989, a *People's Daily* editorial labeled this patriotic democracy movement an antiparty, antisocialist disturbance and tried to compare it to the ten years of turbulence associated with the Cultural Revolution. Moreover, during the dialogue between the government and the students on April 29, Yuan Mu (a government spokesperson) also claimed the two movements were similar. We assert they are completely different. . . .

The Background of the Movements

The ten years of the Cultural Revolution were used by people within the party to strive for certain benefits for themselves. It was instigated by the errors of the leadership. They used the struggle between cliques and personality cults to protect their own beliefs. The patriotic democracy movement, on the other hand, rose to the surface because of a deep-rooted social crisis. The patriotic movement is self-generated, arising from all kinds of social contradictions. The purpose of the movement is to hasten the democratization of China and to promote reforms in the political system; to wipe out official corruption; and to allow intellectuals, workers, and peasants to benefit from the realization of national prosperity and strength brought forth by the real reforms. Actually, no "special group of instigators" is responsible for the movement as was rumored by the government.

Qualities of the Participants

The participants in the Cultural Revolution, which was based on a personality cult, were predominantly Red Guards. They were uneducated, foolish, and ignorant. Under these circumstances, participants were easily misled and tragedy ensued.

By contrast, the patriotic democracy movement was informed by ten years of reforms and openness, which gave students and intellectuals an opportunity to learn about and analyze liberal and democratic ideas from the West. They applied democratic principles in developing the patriotic democracy movement in China. Their analysis of the situation in present-day China produced a series of theories and recommendations to equip students and citizens, including members of the middle class, with a relatively liberal democratic way of thinking.

They . . . realized they were working for democracy and the freedom of their motherland. . . . This was absolutely not the effort of any group "to use the people." One should be aware that participants in the movement are intelligent, and their intelligence is not lower than the bureaucrats'!

Social Purpose

Ten years of disturbance resulted in forming groups and cliques and setting up a comprehensive but exclusive network. The patriotic democracy movement is in no way trying to stir up society with this kind of closed network, but is using democratic and liberal ideas to arouse the consciousness of the masses. For them, it is a democratic awakening movement. It facilitates speeding up the process of implementing a democratic system in China, and it fulfills the historical mission of demanding freedom of speech.

Contradicting the Party

During the ten years of the Cultural Revolution's disturbance, in some schools, government agencies, and factories, and in the minds of people stripped of power, the party committee started the revolution with the purpose of creating a power struggle and fulfilling their personal wants by gaining control. At the present time, however, in this movement we still support the correct leadership of the Communist party. What we oppose are only those parts that are wrong.

We urge that the party not indiscriminately exert power [over] all sectors of society, nor should it intervene in the regular exercise of everyday affairs. We in no way oppose the correct leadership of the party. Instead, we firmly oppose anything imposed upon us that falsely accuses us of being antiparty or against the people. We do not act with ulterior motives. We will not accept any accusation under the disguise of upholding the "Four Principles," and we denounce such acts.

The Background of the Disturbance

As we reflect back on the recent past, we can see that ten years of disturbance brought to the Chinese people a situation of catastrophic dimensions. Intellectuals were persecuted in huge numbers. Our political democracy suffered extensive damage, as did the legislative system. The economy of the nation was almost on the verge of collapse. Education virtually came to a halt. But the democracy movement stabilized the democratic and legislative systems. The masses are experiencing extensive democracy and freedom. With our movement, government officials will be held more accountable, and education will flourish. Eventually these reforms will lead to prosperity and strengthen all the Chinese people.

In summing up the above, if we examine who is part of the patriotic democracy movement and compare that to who participated in the Cultural Revolution, we see that the goals and results of the two are really completely different. We hope that people from various parts of our society can distinguish right from wrong. Some people in our government are trying to discredit the movement by vague accusations and unsubstantiated allegations. . . . Unite and fight for our common cause!

64

Cadres from the Public Security Bureau, Procuratorate, Courts, and Judiciary Support the Just Actions of Our Students

CCP MEMBERS AND CADRES FROM THE JUDICIARY DEPARTMENTS

May 3, 1989

Source: Wall poster or leaflet, in *ORSD*, 1:60.

In the last few days, we have heard and seen the unrelenting and just actions of the university students in the capital to promote democratization. We have been deeply moved and hereby offer our most heartfelt respect to them.

Dear students, please believe that all political and judicial cadres who have brains and a sense of justice and who have committed themselves to strengthening the Chinese nation would not blindly follow the ossified thinking that opposes the people and students . . . .

Because of the sensitivity of our positions, it is not yet suitable for us to adopt the same form of participation as you have in this powerful democratic movement. But we absolutely would not oppose the tide of history, nor merely experience these events vicariously. We have already faithfully reported to our colleagues the programs, slogans, and actions of the students; and we have adopted whatever means we could to support you students.

Without qualms, we support you. History will bear witness to those who do not fear sacrificing themselves for a democratic, prosperous, and civilized new China.

"Support the reform and oppose backwardness!"
—Banner, May 4, in *56 days*

65

Let's Cry Out to Awaken the Young Republic— May Fourth Declaration of the Autonomous Student Union of Universities and Colleges in Beijing

ASUCUB (Autonomous Student Union of Colleges and Universities in Beijing)

May 4, 1989

Source: *Tiananmen 1989*, pp. 320–21.

Fellow students and compatriots: on this same day seventy years ago, students amassed in front of Tiananmen Square. With that event, a great new chapter in the annals of China began. Today we have come together in crowds to the square not only for the purpose of commemorating that great day, but also for advancing the "May Fourth" spirit of democracy and science. . . .

For more than one hundred years, the elites of the Chinese nation have been continuously searching for a way to modernize ancient and poor China. After the

(Versailles) Paris Conference [1919], in the face of the imperialist powers carving up and trampling on China, and the dying . . . corrupt forces of feudalism, our predecessors stepped forward. They bravely upheld the banner of "democracy and science" in the mighty "May Fourth" Movement. The "May Fourth" Movement and the new democratic revolution that followed were first steps by Chinese students toward a patriotic democracy movement and the modernization of China. . . .

Because of the social and economic conditions in China at that time and the weakness of the intellectuals, the "May Fourth" Movement's ideals of democracy and science were not immediately realized in China. A thousand years of history tells us that "democracy and science" cannot be achieved in one stroke. . . . Inevitably, the surviving remnants of feudalism have influenced the Marxist ideals of the Chinese Communist party [as implemented] within the Chinese economic and cultural environment. Therefore, while on the one hand new China marched continuously toward modernization, on the other, it greatly ignored the construction of democracy. Although the role of science is emphasized, the spirit of science—people's livelihood—has not received much attention.[1] At present, corruption is very serious in China, such as in government institutions; knowledge has lost its value, and inflation is high. All these are major obstacles to our government's efforts to deepen reform and continue modernization. Without the spirit of "democracy and science" and the procedures to implement them, . . . feudal elements and the dregs of the old system will reemerge in social life and fundamentally thwart large-scale socialized production. . . . It has thus become a top priority that . . . during its modernization, China accelerate the reform of the political and economic systems, protect human rights, and strengthen the legal system.

Fellow students and compatriots: The spirit of democracy is to draw on collective wisdom and absorb all useful ideas, to give full play to the abilities of everyone, and to protect the interests of everyone. The spirit of science is to respect rationality and to have science as the basis of the country. Now we all the more need to summarize the experiences and lessons of the student movements since "May Fourth" in order to make democracy and rationality become a system and a procedure. . . . We urge the government to accelerate the reform of the political and economic systems, to adopt actual measures to protect the people's various constitutional rights, to pass a law of the press, to allow private newspapers to exist, to eradicate "official profiteering" so as to strengthen the building of a clean and honest government, to pay attention to education and knowledge, and to make science the basis of our country. Our ideas are not contradictory to those of the government. Our goal is only one: realization of modernization in China.

---

[1]People's livelihood was one of Sun Yat-sen's "Three People's Principles." The CCP's interpretation of this principle is that the government must ensure that the people's basic needs are supplied. The argument made here is that the purpose of science is to improve the people's basic livelihood. Otherwise, why bother being scientific?

This student movement is the largest patriotic democracy movement since the May Fourth Movement and a continuation and development of it. This student movement is really ... successful in that more than one million college students (not including hundreds of thousands of Beijing residents) have gone to the streets, shouting our own slogans and expressing our own wishes. The success of the student movement is also attributable to the large number of seniors and graduate students who compose the leadership and main force of the student movement, making the whole movement more mature and more rational. In the student movement, we have also established an "autonomous student union" elected by the student representatives from forty-seven colleges and universities and based on the mass organizations voluntarily sponsored by their students. This is a totally new organization, and it is a heroic undertaking in this student movement. It shows the high degree of democratic awareness of the students and their self-consciousness in applying democratic means to achieve modernization. This organization will certainly be of great benefit to and promote future democratic reform. What is especially encouraging is that hundreds of thousands of city residents and people of all walks of life have helped and supported our actions in various ways, which is also unprecedented. . . .

This victory is, however, very small. Not only can the civilization of several thousand years not provide a ready-made scheme for making the country rich and the people strong, but also the political and economic systems and the agricultural civilization that underlies them have affected and will continue to affect our modernization for a considerable length of time. Therefore, our tasks at present are; first, to try to implement a democratic system in the birthplace of the student movement—the campus—by democratizing and institutionalizing campus life. Second, the students must actively participate in politics, firmly demanding to have a dialogue with the government, promoting the democratic reform of the political system, opposing corruption and degeneracy, and facilitating passage of the law of the press. We believe that these short-term goals are only a first step toward democratic reform. . . .

Fellow students and compatriots: the prosperity of our nation is the goal of this patriotic democracy movement. Democracy, science, freedom, human rights, and legality are the shared ideals of our hundreds of thousands of college students in this struggle. . . . What should we be afraid of? . . .

Let's cry out to awaken the young republic!

66
Statement

ASUCUB

Early May 1989

Source: Wall poster or handbill, HKFS.

To show the students' sincerity in having a dialogue with the government, to reduce sacrifices by the students, and for the sake of the general situation of the whole country, we hope college students boycotting classes in Beijing will resume classes beginning on May 5.

According to an opinion poll conducted . . . in Beijing University, 853 dormitories favored the continuation of boycotting the classes while 301 dormitories opposed it. The Autonomous Student Union of Beijing University has maintained that the boycotting of the classes by Beijing University students is not indefinite, and they will keep their seat as one member of the Standing Committee of the ASUCUB.

The Autonomous Student Union of Beijing Normal University has declared that the students in that university will temporarily resume classes on May 8.

67
Statement

ASUCUB

Early May 1989

Source: Wall poster or handbill, HKFS.

On May 4, the first stage of the student movement temporarily ended, but this does not mean the end of the student movement, nor of the democracy movement. As a small group in the vanguard of this democracy movement, what should we do next? Our answer is: We should carry out democratic construction on campus, such as demanding a confirmation of the elected Autonomous

Student Union, keeping the freedom forum,[1] and maintaining the democracy wall on campus. We should not lose what we have gained. We should also continue our propaganda work among city residents by explaining the basic knowledge of democracy, freedom, and law. We can carry out our propaganda work in various forms of art and literature. Let's use our brains. . . .

68

My Innermost Thoughts—To the Students of Beijing Universities

BEIJING UNIVERSITY STUDENT

May 1989

Source: Courtesy of HKFS.

Students, comrades:
    Having resigned from my position in ASUCUB and in the Autonomous Student Union of Beijing University, and with the approval of these two organizations, I would like to express the following personal views.

About Myself

An Ordinary Story

I grew up in a place along a small clean river in the city of Dujiangyan in Sichuan, and I was nurtured by the honest people there. In the fall of 1982, I began my life at Beijing University. After seven years, I have learned the solitude of Beijing University people.
    To make an evaluation of myself, I am not superior to any ordinary person, either in terms of intelligence and conscience, or in terms of self-respect. Moreover, I am a science student who has never systematically studied politics, society, and law. It is indeed a tragedy of history that I could play an important role in this democracy movement. What would Don Quixote say?

Passion and Conscience

The sole reason that I stood up at the open "democracy salon" attended by two thousand students in the triangle ground on the evening of April 19 was probably

---

[1]The freedom forum consisted of irregularly held discussion groups and panels.

the warm blood of a youth and the conscience of a citizen.

At that salon, I told the audience that in the previous student movements, I was always an enthusiastic "bystander." I think this is an objective evaluation. Although I stayed in the local police station of Zhongshan Park for twelve hours along with many other students, workers, peasants, high school students, and journalists because I was involved in resisting the military police in Tiananmen Square on New Year's Day, 1987; and although I was one member of the "Action Committee" during the "Chai Qingfeng Incident" at Beijing University in 1988,[1] I have always opposed violence and secret actions. I resisted the police because I wanted to have a look at the prison and to see how the Chinese news media distorted the facts. I participated in the "Action Committee" for only a short while, and then I left. I am open and aboveboard, and I want to do things that are open and aboveboard.

Before that salon, I had told my wife (later, she also participated in the Preparatory Committee of Beijing University)[2] I only had a few words to say, and I would not participate in more activities. At that time my reason for getting involved was that my computer was broken. Later, the cries from the students aroused my hot passion, conscience, and sense of responsibility. My only thought at the moment was that I should not let my fellow students down.

That evening I realized my duty to strive later on to defend democratic checks within the Autonomous Student Union.

Rights and Dignity

As a student, I don't know how to express my wishes, or to which student organization; nor do I know which organization to rely on to defend my rights as a student. I don't know how much research money I can use for my own interests, nor do I know to whom I should turn for upholding justice after being insulted by the university security guards. I can only exercise patience. After seven years at Beijing University, I have learned how to exercise patience all too often. This exercise has toughened me for struggle.

As a citizen, I am not clear for whom I should vote. The only candidate I know is Li Shuxian [Fang Lizhi's wife]. The reason is known to most Beijing University students. I am not clear what the People's Congress that I participated in electing has done or is doing for me. I have always been puzzled since I was first able to vote at the age of eighteen. Being puzzled has motivated me to explore.

As a student, I demand my natural right: to organize a democratic student

---

[1]Chai Qingfeng, a graduate student at Beijing University, was killed outside the university campus. This provoked student reactions, including protests over inadequate protection of the university community by local authorities.

[2]The Preparatory Committee of elected student representatives was formed during the 1989 democracy movement.

organization in which I and my fellow students may participate.

As a citizen, I demand my natural right: To organize a democratic government in which I and my fellow countrymen may participate.

If the existing student union believes that it is democratic, then please clear away my doubts.

If the existing government believes that it is democratic, then please resolve my perplexity.

I demand that the university authorities not disregard my rights and dignity as a student.

I demand that the government not disregard my rights and dignity as a citizen.

Causes, Consequences, and Procedural Democracy

Necessity and Contingency

It is by no means accidental that such a democracy movement is bursting out in mainland China on such a grand and spectacular scale. If we look at the present world, it is not difficult to find two major trends: political pluralization and privatization of ownership. The achievements of "open" political reform in the Soviet Union, the legalization of "Solidarity" in Poland, the acceptance of a multiparty system in Hungary, the privatization of "socialist" India, and the adoption of private ownership in the socialist countries in Africa . . . all these provide powerful evidence of these two trends. The reforms carried out in recent years in China are also more or less in accord with these two trends.

Nevertheless, many accidental factors in this student movement have determined its structure and significance. This movement originated in the commemorative acts for Hu Yaobang by the people, particularly by intellectual circles. It has since developed into a democracy movement. One fundamental weakness of this movement is lack of adequate ideological and theoretical preparation. This weakness has meant that this movement can only be a prelude, not a mature melody. It has also meant that the various autonomous student organizations established in haste can only "follow the senses."[3]

On the other hand, many accidental factors have created a favorable environment for this student movement and enabled it to achieve many major breakthroughs. . . .

1. We have set up autonomous organizations that have partially achieved legal status. In a society without a law of association, the legal status of an organization can only be determined by the people.

2. We have used legal weapons to show our awareness that the basis of democratic politics is the legal system. This student movement is also a popular movement to defend the constitution.

---

[3]*Genzhe ganjue zou* is a phrase from a Taiwan song popular in China, the theme of which suggests students should follow their feelings instead of political leaders.

3. We have won the sympathy and support of people from all walks of life, particularly from journalists. Even some high school students have gone to the streets.

4. The government has made several substantial compromises, showing that it cannot totally disregard the cries of the students and people.

Example 1: Several large-scale demonstrations and sit-ins have actually negated the sanctity of the "Ten Regulations" [issued in late April by the Beijing Municipal Party Committee].

Example 2: The government had to express its willingness to "welcome the students' representatives to have a dialogue with the government."

Resurrection

This student movement is the most magnificent bursting out since the May Fourth Movement seventy years ago. This is the beginning of a new enlightenment movement of new democracy with the students as its core. It is the bugle call for a thorough democracy movement participated in by the people from all social strata in the future. The democracy movement in the future will lead to a constitution in China that takes "science and democracy" as a fundamental starting point. [On the basis of] this constitution, China will eliminate the influence of more than two thousand years of feudal politics and will quickly march toward achieving the goal of making the country powerful and the people rich.[4]

This student movement has also awakened the national spirit. It is rescuing China spiritually. Many people said that they have again found the spirit of sacrifice, and the hope and future of China. This movement will end the crisis of belief and awaken the people to worship the spirit of "science and democracy."

The Way to Paradise

First step: campus democracy. The democratic forces currently in China are mainly on the campuses. The intellectuals are the most outstanding stratum. They are thoroughly proletarian, and are full of the spirit of sacrifice. In the meantime, they are equipped with the highest cultural quality and the clearest democratic consciousness. The students are the vanguard of the democracy movement. . . .

Campus democracy is a breakthrough in the process of democratization in China. It is the students themselves who first need democratic enlightenment. This student movement has fully demonstrated that the students who are striving for democracy, and even the student leaders, are themselves not familiar with democracy. Many students do not understand that they bear the responsibility of participating in and supervising the work of the student union, as they are accustomed to being commanded. The autonomous student unions have gradually cut themselves off from many students and become a machine kept constantly on the

---

[4]These goals were first expressed in the late nineteenth century by reformer Yan Fu.

run in issuing orders. No set of organizational rules widely accepted by the students has emerged, and the democratic mechanism is even more vague. The fundamental issue is the quality of individuals. Nevertheless, I still have reason to believe that we can see the embryonic form of a democratic regime in China—the democratic student union on campus.

Campus democracy itself will require a long struggle. It not only means the struggle for legalization of the autonomous students' organizations, but also covers another major part of the campus: teachers and educational institutions. I believe that before this century is over, we will be fortunate to see our campuses managed by such organizations as "Faculty Councils." The college graduates later should not merely have scientific knowledge, but also democratic consciousness. They will form a nucleus in the process of democratization in China.

Second step: enlightenment about democracy. From the students on campus to the intellectuals, then to the workers, peasants, businessmen, and so on, we can gradually form democratic regimes at various levels according to the experiences we gain from consolidating campus democracy. This will spread quickly in the society. We should go step by step. The first areas for achieving victories are probably in the news media and in the press, because the modern technology of communication has profoundly affected modern democracy. When the people have seen and heard about the outside world and felt the strong contrasts, a certain consciousness of democracy is naturally reinforced. This is favorable to the task of this stage: enlightening the democratic consciousness of all.

Third step: constitutional debate. By a most optimistic estimate, I expect to see the aforementioned constitution, with "science and democracy" as its fundamental starting points, emerge within fifty years. From now on, we must study and spread the ideas of such a constitution. The constitution of the United States, based on "democracy and economy," may be seen as the product of the second industrial revolution. It has given half the votes to all the people, and the other half to property owners [*sic*]. Thus, the United States has become prosperous, but it has not fully and scientifically solved the problems of the whole society.

Fourth step: building a state on [the basis of] the rule of law. A government established under a new constitution will surely help ancient China quickly enter the ranks of modernized powers in the world.

Current Tasks and Methods

As early as about May 1, the Autonomous Student Union of Colleges and Universities in Beijing made a prediction: The first stage of . . . the student movement in Beijing would be completed by May 4. The high tide of the student movement in the rest of the country would be after May 4. Based on this judgment, I think the focus of struggle after May 4 should be:

1. Resuming classes and having a dialogue. The method could be to allow

some of the students to continue to hold sit-ins, or even a hunger strike, to demand a dialogue.

2. Speeding up the process of legalization of the autonomous student organizations. The methods are soliciting signatures from all students, establishing student councils (participated in by the representatives from each class or dormitory), or directly electing a new student union. In this area, the university authorities and the government seem to be loosening up.

3. Strengthening contacts with people of all walks of life throughout society, forming an alliance with students of all the universities, and doing propaganda work among the people in order to support the *World Economic Herald* and strive for publication of private newspapers.

"Don't force us to tell lies!"
"Freedom of the press is good for stability!"
—Journalists' banners, May 5, from photo

69
Without Freedom of the Press, There Will Be No Real Stability

HU JIWEI

Source: *World Economic Herald*, May 8, 1989, in *Tiananmen 1989*, pp. 311–14.

. . . Now I want to further elaborate on the point that freedom of the press is a stabilizing factor.

First, the constitution is the fundamental law of our country. It is the legalization of the fundamental guidelines and policies of our party. If freedom of the press within the scope of the constitution can be guaranteed, the people will feel that the constitution is not a mere scrap of paper, but a fundamental law that actually functions. Hence, the people will strengthen their constitutional consciousness. They will respect and obey the constitution, and get united under the banner of the constitution, thus providing a fundamental protection of social stability. Otherwise, if constitutional principles and rights are frequently violated, the people will feel they lack constitutional protection of political [rights], thereby losing a sense of political security. If so, how can we have actual stability and unity? It is known to all that the ten years of the Cultural Revolution were the most unstable period in our country: They began with an open trampling upon the constitution, and a complete destruction of freedom of speech and the press. Isn't this a profound lesson?

Second, full freedom of the press . . . will enhance the degree of openness of information, strengthen political transparency (*toumingdu*) [the Chinese version of *glasnost* introduced by Zhao Ziyang], and expand and deepen supervision by public opinion. The party and government leaders will naturally be more cautious and prudent in the decision-making process. This will help reduce errors and make it easier for people to criticize and correct errors if they are made. Also, those who tend to violate the laws and discipline, and who engage in corruption, will be scrupulous or restrained. It will be easier, too, to expose and punish those who do indeed violate the laws and engage in corruption. Many bureaucrats now are afraid not of internal criticism but of being exposed in the newspaper; afraid not of going to court but of being shown on TV. Here we can see that freedom of the press is itself an effective force in eliminating destabilizing factors. Conversely, without freedom of the press, the people will feel hopeless and powerless when witnessing errors in decision making and widespread corruption. If their criticism is light, it is not effective. If their criticism is severe, then it will not be published in the newspaper. Apart from the criticisms by ordinary people, it is difficult even to publish the speeches by the deputies to the National People's Congress and members of the Political Consultative Conference in the newspaper if they contain some fairly sharp criticism. When such a situation persists for a long time, many people will adopt a passive attitude and discipline themselves against speaking out, thinking, or being angry. They will simply shut their eyes. This provides a false impression of stability and unity, but this kind of stability and unity is maintained at a cost of people being numb, cold, detached, and depressed. This false stability and unity in silence brews serious danger. Can any leader with a modern political mind be satisfied with this?

Third, freedom of the press can facilitate mutual understanding between the people and government, and among all social strata and interest groups. This will make the situation at the lower level known to the higher authorities and vice versa, . . . removing feelings of estrangement and promoting political development and people's unity. Freedom of the press is commonly regarded as an "air vent" in the world: It provides a safe channel for the people to sound off their grievances and dissatisfaction. It can, therefore, passively help maintain social stability and avoid outbursts of radical feelings. It is both a leadership art and political wisdom to let the people speak and let the newspapers publish more of the people's views. It is also politically magnanimous and boldly visionary to do so. Even more, it is a constitutional concept. This is the solid foundation for a modern society to maintain real stability and unity.

Fourth, freedom of the press can maintain social justice and play a role in upholding righteousness and opposing evil. Contradictions can then be moderated and will not easily intensify. It can also help prevent or reduce unjust charges or verdicts and provide opportunities for the victims to appeal. . . . This may also prevent some unnecessary tragedies from happening and play a positive role in promoting stability and unity.

Fifth, freedom of the press will help maintain the democratic authority of the party's Central Committee and the State Council. Every government in every country wants to establish its authority. The issue is that only when this leadership authority is established in an environment of freedom of the press can it become a democratic authority truly supported by the people. A leadership authority established when there is no freedom of the press will only be an autocratic authority, at most an authority under which people dare to be angry but not to speak. Democratic authority is the greatest stabilizing element, autocratic authority the worst. In view of the general situation in the world, all the countries that have a degree of freedom of the press are relatively stable: Military coups are difficult to carry out, and political turmoil caused by illegal accession to power or illegal dismissal are few. On the other hand, the political situation in the countries without freedom or freedom of the press is unstable. Even if the economy in such countries is relatively advanced and the people relatively rich, they never have peace of mind. Even government officials live in fear and trepidation. . . .

70

A Summary by the Dialogue Delegation of University Students in Beijing

REPORTER, *XINWEN DAOBAO*

May 11, 1989

Source: *Xinwen daobao* (News herald), in *ORSD*, 1:89.

To facilitate a smooth process for an open dialogue on the basis of equality and sincerity between the representatives of the Chinese Communist Party Central Committee, the Standing Committee of the National People's Congress, and the State Council, and students at colleges and universities in Beijing, the students' dialogue representatives, elected through a democratic process by the students from more than twenty colleges and universities in Beijing, on May 3 organized a student dialogue delegation. [This delegation] was made up of Beijing college students at the Chinese University of Political Science and Law. After the delegation was formed, it presented a letter of petition to the CCP Central Committee, the Standing Committee of the National People's Congress, and the State Council demanding a dialogue; and it established organizational units. These days, the delegation has continuously held meetings at the Chinese University of Political Science and Law to discuss the dialogue's content. They have been interviewed by dozens of domestic and foreign news agencies. They have also listened to the opinions of people from all over the country.

At the May 3 organizational meeting, the representatives from various colleges and universities democratically chose [XXX], a representative from Chinese University of Political Science and Law, and Shen Tong, a representative from Beijing University, to be the conveners of the meetings of the dialogue delegation. At the May 5 meeting, the dialogue delegation decided to form three panels, to which they appointed core members according to their special skills. The first panel is responsible for discussing this student movement. The core member is [XXX], a representative from Qinghua University; the second panel is responsible for discussing how to further reform. The core member is [XXX], a representative from Chinese University of Political Science and Law. The third panel is responsible for discussing Article 35 of the constitution. The core member is [XXX], a representative from the Chinese University of Political Science and Law.

On May 6, the dialogue delegation finished a draft of the petition letter and presented it to the petition bureau of the General Office of the party Central Committee, of the Standing Committee of the National People's Congress, and of the State Council at 6:00 P.M. on the same day. . . . The representatives from various colleges and universities generally hope to get a dialogue going before May 14.

The delegation conducted continuous panel discussions on May 6, 7, and 8. During the first panel, the representatives unanimously agreed that this student movement is a patriotic democracy movement. The fundamental causes of this movement are that reform of the political system lags behind reform of the economic system; that policies to reform the economic system lack continuity and stability, hence leading to a situation in which crises abound, official profiteering is widespread, corruption is grave, and the political and social environment is very unstable. The direct cause of this student movement is the fact that Comrade Hu Yaobang died before he was cleared of a false charge. Some students on this panel believed that the concerned authorities should be held legally responsible for the April 26 editorial of the *People's Daily* and for the distorted reports of the student movement in the official news media.

The second panel mainly discussed the theme of furthering reform. The members of this panel believed that the tenure system, autocracy, official profiteering, and corruption are all phenomena demonstrating the irrationality of the system. They believed that during the dialogue they should focus on a few concrete issues based on this general theme so as actually to help the CCP Central Committee and the government implement political and economic reform.

The third panel primarily discussed the three basic rights of citizens as granted in Article 35 of the constitution: freedom of assembly, speech, and demonstration. The students hope to have a dialogue with the CCP Central Committee, the State Council, and the Standing Committee of the National People's Congress on three issues: legalization of the Autonomous Student Union, correcting the wrong treatment of Qin Benli, chief editor of the *World Economic Herald*, by the Shanghai Party Committee, and abolishing or revising the Ten Regulations concerning demonstrations issued by the Beijing People's Congress. . . .

71

Resolution for Facilitating Immediate Dialogue between the Student Unions and University Authorities

ASUCUB

May 9, 1989

Source: Handbill, Courtesy of HKFS.

To cooperate with the government in promoting dialogue, the autonomous student union in every college and university should actively seek dialogue with [its respective] university authorities as soon as possible.

The dialogues [should address] the issues of: (1) legalization of the autonomous student union; (2) keeping the democracy wall on campus; and (3) keeping the freedom forum on campus. . . .

72

Letter to Qinghua University Students

DIALOGUE PREPARATORY COMMITTEE OF QINGHUA UNIVERSITY

May 11, 1989

Source: Mimeograph, in *Tiananmen 1989* , pp. 348–49.

. . . Today we have already resumed classes. But we are far from the goal of our struggle—a democratic and free China. We are facing a long, endless struggle. Moreover, the context of our movement is the new enlightenment movement in China. History will reserve a place for us. As long as we recognize the historical significance of this movement, we should not easily relinquish our struggle nor let this movement abort. . . .

The members of the Dialogue Preparatory Committee of Qinghua University are continuing their struggle, and we still need help from the vast number of students. Democracy means that we are in charge. Who will strive if we do not? [For this purpose,] we hereby establish the following departments of the committee, and we hope students will volunteer to work in them:

1. Information and Theory Department
2. Propaganda, Agitation, and Public Lecture Department
3. Liaison and Intelligence Department
4. Public Opinion Department
5. "The Voice of Qinghua People"

73

On the "Historical Achievements" of the *People's Daily*

ANONYMOUS

May 12, 1989

Source: *Xinwen daobao* (News herald), no. 3, May 12, 1989, in *Tiananmen 1989*, pp. 246–48.

On April 26, 1989, the *People's Daily* published the famous antiturmoil editorial [Doc. 43]. In our country, which has time and again claimed to have perfected the legal system, someone can, without following a legal procedure, simply write an editorial that accuses one million college students throughout the country of engaging in illegal organizations, using big-character posters to vilify and attack the party and state leaders, distributing reactionary handbills, and creating turmoil at the instigation of a few persons. Then the editorial ordered the whole party and all the people to engage in a political struggle to criticize and condemn the students. Is this rule by law or rule by man? By distorting the facts, one editorial can lodge accusations against the students. What period did such practices belong to? We can easily find the answer simply by looking at the history of the *People's Daily*.

Now let's recall how the *People's Daily* stirred up turmoil in the "ten years of turmoil" [i.e., the Cultural Revolution]. . . .

On April 2, 1966, the *People's Daily* carried an editorial concocted by Qi Benyu entitled "On the Essence of 'Hai Rui Scolding the Emperor' and 'Hai Rui Dismissed from Office.' " This signified the prelude to "ten years of turmoil." On June 1, 1966, the *People's Daily* carried an editorial entitled "Sweep Away All Ghosts and Monsters," calling on everyone to attack everything. Thereupon, activities to sweep away everything went on all over the country like a mad tornado. On June 3, 1966, the *People's Daily* carried an editorial entitled "A Big Revolution to Touch People to Their Innermost Being." It called upon [everyone] to engage in physical attacks to touch the souls of a handful of people, after which bloodshed and violence spread throughout the country. On June 16, 1966, the *People's Daily* editorial entitled "Freely Mobilize the Masses and Thoroughly Knock Down the Counterrevolutionary Black Gangs" called on [everyone] to beat to death, to cripple, and to harm many black gangs. Thus began large-scale bloodshed. On January 1, 1967, the *People's Daily* editorial entitled

"Carry the Great Proletarian Cultural Revolution Through to the End" called on [everyone] to launch a general attack on a handful of persons, after which a mass rally of ten thousand people was held in Beijing that declared "twenty charges" against Liu Shaoqi, chairman of the [People's] Republic. On January 11, 1967, the *People's Daily* carried an important editorial entitled "The 'January Storm' that Initiated the Power Seizure," after which power seizures, chaos, violence, bloodshed, and death were seen everywhere, and the "ten years of turmoil" in China reached a climax. On June 1, 1967, the *People's Daily* carried an editorial entitled "Great Strategic Measures," again calling on the whole country to knock down Liu Shaoqi. On August 5, 1967, the *People's Daily* editorial entitled "Bombard the Bourgeois Headquarters" called on the country's proletariat to attack a handful of persons. A mass rally of one million people was held in Beijing to attack the chairman of the [People's] Republic, pushing the turmoil all over the country to an even higher level. On August 17, 1967, the *People's Daily* published an article that accused Peng Dehuai of usurping the party and military leadership and opposing the party and socialism. It called on the proletarian and revolutionary people in the country to expose and criticize again a handful of persons in the military. On August 24, 1967, the *People's Daily* published a commentator article accusing Luo Ruiqing of being a conspirator and careerist and of continuing to create turmoil in the army. On July 22, 1967, the *People's Daily* published an article that set off a new round of turmoil by "dragging out a handful" throughout the country. On November 6, 1967, the *People's Daily* editorial called on the people of the whole country to start a new upsurge of "purifying class ranks." A large number of people accused of being so-called hidden class enemies engaged in conspiracy were locked up, denounced, and even died in the turmoil. On February 2, 1974, the *People's Daily* editorial entitled "Carry the Struggle of Criticizing Lin Biao and Confucius Through to the End" directed its spearhead at Premier Zhou Enlai. Thus began a new round of turmoil in China, which had by this time just regained a little stability. On June 18, 1974, the *People's Daily* again carried an editorial to push the new round of turmoil even deeper. With it, a struggle between the Confucian and Legalist schools started on the vast land of China. On November 8, 1974, the *People's Daily* editorial entitled "Continue to Criticize Lin Biao and Confucius" called on [everyone] to carry out deeply and perpetually the struggle between the Confucian and Legalist schools. On March 10, 1976, the *People's Daily* editorial entitled "Reversing the Previous Verdicts Enjoys No Popular Support" again attacked Comrade Deng Xiaoping. In early April 1976, tens of thousands of people and students went to Tiananmen Square to commemorate the great communist fighter, Premier Zhou Enlai. At the same time, they used the methods of writing elegies and small-character posters, and making speeches to expose the . . . crimes of the "Gang of Four" in bringing calamities to the country and the people. On April 5, the activities of commemoration reached a climax. That evening, the "Gang of Four" assembled a large number of military police and the militia to surround the square. After the public announcement by Wu De, mayor of Beijing, was broadcast over the radio, they began a cruel and bloody crackdown. People were beaten by bludgeons and the square was splattered with blood. After the crackdown, the *People's Daily* published a strongly worded article entitled "The Counterrevolutionary Political Incident on Tiananmen Square," describing the "Tiananmen Square Incident" as a counterrevolutionary turmoil schemed, planned, and organized by a few persons. [This] article called upon [everyone] to take a clear-cut stand in this serious political struggle. The article said that "a few persons are mudslinging, hurling abuses, and attacking the party and state leaders in the name of commemorating Premier Zhou Enlai. They attacked the Great Hall of the People, beat up PLA soldiers, burnt army trucks and barracks." This article described the defenseless people who were commemorating Premier Zhou Enlai as rioters who engaged in beating and arson. The *People's Daily* viewed the "Tiananmen Square Incident" as a counterrevolutionary political incident with preparation, planning, and organization. This "counterrevolutionary incident" was stirred up by a few persons behind the scenes. The article also clearly pointed out that this behind-the-scenes backer was none other than Deng Xiaoping. On the same day, the *People's Daily* published two "resolutions" by the CCP Central Committee that removed Deng Xiaoping from all his posts in both the party and the government. They placed him on probation within the party to see how he behaved. After April 7, the *People's Daily* published one editorial after another, in addition to many reports, calling on the people of the whole country firmly to carry out this political struggle. Suddenly, the newspapers and radios all over the country followed the *People's Daily* in producing many reports to distort the facts and to deceive the people of the whole country. Thus, "attacking the rightist tendency to reverse previous verdicts" unleashed major turmoil in China. Although Deng Xiaoping received unjust treatment, he found it very difficult to vindicate himself and to redress the injustice because he did not control the newspapers and radios. At that time, the sheer nonsense in the editorials of the *People's Daily* and the reports that distorted the facts aroused great indignation and protests from the people. On April 12, 1976, the *People's Daily* received a protest letter from a worker. In it this worker angrily called the *People's Daily* a "rumor-mongering daily." This worker emphatically pointed out that the party newspaper had degenerated into the mouthpiece of a handful of fascists and conspirators.

The historical achievements of the *People's Daily* are far more than these. According to incomplete statistics, in the decade between 1966 and 1976, the *People's Daily* published a considerable number of instigating and vilifying editorials, lodging all kinds of charges against the people. From the chairman of the [People's] Republic to ordinary citizens, anyone could be accused by the *People's Daily* and then be put to death. Almost all the large-scale turmoil and bloodshed started with the *People's Daily* sounding a bugle call to stir up the people. There were innumerable reports that distorted the facts. At that time, the

People's Daily was a political prostitute of Lin Biao, Chen Boda, Kang Sheng, Yao Wenyuan, Zhang Chunqiao [all Cultural Revolution leftists], and their like. This political prostitute has totally degenerated. She has only one firm political belief, that is "love for power, not for truth." Now the *People's Daily* has again applied this revolutionary tradition. On April 26, 1989, it carried an editorial entitled "It is Necessary to Take a Clear-Cut Stand against the Turmoil," which has shocked the whole country. Such a peculiar newspaper is really rare in the world. Only in China can such a newspaper be produced. The *People's Daily* has distinctive Chinese characteristics. It is China's major invention since the "Four Inventions" [i.e., gunpowder, the compass, papermaking, and the printing press].

       "Don't believe us. We tells lies!"
       —Journalists' banner, May 4, from photo

IV

May 12–May 19
The Hunger Strike:
From Protest to Uprising

David Zweig

> "Mother, I'm hungry, but I can't eat"
> —Banner during hunger strike

The hunger strike was the apogee of the spring 1989 mass movement. The April 26 *People's Daily* editorial motivated only a small percentage of the general public to join the demonstrations, except to supply food and funds to the students.[1] But the outpouring of sympathy triggered by this "act of selflessness"[2] and the government's refusal to meet with the students, which prolonged the hunger strike and brought many to near death, mobilized millions of people to march in Beijing. Their participation turned a student protest into a popular uprising when citizens acted in consort to deny the PLA access to the center of Beijing. During this period a critical shift occurred that led to a near-revolutionary situation.

The hunger strike both radicalized and fragmented the student movement and social groups in Beijing. Student leaders who had planned and organized many of the actions, including the hunger strike, lost control over the mass of students to a more radical group who opposed any concessions to the government.[3] Other

---

[1]Citizens did play a major role in helping students break through the police cordon on April 27, but they were comparatively passive until the hunger strike. See the description of the April 27 march in Li Qiao et al., comps., "Death or Rebirth? Tiananmen: The Soul of China," in *Beijing Spring*, ed. Oksenberg et al., Doc. 1.

[2]Lucian W. Pye, "Tiananmen and Chinese Political Culture: The Escalation of Confrontation from Moralizing to Revenge," *Asian Survey* 30, 4 (April 1990): 331–47.

[3]Zweig interviews with Cai Jingqing, Cambridge, Mass., August 1989, and with Shen Tong, Cambridge, Mass., October 1990; and Tony Saich, "When Worlds Collide: The Beijing People's Movement of 1989," in *The Chinese People's Movement*, ed. Saich, pp. 25–49.

forces, such as Beijing intellectuals, who to that point had failed to take an open position, flocked to the square and spoke publicly on behalf of the students. More radical elements among them chose to attack Deng Xiaoping directly and call for his retirement. Even government and party bureaucrats became more daring, as thousands of them marched on May 17 and 18. Before the hunger strike ended, some of them would openly side with Zhao Ziyang against the hardliners in the leadership.

The hunger strike brought a core group of retired party elders (the "old guard") back into the political fray,[4] and their increased involvement in the political struggles dramatically affected the final outcome. After pressuring many of them to retire from their posts in 1985 and 1987, Deng now turned to them for support in mobilizing the troops and imposing martial law. Most had good reasons to fear this popular movement. Allegations that the movement was being manipulated by "class enemies" accorded with their world view. Attacks in the posters on "old-men politics" challenged their right to control events from behind the scenes. Changes in the makeup of the second echelon of leaders demanded by the marchers would break their ties to the top, formal decision-making bodies, while attacks on corruption threatened their children. As the students prepared for the hunger strike, Deng, with the support of these party elders, decided to move eight armies toward Beijing. When thousands of party officials joined demonstrators to call on Deng Xiaoping and Li Peng to step down, the old guard knew that if Deng fell, so would they all. The intensified challenge increased Deng's ability to rally them around himself and, several days later, to support martial law.

The flurry of meetings among students, civilians, and leaders during this period suggests that although troops had already begun to move toward the city on May 12, the decision to declare martial law may not have been a foregone conclusion. During the hunger strike, however, the last chances for a negotiated solution came and went. When it began, members of the Dialogue Delegation, the Hunger Strike Committee, and ASUCUB, as well as of private economic and political organizations, met with leading party officials to try to reach some solution. Later, student leaders met to resolve the exploding crisis on national television with the leader of the hardliners, Premier Li Peng, who carried the mantle for some of the more antireform members of the old guard. Yet by the time of this meeting, the decision to declare martial law had been taken, and Li Peng had won in his long-standing confrontation with Zhao.[5] With little need to

---

[4]This group included Chen Yun, Peng Zhen, Li Xiannian, Wang Zhen, Deng Yingchao, Bo Yibo, Song Renqiong, and Deng himself.

[5]According to inside sources who were involved in the political activities at the center, the old guard met on May 16 and decided to declare martial law. On May 17, the Politburo Standing Committee met to ratify this decision. Zhao's refusal at this second meeting to endorse the declaration of martial law ensured his political demise.

compromise with the reformers, the hardliners called in the troops.

Tragically and unfortunately, the hunger strike strengthened hardliners in the party and undermined the very reform process that the students wanted to promote. Zhao's refusal to support the declaration of martial law ensured his political demise and destroyed the remaining consensus between radical reformers in the party, who favored meeting student demands, and hardliners, who preferred slowing the reforms and opposed major concessions. With the challenge to the party's and his own rule taking on such major proportions, Deng sided with the hardliners, even though it cost him the leading implementor of his reform program, and perhaps much of his own reform program as well. Once the CCP proved unable to resolve either its internal conflicts or the students' challenge to its rule, the army became the main arbiter between state and society, allowing the military to play a larger role in Chinese politics than at any time since the early 1970s.

The reemergence of the party elders, whose political dormancy had been necessary for radical reforms to ensue, not only harmed the student movement but also strengthened hardliners in the party. For several years they had demanded that more attention be paid to class struggle, central planning, ideological remolding, and the inequalities and social unrest developing under the reforms. They supported a gamut of policies aimed at slowing a decade of social and political liberalization. While their complaints had been ignored, Zhao's demise shifted the political spectrum from a balance between moderate and radical reformers to one between moderate reformers and hardliners for whom the reform program had already gone too far. Finally, efforts to save Zhao on May 18 and 19 doomed a generation of proreform activists who had been channeling new ideas into the leadership since the late 1970s. The political involvement of members of Zhao's most important think tanks in what was labeled as "counterrevolutionary" actions ensured the political banishment of these advocates and practitioners of radical reform.

Society Joins the Battle

The hunger strike, and the leadership's inability to respond to it, turned a traditional student movement into a political struggle for the control of Beijing and led the movement to shift its attack from a critique of corruption and flaws within the current system—which historically had been at the heart of student movements—to a more direct attack on certain leaders and calls for their overthrow.[6] Once Deng perceived this shift as a challenge to the entire system he

---

[6]One Chinese observer of the entire movement interviewed in Beijing in June 1989 felt the students had not understood the dangers of changing their movement from a student movement into a political movement, and then into a political struggle. For a similar analysis see Jeffrey N. Wasserstrom, "Student Protests and the Chinese Tradition, 1919–1989," in *The Chinese People's Movement*, ed. Saich, pp. 3–24. For an excellent discussion of traditional student movements, see Lee Feigon, *China Rising: The Meaning of Tiananmen* (Chicago: Ivan R. Dee, 1990), chap. 1.

declared martial law, and the resulting confrontation with the citizens turned the movement into a popular rebellion against an immoral government. The hunger strike altered the scale of the movement by dramatically increasing the number of participants and social groups involved in antigovernment marches. On May 13, radical intellectuals from many autonomous social groups and private companies, including Zhou Duo from the Stone Corporation and Wang Juntao and Chen Zemin of the Beijing Social and Economic Research Institute, joined the students for a face-to-face meeting with party representatives. On the night of May 13, a poster by Yan Jiaqi, Bao Zunxin, Su Shaozhi, and other establishment intellectuals called for intellectuals to march in support of the hunger strikers. A similar poster at People's University announced a planned march for May 15.[7]

The hunger strikers' use of the traditional theme of Confucian loyalty to the state presented a dilemma for the regime. In the eyes of the people, China's children,[8] like Confucian "speaking officials"—who at the cost of their own lives told the emperor when corruption endangered the system—risked their lives to warn the new "emperor," Deng, that corruption threatened his government's legitimacy. "When history demands us to do so, we have no choice but to die," their hunger strike vow declared (Doc. 82). To justify the unfilial act of taking the life their parents had given them, the students declared that love of country was primary. "Farewell moms and dads, please forgive us. Your children cannot be loyal to their country and filial to you at the same time" (Doc. 82). The pathos was intense: "It is with the spirit of death that we fight for life." ASUCUB urged students to do propaganda work (Doc. 75), with the result that mothers and fathers throughout Beijing, who witnessed the apparent inhumanity of a government that lets its children starve without talking to them, flooded the streets in unprecedented numbers.

Whether the result of footdragging by hardliners, or of incapacitation caused by internal bickering, continued intransigence by the rulers changed the complexion of the movement. Its pace quickened and days became hours, as each tick of the clock brought the death of China's students closer. The wail of ambulance sirens taking collapsed students from the square to nearby hospitals compounded the government's guilt. Official silence emboldened twelve prominent intellectuals to declare on May 14 that they would join the hunger strike unless the movement was declared "patriotic." On May 16 they established the "Union of Intellectuals" in Beijing and issued their May 16 Statement (Doc. 84). This act reflected a break between establishment intellectuals and the state they had served, and upon which they had been totally dependent. In their "May 17 Declaration" (Doc. 91) they attacked the government's inhumanity.

---

[7]See *56 Days*, p. 113.
[8]In the eyes of most Chinese, college students in their late teens or early twenties would still be children.

Television, which had until then played no role in the movement, began to beam pictures of collapsing hunger strikers nationwide.[9] When visiting the square, reporters for China Central TV could not tolerate the students' verbal assault on them for their political cowardice and unwillingness to stop serving the government. "Our throats had been cut," they explained. So for years they had remained silent. Now the students' bravery forced them to recognize "that we are the tool of propaganda" and gave them the courage to reflect the true nature of the movement in their media coverage (Doc. 83).

Expanded media made this into a nationwide movement. By beaming into millions of homes across China images of suffering and brave children, facing death at the hands of a cruel regime that rejected their seemingly harmless demand for dialogue, the media turned what was largely a Beijing movement into a nationwide crisis. Chinese friends of this author in Nanjing reported that their mothers wept at this sight on television. Appeals were directed at people all over the country to save the students (Doc. 87). Even Chen Xitong, the hardline mayor of Beijing, recognized that the hunger strike had nationwide repercussions, "producing a large scale of involvement and a serious disturbance never seen since the founding of the People's Republic."[10] Thousands of students nationwide traveled to Beijing. According to Chen, over 200,000 came to support the hunger strikers. The hunger strike also led to sympathy marches and hunger strikes in dozens of cities across China.[11] One intellectual, Liu Xiaobo, tried to make it a global movement by appealing to overseas Chinese to donate money (Doc. 88). Funds for the students, and supplies such as the brightly colored pup-tents, flowed in from Hong Kong in support of the hunger strike. The television media's ability to report openly and truthfully on the hunger strike—which suggested that the party had completely lost control over the media—may have convinced Beijing's citizens that victory was at hand and emboldened them to confront and stop the martial law troops.[12]

The hunger strike brought the movement to a near revolutionary pitch. On May 17 and 18, the largest spontaneous demonstrations in modern China's history took place. People from all walks of life marched. Government and party workers, whose participation signaled the growing defection of the regime's critical supporters, joined in. The Foreign Ministry was represented. While no top party officials joined, some bureau chiefs who held supervisory posts marched under banners representing their units.[13] According to a Western report,

---

[9]For a discussion of how China Central TV got free of the Propaganda Department, see Simmie and Nixon, *Tiananmen Square*, p. 124.

[10]Chen Xitong, "Report to NPC on Quelling the Counter-Revolutionary Rebellion," in *Beijing Spring*, ed. Oksenberg et al., Doc. 2.

[11]For in-depth descriptions of events in several cities, see *The Australian Journal of Chinese Affairs*, nos. 23 and 24 (1990). See also *56 Days*, pp. 117–21, 124–27.

[12]Andrew G. Walder, "The Political Sociology of the Beijing Upheaval of 1989," *Problems of Communism* (September–October 1989): 38.

even PLA soldiers, whose job is to protect the Communist party, were there.[14] There was fervor in the streets. Construction workers from Shanghai, working in Beijing, spoke with pride of how they gave blood for the students, while one hotel worker recalled how after visiting the square on May 17, he organized his fellow workers to march on the 18th. According to one Chinese observer, "It was a time when people lost themselves, it was not normal. It was crazy."[15] Taxi drivers in Beijing still recalled in the spring and summer of 1990 how they had stopped driving during the hunger strike to go to the square every day. Even Mayor Chen Xitong admitted the power of the hunger strike. According to his official report on the movement, not participating became "unpatriotic," a sign of indifference "to the survival of the students." Disgusted individuals withdrew from the CCP and the Communist Youth League (Doc. 95). Intellectuals began to withdraw from the CCP in Nanjing on May 14.[16] Workers attacked the government (Doc. 89) and marched in large numbers, even as Li Peng personally went to Beijing's largest factory, the Capital Iron and Steel Plant, to head off massive workers' protests.

Even if one were to argue that the real threat of popular rebellion against Communist rule was only in the minds of the rulers,[17] the establishment of an autonomous governing organization in the square represented a demand for autonomy that challenged the essence of Communist rule. The occupation of the square by ASUCUB signified a demand for "civil society," where independent citizens have the right to organize and defend their own interests, separate from those of the state.[18] On May 20, the Beijing Workers' Autonomous Union (BWAU) declared that "supporting and protecting the student hunger strikers" was its primary goal,[19] a sign of their willingness to rally with other social forces against the state.

Students expressed this desire for autonomy in several ways. Much of the

---

[13]A bureau or *ju* official is responsible for several departments (*chu*) and could have supervisory authority over several hundred party members. While it was one thing for party workers to march, or for a party official to let his staff march, it was a far more significant statement and much greater challenge to the regime if a party official who supervised other party members joined in.

[14]Fathers and Higgins, *Tiananmen*, p. 66.

[15]Interviews by David Zweig in Beijing, June 1989.

[16]*56 Days*, pp. 116–17.

[17]Whether the students really wanted to overthrow party rule remains unclear. In most instances they have denied this government contention, and the government can only point to a very few cases where anyone in the marches called for the overthrow of the CCP. In an interview with Ted Koppel on "Nightline," Wu'er Kaixi clearly stated that the students' goal had always been to overthrow the party; but in a later conversation with the author, he claimed that problems in the translations had led him to say this.

[18]For an analysis of the spring movement as a search for civil society, see Sullivan, "The Emergence of Civil Society in China, Spring 1989," in *The Chinese People's Movement*, ed. Saich, pp. 126–44.

[19]"BWAU Preparatory Committee Public Notice No. 1," May 20, 1989, from photo.

basis of their activism was, in fact, a desire for private freedom. Oppressed by an authoritarian family system, they also sought escape from a state that had recently reimposed controls over job placement.[20] Among students in the square, a popular theme was the lone wolf, walking across the desert (Doc. 98). For Chinese students, the wolf was not lonely; it was free. Students also expressed their desire for autonomy by refusing to place their hope for success in this movement on any reform leader. Unlike many establishment intellectuals who remained tied to the party system, the students presented themselves as a new force in conflict with the state. This demand for autonomy could only be seen by hardliners as a total repudiation of party leadership, in essence, as "counterrevolutionary" behavior.

The Increasing Threat to Hardline Elites

While critics of the current regime may feel that any effort to address the leadership's perception of threat legitimizes the regime's refusal to meet with the students and its use of force, any objective effort to understand why it behaved in a manner we perceive as "irrational" or "fascist" must begin with an effort to understand its interpretation of reality.[21] Students had accused party elders of employing the old-world view of seeing class enemies everywhere and of responding to threats through the old methods of "class struggle" (Doc. 76). This perspective, they argued, had undermined the reforms; in 1989 it triggered the old guard's hardline response to the students' demand for dialogue, and the decision to use force on June 4.

While the scale of the demonstrations mounted, the content of the posters and slogans appeared increasingly menacing to the inner circle of hardliners, to their dependents, and to Deng Xiaoping. Various factors—including the scale of the protest and the swiftness with which students nationwide reacted to the hunger strike through marches, the demands for dialogue with school leaders, and the boarding of trains for Beijing—caused China's leaders to recall the early days of the Cultural Revolution.[22] Posters that correctly asserted the sharp differences between the Cultural Revolution and the current movement, while failing to

---

[20]While the government had in spring 1988 made university graduates responsible for finding their own jobs, by April 1989 it had reimposed the system whereby the government allocated jobs. Students had feared that under the reformed system they might not get good jobs, but they were at least free to choose.

[21]The best effort to understand the perceptions and misperceptions of the leaders and the students is Melanie Manion, "Introduction: Reluctant Duelists: The Logic of the 1989 Protests and Massacre," in *Beijing Spring*, ed. Oksenberg et al., pp. xiii–xlii.

[22]According to *56 Days*, pp. 116–21, on May 14 students at Yan'an University began a class boycott and stopped eating in the cafeteria; in Shanghai, students at Fudan University began a hunger strike; seven hundred students from Tianjin rode their bikes to Tiananmen Square. On the 15th the protests grew even more widespread.

convince the leadership, showed that students recognized these as real issues with which they had to deal. Direct calls for Li Peng to step down, which intensified as the hunger strike dragged on, threatened party elders who had actively promoted him. Within the Standing Committee of the Politburo, Li and Yao Yilin had thwarted rapid reform on behalf of the party elders who feared that Deng's reforms were leading China away from communism. Demands from citizens that Deng totally withdraw from politics threatened their ability to manipulate politics to their own advantage and challenged their view that only a strong central leader could ensure the success of China's modernization.

Even before such direct attacks on Deng appeared, he and the party elders felt that the challenge to their control and the possible chaos that could result from a Cultural Revolution–type eruption necessitated drastic measures. China's recent history no doubt convinced them that political chaos would destroy China's chance for economic modernization. Deng had often expressed such views. Measures that appeared to outsiders far out of proportion to the problem suddenly seemed quite necessary from their perspective. Nevertheless, serious challenges confronted the leadership. A poster that appeared at Beijing University on May 11 calling for a hunger strike and the occupation of Tiananmen Square was certainly reported to the leadership[23] and may explain in part why troops from eight armies around the country were ordered to move toward Beijing on or around May 12.[24] Some analysts suggest that Deng mobilized these forces as a warning to Zhao Ziyang, who may have contemplated his own military coup.[25]

Yet the actual decision to launch the hunger strike on May 12, Gorbachev's impending visit, and nationwide sympathy marches and hunger strikes no doubt increased the resolve of Deng and the party elders to deal forcefully with what for them appeared to be a deteriorating situation. Thus, by May 16, even before the direct attacks on Deng began, the party elders had already decided to declare martial law.

Another major threat to the old guard, party hardliners, and their dependents involved the attack on corruption, a core part of this and other student movements dating back almost two thousand years. Accusations that party leaders had formed a "new class" grew more vociferous at this time. The link between

---

[23]Ibid., pp. 106–7. It is possible that the government fabricated this poster to justify its military mobilization, but given that so many people were copying down posters, it may simply have noticed this one and included it in the official chronology because of its threatening nature.

[24]There is considerable debate among Chinese as to whether the order was given on May 12 or May 14.

[25]Su Shaozhi said that in the second week of May, Defense Minister Qin Jiwei offered to carry out a military coup on Zhao's behalf. After considering it, Zhao chose not to accept his offer, whereupon Deng mobilized eight armies as a warning to Zhao that Deng really controlled the military. Had Qin made such an offer, however, he would have been purged after the crackdown; yet he remained in his post as of mid-1991.

corruption and political reform and the need for public disclosure of economic activities were part of the May 16 Statement (Doc. 84). On May 17, the BWAU accused the party of getting rich at the people's expense, and it questioned the utility of foreign investment if it merely became the personal property of the elite (Doc. 89). Another poster ridiculed the leadership's request that people tighten their belts in these difficult times, while at the same time members of the ruling elite dissipated themselves in luxurious living (Doc. 85). This theme struck a chord for many Beijing residents. On June 5, an old man standing near Jianguomenwai pointed at all the new tall buildings, such as the CITIC and Noble House towers, and demanded that this author tell foreign governments to stop giving loans to China's leaders; they had built big buildings for themselves, he claimed, while the monies had not helped the common people. Earlier posters had listed the high posts of many children of top leaders. Since the mid-1980s they had been able to gain important business contacts that kept them and their parents in good financial condition. The demands that top leaders reveal their incomes and end the business careers of their children reached a crescendo during the hunger strike. Thus, one of Zhao Ziyang's major concessions to the students, no doubt horrifying to other leaders and their children, was his willingness to reveal his income and force his children to retire from business.

Yet the attack by both students and workers on the children of high-ranking officials may have contributed to the violent denouement of June 4 by alienating a group that had limited the hardline reaction to earlier student movements. According to reports in 1987, Deng's son, Deng Pufang, had played a key role in convincing his father to stop the "anti–bourgeois liberalization" campaign in spring 1987 because it would harm foreign investment. With the "Prince's Party" (*taizidang*) now a major target of the democracy movement, children of leading cadres had to reconsider their stance toward the popular demands for political reform. Some of them had failed in their bids for public office in the 1987 elections, leaving business as their sole path to power and profit. For them, demands for public disclosure of incomes and a free press that could investigate their corrupt business deals were deeply threatening. As a result, a force for moderation and restraint during previous popular movements now saw this one as a major challenge to its security and position. In fact, some rallied to their parents' side and may have lobbied for a military crackdown.

Once direct attacks on Deng Xiaoping intensified, supporting Deng's position became critical to the ruling group. According to foreign observers, marchers on May 17 shouted "Down with Deng Xiaoping! Go Play your Bridge!"[26] In their May 17 Declaration, Yan Jiaqi, Bao Zunxin, Li Nanyou, and Yang Lujun called the student movement "a patriotic prodemocracy movement that is to bury China's last autocrat and China's last imperial regime" and stated that "Autocrats must resign from their positions" (Doc. 91). The government's internal

---

[26]Simmie and Nixon, *Tiananmen Square*, p. 116.

analysis of the events cited two sections of the May 17 Declaration that it claimed "directed the spearhead of the attack directly at Comrade Deng Xiaoping."[27] On May 18, a Beijing University poster challenged Deng's right to make decisions, such as the April 26 editorial, calling on him to admit the enormity of his error (Doc. 96). As a result, Yang Shangkun beseeched Zhao during these critical days to maintain his loyalty to Deng, stating that the critical question was where Zhao stood on the question of Deng Xiaoping, and whether he would keep his promise to safeguard Deng Xiaoping's prestige.[28] With the party general secretary unwilling to do so, the threat to the ruling group took on a new intensity.

The Failure of Negotiations

During the week of the hunger strike, a flurry of meetings between the students and the government ensued. On the night of May 12, a group of intellectuals met with the head of the United Front Work Department in the Central Committee, Yan Mingfu, a close ally of Zhao Ziyang, and persuaded him to meet the following day with student leaders.[29] Thus, on May 13, members of the Dialogue Delegation, representatives of the Hunger Strike Committee, and independent intellectuals met with Yan and other officials from the Communist Youth League. On the 14th, many of these same people met again in a more formal meeting with Yan Mingfu and Li Tieying, minister of the State Education Commission, a close ally of the conservatives. Even after this meeting failed, interactions continued between some student leaders and some government officials. Finally, on May 18, Li Peng met with a group of student leaders.

While the students' goal was to gain formal recognition for their organization, get the party to revoke the April 26 editorial, and persuade the government to meet with them as equals, the stakes of these meetings intensified for various reasons. First, initial efforts went into getting the students out of the square before the May 15 arrival of President Gorbachev of the Soviet Union, whose visit signaled the end of thirty years of Sino-Soviet hostility. For reformers in the party, disruption of the Gorbachev visit would embarrass China and strengthen the hardliners' position, both in their resistance to negotiate with the students and in the ongoing succession struggle. For hardliners, these disruptions were clear

---

[27]*56 Days*, p. 128.

[28]See "Main Points of Yang Shangkun's Speech at Emergency Enlarged Meeting of the Central Military Commission," in *Beijing Spring*, ed. Oksenberg et al., Doc. 50.

[29]See Shen Tong, with Marianne Yen, *Almost a Revolution* (Boston: Houghton Mifflin, 1990), p. 240. In an interview with the author, Shen emphasized the importance of the May 13 meeting as the first time the students realized the depth of the leadership split and the need to evacuate the square to protect Zhao Ziyang. Yet elsewhere Wu'er Kaixi has been quoted saying that the students did not care at all about the leadership struggle, only about "rocking the system." See Fathers and Higgins, *Tiananmen*, p. 57.

indicators of the failure of Zhao's softer line toward the students and probably helped them in their struggle against Zhao. Second, as hunger strikers began collapsing, the risk to the students' health made ending the hunger strike all the more important. Yet despite efforts by various actors to resolve the crisis without using military force, the two sides faced enormous difficulties, including splits within each group participating in the dialogue, mutual misperceptions, cultural and personality difficulties, and this dramatic increase in the stakes.[30]

The hunger strike was a high-risk strategy in the students' ongoing negotiations with the government. The Dialogue Delegation had been pushing for a meeting on May 8, but the government had put off that meeting without setting another date. Thus, while the hunger strike reflected a growing impatience with the government's refusal to carry on a dialogue "on the basis of full equality" (Doc. 74), the students knew that if they opted for using the hunger strike as leverage, they had to show that it did not threaten social stability or create "turmoil," and that their political activities were legitimate and patriotic. To prove that their actions were not antiparty, they tried to control both the public statements made on their behalf (Doc. 79) and slogans used by demonstrators (Doc. 92). To prevent "chaos," students tried to prevent disruptions in the commercial districts and violent or illegal acts (Doc. 92). They organized traffic in and around the square. By rallying the people around them and creating an autonomous society in the square, they increased their leverage against the government and popular support for their right to demand a dialogue based on equality between the government and the students. Beijing citizens who came to the square strongly supported this effort (Doc. 97).

But splits within the two camps complicated the negotiation process. Despite splits within the party, the hunger strike's potential to disrupt Gorbachev's visit forced reformers in the party to meet with the students. At the May 13 meeting Yan Mingfu shared information about the intraparty split as a way to get the students out of the square. But he could offer little in return for any evacuation, except the knowledge that a continued strike would only make things worse. In response to continued student demands, Yan arranged a meeting for May 14 in which hardliners and reformers could meet with the students. But again, Yan was unable to offer the students any concrete incentives for leaving the square, let alone persuade party hardliners to concede to any of the students' demands. He was even unable to conduct the meeting in a way that met student demands. While students had demanded that the meeting be televised live, the government said that for technical reasons it could only broadcast the meeting after a several hour delay. Yet despite Hu Qili's reported insistence that the meeting be aired on CCTV, this did not occur, nor was it broadcast into the square, as had been

---

[30]For an application of "negotiations theory" to the Tiananmen crisis, see Benedict Stavis, "Impediments to Peaceful Conflict Resolution: China's Spring, 1989," ms., November 1989.

promised. The hardliners did not want to negotiate on national television with members of an autonomous student organization, for such a meeting would trigger nationwide demands for similar dialogues with other "autonomous" associations. Thus this meeting too failed, for once students outside the meeting room discovered that it was not being broadcast in any format, they threatened to break into the meeting unless the Dialogue Delegation adjourned it. Yan Mingfu merely sighed in frustration and disappointment when the Dialogue Delegation announced its withdrawal.

Some might argue that had the government spoken with one hardline voice, the students might have recognized more clearly the price they would pay for their continuing resistance. Zhao's conciliatory voice, as in his speeches of May 3 and 4, may have suggested to the students that if they held out, the government might concede. With both conciliatory and hardline messages emanating from the government, students must have been confused as to the leadership's intentions. This view, attributed by Yang Shangkun in his May 24 speech to former President Li Xiannian, was that having "two headquarters" in the CCP's Central Committee persuaded the students to increase their demands rather than concede to government pressure.[31] Perhaps a consistently hardline policy from April 27 would have clearly signaled the probable costs of continued protest, thereby avoiding the bloodletting of June 4. On the other hand, students felt compelled to insist on the overturning of the April 26 editorial as the only way to ensure that the leadership would not "settle issues after the harvest." Moreover, the government's efforts to manipulate the students during the early days of the hunger strike showed that it was incapable of making any real conciliatory offer to the students.

But conflicts and poor communication among the wide assortment of groups that formed the student leadership greatly complicated the negotiations as well. There was no real central leadership among the students, especially after the hunger strike began. Escalating conflict between, on the one side, the Dialogue Delegation (represented by Xiang Xiaoji and Shen Tong) and ASUCUB (represented by Wang Dan, Wu'er Kaixi, and Feng Congde), and, on the other side, by the more radical hunger strikers led by Chai Ling, Li Lu, and Zhang Boli, made it harder for the students to present a consistent set of demands. According to some accounts, leaders such as Wang Dan, Wu'er Kaixi, and Shen Tong were determined to establish a constructive dialogue with the government; they prepared sincerely for the May 13 and 14 meeting.[32] According to Shen Tong, only those who had heard Yan Mingfu's message at the May 13 meeting understood

---

[31]See "Main Points of Yang Shangkun's Speech," in *Beijing Spring*, ed. Oksenberg et al., Doc. 50.

[32]See Woei Lien Chong, "Petitioners, Popperians, and Hunger Strikers: The Uncoordinated Efforts of the 1989 Chinese Democratic Movement," in *The Chinese People's Movement*, ed. Saich, pp. 106–25.

the necessity of getting the students to leave the square. Thus, Chai Ling and Li Lu, who had left the meeting early, were not supportive of subsequent efforts by Wu'er Kaixi, Wang Dan, and other, more moderate leaders to get the hunger strikers to evacuate the square before the Gorbachev visit. Even Zhao's declaration that the government would not "settle accounts" with the students (Doc. 90) did not elicit a positive response from the hunger strikers. Some who felt the government had forced them into the hunger strike mocked Zhao Ziyang's promise that the leaders would not take revenge and refused to respond until the government apologized for its immoral behavior (Doc. 90). Also, Wang Dan and Wu'er Kaixi, who represented the hunger strikers at the May 14 meeting, disrupted it themselves when they played a tape of their own demands, after telling the Dialogue Delegation that they only wanted to be quiet observers.

For some analysts, China's political culture, with its penchant for farce, ritual, and moral posturing, explains the inability to find any solution short of martial law. According to Lucian Pye, when Premier Li Peng met on May 18 with a group of hunger strike students,[33] he was culturally incapable of negotiating with them. Instead he lectured them about the dangers hunger posed to their health, demanded that they leave the square, and compared them to his own children whom he must educate. His patronizing manner infuriated the students who, from the perspective of political culture, were involved in the psychological act of rejecting parental authority. According to Ben Stavis, "psychological tensions deeply rooted in family relationships were writ large on the national political scene."[34] The government offered no political quid pro quo, and halfhearted efforts at dialogue were viewed as mere orders to students which they had to reject.

Li Peng's intransigence, however, may have resulted more from political circumstances than from cultural predilections. By May 18, Zhao's refusal to abide by the decision to declare martial law meant Li had finally defeated his arch rival, so Li may have expected the students to capitulate in light of his now dominant power. When they did not, his temper flared. People who know Li Peng well argue that his character flaws—an imperious attitude as a defense against a feeling of inferiority, and inability to work closely with colleagues— were already apparent in Yan'an.[35] A cultural explanation ignores Li's incompetence, arrogance, and hunger for power. Further, if culture explains Li's refusal to negotiate with the students, how does one explain Zhao Ziyang's willingness to do so? As a political underdog in a losing struggle, he had reasons to negotiate; but then politics, not culture, explains his behavior.

Similarly, it is simplistic to attribute the students' behavior entirely to a desire to reject parental authority. Students did see this movement as a rebellion against

---

[33]For the text of the meeting see Oksenberg et al., eds., *Beijing Spring*, Doc. 36.
[34]Stavis, "Impediments to Peaceful Conflict Resolution."
[35]Zweig interviews in Beijing in 1989.

a paternalistic and oppressive system, but other factors were also at work. For example, while Wu'er Kaixi's statement to Li Peng at the May 18 meeting that Li was "late" was seen as a reflection of his arrogance and disrespect for authority,[36] Wu'er Kaixi claims he was not lecturing the premier. His point was that because Li had waited so long to hold an honest dialogue with the students—they had called for him to "come out" back on April 22—the movement had reached a point where student leaders could no longer promise that they could get the hunger strikers out of the square.

Declaring Martial Law Cracks the Leadership

While the leadership was deeply divided over the future direction of political and economic reform, as well as over the impending succession to Deng Xiaoping, the hunger strike pushed the elite conflict to its apogee.

Although Zhao Ziyang's political problems were severe before the student movement, and rumors suggested that he was to lose his post as general secretary and his preeminent place in the line of succession,[37] his refusal to support martial law ended his political career. Zhao tried several times during the hunger strike both to get the students to leave the square and to persuade the hardliners to alter their position. On May 15 he wanted to go to the square but was reportedly thwarted by demands that he accept party discipline. The next day he reportedly demanded that the Politburo Standing Committee accept a major investigation of the financial perquisites and ill-gotten wealth of top leaders and their children. Instead, the old guard voted to declare martial law. Then, on May 17 he rejected the counsel of elders and voted against martial law. Yet as general secretary, Zhao was obligated to support and announce any decision of the Standing Committee of the Politburo. His rejection of the majority decision and refusal to announce martial law on May 19 flew in the face of party discipline and effectively ended his career. Even after Yang Shangkun phoned to dissuade him from rejecting Deng's decision, he refused to support using force against peaceful demonstrators.[38]

For hardline members of the second generation, including Premier Li Peng, Politburo Standing Committee member Yao Yilin, Beijing Mayor Chen Xitong, Beijing First Party Secretary Li Ximing, State Education Commission Minister Li Tieying, and State Council spokesman Yuan Mu, the student movement provided further ammunition to remove Zhao and his colleagues from office, as well as

---

[36]I helped project this image with my comment on Wu'er Kaixi on the ABC special by Ted Koppel, "Tragedy at Tiananmen," June 27, 1989.

[37]See Lowell Dittmer, "China in 1989: The Crisis of Incomplete Reform," *Asian Survey* 30, 1 (January 1990): 25–41.

[38]See "Main Points of Yang Shangkun's Speech," in *Beijing Spring*, ed. Oksenberg et al., pp. 320–27.

a chance for personal promotion. Since late April they had worked together closely. Then they had played a major role in the critical days surrounding the April 26 editorial. During the hunger strike they continued to frustrate Zhao's efforts to negotiate with the students and peacefully resolve the crisis. Some Chinese argue that they actively sabotaged negotiations because, while successful negotiations could save Zhao, a crackdown would increase the power of the hardliners and the old guard who backed them.[39]

The decision to declare martial law also meant the political demise of many of Zhao's young advisers. Soon after arriving in Beijing in 1979, Zhao had established close ties with a group of young economists and sociologists who had united in 1978 because of their belief that only radical reforms could save China. Most went to three institutions—the Research Institute for Restructuring the Economic System (Tigaisuo) under Chen Yizi in the Commission for Restructuring the Economy; the Development Institute in the State Council's Research Center for Rural Development under Du Runsheng; and the Research Institute for International Problems, under Zhao's former personal secretary, Li Xianglu, in the China International Trust and Investment Corporation. Several had also gone to work in Bao Tong's Office for Political Reform in the CCP's Central Committee.

Soon after Zhao voted against martial law on May 17, Bao Tong informed all bureau-level officials under him that Zhao's political position was now untenable. In accordance with party discipline, however, Bao insisted that this information not leave the room.[40] But someone ignored his request, and a meeting of representatives of the three research centers was called. According to one attendee, they were all stunned to have lost another reform-oriented general secretary. But rather than sit back and accept this defeat as they had in 1987 when Hu Yaobang was sacked, they decided to try and save the situation. On May 19, they drafted a "Six-Point Declaration," blaming the turmoil on the government's procrastination, attacking factional struggles as the root of the leadership's alienation from the people, and denouncing the declaration of martial law, which they said would split the nation. They called for full disclosure of inner-party political machinations, the convening of a special meeting of the National People's Congress to overturn martial law, and a National Party Congress to investigate the Politburo's work during the crisis. They also asked students to end the hunger strike.[41] They read their declaration in the

---

[39]A PLA officer actively involved in these events said this view was common in China. According to other Chinese, Deng's concern that they had used the crisis for their own advantage explains why none of them were promoted to higher leadership positions at the Fourth Plenum in 1989 after the crackdown.

[40]Interview in China, July 1990. Since he did not pass on the information himself, efforts to connect Bao personally to the public disclosure that martial law had been declared have failed. Bao Tong has not been charged with antiparty activities as of this writing.

square and published it in a fake edition of the *People's Daily* that was circulated around the square. By publicizing the declaration of martial law, this report led the students to end the hunger strike and to send people to all major suburban thoroughfares to mobilize citizens to stop the troops.

President Yang Shangkun in his speech to the party's Military Affairs Commission on May 24 denounced the Six-Point Declaration and the "three institutes and one association" that promulgated it.[42] Several writers of this declaration were arrested, and leaders of two of the three institutions fled the country.[43] These organizations were unable to continue their work—the Development Institute and its parent body were closed in December 1989, the Tigaisuo was closed in late fall 1990, and the third exists in name only. While continued need for change has already forced hardliners to renew economic reform, the demise of these units exemplified the end of the ten-year reform era and the once powerful reform faction that led it.

Conclusion

The events described above show how well China's critics understood the deep-rooted problems in their own system and how these problems have historically undermined China's modernization and democratization. Document 76 argues that conflicts between the vestiges of Mao's totalitarian system and society's demands for pluralism generated by economic reform triggered popular explosions. Yan Jiaqi blames the crisis on continued autocracy (Doc. 91). And Document 93 emphasizes how most party members give up independence of thought and accept blind idolatry to the leader, party structure, and party ideology in return for a party card and the profit-seeking opportunities it affords. Preferred solutions include calls for increasing the pace of political reform to remove "feudal privileges" that "have infiltrated the world of exchange" (Doc. 84) and a multiparty system to incorporate the proliferating interests within socialist society (Doc. 80).

These events also demonstrated the depth of the chasm dividing state from society. Only leaders alienated from the people and driven by powerful self-interest could have remained unresponsive to the people and allowed young people to edge toward the brink of death. Some leaders may have believed that only a strong central moral and political authority could hold China together and create the stability needed for modernization. But their desire for power, which

---

[41]See "Six Statements Concerning the Present Situation," in Han Minzhu and Hua Sheng, eds. *Cries For Democracy: Writings and Speeches from the 1989 Chinese Democracy Movement* (Princeton: Princeton University Press, 1990), pp. 250–51.

[42]The "one association"—the Beijing Young Economists Association—was an informal organization to which many of these young reformers belonged. Yang Shangkun, in Oksenberg et al., eds., *Beijing Spring*, Doc. 50.

[43]As of July 1991, several of those involved in publicizing the information about martial law remained in prison and may yet be found guilty of political crimes.

prevented the second generation from stepping down to placate popular protests, created far greater instability in China's political system. For some analysts, this desire for power is at the root of the CCP's problems (Doc. 93).

The hunger strike showed the need for significant political reform. A more open political system, with a modicum of popular representation, might generate more, not less, stability; but the price for such a system would be the full retirement of party elders and the political demise of some members of the hardline second generation. Instead, the reform faction collapsed, and with it another episode in China's historic search for modernization.

The state-society split illuminated by the hunger strike drove millions of people who previously had not been politically active onto the streets in a public display of antigovernment protest that became a popular revolt. Such a spontaneous mass mobilization and free media expression had not occurred in China since the May Fourth Movement of 1919. Eventually, the perceived threat to elite power and privilege drove hardliners to move troops toward Beijing. As the troops approached the capital, a flurry of negotiations ensued that failed for various reasons analyzed in this chapter. The return of the party elders with their class struggle mentality, elite and student factionalism, youthful organizational inexperience, mutual misperceptions, prideful posturing and public moralizing on both sides, as well as an unfortunate mix of personalities and power made an acceptable solution unattainable. As a result, both sides dug in and aggravated the crisis.

The declaration of martial law did not end the crisis. Imposing martial law and infiltrating the media offices turned off the flow of antiparty propaganda that had been filling the air waves throughout the hunger strike. These moves also forced students and citizens to turn their attention from directly challenging the government to dealing with the army. To this extent, the popular rebellion subsided. But as will be seen in the next section, enormous challenges still faced the Chinese Communist party and the hardliners who were now in control. The decision to send in troops increased the chances for a split in the military. Soldiers became vulnerable to direct citizen appeals to abandon the government, while some old military leaders sided with the students. If popular pressure cracked the army, the old guard would lose its last source of power. Zhao's political allies still sought ways to overturn martial law. The students introduced new and inventive ways to rally mass support. For almost two weeks China sat in a state of paralysis as the tragic denouement drew closer.

"Jueshi" (Fasting)

"Wu ziyou, wu ningsi" (Give Me Liberty or Give Me Death)
—Slogans on white headbands of hunger strikers

74

Declaration of the Hunger Strike

PETITION GROUP OF THE STUDENT HUNGER STRIKERS
OF BEIJING COLLEGES AND UNIVERSITIES

May 12, 1989

Source: Handbill or wall poster, courtesty of HKFS.

In the great April patriotic democracy movement, we petitioned through a series of peaceful actions—the sit-in of April 20 in front of Xinhua Gate, the petition of April 22 in Tiananmen Square, the march of April 27 around the city, and the demonstration on May 4—for direct and open dialogue with the government on the basis of full equality. The government, however, brazenly responded with cheating and mudslinging. On May 6 we again petitioned the government for a definite response by May 8. The government delayed answering our petition, saying that it would reply on May 11. On May 11, however, the government said it would do its best to respond definitively within the week. We can no longer tolerate such a deceitful attitude and one delay after another. To make a determined and forceful protest, we have decided to hold a hunger strike to urge the government to hold an immediate and real dialogue with students from the Dialogue Delegation of Beijing colleges and universities.

"We have no other alternative but to go on a hunger strike for the people."
—Slogan, in *56 Days*

75

Announcement

ASUCUB

May 12, 1989

Source: Poster or handbill, courtesy of HKFS.

. . . Because the hunger strike that was spontaneously organized by some students begins at 4:00 P.M., May 13, ASUCUB asks students in every college and university to take immediate action to support the student hunger strikers, protect their safety, and ensure victory to the hunger strike. Concrete measures to be taken are as follows:

1. The students should rally under the Monument [to the People's Heroes] before 8:30 P.M. tomorrow evening. Pickets and organizational discipline should be strengthened. Students should be grouped around their university flags and sit in around the student hunger strikers. They may gradually leave by 8:00 A.M. on May 14. A new rally should be organized again between 8:30 and 9:00 P.M. on May 14.

2. During the day, some student groups should be organized around the hunger strikers to take care of them and provide for their safety. (Schools whose students have joined the hunger strike are mainly responsible for doing this work.)

3. During the day, do good propaganda work among city residents. Make many street speeches and distribute handbills. From the daytime of May 13, every college and university should produce propaganda materials.

4. Points for propaganda include:

a. Strongly demand a dialogue between the government and student delegations. Explain the truth about what the student delegation is doing and about the student movement.

b. Demand the removal of the government's accusation that the students are "creating turmoil." Explain to the residents that the students face possible government revenge, and some universities are already under much pressure.

c. Welcome the recent moderation in the government's position (the May 4 speech by Zhao Ziyang, the May 5 speech by Li Peng, and the agenda of the Standing Committee of the National People's Congress).

76

While the Students Are Having a Hunger Strike

ANONYMOUS

About May 13, 1989

Source: Handbill or wall poster, courtesy of HKFS.

It is extremely depressing to see that citizens must inflict harm upon themselves in order to express their wishes in modern China. Regardless of the consequences, however, the student movement already marks the end of an old era and the beginning of a new one. The traditional way of thinking can only bring about national disaster and popular suffering.

The old generation of revolutionaries fought on horseback for a new republic. After establishing the republic in 1949, they still ruled on horseback, using a wartime mobilizational system with the following features:

1. A pyramidal, one-way structure of power relationships, with a political group represented by one leader at the top, placing itself above society;

2. A one-way administrative chain of command covering every corner of social life;

3. Personnel management, institutions, procedures, structures, and rules that are regarded only as expedient measures and are easily and arbitrarily changed;

4. An ideology of all-encompassing unity (*da yitong*)[1] ideology which requires the unconditional loyalty of every member of society;

5. Political campaigns form the basic pattern of behavior. This system, which has seriously clashed with all new interests emerging under modernization, frequently leads to social turmoil and political instability;

6. Severe and cruel punishments to maintain iron discipline.

This system suits the needs of war, not construction and modernization. During the modernization process, a new system must be established that can ... integrate all kinds of interests to achieve political stability. Such a system can only be a constitutional democracy that contains the following principles:

---

[1]This term used by Chinese intellectuals, such as Jin Guantao, reflects the problem of Chinese monism—nothing is allowed to exist independent of the system or established rules; and the system can always adjust to incorporate any deviations against the ruling ideology. Thus, rebellions come and go, dynasties rise and fall, but the system remains the same.

1. Individuals as the basic starting point and end-result of political activity, and inalienable human rights;
2. A representative system of government with general elections;
3. A government with a responsible cabinet;
4. A political system with checks and balances;
5. Legalized and regularized political struggles among political parties that are open and nonviolent, with freedom of assembly;
6. Social pluralism and limited government;
7. Freedom of speech and the press, which would allow the open flow of information.

At this moment of change from the old ways of thinking to the new, China has lost its direction. Although in theory "taking class struggle as the key link" has been abandoned, the stubborn way of thinking that views problems through the lens of class struggle, considers solutions based on class analysis, and handles various social relationships through the coercion inherent in class struggle, still prevails. This is an extremely stubborn way of thinking. Some people still imagine that "one class must oppress another." Every little disturbance heightens these perceptions, and painstaking efforts are made to find "a handful of enemies." Struggles are launched to beat back "the anti-party and antisocialist adverse current." But facts show that a contradiction does not end but rather just begins when one side prevails over the other.[2]

Since Mao Zedong, it has almost become a convention to equate the leader himself with the party and state. This is the main source of all turmoil and disasters in our society. If a leader sets a bad example, then subordinates follow it. Every party branch secretary can then automatically attack dissidents in the party's name. All flatterers and toadies can rally their forces to "ask the emperor's permission" to suppress the opponents in the name of defending a certain political line. "Either the East Wind prevails over the West Wind or the West Wind prevails over the East Wind"[3] is indeed the logic of power politics. . . .

---

[2]The mentality described here was at work throughout the crisis and explains in part the government's paranoid response to every little antigovernment, antiparty, or anti–Deng Xiaoping slogan or expression that appeared during the movement. For a full outline of the government's perception, see 56 Days.

[3]Here the students use Mao's own words to criticize Mao in a more sarcastic way.

77

Letter to the People of the Whole Country

AUTONOMOUS STUDENT UNION OF BEIJING NORMAL UNIVERSITY

About May 13, 1989

Source: Leaflet, courtesy of HKFS.

1. Since the student movement began on April 15, a series of erroneous and inappropriate decisions made by the party and government have led students to initiate marches, class boycotts, and a hunger strike, one right after the other, and each with serious consequences. The party and government have not responded quickly or appropriately, so the situation deteriorates. party and government decision makers must be held responsible for all consequences that arise from this.

2. . . . We demand improvements in China's democratic and legal system. We do not want to cause turmoil. . . . We hope people throughout the city and country, from all walks of life, will join us in adopting a cool and restrained attitude in support of the student movement and maintain normal order in their work and their lives.

3. We clearly know that our goal cannot be achieved in a short period of time, and that the hunger strike is only a temporary but necessary method. We sincerely hope that the party's and government's top leaders can meet the hunger strikers' reasonable demands as soon as possible to avoid an even more serious situation whose consequences would be too ghastly to contemplate.

78

Letter to the Capital Workers

COMMITTEE IN SUPPORT OF THE STUDENTS' ACTION,
CHINESE WORKERS' MOVEMENT COLLEGE, AND TEMPORARY
COMMAND CENTER OF THE CAPITAL WORKERS' PICKET GROUP

May 13, 1989

Source: *ORSD*, 1:31.

To the great capital worker comrades:
Democracy and dictatorship have arrived at the hour of a struggle to death.
The Li Peng government has become isolated and reactionary by publicly
hoisting the banner of opposing the people and democracy. Now the Li Peng
government is moving a large number of armed troops into Beijing. We can
see that this grand democratic movement is going to be swept away. This
morning, 300,000 university students declared a general hunger strike.[1] Most
of the students are facing the threat of a strong and brutal suppression. Only
the capital's working class can save this great democratic movement. We
urgently appeal to capital workers and citizens to take immediate actions.

1. Make use of all kinds of nonviolent means to prevent the troops from
entering the city and publicize to the troops the truth of this patriotic democratic
movement and its great historical significance, and also try to win support of the
troops.

2. Organize workers' picket groups immediately to maintain order in the
capital. Prevent illegal behavior like beating, smashing, robbing, and burning
so as to ensure the continuation of the struggle of the students' hunger strike.

---

[1]According to observers, the number of hunger strikers was 3,000, but the document
may have incorrectly used the figure of 300,000.

79
Statement

ASUCUB

About May 13, 1989

Source: Leaflet or poster, courtesy of HKFS.

No one can release news in the name of the Autonomous Student Union of Colleges and Universities in Beijing. News releases can only be made with written authorization and within the guidelines set out by the authorization. Otherwise, if an unauthorized news release brings about adverse effects, the responsible individual will be investigated.

80
The Socialist Multiparty System in China

YANG XX

May 12, 1989, posted May 19, 1989 at People's University

Source: ORSD, 1:47.

Note: This article's author, a student in the Chinese department, thinks a lot but lacks theoretical sophistication. The author offers his thoughts on the "socialist multiparty system," hoping to hear others' views. He also hopes that fellow students and researchers will discuss this topic more.[1]

Viewing the multiparty system as a copyright of capitalism and unrelated to socialism is an old biased view. There are democratic socialist countries like Sweden, but we never admit that they practice socialism. (Actually we have no convincing arguments disproving that they are socialist. If we accept "socialism with Chinese characteristics," why not accept a Swedish socialism?) Hungary's political agenda now includes discussions on the multiparty system, and Poland

---

[1]Yang describes himself as a Ph.D. candidate at People's University, Beijing.

is talking about political pluralism. However, opposing voices from the German Democratic [Republic] call this "revisionist." Other Communist countries (including the USSR and China) reject the rationale of a multiparty system. China's leaders reject the multiparty system, saying it is ill-suited to China. True, the CCP's position as the ruling party is irrefutable, but this is not a convincing reason to reject other political parties—real independent parties, not China's current so-called democratic parties and organizations.[2] The following are my preliminary thoughts on the socialist multiparty system.

1. If capitalism can have a multiparty system, can't socialism? . . . It can for the following reasons:

Party politics is the common political form of a modern civilized society. When different interest groups exist in society, political parties representing these interests naturally come into being. Since individual interests vary, there must be more than one political party. Multiparty politics are based on this.

The CCP has always insisted that under socialism all people share the same interests, thus justifying one-party dictatorship. Actually, people's interests under socialism are not always the same, and different societal interests exist. In China there are at least four social strata—workers, peasants, merchants, and intellectuals—that form the "class" basis for different political parties. The CCP's claim to represent everyone's interests is not true. It simply cannot represent the people. It has changed into a party alienated from and oppressing the people, practicing bureaucratic rule. . . . Without any competitors, the CCP does not fear losing control, so it acts as it pleases and corruption becomes widespread. Placing its interests ahead of the people's and the country's, it enjoys unlimited privileges that it is terrified to lose. Thus, because a system with checks and balances among parties includes the constant threat of losing power, the Communist party is unwilling to practice a multiparty system or allow its emergence. This is the party's ultimate intention. So its argument that a multiparty system is "inconsistent with China's reality" is just an excuse. . . .

Some people worry that a multiparty system will change the nature of the socialist state. This concern is unfounded. Hasn't the state's nature in capitalist countries remained unchanged despite the fact that its multiparty system incorporates even socialist and Communist parties? This is because people with different interests can share the same ideology. More precisely, different political parties in capitalist countries may represent specific interests, but all share a fundamental belief in capitalism. Can't such logic be applied to socialism?

Socialism reflects ideology, not interests, because under socialism people may have different interests. But if capitalism can accommodate different political parties, why can't socialism? Different political parties may represent different interests, but all can be strongly committed to socialism.

In theory, a socialist society is the most humane, democratic, prosperous, and

---

[2] China has eight "democratic" parties that are remnants of pre-1949 political parties.

rational society, which incorporates the best parts of all societies (including capitalist society) and rejects corruption and decadence. While socialism today is far from perfect, it is always improving; thus, people naturally aspire toward it. And even if some people in a multiparty system want to change the nature of the socialist state, the multiparty system's checks and balances will prevent such changes. So a socialist multiparty system is practical and obviously needs to be introduced.

2. Seventy years after the 1917 October Revolution established the first socialist country, we are faced with the unpleasant fact that all socialist countries lag behind capitalist ones. As a rule, these countries are poor and undemocratic. Not surprisingly, some people say that socialism is really social feudalism and societal regression.

The ruling parties of most socialist countries are awakening. A reform wave has swept the USSR, Eastern Europe, and, in Asia, China and Vietnam. The reforms announce the failure of past socialist efforts. Twenty to thirty years of reform in Eastern Europe and ten years in China have brought some achievements, but new problems (for example, inflation and corruption) create many difficulties, shattering people's faith in socialism and turning their hearts blindly toward Western capitalism.

Why have so many problems arisen even as these countries reform? Probably the reforms are not comprehensive enough. Almost all reforms, in China, the USSR, or Eastern Europe, focus on economic reform, leaving politics untouched. But the resultant stagnant political reform undermines economic reform and hampers economic development. Only political reform can relieve these countries from the crises they face.

Democracy is the most critical part of political reform, for without it corruption cannot be eradicated and economic development will stagnate. But in a one-party dictatorship, democracy is bestowed on the people by powerholders who can withdraw it. Therefore, democracy cannot be guaranteed, and true democracy can only be attained through political pluralism whose highest form is the socialist multiparty system.

3. The socialist multiparty system's superiority is apparent. But people's reservations about its introduction in China have some validity given the CCP's determination not to share political power. Yet the people and the CCP are both impatient with the status quo. Corruption causes the CCP serious problems, while growing popular discontent threatens the party's legitimacy. The current massive student movement is a warning that a socialist multiparty system is becoming more likely. The CCP will certainly not allow us to organize a new political party, which would compete with it, even if we proclaim socialism as its guiding principle. And once attacked as an illegal and counterrevolutionary organization, it will be disbanded.

Are we helpless? Certainly not. One strategy is to win over the existing democratic parties. We can use their legal status and resistance to direct CCP control so as to encourage their independence. This is possible now when people nationwide are demanding democracy, for it will be difficult for the CCP to withdraw their legal status after they declare their independence. At worst, the CCP can withdraw financial support, which overseas patriotic compatriots would replace if they were to achieve genuine independence.

Comrades in the democratic parties believe in socialism. Their parties are socialist parties. The existence of independent democratic parties creates the preconditions for a socialist multiparty system, which is where the hope for China's democracy and modernization lies.[3]

"International Opinion, Please Support Us."
"Democratic Factions in Various Fields, Please Support Us."
—Slogans, in *56 Days*

81

The Authorities Have Completely Broken Their Promises: A Statement about the Government's Response to the Students' Demands for a Dialogue

AUTONOMOUS STUDENT UNION OF PEOPLE'S UNIVERSITY

May 13, 1989

Source: *Tiananmen 1989*, pp. 346–47.

On the evening of May 12, the party's Central Committee, the Standing Committee of the National People's Congress, and the State Council finally produced "An Answer to the Demands for a Dialogue," the main contents of which are as follows:

1. A discussion meeting (not a dialogue)[1] will be held next Monday (May 15);
2. The number of student representatives is limited to twenty;
3. Only government representatives at the ministerial level will participate;

---

[3]One of Zhao Ziyang's staunchest allies, Yan Mingfu, director of the United Front Work Department of the CCP Central Committee, was responsible for the democratic parties. Because of his involvement in this movement, he was a target of the post-Tiananmen crackdown.

[1]A discussion meeting (*taolun hui*) is presided over by someone, usually a party secretary, who controls the discussion. A dialogue (*duihua*) is between equals.

4. The process of the discussion meeting can only be partially reported; and

5. The students must present a list of student representatives before 10:00 A.M. on the morning of May 13 (today).

The content of the "answer" is nothing but a reproduction of the "April 29 Dialogue,"[2] which was manipulated singlehandedly by Yuan Mu and his like. It repeats the clumsy tricks played by Yuan Mu at the news conference on May 3. This answer by the government merely shows that it lacks the most rudimentary sincerity toward having real dialogue on the basis of equality as strongly demanded by the students. They have still persisted in their own ways with regard to the cries for democracy and freedom, and they have turned a deaf ear to the demands of the students. The Autonomous Student Union of the People's University hereby strongly protests the government's attitude.

It is well known that since the "dialogue" of April 29, the government has time and again delayed responding to the students' demands for a dialogue. When ASUCUB presented a letter of petition, the government said it would give an "answer" on May 8. Then it delayed the time of the answer until May 11, claiming that it "needed to continue to study it." However, . . . [it was not] until yesterday (May 12) that it concocted the aforementioned "answer." Such abominable behavior on the part of the government, which treats state affairs as a trifling matter, is an attempt to hoodwink the people. It is a direct and brazen confrontation with the Chinese people. It fully manifests their incompetence and backward political awareness.

. . . [O]verseas Chinese groups and Chinese students have supported the student movement and expressed deep indignation over the abominable attitudes of the government. Large petition groups from the colleges and universities in Shanghai, Tianjin, and other provinces have recently arrived in Beijing. The Chinese in Hong Kong and Macao are also showing support for the patriotic student movement in the mainland. The government's lack of sincerity and the authorities' promise-breaking behavior have been fully exposed to the people all over the world.

It is outrageous that the authorities still take such a rigid and uncompromising confrontational attitude toward this popular patriotic movement. The Chinese people cannot help asking: Where on earth is the sense of duty of those bureaucrats, who stand high above the masses, to make the country strong and the people prosperous? Where is their moral conscience? . . .

"Mom, We Are Not Wrong!"
—Slogan from photo

---

[2]For this dialogue see Oksenberg et al., eds., *Beijing Spring*, Doc. 27.

82

Hunger Strike Declaration of May 13

ALL THE STUDENTS OF THE BEIJING UNIVERSITY HUNGER STRIKE GROUP

May 13, 1989

Source: *Xinwen daobao, haowai* (News herald, extra), HKFS.

In this bright, sunny month of May, we are on a hunger strike. In the finest moment of our youth, we must leave behind everything beautiful about life. But how reluctant, how unwilling we are!

The country has reached this juncture: Rampant inflation; widespread illegal business deals by corrupt officials; the dominance of abusive power; bureaucratic corruption; just and talented people fleeing abroad, while law and order deteriorate. Compatriots with a conscience, at this critical moment in our people's life and death, listen to our voice:

This country is our country;

These people are our people.

The government is our government.

Who will shout if we don't?

Who will act if we don't?

Although our shoulders remain tender, although our death is hard to face, we must part with life. When history demands it, we have no choice but to die.

Our purest feelings of patriotism and loyalty are labeled "chaotic disturbances" with "ulterior motives" "manipulated by a small gang."

We ask all honorable Chinese—every worker, peasant, soldier, ordinary citizen, intellectual, as well as prominent individuals, government officials, police, and those who fabricated our crimes—to place their hands on their hearts and examine their conscience: What crime have we committed? Are we creating "chaos"? We walk out of class, march, hunger strike, sacrifice everything, yet our feelings are betrayed again and again. We bear hunger pangs to pursue truth and get beaten by police. We kneel for democracy and are ignored. Our request for dialogue on equal terms is met with delay after delay. Our student leaders face personal dangers.

What can we do?

Democracy is the essence of life; freedom is our basic human right. But we must pay for them with our lives. Can Chinese be proud of this?

We have no alternative but the hunger strike. We must strike.

We fight for life with this spirit of death.

But we remain children! Mother China, please look hard at your children.

Hunger ruthlessly destroys their youth. Are you not touched when death approaches them? . . .

Dear parents, although we suffer from hunger, don't be sad. Uncles and aunts, although we bid life farewell, don't be heartbroken. We have only one request: don't forget that we do not seek death! Democracy is not a few people's private affair, and democracy cannot be attained in one generation.

. . . Farewell moms and dads, please forgive your children who cannot be loyal to their country and act with filial piety at the same time. . . .

83

Statement of Support for the Students by Some Editors and News Reporters of CCTV

SOME EDITORS AND NEWS REPORTERS OF CCTV

May 14, 1989

Source: Mimeograph, in *Tiananmen 1989*, pp. 314–15.

Students and compatriots of all walks of life in the capital and nationwide:

We are editors and reporters at China Central TV. Since students in the capital began their petitions in mid-April, people everywhere have claimed that "CCTV stands facts on their heads." This is true. For various reasons we kept silent. As some reporters said, "We keep silent, but we all swallow our humiliation."

A few years ago, some of us were students like you, ardent and promising youths. We wanted to become news reporters, who with a clear conscience would fight for honest news. Have we become insensitive in such a short time? Has our blood become cold, too? No. Our throats have been cut. The news's essence has been stripped because the leadership was able to check [our work] at every level. As the party's mouthpiece, we know we should speak not only for the party but also for the people. When the party errs we must remind it and make it listen carefully to the voice of the people. With these hopes, we tried time and again. But we achieved nothing, and now our throats have been cut. We must admit to being propaganda tools.

On the night of May 13, when our cameramen went to the square to film the hunger strikers, students shouted, "CCTV, get out!" Hearing this broke our hearts, causing pain and shock. Any news reporter with a conscience must feel sad at being a propaganda tool. We can keep silent no longer. We firmly support the students. We strongly demand a dialogue between the students and the government. . . .

84
May 16 Statement

BA JIN, AI QING, LIU ZAIFU, AND FAN ZHENG[1]

Source: Li Qiao et al., comps., "Death or Rebirth?" in *Beijing Spring*, ed. Oksenberg, et al., Doc. 1.

The "May 16 Directive" of 1966 is universally acknowledged by the Chinese people as a symbol of autocracy and darkness. Today, twenty-three years later, we find democracy and enlightenment strongly appealing. History has finally reached a turning point. At present a patriotic democracy movement led by young students is rising across the country. Over the short period of less than a month, in one wave after another, large-scale demonstrations have swept through Beijing and other cities. . . . This is a national awakening that not only draws on the spirit of May Fourth, but also goes beyond it. It is a great historical moment that will determine the fate of China.

Since the Third Plenum of the Eleventh Party Congress [December 1978], China has embarked on a course of national revitalization. But there are problems. The weakness of political reform has affected the economic reform, when the latter has only begun to show results. The problem of corruption is getting worse, and the social contradictions are intensified. The reforms in which the people put so much hope face a grave crisis. . . .

1. We believe that in dealing with the current student movement the party and the government have not been rational enough. This is especially clear in the recent use of pressure tactics and threats of force against the students. We should draw a lesson from history. The Beijing government in 1919, the Guomindang government in the 1930s and 1940s, the Gang of Four in the late 1970s: all these dictatorial regimes used force against student movements, and in each case it led to their disgrace in the eyes of history. History tells us, "Whoever would crush the student movement is doomed." Recently the party and the government have shown a welcome increase in the use of reason, and the tension has been alleviated somewhat. If we apply principles of modern democratic governance, respect the people's will, and respond to changing times, then we will see a democratic

---

[1]The authors are four of modern China's most famous literary figures.

and stable China. If we do not, then a very hopeful China will be pushed into an abyss of genuine turmoil.

2. If we want to solve the current political crisis democratically, the first step must be to recognize the legality of the autonomous organization that consists of the democratically elected representatives of the students. Not to do so is to violate the constitutional right of freedom of assembly. To label the student organization as "illegal" can only lead to intensification of conflict and further crisis.

3. The immediate cause of the current political crisis is the corruption these young students have rightly opposed with their patriotic movement. The greatest mistake of the past ten years of reform is not the failure of education but the neglect of political reform. Totally untouched, the "official standard" and feudal privileges have infected the world of exchange, and that has led to rampant corruption. This has not only devoured the fruits of economic reform but also shaken the people's faith in the party and the government. The party and the government should take this lesson to heart and, in accordance with the people's will, immediately advance the political reform, abolish official privilege and profiteering, and guarantee that corruption will be eliminated.

4. During the student movement, the press, represented by the *People's Daily* and the New China News Agency, have concealed the truth, depriving the people of their right to know. The Shanghai Party Committee dismissed Qin Benli from his position as editor-in-chief of the *World Economic Herald*. These totally wrong measures are greatly contemptuous of the constitution. Freedom of the press is an effective tool for eliminating corruption, maintaining national stability, and promoting social development. Absolute power corrupts absolutely. If we do not implement freedom of the press and do not allow unofficial publications, then all the promises of openness and reform are nothing but empty words.

5. It is a mistake to call the student movement antiparty, antisocialist political turmoil. To recognize and protect the right of citizens to express different political opinions is the basic meaning of freedom of speech. Since Liberation, the true purpose of all the political campaigns has been to suppress and attack different political opinions. A society with only one voice is not a stable society. The party and the government must review the lessons of the "anti-Hu Feng campaign," the "anti-Rightist campaign," the "Cultural Revolution," the "anti-spiritual pollution campaign," and the "anti-bourgeois liberalization campaign." They must allow a broad expression of opinions and engage in discussion with the young students, intellectuals, and the whole people about state policy. Only then will it be possible for a genuinely stable and unified political system to take shape.

6. It is a mistake to say that there is a "small handful of long-bearded manipulators" [i.e., older intellectuals] behind the scenes. All the citizens of the People's Republic of China, regardless of their age, are politically equal. All have the political right to participate in discussion about government. Freedom, democracy, and the rule of law are not things that will someday simply be granted to the people from above. All truth-seeking, freedom-loving people must

strive to achieve what the constitution promises: freedom of thought, freedom of speech, freedom of the press, freedom of publication, freedom of association, freedom of assembly, and freedom of demonstration.

We have arrived at a historical turning point. We, the long-suffering people, cannot afford to miss this opportunity. There is no place to which to retreat.

. . .

85

Convene the Special Session of the National People's Congress and Let the People Make the Judgment: Letter to the Citizens of the Whole Country

ANONYMOUS

Mid-May 1989

Source: Handbill and/or wall poster, courtesy of HKFS.

To all citizens:

We have petitioned and held demonstrations. But what do the top decision makers and their hack government do? While our students verge on death, they stand high above the masses and ignore the students. China's people burn with worry and anxiety, but they cruelly keep silent, concealing their vicious plans.

We have petitioned, made suggestions, appealed, urged, and entreated the government. . . . We have done all we can as citizens, but what is the result? . . .

Look at Li Peng. Is it legitimate for him to be prime minister and be ulti-mately responsible for the national economy and people's livelihood? Li Peng did not get this key position because of talent, skills, or achievements. His mediocrity, weakness, and incompetence since becoming prime minister, partic-ularly in the last month, prove this. Is it legitimate for Deng Xiaoping to be the country's sole decision maker as chairman of the Military [Affairs] Commis-sion? He places himself above the party, the government, and the National People's Congress. He orders people by gesture, and all bureaucrats around him are obsequious. This proves the illegitimacy of his power. Even the party has no democracy or legality. Hu Yaobang and Zhao Ziyang were removed from office without votes by either party members or the National Party Congress, but according to the decisions of one emperor. Isn't this illegitimate? How could this illegitimate ruling clique have qualities and credibility to speak of democracy before the people?

This regime is like a rotten tree whose corrosive and poisonous elements have invaded the people's bodies and endangered the national spirit. Policy failures and difficulties occur frequently. The leaders must stop singing loudly about the "excellent situation" they have fabricated. As they talk of the country's difficulties and ask people to tighten their belts and pull through these difficulties with them, they live in luxury and dissipation, take bribes, and break the law. They give the people's wealth to powerful officials to squander, while asking the people to pay for them. . . .

They must be responsible for dereliction of duty. They must sincerely apologize to the populace. Arbitrary, dictatorial, fatuous, incompetent, complaisant, or obsequious officials must step down. Urging or entreating them is a waste of time. Our priority is immediately to exercise the people's rights and, based on constitutional law, act as the country's real masters and judge state affairs. We loudly appeal to people: Immediately convene the special session of the National People's Congress with elections based on democracy and law. Elect real public servants who, under popular, strict, and effective supervision, will observe, execute, and defend the solemn constitution. . . .

86

Letter to People's Policemen

Mid-May 1989

Source: Leaflet passed out on a Beijing Street, in *ORSD*, 2:84.

Dear people's policemen:

You have worked hard and are tired. During this great patriotic democracy movement, you have assumed the difficult task of maintaining social order and allayed student fears of attacks from the rear, allowing them to sit quietly and concentrate on petitions. Among these petitioners are your brothers and sisters. They act for no private purpose, only for the Chinese people. They strive for the democratic rights due to the entire populace, including yourselves. We all seek the same fundamental goals, and there is no conflict of interest between us. Yet due to the government's foolish attitude, several distressing clashes have recently taken place between students and police. As policemen, your duties are to obey orders and carry out assignments. We fully understand your situation and cannot ask you to stand by the people

THE HUNGER STRIKE 219

without hesitation or worries; we only hope that you act as Chinese with consciences when you fulfill your assignments and do nothing that lets down the people and your brothers and sisters. Don't fall prey to factional struggles or become government tools in crushing the students. Otherwise you will remain forever criminals condemned by the people.

"We Will Be Remembered in History"
—Slogan from photo

87

Letter to Compatriots of the Whole Country on the Current Situation

TEACHERS OF BEIJING UNIVERSITY

May 16, 1989

Source: *ORSD*, 1:90.

To all workers, peasants, PLA soldiers, intellectuals, and compatriots from all walks of life:

Since May 13, for three days and nights, several thousand Beijing college students have been holding a hunger strike in Tiananmen Square to strive for democracy and freedom. Several hundred students have already fainted and been sent to the hospital for emergency treatment. The gravity of the situation is increasing. Thus, we appeal to all compatriots nationwide:

1. From the very beginning, the student movement has been a patriotic democracy movement whose aim is democracy and freedom, punishing profiteering officials, wiping out corruption, promoting political and economic reform, and holding a dialogue with the government on these issues. However, the government's nonchalant attitude forced the students to hold a hunger strike. Beijing intellectuals and citizens have already demonstrated in support of the students. Compatriots nationwide must use all legal means to give the students moral and concrete support.

2. The source of the present situation is the government's carefree attitude toward the students and its unwillingness to openly and sincerely talk with them. . . .

3. Rarely in Chinese or world history have so many tens of thousands of

students held hunger strikes or boycotted class. Their unified actions represent the people's will. Their brave actions and sacrifices have remolded the national spirit. We call on all Chinese with a conscience to abandon selfish considerations and act immediately to save our students, to save our good, honest, and brave children.

"Sacrifice Ourselves to Rejuvenate the National Spirit"
—Slogan from photo

88

Letter to Overseas Chinese and All Concerned People Worldwide

LIU XIAOBO

May 17, 1989

Source: Letter written in Tiananmen Square, in *ORSD*, 1:14.

Ladies and gentlemen:

More than a month ago, in April 1989, the students' patriotic democracy movement began. It has now reached its most difficult and yet promising point. The hunger strike has been underway for over one hundred hours, and more than six hundred students (note: now more than two thousand) have been hospitalized for emergency treatment. If the government delays further in publicly responding to the students' demands, the hunger strike will continue indefinitely, with irretrievable losses to the students and the country.

I sincerely appeal to overseas Chinese and all foreigners who care about China to donate money to the hunger strikers. I appeal to the Chinese government to respond with humanity to the students' minimum demands as soon as possible:

1. Correct the wrong judgment of the student movement made by the *People's Daily* editorial of April 26, 1989.

2. Hold an open, direct, independent, and sincere dialogue with the students' delegation as soon as possible. . . .

As a young teacher in the department of Chinese language and literature, a Ph.D. in literature, and a citizen who enjoys the same political rights as the college students,[1] I have spent four days and nights with the hunger strikers. From both a political and a humanitarian perspective, their behavior has been consistent with the Constitution of the People's Republic of China, and with the Human Rights Declaration of the United Nations. . . .

"Our Workers Have the Strength"
—Slogan from photo

89

Letter to Compatriots of the Nation

BEIJING WORKERS' UNION

May 17, 1989

Source: *ORSD*, 1:28.

The lawlessness and brutality of corrupt officials has become extreme. Even in the vastness of mainland China there is no place for truth! But no reactionary force can stop the tide of the people's anger; they will never again fall prey to the government's lies, for the words on our flag are science, democracy, freedom, human rights, and legalism.

On April 21, 1989, the Beijing Workers' Union was established to protect workers' rights. That day we published two documents: "A Letter to People of the Entire City" [Doc. 18] and "Ten Questions" [Doc. 19]. The April 26 *People's Daily* editorial falsely declared these two documents reactionary. Since you dare not answer our ten questions in your paper, would you please publish our two documents? Or are you cowards? For forty years didn't you shout, "Believe in the people!"? We solemnly demand that the April 26 editorial be rejected entirely and its author and hidden supporter be seriously punished.

---

[1]Mr. Liu was a visiting scholar at Columbia University in New York. When the movement began, he returned to China to join the movement. On June 2, he was one of four intellectuals who began a hunger strike at the base of the Monument to the People's Heroes in Tiananmen. He also was deeply involved in negotiating with the army to let the students march out of the square on the morning of June 4. His contacts with dissidents in New York figure prominently in Beijing Mayor Chen Xitong's contention in his June 30 report that foreigners were deeply involved in the movement.

We have investigated workers' oppression using Marx's analytical framework from *Das Kapital*. After deducting workers' wages, welfare, medical costs, social accumulation, capital depreciation, and reinvestment funds from the total output, we astonishingly discover that China's "public servants" swallow the remaining assets drawn from the people's sweat and blood. The sum consumed [by them] is vast. So cruel, but typically Chinese. The people's servants use the people's hard-earned money to build deluxe villas nationwide (guarded by soldiers and called "closed military areas"), buy deluxe foreign sedans, and travel to foreign countries (called study tours, but including their children and nannies! Male officials womanize and women officials do the same . . .). Their shameful criminal acts are too numerous to count.

Concerning its impact on the country and people's welfare, Comrade Fang Lizhi's view on "how to attract foreign investments" is accurate.[1] We support it because these foreign investments, as in past years, will "legally" (through official corruption) become private property. The country is the victim; beneficiaries are "a small group";[2] the debt payers are the people.

We strongly protest forcing people to buy government bonds. We demand that the government publish the total income and expenditures of these bonds (including the purpose for which they were used); immediately repay the capital and interest on these bonds to the people who hold them; and close the bond market—a major market for official business and the root of much official corruption! We repeat: Increase salaries, stabilize prices, and end the system where two generations (or even three) get the same wage; investigate high officials in the Central Committee, the Central Advisory Commission, and various ministers in the State Council and the Central Military Commission.

The first group to be investigated is those who have deluxe villas, like Deng Xiaoping, Zhao Ziyang, Li Peng, Chen Yun, Li Xiannian, Yang Shangkun, Peng Zhen, Wan Li, Jiang Zemin, Ye Xuanping, and their family members.[3] Immediately confiscate their total property. The investigation should be carried out by an "All-People's Investigation Team" with the results immediately publicized to the people.

University students have matured; the good discipline maintained by the

---

[1]Fang reminded foreigners to consider China's poor human rights record when deciding whether to invest in China. See *Asian Wall Street Journal*, April 25, 1989.

[2]This reference to a "small group" mocks the fact that the CCP always blames social unrest on a "small group" of counterrevolutionaries.

[3]Zhao Ziyang's inability to rein in the corrupt activities of his two sons, particularly one who reportedly made a fortune in Hainan Island, hurt his popularity with many Chinese. Note also that even before he became general secretary of the CCP, Jiang Zemin, then mayor of Shanghai, was criticized for corruption. Finally, Ye Xuanping was governor of Guangdong and the son of Ye Jianying, China's most important military leader since the fall of Lin Biao in 1971. He played a critical role in arresting the Gang of Four in 1976 and returning Deng to power in 1978.

millions of people in Tiananmen Square proves it. The people have awoken. They understand that in every society or historical period, there are only two classes, the rulers and the ruled. Those classes, parties, social groups, and individuals who follow historical tides are progressive and revolutionary; the opponents are regressive and reactionary. This is why Chinese people, who since the Qin emperor have lived in a society governed by the rule of man, have always loved, needed, praised, and cherished "upright officials." Forty years of political campaigns have been an important weapon for oppressing the people, and history shows that they like to "settle accounts after the fall," but history in the end cannot be changed.[4]

We particularly must guard against political careerists in the Central Committee who would use this democratic movement for their own goal of taking power.[5] Deng Xiaoping really used the popular movement of April 5, 1976,[6] to return to power, but soon after he showed his evil intentions. The "achievements of reform" that they trumpet are false and superficial. Most people's living standards have declined, and the people will still have to repay a heavy foreign debt.

Fellow workers, rally around the Workers' Union. Under its direction we will push the democratic movement to new heights. The union has decided to march to Tiananmen Square at 2:00 P.M., May 22, to present a peaceful petition in support of the students' movement. The slogan of the march is "Even in the vastness of mainland China there is no place for truth!"

---

[4]Literally this statement means to "settle accounts after the autumn harvest," because only after the state knew what the harvest would be could it decide what actions to take. But it also means "take vengeance when the time is ripe." This is also the subtitle of Asia Watch's report on post-Tiananmen China, *Punishment Season: Human Rights in China after Martial Law* (New York: Asia Watch, 1990).

[5]This refers to Li Peng and the leadership of Beijing Municipality. Reports from China suggest that Deng was aware of this problem—that some people tried to use this movement to their own advantage—so Li Peng, Chen Xitong, and Li Ximing (first secretary of Beijing) were not promoted after the crackdown.

[6]This refers to the political movement in late March and early April 1976, following Zhou Enlai's death. Hundreds of thousands of Beijing citizens brought wreaths to Tiananmen to honor Zhou, attack the "Gang of Four," and support Deng Xiaoping, whose political career was in trouble. But after the Beijing militia forcibly cleared the square on April 5, Deng was accused of organizing a counterrevolutionary movement and purged from all party posts. In 1978, when he was rehabilitated, he overturned this verdict.

90

Who Owes Whom a Debt of Gratitude?

PROPAGANDA GROUP OF CHINESE UNIVERSITY OF POLITICAL
SCIENCE AND LAW

May 17, 1989

Source: *Tiananmen 1989*, p. 249.

This morning, the radio broadcast Zhao Ziyang's speech made on behalf of the
Politburo, in which he affirms that "The party and government will never settle
accounts with the students later." What tolerance and magnanimity! What a
good, kind feeling! We should be moved to tears by this.

Yet we must ask one question. Who owes whom a debt of gratitude? For the
people's prosperity, the nation's strength, democratization, and the party Central
Committee's positive evaluation of the student movement, thousands of students
already neither eat nor drink. Their actions have won understanding, sympathy,
and support from people of all social strata and all walks of life. Yet our party's
leader says only that he "won't settle accounts in the fall" or compel students to
"repay debts."

We may ask: Is such a tone what people want? Can such a tone express most
party members' feelings? . . . If we want to talk about "settling accounts" and
"paying debts," it is the concocters of the *People's Daily* editorial who owe the
students and people a debt, because they have hurt their feelings. Their nonchalant, heartless attitude has endangered many young lives. If they refuse to apologize to the people right now, the students and people have the right to square
accounts with them—not later, but now. . . .

91

May 17 Declaration

YAN JIAQI, BAO ZUNXIN, LI NANYOU ET AL.

May 17, 1989

Source: *Tiananmen 1989*, p. 325.

Since 2:00 P.M. on May 13, and for nearly one hundred hours, approximately three thousand students have been on a hunger strike in Tiananmen Square. More than seven hundred have already fainted. This is an unprecedented tragedy in our motherland's history. Our fellow students asked that the April 26 *People's Daily* editorial be overturned; they asked for a live broadcast of their dialogue with the government. Before our very eyes, our motherland's children pass out one after another, while the students' just demands are ignored day after day. So the hunger strike cannot stop. Our country's problem is exposed worldwide—the autocrat has unlimited power, and the government has forsaken its responsibilities and humanity. This irresponsible and inhumane government belongs not to the republic but to the autocrat.

The Qing dynasty collapsed seventy-six years ago; yet China still has an emperor without a crown, an aged and muddle-headed autocrat. Yesterday afternoon, party General Secretary Zhao Ziyang announced that every important policy decision in China must be approved by this senile autocrat. Only his words can overturn the April 26 *People's Daily* editorial. While students use this hundred-hour hunger strike to fight, China's people cannot wait for the autocrat to admit his mistake. We can rely only on the students and the people themselves. Today we declare to the whole country and the whole world: the students' hundred-hour hunger strike has been victorious. Their actions declare that this movement is not chaos but is a patriotic democratic movement to bury China's last autocrat and last imperial regime.

Let's shout: Victory for hunger strikers! Long live the spirit of nonviolent protest!

Down with autocracy! Autocrats cannot escape punishment!

Away with the April 26 editorial!

Gerontocratic politics must end!

Autocrats must resign! . . .

92

Urgent Announcement about May 17 Demonstration

GENERAL HEADQUARTERS OF THE DEMONSTRATION

May 17, 1989

Source: Mimeograph, in *Tiananmen 1989*, p. 293.

To consolidate and defend this great student movement's achievements and ensure that today's demonstration goes well, we announce the following points to be observed during the demonstration:

1. Extremist slogans that violate the constitution are strictly forbidden.
2. Violence and illegal actions are strictly forbidden.
3. Assaults on government institutions, stores, and public facilities are strictly forbidden.
4. Entry into downtown commercial districts, such as Wangfujing, Xidan, and Qianmen, is strictly forbidden.
5. All groups participating in the demonstration must organize their own pickets.
6. All people must guard against trouble-makers and saboteurs with ulterior motives.
7. The demonstration will proceed along the Second Ring Road, and people should join the demonstration at a nearby location.

The prime task of the teachers and students of all the colleges and universities is to make sure the demonstration proceeds smoothly.

93

A Sketch of the Chinese Communist Party

ANONYMOUS

Mid-May 1989

Source: Big-character poster, People's University, in *ORSD*, 1:55.

The party leaders: dominators of the party.[1]
Individual worship, a movement to make them into gods, and the influence of traditional culture on the masses have contributed to the alienation of these leaders who consider themselves the gods of the people. Their egocentricism and autocracy have made them dictators of the people.

The party cadres: humble servants of the party dominators, patriarchs of the people, and newly emerged arrogant nouveau riche. They demand that the people be subservient to them. They gain personal privileges by abusing their power and violating the law.

The party organization: a gangster organization dominated by patriarchalism and constant factional struggles. Anyone pro[party] is allowed to live, while anyone anti[party] is dead.

The quality of the party: 75 percent of the forty-seven million "vanguards" [party members] have only received an elementary school education.

Loyalty to the party: subservience and blind faith as a result of [intellectual] castration and loss of the ability to have any independent thought.[2]

Party membership: A party card offers the transactional power of personal relationships with functional and social value. [It] is a symbol of one's progressiveness, as well as a short-cut for achieving one's self-interest. "Joining the party" has created a whole bunch of schizophrenic hypocrites who end up with

---

[1]The original text uses numerous idioms composed of four Chinese characters.
[2]The use of sexual terminology in Chinese political discourse and literary works increased dramatically after 1978. Liu Xiaobo's Ph.D. graduation paper given at Beijing Normal University, for instance, described Chinese contemporary literary works as "impotent." The book *Yiban shi nanren; yiban shi nuren* (Half of woman is man), by Zhang Xianliang, also contained explicit descriptions of sexual impotence that some readers considered a metaphor on sexual repression in Chinese society. Strong undertones of sexual liberation were evident in Tiananmen Square where banners depicting cave-like naked men and slogans comparing Chinese politics to bikinis (namely, that the "three areas" covered by the swim suit were comparable to the party's slogan of "one guiding line and two cardinal points") adorned the hunger-strike areas.

extremely different personalities after becoming party members. "Joining the party" has seriously distorted the mental state of the people in China and has destroyed their personalities.

The will, interest, and principles of the party: irrefutable, sacred orders, and hollow dogmas according to which the party leader could instigate the "Cultural Revolution" and the "rectification campaigns" that have seriously endangered the survival of the nation and caused the suffering and death of many people. With the disguise of those orders and in the name of the "holy" banner, the [party] cadres are involved in tricking the people and making dirty deals.

The party's four-izations (derived from the word "modern-ization"): the idolization of the party image; the absoluteness of the party's function; the party's monopoly of authority; the corruption of party cadres.

The party: the omnipotent "leviathan" and the almighty god both in heaven and on earth. The party leaders give orders to generate the machine, and the cadres and the party members act as cogs and screws. What a great number of (Chinese) elites have been strangled to death by this machine!

The "grandeur" of the party: "She can correct her own mistakes!"

Blood can clean up the shame of the authorities; it can nurture a generation of genuine Communists; but it can also breed nouveaux riches and dictators!

94

A Million Beijing Residents Demonstrate in Support of the Students and Demand that Deng Xiaoping Step Down

EDITORIAL BOARD OF *XINWEN DAOBAO*

May 17, 1989

Source: *Xinwen daobao* (News herald), May 18, 1989, courtesy of Robin Munro.

On May 17, hundreds of thousands of the capital's residents demonstrated in support of the students. They used various expressions to demand that Deng Xiaoping step down. Although as early as April 15, big and small posters at several universities had already directly criticized Deng Xiaoping, this was the first time city residents widely expressed their forceful aversion to Deng.

People uninhibitedly shouted this head of state's name. One fat woman led workers in shouting: "Xiaoping, Xiaoping, is over eighty. His body's OK, but not his mind. . . ."

Many demonstrators have, without consultation, held up banners with calligraphy saying: "Holding court from behind a screen."[1] A group of people from the Youth Film Studio added a sentence: "While holding court from behind a screen, he brought calamity to the country and people." People from the Chinese Encyclopedia Press demand: "Remove the screen and give back the court. . . ."

Many posters refer to him, but they no longer ask: "Xiaoping, how are you?" Atop one truck a poster reads: "One man retires and the nation feels honored."[2] A group from China Central TV holds a banner with the antithetical couplet: "One man cannot hoodwink the public; millions of people send off the 'god of diseases'."[3] The poster from Factory 503 of the Ministry of Aviation and Aerospace reads: "Retire and enjoy life. . . ."

In the evening, as groups of workers from the Railway Ministry and construction workers pass through Tiananmen Square, a worker carries aloft a certificate of "glorious retirement" which catches the attention of everyone in the square. On the certificate in ink are the names of Deng Xiaoping, Zhao Ziyang, and Li Peng. . . .

One worker told a reporter, "He is too old." This probably refers not just to Deng's age, but Deng's age is clearly an issue of interest for many people. One banner humorously reads: "Friendly competition between China and the Soviet Union—Score: 85 to 58. China holds a temporary lead." This scroll tells people the exact age of [Deng Xiaoping and China's] visitor, Gorbachev.

Deng was once a leader held in high esteem, so his skill at bridge, like Zhao Ziyang's at golf, were both topics journalists loved to discuss. Unfortunately, after General Secretary Zhao's hobby of playing golf was criticized, Chairman Deng's hobby was also raised. Students from Qinghua University shouted, "Step down and go play bridge."

Residents also insisted that Li Peng resign, with many yelling: "Li Peng, step down." This reporter finds many similar banners in different groups with the words: "Wanted—Prime Minister." "Prime Minister—where are you?" "Prime Minister Zhou Enlai, where are you?" In front of one group was a big portrait of Zhou Enlai. People expressed their anger over Li Peng's reluctance to come out and talk with the students. They expressed dissatisfaction with Li Peng by

---

[1]This reflects the constant comparison of Deng Xiaoping to the Dowager Empress Ci Xi, who ruled China for the latter part of the nineteenth century as the invisible power behind her emperor son.

[2]Because of the respect for old age in Chinese society, retirement is seen as the pinnacle of one's contribution to society.

[3]This couplet plays on a poem Mao wrote to honor a village that eliminated schistosomiasis in the 1950s. In this poem, Mao refers to the villagers sending off this "god of disease." Here the demonstrators are "sending off" Deng Xiaoping, who has become the source of the problems "plaguing" China.

mourning Prime Minister Zhou Enlai. The relationship between Li Peng and Zhou Enlai is not just that they were both prime ministers at different times, but that Li Peng is Zhou's adopted son. In contrast, attitudes toward Zhao Ziyang were more moderate. . . .

In addition to demonstrators from colleges and universities in the capital and other provinces, people from the media, hospitals and medical institutions, democratic parties, religious circles, scientific research institutes, and law firms, there are also many groups of workers, high school students, private businessmen, and people from financial circles. Most noticeable are the groups of people from the Capital Iron and Steel Plant, Central Radio and China Central TV, the Party School of the Beijing Party Committee, the Ministry of Public Security, the United Front Department of the Central Committee, workers from Kunming Municipality, unemployed youths with criminal records, peasants, noncommissioned PLA officers, China's National Men's Volleyball Team, deaf workers of Shanlu Factory, Christians, and about one hundred Buddhist monks wearing patchwork outer garments.

95

Proposal for Quitting the Communist Youth League

SOME COMMUNIST YOUTH LEAGUE MEMBERS

May 18, 1989

Source: Big-character poster at Beijing University, in *ORSD*, 1:62.

Given the corruption in the Communist party and the despair its actions have caused the people during this student movement, we, as members of the preparatory ranks of the Communist party—the Communist Youth League—suggest that all members of the Beijing University Communist Youth League, possessing reason and conscience, give up all hope and quit the league to express our new awareness, our true intentions, our support for the student hunger strikers, and our opposition to the government's inhuman silence.

96

Deng Xiaoping Should Admit Mistakes:
Open Letter to the CCP

A CHINESE COMMUNIST PARTY MEMBER

May 18, 1989

Source: Big-character poster at Beijing University, in *ORSD*, 1:59.

To the Central Committee and all comrades in the party.

The students face peril! The situation is perilous! The country faces peril!

Yet the Politburo and the State Council still evade the student hunger strikers' reasonable requests, thereby intensifying the contradiction and its dreadful consequences.

As party members we are terribly anxious and appeal to Comrade Deng Xiaoping openly to admit his mistake and acknowledge that labeling the student movement as "turmoil" on April 25 was a total error of judgment. According to the party constitution, Deng, who is neither the general secretary nor a member of the Politburo's Standing Committee, has no decision-making authority. The April 25 speech, which was directly proclaimed to the entire party as his personal order, seriously violates organizational principles. This imperious behavior makes all claims of inner-party democracy into rhetoric. We hope Comrade Deng Xiaoping will treasure his past and, for the greater good, review his mistakes and solve this problem. Don't let one mistake negate all your past glories.

We hope the Politburo will find its party essence, conscience, and courage, follow the people's and the party's will, implement truly collective decision making, immediately and unequivocally acknowledge this patriotic, democratic student movement, face up to and comply with the well-grounded demands of the students (and the people), and, without delay, push forward the democratization of the motherland and the establishment of a legal system.

History has given us few chances. The Central Committee and the entire party must act instantly and choose wisely for our suffering race.

97

Most Believe the Student Movement Is a Patriotic Democracy Movement: Public Opinion Poll Conducted by *Beijing Youth News*

May 18, 1989

Source: *Beijing qingnian bao* (Beijing youth news), May 18, 1989, in *Tiananmen 1989*, pp. 300–301.

On May 17, about a million Beijing residents joined street demonstrations supporting the student hunger strikers. This paper's editorial board immediately conducted a public opinion poll. Even before the ink was dry, 500 questionnaires were distributed between 11:00 A.M. and 12:00 P.M. among residents in Tiananmen Square. Respondents included workers, office workers and cadres, intellectuals, and private businessmen. According to the 423 questionnaires returned, more than 95 percent of respondents believe that the student movement is a patriotic democracy movement. More than 80 percent think that today's large demonstration will force the government to make some concessions and promote the democratic process.[1] The following are response figures to some questions on the questionnaire:

1. You believe the student movement is:
   a. a patriotic democracy movement (387)
   b. student trouble-making (3)
   c. turmoil (0)
   d. don't know (0)

2. Your attitude toward the hunger strike by the students:
   a. supportive (277)
   b. understanding (193)
   c. cannot understand (17)
   d. don't care (0)

---

[1]This survey is important because it shows that most Beijing residents actually believed they could defeat the government and force it to negotiate with the students, while at the same time never thinking that the government would use force. Herein lies one source of the tragedy that unfolded.

3. During this movement, you have:[2]
a. participated in the marches (262)
b. made donations (240)
c. cheered and supported the students in your heart (240)
d. not participated (5)

4. Who do you believe should come out to have a dialogue with the students?
a. Deng Xiaoping (241)
b. Zhao Ziyang (248)
c. Li Peng (257)

5. What will be the result of the hunger strike and demonstrations?
a. the government will agree to the students' demands (280)
b. a compromise by both sides (48)
c. a government crackdown (7)
d. national turmoil (11)
e. don't know (46)

---

[2]In this case the total number can be more than the number of respondents because people could participate in more than just one way.

V

May 19–June 3
Sliding Toward Tragedy:
Martial Law

Kathleen Hartford

Around midnight on May 19–20, the government-controlled loudspeakers on Tiananmen Square suddenly crackled into life, and a deep voice boomed across the expanse where students were camped waiting for something to happen after several tense hours of reports about tens of thousands of troops moving into the city.[1] After listening for a few moments, the crowd roared into life with a spontaneous and angry chant: "Li Peng, step down!" (*Li Peng, xiatai*). The remainder of Premier Li Peng's speech calling for an end to the occupation of the Square was drowned out by the chant taken up by tens of thousands of voices.[2] Not until the next day did the government declare the imposition of martial law in Beijing,[3] but the battle lines were drawn that night. For the next two weeks, the

---

[1]Some of the information in this introduction is taken from interviews and conversations with participants or firsthand observers, both Chinese and Western, who must remain anonymous. Aside from interviews conducted individually, I have also relied on an interview conducted at Harvard University on July 13, 1989, by the China Scholars Coordinating Committee (CSCC) with a Chinese participant who occupied middle-level leadership positions in the Tiananmen student movement. I also gratefully acknowledge the help rendered by Steven Chang, who filled in much background information based on his on-the-spot observations.

[2]For the text of the speech, see Oksenberg et al., eds., *Beijing Spring*, Doc. 46, or Yi Mu and Mark Thompson, *Crisis at Tiananmen: Reform and Reality in Modern China* (San Francisco: China Books and Periodicals, 1990), pp. 176–80.

[3]The martial law declaration specified "some districts of Beijing" in order to get around a constitutional provision that would have required approval by the National People's Congress. All the urban portions of Beijing Municipality, however, were covered by the martial law decree.

world witnessed yet another in the succession of incredible spectacles in the popular movement, as all the regime's steps short of massive violence failed to reassert its control over the capital, while the popular antipathy toward Li Peng and the aging but still dominant Deng Xiaoping coalesced in demands for their removal.

The Flow of Events

By May 19, everyone was expecting something momentous to happen. In the early hours of that Friday morning, both Zhao Ziyang and Li Peng had appeared at the hunger strikers' camp. Li departed after mumbling a few words, but Zhao stayed to talk with the students for about twenty minutes, addressing them through a bullhorn and then autographing books and T-shirts passed to him.[4] Probably most of the students did not realize at the time the significance of his words, "We have come too late." For Zhao already knew that those who favored conciliation had lost. By mid-day on the 19th, most of those connected with Central Committee and State Council organs knew that the decision for martial law had been made.[5] The word spread beyond strictly official circles; that afternoon, several leading intellectuals met in a hush-hush conference with the student leaders, and by that evening many of the student leaders probably knew martial law was coming, although the general body of students may not have.[6] All knew that massive concentrations of troops were ringing the city. Many certainly knew that Zhao was now out of the picture, for this was revealed, along with other privileged information, by cadres in units working for him (Doc. 101). Until then, students had been uncertain whether Zhao was good or bad; even when he first appeared at the hunger strikers' bus, some insults had been thrown at him. Only his fall persuaded them to support him, and by then it was indeed too late.

Knowing before Li Peng's speech that the government would not entertain any conciliating measures, student leaders began debating whether to call off the hunger strike. It was obvious that continuing would not elicit dialogue or compromise, but some students preferred martyrdom to practicality. The argument

---

[4]The text of some of his remarks may be found in Yi and Thompson, *Crisis at Tiananmen*, pp. 180–82.

[5]See Jiang Zhifeng, *Countdown to Tiananmen*, pp. 209–10.

[6]CSCC interview, July 13, 1989. The interviewee said that students knew by that afternoon that martial law would be declared the next day. Chai Ling, in a June 2 interview with Philip Cunningham, stated that the student leaders "did not anticipate the decision of Li Peng to suppress us" when they ended the hunger strike. (My thanks to Philip Cunningham for supplying an English transcript of this interview.) Memories may err even after a short time as to the details of events, and different groups of student leaders may have had different information. In addition, those like Chai Ling who had been fasting for a week were not likely to be as keyed into events and details as those who had not been on hunger strike.

lasted hours and was ferocious at times, but finally at around 9:30 P.M., the student broadcasting station announced Zhao's resignation and the end of the hunger strike, and called for a general strike to begin on the 20th.[7] Attention now turned to meeting the challenge of the troops moving on Beijing.

Popular attention shifted from support of hunger strikers to defense of Beijing against the martial law troops. For several nights running, the Beijing citizenry poured into the streets to persuade the army away. They set up roadblocks and barricades on the major routes into the city. They lay on the road in front of trucks bearing troops, let air out of the tires when troop carriers stopped, and pressed food and pleas upon the young and largely bewildered soldiers, urging them not to harm the students, telling them what the movement was all about (docs. 115, 137). Student marshals made sure that order was maintained and peaceful means used. The trucks turned back, many of them bearing weeping soldiers out of the city. The main body of troops, which had increased to some 300,000, was withdrawn from the outskirts of Beijing, a move that was taken by the less sophisticated public as indication of a popular victory. Troops had, however, been successfully moved into the offices of the Central Broadcasting Station, *People's Daily*, New China News Agency, and other major news organizations, permitting the gradual reimposition of propaganda controls. Foreign television's satellite links out of China were cut.

From May 20 to 23, popular morale was at a peak, largely from the euphoria over having repulsed the army's efforts to enter Beijing. Mass marches in cities throughout China demonstrated the breadth of popular opposition to martial law in Beijing. From May 21 to May 23, huge marches took place in Beijing (a million or more participated on May 21, and several hundred thousand on May 23) and other cities. Wildcat strikes by workers took place in Beijing, Wuhan, and other scattered locales. A clash between armed police and residents in the southwestern Beijing suburb of Fengtai on May 23 resulted in serious injuries to about forty persons.

The period from May 24 to May 27 provided a breather of sorts to both the populace and the regime. New autonomous associations of intellectuals and others were formed, and the embryonic Beijing Workers' Autonomous Union began churning out propaganda in support of the students. As others organized, the students' organization on the square began to shift and erode. More students from outside the city poured in, and the original core of leadership from Beijing universities began to fragment over strategy, with some favoring a withdrawal from the square and others arguing to remain until the government had acceded to all their demands. The breather afforded some opportunity for reflections on

---

[7]CSCC interview, July 13, 1989; Simmie and Nixon, *Tiananmen Square*, p. 127. Later that same night some of the students tried to muster a hunger strike by 100,000 people but gave it up before daybreak.

the shortcomings of the movement, which came from both students and older intellectuals.

Meanwhile, Deng Xiaoping, who was rumored to have gone to Wuhan for a series of meetings gathering the support of regional civilian and military leaders in a manner reminiscent of Mao's old tactics, apparently returned to Beijing on May 24 ready for action and began working out plans for armed suppression of the popular movement.[8] The hope that the party and army establishment would resist the imposition of martial law in Beijing had to give way before the train of events. Already on May 22, a Politburo meeting had prepared a set of accusations against Zhao Ziyang, who had dropped out of sight after his visit to the students' Tiananmen encampment in the early morning of May 19. Some of his closer associates were also accused of "antiparty" activities. On May 24, Wan Li, chairman of the NPC Standing Committee, who had been on a visit to Canada and the United States, arrived in Shanghai; but instead of proceeding to Beijing to convene a special session of the NPC and repudiate martial law, as many had hoped, he was immediately spirited off to a hospital. In a May 27 television broadcast, he announced his support of the martial law declaration.

The people's faith that military commanders would refuse to support martial law also faded in the face of the facts. Initially some of the country's major veteran army commanders had denounced the idea of forcible suppression of the students and urged that the army not force its way into Beijing (Doc. 132). But Deng, with the help of Yang Shangkun, recovered quickly. By May 26, some had repudiated their previous opposition, and all the military region commanders had gone on record in support of martial law.

From May 28 to June 3, the student presence in Tiananmen Square subsided considerably, with only about ten thousand remaining there as of May 29. The new leadership of the student organizations cast about for a way to regain the initiative. Some argued for a "long march" of students to propagandize their cause outside Beijing; others declared their intention to remain in the square until the NPC's Standing Committee session convened on June 20. Temporarily, some new excitement was generated by the erection on the night of May 29 of a statue of the "Goddess of Democracy." Enthusiasm was revived by the initiation of a limited-term hunger strike by the popular Taiwan music star Hou Dejian and three other prominent figures on June 2.

Tensions within Beijing mounted during the last few days of this period as the government stepped up military and police pressure. Three leaders of the Beijing Workers' Autonomous Union (BWAU) and several members of the "Flying Tigers" motorcycle corps (which had carried messages and bulletins on events from the city outskirts to the student command center in Tiananmen Square) were arrested. Government-sponsored demonstrations against "turmoil" took place in the Beijing suburbs on May 31 and June 1 and 2. Troops in plainclothes

---

[8]Jiang, *Countdown to Tiananmen*, pp. 243–44.

were intercepted trying to move into the square on June 2. Their weapons were confiscated by student marshals; these were placed on exhibition in a bus that was driven around the city (to publicize the government's provocations) before being parked in Tiananmen Square as a display.[9] Tens of thousands of unarmed troops were marched toward Tiananmen on June 3 but were stopped at various points by citizens and students. Several thousand troops and armed police entered the square via Zhongnanhai, tear-gassed part of the crowd, and began clubbing civilians. A few hundred troops ran out through another gate, beating up more civilians. Several thousand more armed police exited from the Great Hall of the People that afternoon, attempting to link up with the others to fragment the crowd, but they were foiled by the citizenry.[10]

The final thrust began with armed troops that night. Beginning at around 6:00 P.M., the media and loudspeakers throughout the city repeatedly broadcast emergency orders for all citizens to stay off the streets and out of the square. A last core of about five thousand students, forlorn and frightened, but determined, remained huddled on the square around the Monument to the People's Heroes. At 10:00 P.M. the troops began to move, and the slaughter began.

Why the tragedy? At first, most of the advantages seemed to rest on the movement's side. Not only did the citizens of Beijing successfully block the army's entry, but the range of participants and intensity of participation grew in Beijing and throughout China. Groups other than students constituted themselves as formal organizations, formulated demands, and issued manifestoes, while prominent military and civilian leaders deplored martial law and pleaded for a peaceful settlement. Many outside observers, and—as the documents in this section reveal—some in China, thought that "people power" really had defeated the hardliners. But while an apparent standoff continued on the surface, the government's waiting game paid off. The popular movement, particularly its student core, began to founder on organizational conflicts, lack of strategic vision or political analysis, and inability or unwillingness to move either forward or back. Meanwhile, the forces favoring suppression of the movement, which had initially appeared isolated and outnumbered even at the top, soon began gathering momentum, especially once the intervention of Deng Xiaoping and other semiretired revolutionary veterans tipped the scales.

Participation Expands

During the Tiananmen hunger strike, cities throughout China had seen sympathy demonstrations and hunger strikes. The declaration of martial law, however, prompted not only nationwide but worldwide demonstrations, along with strikes and more violent actions in some Chinese cities.

---

[9]CSCC interview, July 13, 1989.
[10]Liu Binyan, with Ruan Ming and Xu Gang, *"Tell the World": What Happened in China and Why* (New York: Pantheon 1989), pp. 57–58.

From May 20 to 23, numerous sympathy demonstrations were held in Xi'an, Shanghai, Nanjing, Kunming, Tianjin, Hangzhou, Wuhan, Guanzhou, and many smaller cities. Later demonstrations occasionally drew large contingents of marchers. In Tianjin, an "intellectuals' demonstration" on May 25 drew so much support from other citizens that a turnout of several hundred thousand, maybe even a million, was estimated. Hangzhou saw a large demonstration on May 26. For May 28, the Beijing students had appealed to Chinese around the world to demonstrate (Doc. 166), and the appeal was answered with action. Besides marches drawing around 100,000 each in both Beijing and Shanghai, demonstrations were also held in Taiwan, Hong Kong, Australia, and the United States. The Hong Kong demonstration drew 300,000 participants.[11] As overseas Chinese attention focused on the crisis in China, the potential impact on the chances of China's reunification with Taiwan and Hong Kong did not go overlooked by either side (Doc. 161).[12] Demonstrations in some cities persisted, although drawing fewer participants, right up until June 4.

Students from many of the provincial cities decided to go to Beijing to support the sit-in there, and although the Beijing authorities tried to block their entry, many got through. A large contingent came from Tianjin, where students had set off for Beijing by bicycle early on May 21.[13] By late May, thousands of students from colleges and universities throughout China were camping in Tiananmen Square.

Demonstrations and sit-ins were no longer the only form of participation: wildcat strikes in some urban centers caused considerable disquiet among officials. In Hangzhou, posters had appeared on May 20 calling for a general strike to oppose the martial law declaration in Beijing. Later, as troops and supplies were being moved toward Beijing from all over the country, students and workers disrupted rail traffic. The popular reaction in Wuhan was especially intense, so much so that "martial law–type restrictions" were imposed on May 22. Unfortunately we know far too little about events in most locales outside of Beijing; aside from accounts of a few Western scholars, students, and business people who happened to be on the scene in such places, and whose opportunities for observation were relatively limited, most information on those events comes from reports of arrests after the crackdown.[14]

What is apparent even from this scattered information, and the much better documented events in Beijing, is that by late May, students were not the only

---

[11]*The New York Times*, May 29, 1989, p. 1.
[12]For a discussion of the priority accorded the Taiwan and Hong Kong questions by Deng himself, see Jiang, *Countdown to Tiananmen*, pp. 263–66.
[13]Josephine Fox, "The Movement for Democracy and Its Consequences in Tianjin," *The Australian Journal of Chinese Affairs*, no. 23 (January 1990): 140.
[14]For a good collection of Western accounts from various parts of China, see the July 1990 issue of *The Australian Journal of Chinese Affairs*. On the arrests, see Asia Watch, *Punishment Season*, pp. 83–150.

organized group calling for change. Once martial law was declared, more and more groups got actively involved and began organizing themselves as "autonomous" (i.e., outside of government control) "federations" or "unions."

Beijing workers were the first. Han Dongfang, a railway worker, and a small group of other workers set up a tent on the northwestern edge of Tiananmen Square and declared the official formation of the Beijing Workers' Autonomous Union (BWAU) on May 19 (a loose group had been active for some time). Their activities during this period, like those in the previous periods, were initially oriented only toward supporting the student protest. The BWAU's inaugural declaration called for a one-day general strike if the Politburo failed to accept the students' demands by May 20 (Doc. 100). According to Asia Watch, the BWAU's "small broadcasting system" in the square "nightly transmitted items of news, commentary, and political analysis which attracted audiences of several thousands, sometimes until dawn."[15] Eventually, however, the BWAU began calling on workers to organize to pursue their own interests, in Beijing and nationwide (docs. 116, 145). Workers in some Beijing enterprises began to form their own autonomous unions as well; one example is the Construction Workers' Autonomous Union, which declared its existence on May 21 (Doc. 119).

Before the declaration of martial law, students had been leery of direct involvement by others, particularly workers, in their movement for fear of rendering themselves vulnerable to government charges of conspiracy. Once martial law was declared, there was little to lose, and much to gain, from encouraging cooperation between students and workers. Students appealed to workers not to be coopted by the government into actions that would split the movement (Doc. 130). But students also invoked the model of both Polish Solidarity and the joint student-worker campaign to block the Yangzi River Bridge in Wuhan, in exhorting workers to organize themselves against the government (Doc. 107). In cities outside of Beijing, some students organized propaganda teams to go to factories and mines to mobilize workers in a united front with the students (Doc. 110).

But workers did not necessarily wait for word to arrive via student spokespersons before organizing themselves. The reports on arrests and sentencing after the crackdown give a sense of the widespread phenomenon of worker autonomous organizations while martial law was in effect in Beijing. Such unions were set up not only in Beijing but also in Changsha, Jinan, Xi'an, Nanjing, Shanghai, and Hangzhou. Workers also formed various support groups for the students and popular movements (democratic associations, support associations, worker pickets, dare-to-die corps, etc.) in Dalian, Chongqing, Xi'an, Shanghai, and Jinan; and one "self-employed worker" wrote for and edited some newspapers that circulated in Kunming.[16] It is impossible to tell

---

[15] Asia Watch, *Punishment Season*, p. 123.

[16]Ibid., pp. 123–50. This is certainly not an exhaustive list; many arrests and sentences were reported only in local newspapers, and the reports were never picked up by human rights monitors in the West. Moreover, some groups may have been formed whose principals were not detected, or whose arrests were never even reported.

how many actually joined such organizations. Generally speaking, their membership was small, even in Beijing,[17] for all workers knew how grave a risk they ran
in constituting themselves outside of the officially government-sponsored
unions.

Many of those who played leading roles were marginal to workers as a whole:
unemployed, partially employed, migrants, or private entrepreneurs, and those with
some sort of police record (sometimes for political offenses) form a substantial
majority of the most heavily publicized arrests.[18] Nonetheless, the specter of workers
losing their chains was undoubtedly a worrisome one to the CCP hardliners.

In retrospect, it is intriguing to speculate whether a Chinese Solidarity-type
movement might have sprung up, had students been less standoffish toward their
proletarian brethren. But even those students who proposed to propagandize the
workers sometimes sounded as condescending—and often more ignorant—in
their approach as the authorities they opposed. The BWAU's geographic
marginalization at the far northwest corner of Tiananmen Square symbolized a
much deeper marginalization imposed by the student movement. Despite the
risks they were taking on students' behalf, BWAU participants generally could
not get through the lines of student pickets for direct communication with the
student leaders. Worker organizers were the first to be arrested among those
sitting in the square; three of BWAU's members were arrested on May 29. After
about a thousand students demonstrated outside the Public Security offices, these
people were released.[19]

Others besides workers organized as well. The Beijing Autonomous Federation
of Intellectuals was set up on May 23, with Yan Jiaqi and Bao Zunxin as leaders.[20]
The following day, a Union of People from All Circles in the Capital was founded
(Doc. 152), headquartered at Beijing University. An Autonomous Residents' Federation was also set up in Beijing. On occasion, various such organizations could
cooperate with the student and worker organizations in formulating positions (Doc.
162). Even the "Beijing entrepreneurs," though not claiming the status of an organized group, issued a couple of appeals (Doc. 128). Thieves' associations in Beijing
and Xi'an suspended all thefts as a gesture of support for the students (docs. 140,
141). The suspension was not purely rhetorical: those present in Beijing at the time
attest to the sharp drop in incidents of theft and pick-pocketing.

---

[17]On May 29, one leader of the BWAU claimed a membership of 13,000 for that
organization—almost certainly an excessively generous estimate. See Simmie and Nixon,
Tiananmen Square, p. 160.

[18]This, of course, could reflect deliberate selectivity on the part of the government,
which desperately wanted to prove that those participating in "disturbances" were "hooligans" and "ruffians," not upstanding workers.

[19]Eleven members of the Flying Tigers had also been arrested. Jiang, *Countdown to
Tiananmen*, p. 275.

[20]*Ming pao* (Enlightenment), May 25, 1989, trans. in FBIS, *Daily Report: China*, May
26, 1989, p. 35.

But perhaps the most impressive organizational feat was the spontaneous defense of Beijing. Students and workers, young and old, government functionaries, nouveaux riches, and unemployed drifters alike flocked to build and then maintain the barricades stopping the army advance into the city those several nights in May. With a few general guidelines from the students (use reason, not force; offer the soldiers food and water), and perhaps with suggestions from those with some military experience (docs. 105, 131, 136), all pulled together in a remarkably good-natured and effective effort at a very tense time.

The Party: Illegitimate, but Still in Power

For forty years, the CCP had weathered many storms—including those it caused itself—without losing its fundamental legitimacy among the populace. Even more had it been able to count upon the devoted and often blind loyalty of party members and the People's Liberation Army. The declaration of martial law set the seal on the party leaders' loss of legitimacy among the urban population. At first they seemed to have lost the loyalties of the bulwark institutions as well.

Opposition from a variety of civilian party and government institutions was unprecedented if not generalized. Party members publicly announced their resignations from the party and called on others to do likewise. Several hundred party members in Shanghai, some quite highly placed, wrote to the Central Committee criticizing martial law, attributing four decades of errors to intraparty dynamics, and calling for a special session of the Central Committee (Doc. 125). Several provincial leaders dragged their feet on supporting martial law, delaying their telegrams expressing approval of Li Peng's actions. Support for Zhao Ziyang remained strong among some branches of the government, and for several days after his removal (even after Politburo charges were leveled against him), some government agencies still signaled their support directly or indirectly. In marches soon after May 20, members of some government departments, including the Foreign Ministry, paraded openly with banners identifying their units.[21] Approximately a quarter of the members of the NPC Standing Committee were said to have signed a petition to convene a special session to revoke martial law.

Even the official media organizations, occupied by military units on May 20, continued to express their sympathy for the movement and their opposition to the hardliners' response by whatever means they could. Staff from *People's Daily* and New China News Agency marched in some of the mass demonstrations.[22] Unable to call openly for the government to step down, *People's Daily* on May 21 gave front-page play to the Italian government's resignation and followed this the next day with another front-page article quoting Hungarian Premier Nemeth, that "no political forces will be allowed to use troops to solve internal problems"

---

[21]Yi and Thompson, *Crisis at Tiananmen*, p. 69.
[22]Ibid.

in Hungary. *China Daily*, reporting the huge march on May 23, could not repeat the marchers' main slogan of "Down with Li Peng!" but did mention that "the overwhelming majority of the slogans . . . were directed against the chief leader of the State Council." All the media gave prominent coverage to Wan Li's speech in Toronto, which seemed to reject the hardliners' approach to the student movement.[23]

More worrisome still for the party elders was the apparent defection of important segments of the military. From the earliest days of the revolution, the People's Liberation Army had prided itself on its dealings with the people, enjoying the justly earned reputation of "son and brother army." Recruits received heavy doses of ideological indoctrination, particularly concerning the principle of "serve the people." Although the army had been brought in to suppress, sometimes violently, the internecine violence unleashed at the height of the Cultural Revolution from 1967 to 1968, its principal modus operandi was to use persuasion and example, and it preferred to forget that it had ever used force against the civilian population. (Tibetans, unfortunately, were viewed with such contempt that the armed suppressions in Tibet were not thought to count.)

Thus, in enforcing martial law, the regime had to contend with the PLA's self-image at all levels of the military hierarchy. Seven senior PLA leaders, some with reputations dating back to the revolutionary war, appealed to the Beijing Martial Law Headquarters and the Central Military Commission not to suppress the people (Doc. 132). The two surviving revolutionary era marshals, Xu Xiangqian and Nie Rongzhen, were visited by students who appealed for their support, and though both urged students to leave the square and go back to classes, Marshal Xu's staff representative assured the students of the army's unwillingness to cause bloodshed.[24] The commander of the Thirty-eighth Army, which was responsible for the defense of Beijing, refused to lead his troops in the advance on the city (docs. 163, 169). Many of the rank-and-file soldiers and officers expressed their sympathy with the demonstrators and apologized for having to follow orders (Doc. 106). The disarray caused in the ranks during the early days of martial law and the troops' apparent sympathy with the populace may have been one major reason for the decision to withdraw the troops after May 23.[25]

Had Li Peng had to contend with this situation alone, the outcome would have been very different. But Li, whatever his own hardline sympathies, was a relatively minor actor in the behind-the-scenes maneuvers to pull off a crackdown. Deng Xiaoping was central to these, but important weight was thrown into the

---

[23]Gwertzman and Kaufman, *The Collapse of Communism*, pp. 72–73; Simmie and Nixon, *Tiananmen Square*, pp. 147, 149.

[24]Beijing Domestic Service, May 22, 1989, FBIS, *Daily Report: China*, May 22, 1989, p. 52.

[25]See, for example, Jiang, *Countdown to Tiananmen*, pp. 227–28.

balance also by Yang Shangkun, Chen Yun, Peng Zhen, and other senior leaders on the Central Advisory Commission. Through speeches, jawboning, and some very canny politicking, these men pulled in the crucial support from the provinces and the regional military commands. According to one source from within the Central Committee offices, by around May 24 all provincial governors and party secretaries had been to Beijing for individual talks with the "Central Committee," and the wheels were already in motion for suppression of the popular movement by force. By May 25, Deng had the support of six of the seven military regions, "the Headquarters of the General Staff, the General Political Department, the General Logistics Department, and the Headquarters of the Navy and Air Force."[26]

Meanwhile, the occupation of major media and government offices began to take its toll on their staffs' ability to resist: to hold onto their jobs and avoid serious reprisals, they had to submit. Despite the occasional opportunities for criticism by analogy, the media basically fell into line (Doc. 151). Press accounts increasingly reverted to the official line, thus rupturing the most potent link between the Beijing movement and the rest of the country. Within military, police, and other units in Beijing, even while the populace as a whole was flush with victory, the purge process was grinding away, and staff members were cowed into passivity (Doc. 138). Managers of factories and enterprises began to threaten employees with dismissal, withholding of bonuses, and other sanctions if they participated in demonstrations; this helped to reduce the numbers marching by the May 28 demonstration.

While some of the movement's participants were aware of such actions, they did not always take them seriously. Often attention focused instead on the measures that inspired only contempt, such as the progovernment demonstrations of workers and peasants mustered on the city outskirts by a government that did not dare to parade its "supporters" in the urban center. Many, if not all, participants in those demonstrations were attracted by offers of payment, or even ordered there by their employers. On May 24, the Li Peng government offered ten yuan apiece to peasants from Miyun County to attend a march in Beijing in support of the government. Another march, to which the media were summoned, was staged in Daxing County (a Beijing suburb) on May 31, when four thousand workers and peasants shuffled along mechanically mumbling slogans for the benefit of television cameras.[27]

But the patent futility of such public relations stunts distracted many, particularly the students, from the growing consolidation of the hardline leadership's control over the military and the government. As the movement increasingly challenged their legitimacy, the hardliners came to see recourse to naked power as their only option. And power they still had. By contrast, the popular

---

[26]Ibid., pp. 243–44, 252.
[27]Ibid., p. 248; Simmie and Nixon, *Tiananmen Square*, pp. 161–62.

movement had neither the organization, the power, nor the analysis to contend with this reality.

The Popular Movement: Disillusion and Dissolution

From the outset, the leadership of the student movement was at best fluid, at worst unstable. After the declaration of martial law, the instability grew even as bureaucratism among the student organizations increased. As the initial crisis of the army's advance on the capital was surmounted, the student leadership fragmented, and organizational coherence disintegrated. Students were left largely leaderless, while the larger popular movement totally lacked any central leadership. There was no lack of criticism of this state of affairs, but all seemed powerless to remedy it.

The structure of student organization at the beginning of martial law consisted of three organizations: the Autonomous Student Union of Colleges and Universities in Beijing (ASUCUB), the hunger strikers, and the union of students from universities outside of Beijing. Wu'er Kaixi and Wang Dan led ASUCUB. Chai Ling was one of the main leaders of the hunger strikers. Shortly after the imposition of martial law, the leaders fell out over the question of whether to maintain their occupation of the square.

Wu'er Kaixi first called for students to evacuate the square on May 23. One highly placed observer suggested that this was related to intervention by Deng Pufang, Deng Xiaoping's son, when it became apparent to those surrounding Deng and the top leaders that military suppression would be used.[28] Wu'er Kaixi was removed from his post as leader of ASUCUB, but Wang Dan remained in the secondary leadership position he had occupied all along. The argument over whether or not to leave the square persisted. On May 27, Wu'er Kaixi and Wang Dan announced that the protest would conclude on May 30 with a final mass demonstration, after which students would vacate the square. They proposed—as had been the original plan of the student protest—to return to the campuses to discuss and reflect upon the movement's experiences in order to formulate plans for more effective future actions. By the following day, however, hotter heads prevailed among the occupiers of the square.[29] In a joint statement on May 27, several organizations, including ASUCUB, the non-Beijing students' union, the BWAU, and other nonstudent groups, declared their intention to remain on the square to petition for repudiation of the April 26 editorial and the May 20 labeling of the movement, as well as for the end of martial law, until the NPC Standing Committee convened on June 20 for its regular session (Doc. 162). On May 31 Chai Ling, newly elected commander-in-chief of the students on the

---

[28]Jiang, *Countdown to Tiananmen*, pp. 241–42.
[29]Stefan Landsberger, "The 1989 Student Demonstrations in Beijing: A Chronology of Events," *China Information* 4,1 (Summer 1989): 47.

square, announced four demands: Rescinding of martial law, withdrawal of the army, guarantees of amnesty to all who joined the movement, and an end to press censorship.[30]

Part of the problem of leadership fragmentation stemmed from the changing composition of the groups on the square. After the first few days of martial law, many students from Beijing went to stay in their family homes. Most of those remaining were students from out of town, who had nowhere else to stay. To leave the square, for them, meant to leave Beijing, which they were not willing to do while the excitement continued. Some of them were determined to remain to see the movement through to the end, while others probably had somewhat crasser motives.

While the unity and exalted purposes of the general body of students thus gradually disintegrated, the leadership tended increasingly to develop some of the same unhealthy tendencies that the movement had criticized among the party and government officials. One observer (Doc. 123) warned that "feudalism" was rearing its ugly head, with bureaucratism and corruption emerging among some of the ASUCUB leaders, and constant squabbling occupying the leaders' time. Even those who had taken part in the squabbling—Wu'er Kaixi in particular— criticized the student leaders' tendency to behave undemocratically (Doc. 176).

Some of the more mature intellectuals not only called on the CCP leadership for dialogue with the students, but also appealed to students to act in a more strategic and considered fashion. Some students also made concrete proposals for remedying the organizational problems, though their suggestions seemed to bear no fruit. Three days before the crackdown, one such analyst excoriated the combination of organizational confusion and inefficiency, on the one hand, and undemocratic concentration of decision making, on the other. The result, he maintained, was the inability to act strategically. The same student argued for the establishment of units within the ASUCUB that would separate functions of communications, brainstorming, decision making, and implementation.

To some extent, the organizational problems can be attributed to inexperience and to the rapid unfolding of events, and to students' exhaustion after weeks of little rest. But probably the greater weight of causation must be attributed to most students' deliberate refusal to stoop to consider compromise, alliance-building, and other such mundane matters of political strategy, as well as to their inability or reluctance to formulate some larger theoretical vision that could guide the movement. Chai Ling stated as a matter of pride, "This movement has been accidental and was not premeditated. There is no governing theoretical framework. We just follow our feelings! It is spontaneous and a pure demand for democracy."[31] Too many preferred to remain on the moral high ground, neglecting to notice until too late that it was situated in a strategic wasteland.

Popular movements throughout the world in this century have time and again

---

[30]Ibid.
[31]Chai Ling, interview with Philip Cunningham.

confused spontaneity with authenticity and moral rectitude. Anti-authoritarians will often equate theoretical analysis, careful goal-setting, and strategic planning with authoritarian manipulation. This is not surprising given the cynicism with which those in power regularly pervert ideological discourse and political organization to their own ends. Yet those in the Chinese popular movement, and particularly the students, who insisted on spontaneity of action and eschewed any cooperation with existing organizations, preserved purity at the expense of effectiveness. While many attempted to analyze the fast-moving events of late May in order to assess the options for action, the movement never functioned *as a whole* because no analysis developed sufficiently or gained enough adherents to coalesce into a unifying guide to action. Those "ideas" that did galvanize crowds to move with some semblance of unity can hardly be glorified with the name of "principles." While they could muster unanimity, they trapped the movement in a reactive stance. What preoccupied not just the students but virtually the entire population of Beijing after the declaration of martial law were just two things: Getting rid of a handful of party leaders seen as responsible for martial law, and defending the students and the square against a reassertion of government control.

The popular animus against Li Peng was particularly strong, but Deng Xiaoping and Yang Shangkun also came in for a large share of hostility. From May 20 on, the most frequently stated demand was the resignation or removal of Li, Deng, and Yang, occasionally combined with the call to restore Zhao Ziyang to his position as party general secretary. Reasons given for eliminating the dastardly three ranged from their having ignored the health and welfare of students, to their violations of constitutional and legal principles, to their staging a "counterrevolutionary military coup" (docs. 112, 117, 139). One group delved into the past in drawing up their indictment of Deng, listing offenses ranging from the anti–spiritual pollution campaign, to his son's alleged criminal activities, to usurping party power, to sitting on the heights "swathed in mystery" (Doc. 148). Even some who remained conscious of the movement's original goals of ending corruption and "feudal autocracy" might, when recommending concrete action, resort to a "dump Li Peng" recommendation (Doc. 158). Behind the energy of the attacks, however, was a relatively simple, and simplistic, factor: these three could be easily identified as involved with the imposition of martial law; therefore, they should be removed. The question of what would come next, or how it would come about, was rarely entertained.

When it was, too often the answer proffered was equally simplistic: bring back Zhao Ziyang. A few might maintain that Zhao was not necessarily any better than the others. One Beijing University teacher pointed out that Zhao would never garner the support of the military, who had no love for him, considering him largely responsible for corruption (Doc. 149). In any event, demands against the Li-Deng-Yang group or for Zhao generally reflected a tendency to react mechanically against steps taken by the authorities, rather than seizing some kind of initiative.

Defense of the square and the students was an equally reactive position. Some raised common-sensical objections to the fixation upon the square. One group of teachers, for example, argued for students to leave the square while they could do so in large numbers, making a public declaration of their continuing goals (Doc. 165). And, as noted above, those like Wu'er Kaixi, Wang Dan, and Shen Tong, who hoped to consolidate the lessons of the movement as a guide to further action, considered the insistence on digging in on the square counterproductive. When the proposal to leave the square was rejected (by a decision-making procedure that was never very clear), the rank-and-file students gradually voted with their feet by leaving as individuals. But because no decision had been taken to leave, there was no other direction in which to go.

Those who remained fixated upon the square, noting the loss of both bodies and momentum for those camped before Tiananmen, cast about for some way of regaining the initiative that was fast slipping away from them. Some proposed to organize a "long march" that would propagandize the movement's aims and build up enthusiasm for assembling large numbers in time for the June 20 NPC Standing Committee session (Doc. 175). A short burst of new enthusiasm, and ingress of curious onlookers, was elicited by the erection of the statue of the "Goddess of Democracy" on the night of May 29 (Doc. 170). Students saw the Goddess as a symbolic occupation of the square, but the preoccupation with refuting the authorities' charge that it had been erected without the proper permits (Doc. 173) indicates how they had been deflected into trivialities at a time when the machinery was grinding toward disaster.

This is not to say that there was a complete dearth of analysis during the martial law period. In fact, the breather afforded by the relative calm after the first few frenetic days of "defending the square" allowed the drafting of numerous documents, some of them quite impressive in their sophistication. The themes that predominated included the illegitimacy of those controlling the CCP and the legitimacy of the protest movement, steps that should be taken to remedy the situation, what changes in consciousness had been or should be wrought by the popular movement, and whether or not those seeking change could or should work within the system by "playing politics."

Discussions on the legitimacy issue focused both on who was really in power, and how those in power should be assessed. A number of documents referred to a military coup or a "Yang Family" coup;[32] others maintained that the enormous troop strength called up was only explicable if military action was needed to solve a power struggle among the leadership. All such speculations, of course, contributed to a sense that those calling the shots in Beijing by late May were illegitimately in power by any standards one might wish to apply.

The range of standards applied was wide indeed. These ranged from holding

---

[32]This refers to the dominant position within the PLA of a small group related to Yang Shangkun.

the authorities responsible for the disruption of public transport in the city of Beijing (Doc. 103) to assigning responsibility for all major disruptions and injustices that had occurred throughout the PRC's history.[33] Discussions on the legitimacy issue also varied in the degree to which they blamed the entire system and longstanding abuses, or individual leaders and recent problems, for the crisis that China faced.

Those who focused on the systemic nature of China's problems pointed out that the movement was up against something much bigger than Li Peng. One underscored the existence of an entire "bureaucratic class with vested interests," while another pointed out that martial law had been imposed in order to defend just such a corrupt bureaucratic class (docs. 155, 171). Others pointed out the chronic tendency for factional disputes to arise within the party and to spill over into general political ills. These analysts often tried to identify the remedies that would have to be applied either within the party (Doc. 157) or in the polity as a whole (Doc. 178) to cure those ills.

In hindsight, those who assumed that deep divisions within the CCP leadership offered some leverage for moves against the "Li-Deng-Yang" group were pinning their hopes on futilities. This was particularly true for those who counted on military noncompliance with orders for a crackdown, hoping that a Chinese version of "people power" à la the Philippines could convince soldiers not to intervene against the movement. Thus, a considerable amount of propaganda was directed toward the soldiers. And students from China Science and Technology University, the same school that sent the delegations to marshals Nie Rongzhen and Xu Xiangqian to appeal against martial law, provided some strategic reasoning for such a move, counseling trying to win over the middle-of-the-roaders in the party and the government.

Futility also plagued those who argued (at times, perhaps only rhetorically) for pursuing legal or constitutional channels for redress. These included calls to bring Li, Yang, or Deng to trial (Doc. 146), or to convene a special session of the NPC to repeal the martial law declaration and/or remove Li, Deng, and Yang from their posts. With regard to the latter course, two hundred intellectuals signed an open letter to the Standing Committee of the NPC asking for a special session to repeal martial law (Doc. 144), while expressing the hope that students would leave the square once martial law was repealed. When the Autonomous Federation of Intellectuals was formed, its two leaders, Yan Jiaqi and Bao Zunxin, also pointed out Li Peng's violations of the constitution and called for the NPC Standing Committee to

---

[33]See Han and Hua, eds., *Cries for Democracy*, pp. 269–71. This Beijing University handbill listed a series of incidents of "turmoil" in the PRC's history that had been caused by CCP policies—including several launched by Deng Xiaoping. However, it laid the blame for the 1957 anti-Rightist campaign at Mao's door, while Deng Xiaoping was in fact one of the major architects of that campaign.

take action.[34] A petition, circulated among NPC Standing Committee members for convoking a special session, gathered about forty signatures. Especially high hopes were placed on Wan Li, NPC chairman, who had expressed relatively positive views about the students' movement during his visit to Canada and the United States. These hopes were dashed by Wan's declaration of support for martial law, by which point any hopes of a successful petition by NPC Standing Committee members also had to be abandoned.

Others argued directly or indirectly against working within the system at all. Some attempted through various means to demystify the party's position in the Chinese body politic. One Beijing University author, for example, made a cogent argument concerning who really owned the Chinese revolution, the party or the people, and pleaded not to let the democracy movement turn into yet another "change of feudal dynasties" (Doc. 167). Many students suspected that any collaboration with the existing powers tainted one. Wu'er Kaixi, for example, complained that older intellectuals had been too caught up in attempts at "reform," meaning effecting change from the top down; the students, on the other hand, had grasped the need for "revolution," meaning building the forces for change from below.

Many who recommended not working within the system considered the point of the popular movement to be the transformation of the popular consciousness rather than some concrete political or legal development. Certainly, to all who observed the events of that spring, the change in popular attitudes was breathtaking, and a number of the documents observe this. One, for example, claimed that this was the first time a revolution in China fought for ideals rather than for material benefits, and it saw the change of consciousness as the main goal (Doc. 133). Some were more specific. Especially impressive was the long declaration by the four celebrities who began a public hunger strike on June 2 (Doc. 178). They pleaded for combatting the mentality of hatred that had characterized so much of Chinese political life for centuries, and that had been exacerbated under the PRC.[35] Another source emphasized the need for Chinese to realize they must rely on themselves, not on "gods" or "emperors," to solve their problems (Doc. 150).

But such arguments increasingly were voiced in a climate in which some kind of forceful crackdown seemed almost inevitable, and any recommendations for action were offered almost in a spirit of fatalism. Chai Ling, who was terrified at the prospect of an imminent crackdown, referred to the possibility of prison for herself and other student leaders (Doc. 172). Two days before the crackdown, however, she still thought that somehow sufficient consciousness could save the

---

[34]"Solve the Current Problems in China along the Track of Democracy and Legal System," in FBIS, *Daily Report: China*, May 26, 1989.

[35]See the declaration of a hunger strike preparatory committee issued on May 26, Doc. 159.

day. As she told Philip Cunningham, "To tell you something from the bottom of my heart: If this movement fails, it will be a tragedy for the whole people. It will mean that the democratic consciousness and qualities of the people are not high enough. Its failure will have been predestined. Its failure would not have been preventable by the student leaders and the several thousand students in the square."[36]

Many of the students' elders, who had seen so many movements fail, had sensed impending disaster from a much earlier date, no matter what actions (short of withdrawal from Tiananmen Square) the movement took. None of them wanted to be proven right. Unfortunately, they were.

---

[36]Chai Ling interview with Philip Cunningham, June 2, 1989.

DOCUMENTS FOR MAY 19–JUNE 3

"You Have Brute Force, I Have Blood"
—From photo

What Do You Lack? On Martial Law in Beijing
by a Commoner
Newspapers are in your hands
Radio stations are in your hands
Guns are in your hands
Prisons are in your hands
Everything is in your hands.
What do you lack, Emperor?
Only the popular will!
Only the truth!
—*Xinwen daobao*, May 22

98
Wolf

Qɪ Qɪɴ

Source: Speech by Wu'er Kaixi, September 16, 1989, Conference on Perspectives on Tiananmen, Brandeis University, Waltham, MA. Translation by Rachel Sing.

I am a lone wolf from the north,
Walking a boundless wasteland.
The bitter north wind blows through,
Endless yellow sand swirls around.
I can only grit my cold teeth,
Responding with a howl.
Not for anything else,
But the lush plain of which legends tell.

[Wu'er Kaixi's explanation]: The fact that this song was so popular among Chinese students reveals the extent to which they have been influenced by anti-authoritarian existentialism and individualism.

The first part of the song describes a lonely, pitiful wolf. The melody is sad. In the second part of the song, the pitch rises and the rhythm and tempo begin to quicken. The song becomes increasingly upbeat. The lyrics say that the wolf grits his cold teeth. This begins to express the song's underlying idea.

The intense dissatisfaction that young Chinese feel is expressed in the first section. It specifically reflects their dissatisfaction with reality.

The first line states: "I am a [lone] wolf from the north." Why is the north significant? Why in recent years has the image of China's northwest had such appeal for Chinese? Everyone knows that South China has been increasingly open and developed. North China has remained extremely backward. When Chinese students sing the first line . . . they unconsciously are expressing a very traditional kind of patriotic malaise. If we were to change the lyrics to: "I am a lone wolf from the south"—well, first of all there are no wolves in the south. . . . That is to say, there is no sense of lonely wolves or individual selves because the south is all high-rise [buildings].

The feeling created in the next few lines: "I walk a boundless wasteland, the bitter north wind blows through, endless yellow sand swirls around," echoes the extreme dissatisfaction with reality which Chinese young people feel—the feeling each of us has of being on a northern plain, of charging forward and encountering only bitter wind and endless sand.

We cannot maintain our inner equilibrium because while we seek a lush plain, we are surrounded by boundless wasteland.

One thing in particular that I would like to point out is that on this boundless wasteland there is only one wolf, and it is "me." This reflects young Chinese people's sense of individualism and self-identity.

You may have heard about young Chinese [men] taking off their shirts and shoes and climbing up to the roof of a tall building to shout, "I am me, I am me!" Many people have found this behavior bewildering, but I can fully understand these students' intense desire to assert their self-identity. Individualism and self-identity have been central to the thinking of Chinese college students in recent years, sometimes to an extreme degree.

In the second part of the song, the lyrics say: "I can only grit my cold teeth, responding with a howl." These lines express a sense of power. They declare to society and the entire world that, "I exist, I am powerful, I am able to howl."

The meaning of the final lines of the song, "Not for anything else, but the lush plain of which legends tell," is so clear that no explanation is necessary: Young Chinese people's commitment to their ideals is profound. And the song tells us that lush plains exist only in legend, not in reality.

Of all the songs popular among Chinese college students, "Wolf" was the most popular. It could be heard at every party on every campus around China. Guys especially liked to sing it. It was also the most popular song on Tiananmen Square. During the days we spent on the square, it could be heard coming out of tape recorders everywhere.

99

Open Letter to the People's Soldiers

QINGHUA UNIVERSITY STUDENTS

Mid-May 1989

Source: *ORSD*, 1:39.

The patriotic students have been holding a hunger strike and petitioning for six days. But what is the result? The peaceful petitioning has been labeled turmoil, and the six-day hunger strike will result in a serious crackdown. Where is rationality? Where is the sympathy for the people from those in power?

They said that there had been turmoil. But why did [the government] remove traffic policemen from their posts the day the students started the hunger strike on May 13? Why did they keep delaying meeting with the students? They have cunning, dirty, and cruel strategies in their minds! The People's Liberation Army soldiers are the sons and brothers of the people. They are not slaves. The soldiers love the people, and the people love the soldiers. Let the soldiers unite with the people to struggle to defeat totalitarianism and promote China's democracy! . . .

100

Declaration of Capital Workers

BEIJING WORKERS' AUTONOMOUS UNION
PREPARATORY COMMITTEE

May 19, 1989

Source: *ORSD*, 1:29.

We have learned that since April, the students' democratic and patriotic movement developed and grew into a national patriotic movement that directly affects the interests of the working class; and that . . . the hunger strike students are already in danger.[1]

---

[1]This document was issued five days after Li Peng had visited the Capital Iron and Steel plant to hear worker complaints. *New China News Agency*, May 14, 1989, in *Jieyan ling fabu zhiqian*, pp. 132–33.

[For these reasons,] we ... declare that the Politburo must unconditionally accept the two appeals of the students within twenty-four hours. Otherwise, beginning at noon on May 20, all the city's workers will strike for twenty-four hours [and then take further action as deemed appropriate].
... Beijing workers have already become organized!

"Kindergarteners proclaim, long live the students!"
—Placard held by child, photo, courtesy June 4th Project

101

Letter to the People

SOME CADRES OF STATE INSTITUTIONS
OF THE CENTRAL GOVERNMENT

May 19, 1989

Source: *ORSD*, 1:60.

... We announce, with outrage and sinking hearts, news that is definitely true: Party Secretary Zhao Ziyang has been dismissed. Li Peng has taken charge of the Politburo and ordered a crackdown on the students tonight. Here is a brief account of events:

On May 13, at the meeting of the Standing Committee of the Politburo, Zhao Ziyang proposed repudiating the April 26 *People's Daily* editorial. His proposal was rejected. On May 15, Zhao intended to announce his personal view to the public at Tiananmen Square. This was considered a violation of party rules and hence was prevented by the Central Committee of the CCP. On May 16, Zhao put forward six proposals in the Politburo Standing Committee meeting chaired by Deng Xiaoping:

1. [The Politburo's Standing Committee would] repudiate the April 26 editorial.

2. Zhao himself would take responsibility for having issued that editorial.

3. Establish a special branch of the National People's Congress to investigate official profiteering by children of top cadres, including [Zhao's] own sons.

4. Publicize the background of cadres above the vice-ministerial level.

5. Publicize the salary and fringe benefits of top cadres.

6. Eliminate such privileges as the special food supply for top cadres.[1]

All of the above suggestions were rejected. The May 17 meeting of the Politburo, by a feeble majority, decided to oust Zhao. Li Peng took over the work of the Politburo. Martial law is now imminent. Suppression [such as] that which followed the [incident of] April 5, 1976, will soon resume.

Yet this is a different time. History cannot repeat itself exactly. It is said that Wan Li [chairman of the Standing Committee of the National People's Congress] firmly supports Zhao Ziyang; and that when Wan Li proposed calling a meeting of the vice-chairmen of the National People's Congress, Li Peng threatened to penalize him with party discipline. Another reliable source revealed that about ten ministries, including the [State] Reform Commission,[2] decided to counteract [Li Peng] by staging a hunger strike. In view of the urgency of developing events, we strongly appeal to everyone to: (1) Definitely avoid bloodshed and refrain from using violence; (2) Carry out a nationwide general strike; (3) PLA soldiers are the people's children and brothers; we should never kill each other.

We strongly demand that: (1) A meeting of the Standing Committee of the National People's Congress be called immediately to dismiss Li Peng; (2) A special meeting of the national representatives of the CCP be called to elect a party general secretary and put an end to old men politics and old men interfering from behind the curtain. . . .

---

[1]Fields in Yuquanshan near the Summer Palace just outside Beijing are used to grow special foods for central leaders. Similar criticisms of such privileges were voiced in the 1940s against the CCP leadership in Yan'an by the intellectual Wang Shiwei, for which he was purged and then executed, reportedly by Wang Zhen. Timothy Cheek, "The Fading of Wild Lilies: Wang Shiwei and Mao Zedong's *Yan'an Talks* in the First CPC Rectification Movement," *The Australian Journal of Chinese Affairs,* no. 11 (January 1984), pp. 25–58; and Ruan Ming, "Hu Yaobang and I."

[2]The State Reform Commission (Tigaiwei) is in charge of reform of the economic system in the PRC. It is the equivalent of a ministry and is under the direction of the State Council, and ultimately Premier Li Peng. The statement here refers to a rumor, or at least a plan, that was never carried out. It reflects the fact that as of May 19, just one day before martial law was imposed, in view of the paralysis of the government, many of China's state-related units wanted to declare themselves to be on the right side, that is, against the leadership of Li Peng and Deng Xiaoping, which they thought was about to collapse.

102

Communist Party Members, Step Forward— To All Party Members

ALL PARTY MEMBERS AMONG GRADUATE STUDENTS, CLASS OF 1986
PARTY BRANCH IN THE DEPARTMENT OF MATERIALS

May 19, 1989

Source: *ORSD*, 1:61.

The patriotic democratic movement has now reached a critical stage. The hunger strike by thousands of students in Tiananmen Square has entered its seventh day. Yet our government leaders have still not made any definite reply to the reasonable demands made by the students. As CCP members, we feel that the government's attitude is wrong and unwise. Ever since April 15, we have participated in the patriotic democratic movement. We are deeply grieved by the government leaders' wrong judgment on the students' movement, which has greatly ruined the image of the party and its members.

We treasure our title as Communist party members. We joined the party for its promotion of communism. Although we have been members for only a few years, party education has taught us the value of the title of a member. CCP members have always stood at the forefront of revolution and the society to serve the people. Our predecessors used their lives and blood to gain honor for Communist party members, whose names have been tarnished in the process of trying to gain democracy and a legal system. Since April 20, we have been subjected to a considerable amount of pressure. We could only join the demonstration as individuals. We thought about our oath, about the obligations and duties of a CCP member. Speaking from our conscience, we feel ashamed before the students and [being called by] the glorious name of a CCP member. Genuine party members uphold and defend its truth, not the reputation of a few leaders who possess the title of CCP member. We'd like to say that they are not true CCP members. The image of the CCP does not belong to those individuals. It belongs to every single party member.

We appeal:

1. All CCP members should step forward for the sake of defending the CCP and the honor of Communists by participating in this patriotic movement as CCP members under the name of their respective party branches.

2. The movement has come to a critical moment. Party members should serve as models to assist in the organization of the autonomous students' associations, to keep a clear head and minimize unnecessary losses on the part of the students.

"One man makes decisions, a group of leaders collectively takes responsibility, and the whole people suffer."
—Xiao Zi, about May 20

103

The Crimes of the Government

PRINTED AND DISTRIBUTED BY BEIJING NORMAL UNIVERSITY

May 20, 1989

Source: Courtesy of HKFS.

According to reliable information, the hypocritical government of Li Peng has ordered all transportation workers to take a vacation indefinitely. The subway is to be closed to the public and used for transporting troops. There are restrictions on using vehicles that belong to any work unit in Beijing. The order goes into effect on May 20, 1989. We all know that today, no bus is running on any bus line. Why has the government done this? They are trying to use this to lodge a false accusation against the vast majority of patriotic students and to show that the breakdown of transportation is the consequence of great turmoil. How vicious their intentions are! Moreover, the shortage of vegetables and milk is singlehandedly created by them. . . . [W]e must be aware of their schemes. The people need daily transportation and normal order in their lives. The hypocritical government of Li Peng has taken psychological advantage of the people and attempted to split and disintegrate the great unity among the people and the students. These are the true features of "a people's government." . . . To carry the democracy movement through to the end, we must immediately expose the government's schemes to the . . . people and ask the transportation workers to return to work. Standing fast at one's post is also support for the revolution. Dear transportation workers, the residents in the capital need you!

104

A Declaration of Emergency to All People in the Country from People in the Capital

PEOPLE IN THE CAPITAL

May 20, 1989

Source: *ORSD*, 1:37.

The governing body is prepared to kill. They publicly trample on the republic's constitution and have openly declared [us] to be enemies of the people. We must struggle to force the ruling party to resign collectively.

People in the capital are against a bloody crackdown and terror and have spiritually prepared to fight to the end. We urgently declare to all people in the country:

1. Start a noncooperation movement in the whole country to oppose the government.

2. Begin urgent nationwide support by providing all kinds of medical and first-aid equipment to the capital.

3. Begin a signature movement among all [NPC] representatives to dismiss Yang Shangkun, Wang Zhen, Li Peng, and Yao Yilin and their own ruling group so as to avoid large-scale bloodshed and to save the republic.

4. Urgently demand that governments in every province, city, autonomous region, and military area support people in the capital and condemn the ruling group; protect the administrative stability of all places and openly object to the ruling group of the military government. Declare the military government to be an illegitimate governing power . . . .

6. Urgently request all governments and people in the world to support and help.

7. Urgently request all people to struggle firmly and thoroughly against the antidemocratic, antirevolutionary group of Yang, Wang, Li, and Yao, who are the main representatives of corrupt power . . . .

> "Martial law troops brought along weapons and tear gas to Beijing not to attack demonstrators . . . but to pay a visit."
> —Slogan in *56 Days*

105

A Statement to Citizens Regarding the Army Entering the Capital

BEIJING UNIVERSITY

May 20, 1989

Source: Handbill, in *ORSD*, 1:38.

All comrade citizens:

. . . Regarding the current situation, we appeal to all people who are trying to block the army from entering the city at various road intersections to take the following points into consideration:

1. The soldiers are not our real enemies. They are the people's brothers. They have been tricked into coming here, and they do not really understand the situation. Recently, some squadrons have not had access to newspapers or television and thus do not know what has really been occurring [here]. So we must tell them the truth and make them understand the people's intentions [in blocking them]. We must persuade them with reason, not force, during our propaganda work. We should try to understand and respect the soldiers.

2. Some individuals have stolen the honor of the government and have tricked the soldiers into coming here while irresponsibly leaving the soldiers with insufficient food supplies. Some soldiers have not eaten anything for quite a few days. The aim of those individuals is to create a conflict between the army and the people. For this reason, we should take care of our soldiers and help solve their food problem.

3. We understand that soldiers are required to obey orders. But we should try to make clear to them that they also have the right to reject orders that run counter to the people's wishes. We must also tell them that we people have no other choice but to block them. We must avoid having conflicts with them. In the meantime, we should also be aware that some plainclothes policemen and those with evil intentions may beat up soldiers to create tensions.

4. If the army needs to retreat to rest, we should let the soldiers go.

106

From the Bottom of Our Soldiers' Hearts— Kindhearted Soldiers from the Third Battalion of the Central Security Guard

A SOLDIER OF THE THIRD BATTALION OF THE
CENTRAL SECURITY GUARD

May 20, 1989

Source: *ORSD*, 1:43.

Dear compatriots:

You have suffered enough! I'd like to say something on behalf of the kind-hearted soldiers of the Third Battalion. From April 20 to the present, the patriotic movement by students, workers, and citizens has lasted for a month. Yes, we are soldiers and must obey orders, and that is why the troops cannot support you fully. But we are sons and brothers of the people, and we are also the offspring of the Chinese nation with a strong patriotic heart. Yes, some of the young soldiers might have left a bad impression on people's minds by obeying their superior's orders, including the advance on the capital. But we'd like to say: compatriots, please do not abandon us. Do not treat us coldly. Do not reject us. Our hearts are linked closely with yours. We are also common people who are suffering. We are also conscientious Chinese.

Our compatriots are struggling for democracy and freedom. Compatriots, do we have any democracy and freedom? Of course, the nature of an army is different [from that of civilians]; however, we do not have the right to enter Beijing to take a look at the students. There were ten soldiers who left their unit [without asking for leave] and went to Beijing, neglecting the possibility of losing their posts. They are a small number—only about ten or a hundred—compared with the millions of people [in Beijing]; however, that shows that they (including us) are really concerned with the people and the students.

Compatriots, do not scold us as running dogs. Do not hate us. We will build up our new image with our own style and by our actions. We belong to the people.

107

Stand Up Bravely, Our Elder Brother Workers

BEIJING UNIVERSITY

About May 20, 1989

Source: Students' handbill, in *ORSD*, 2:56.

Dear comrade workers:

We know that you were forced by the officials to come. They forced you to hold a [progovernment] demonstration and forced you to shout slogans against your own will. This is an insult to [you], and you are filled with pent-up anger.

Your real intention is to knock down Li Peng. . . . It is a big scheme of the Li Peng government to force you into the streets to demonstrate and to shout [progovernment] slogans against your will. Before Liberation, the Guomindang government once forcibly organized workers to demonstrate against patriotic students. This was the old trick used by the Guomindang government to sabotage the student movement and to crack down on the students. Today Li Peng went so far as to "make the past serve the present" by adopting the old "tricks" of the Guomindang government.

During the Cultural Revolution, Lin Biao and the Gang of Four also incited the workers to fight against the students and agitated the masses to fight against each other. Today Li Peng and his ilk again "creatively learn and apply" the dirty tricks of Lin Biao and the Gang of Four.

[They] attempt to . . . use the workers to deceive world opinion. They want to report your fake demonstration in the newspapers and over radio and television for both national and international propaganda. They claim that Beijing workers support Li Peng and oppose the students, and that Beijing workers are willing to have the army control them with guns. Li Peng and his ilk . . . want all Chinese with conscience to condemn our workers in Beijing and [cause] overseas Chinese to laugh at them. Li Peng is insulting your nature and ruining your reputation. Men of integrity, can you swallow such an insult?

. . . During the May Fourth Movement, the older generation of China's workers bravely stood up and held general strikes to support the patriotic students. After that, the Chinese working class stepped onto the stage of history and became the leading force of the revolution. The history of the Chinese working class is a glorious history. In all the patriotic democracy movements in the past, the workers always played a great role. We believe, therefore, that today in the 1980s, educated and [politically] conscious workers will never become puppets . . . manipulated by Li Peng. We believe that the working class in the 1980s will play an even more glorious role than its predecessors.

In 1980, when the government was corrupt and prices were skyrocketing in the European socialist country of Poland, and when that country was at a most critical moment, it was the Polish working class that first staged large demonstrations and a general strike. They did not wait for college students to boycott classes and go on a hunger strike. Polish workers abolished the government's fake [yellow] workers' union and organized their own Solidarity union. They kept up their struggle for three years without fearing jail or suppression by the army, and they have finally achieved their victory. Now the Central Committee of the Polish Communist party has recognized the legality of Solidarity and punished by law sixteen corrupt officials at the ministerial level of the central government. Workers' wages have increased, and democratic power has been enhanced. The Polish workers are the heroes among the workers of the world. What should our workers in Beijing and in China do? We believe that [they] should be more [politically] conscious and braver than the Polish workers. . . . The Polish workers are heroes, but our Beijing workers are by no means cowards. Eight hundred workers from the steel mill in Wuhan bravely stood together with the college students on the Yangzi River bridge in defiance of the crackdown by the military police. Our Beijing workers should be braver than Wuhan workers and do an even more remarkable job. Beijing is a heroic city. Beijing college students are heroic students, and Beijing workers should be heroic workers.

Elder fraternal workers, bravely stand up as men of backbone and integrity. Struggle to wipe out official profiteering, oppose corruption, and demand that Li Peng step down and that martial law be rescinded.

108

Beijing Workers' Autonomous Union
Preparatory Committee Public Notice No. 1

BEIJING WORKERS' AUTONOMOUS UNION
PREPARATORY COMMITTEE

May 20, 1989

Source: *ORSD*, 1:29.

The BWAU is a spontaneous, transitional organization formed by the workers of Beijing at this extraordinary time. Its objectives are to win democracy, oppose dictatorship, express support for and protect the student hunger strikers, and promote democratization in China together with the university students and people from all walks of life. We call for:

1. The employees of all trades in Beijing Municipality to go on strike on May 20 at 12:00 P.M. (except those in electricity, water, gas, mail, and communications) until all troops withdraw from Beijing Municipality.

2. Resolutely preventing troops from entering the city, defending the fruits of this democratic movement, maintaining the present order on Tiananmen Square, blocking all the main roads leading to the city and all the subway exits by using vehicles belonging to [work] units, and maintaining the normal operation of China Central Radio and TV.

3. Working together with people of all walks of life in the city to publicize the truth among all the troops in Beijing.

109

Questions and Answers about the Student Movement

PROPAGANDA GROUP, CHINESE LANGUAGE DEPARTMENT,
BEIJING NORMAL UNIVERSITY

May 20, 1989

Source: Courtesy of HKFS.

Q: How can we evaluate this student movement?

A: This is a democratic movement with college students as the core and people throughout society participating. This is the first cry for democracy and freedom by the Chinese people under highly centralized autocratic rule. It is a general outburst of the grievances and anger that have accumulated for many years. . . .

Q: Why did the government officials repeatedly delay responding to the students' demands?

A: They are intentionally creating turmoil and intensifying the contradictions. They want to use the pretext of quelling the turmoil and depend on the troops to maintain a reign of terror. But the army is the people's army. Those who want to exercise dictatorship and autocracy did not expect several developments: (1) the movement is so broad; (2) the students are so brave; (3) the people are so enthusiastic about showing their support for the students; and (4) the demonstrators have such great skill in struggling.

Q: Will the troops eventually enter the city?

A: [Yes,] but (1) with bloodshed; and (2) once blood is shed, the situation will become worse.

Q: How do students evaluate themselves in this movement?

A: The student-led movement has already reached its limits. From now on the students will gradually change from their leading role as a daring vanguard to that of assistants. Because this movement is one of the "whole Chinese people," it should be led by the older intellectuals. It is also normal that some internal strife has emerged among the student leadership. But the students' daring vanguard role should not yet be weakened. . . .

Q: What is the most urgent task [now]?

A: The most urgent [task] is not only to expose the schemes and intrigues of Li Peng and his ilk, but also to make a clear-cut demand for them to let Zhao Ziyang return to [his role] as the political spokesman for the students. We must openly demand: Give us back Zhao Ziyang! At the moment, Zhao is not under much pressure, and the people are becoming more and more [politically] conscious. So if we exert a bit more pressure, we may save Zhao Ziyang.

Q: How should we view the two victims, Hu Yaobang and Zhao Ziyang?

A: Their fates reflect the extreme abnormality of political life inside the party. A party general secretary, who did not even have the little power that an ordinary citizen might have, [including] the right to ask a lawyer to defend him, has disappeared from the political stage quietly. This will evoke wide repercussions. . . .

Q: What should be the relationship between the people and the party?

A: The people have no obligation to be grateful to a political party, because any political party only acts to coordinate the beliefs of the people. The improvement of some people's lives, on the other hand, is the result of hard labor by the people themselves. It is the political party that should be grateful to the people . . . not vice versa. . . .

Q: What are the drawbacks of the Communist party organization?

A: The Communist party has used iron discipline [instead of] democracy and freedom. This is [its] inherent drawback. One-party dominance by the Communist party cannot lead to competition nor [lead to progressive thinking] by the party. Forty million party members can actually do nothing about reconstructing the party. Party membership simply becomes a ticket to practical benefits.

110
Letter to Compatriots of Changsha Railway Institute

CHANGSHA RAILWAY INSTITUTE

May 20, 1989

Source: Courtesy of HKFS.

Compatriots of Changsha Railway Institute:

Hunan Polytechnic University, Hunan Normal University, Hunan University, Hunan College of Education, and other colleges have already formed a united front. . . . The Student Union has highly praised the persistent struggle of our institute. It hopes we will organize propaganda teams and go to the factories and mines to mobilize the workers in forming a united front with students. At the same time, we should oppose violence and fascism and try to win the support of the security guards.

According to a report by the propaganda team of Hunan Polytechnic University, Beijing workers have declared a general strike today.

Fellow students: Let's get united in mobilizing the people to oppose the fascist violence and crackdown on the student movement.

111

Declaration to Defend the Constitution

SIXTEEN SCHOLARS

May 21, 1989

Source: *Tiananmen 1989*, pp. 325–26.

The peaceful and patriotic democracy movement of Chinese students has been going on for more than a month. On May 20, Premier Li Peng issued the order to impose martial law on certain areas of Beijing, and many troops have been ordered to enter the city. By so doing, they have aroused an all-out strong opposition from people throughout the country. This is leading to a severe political crisis. At this most critical moment, we, as Chinese citizens, make the following solemn declaration. . . .

1. According to Article 35 of the Constitution of the People's Republic of China, Chinese citizens have "freedom of speech, publication, assembly, association, to march, and to demonstrate." Therefore, when college and university students peacefully march and demonstrate, and form an organization of colleges and universities [ASUCUB], and when other Chinese have private or public gatherings to discuss politics, they are all exercising rights granted to them by the constitution. Their rights should be protected by the constitution and the laws.

Also in accordance with Article 67, Section 6, of the constitution, the Standing Committee of the National People's Congress has the right to "supervise the work of the State Council, and the Central Military Commission . . . ." According to one report, Fei Xiaotong, vice-chairman of the Standing Committee of the National People's Congress, has notified many deputies to the National People's Congress of the demands . . . for convening a session of the Standing Committee to discuss the student movement. . . . [A]n urgent session of the Standing Committee must be immediately convened to guarantee the supervisory power granted to it by the constitution.

2. To solve . . . the present crisis, to advance democratization of the Chinese political system, and to continue the policies of reform, the open door, and economic development, peaceful, legal, and reasonable methods of political solution must be adopted. Hence we believe:

a. The government should immediately repeal the martial law order. . . .

b. A full session of the Standing Committee of the National People's Congress should be convened as early as possible. The opening date of the session should be publicized.... The participants should have full power of initiation and resolution. Adequate time should be guaranteed for the session. We hope that the session will be made open to the people.... [T]he freedom of journalists to report it and to interview the deputies should not be restricted.

c. The present crisis can only be solved by the above legal and democratic procedures. The use of other compulsory and abnormal measures will necessarily put China into a long period of turmoil and disputes.

We believe that defending the constitution is an unshirkable duty of every Chinese citizen.[1]

112

Letter to the People of the Whole Country

COLLEGE AND UNIVERSITY STUDENTS OF BEIJING

Mid-May 1989

Source: Handbill distributed on the streets of Beijing, in *ORSD,* 1:21.

Compatriots of the whole country:
The situation in Tiananmen Square is steadily deteriorating. In view of the possible consequences, we believe it necessary for the college and university students of Beijing to proclaim to the people of the whole country:

1. The worsening situation today is entirely the result of the central leaders' wrong policies. The inhuman ignorance and cruelty they had shown in dealing with the petitioning and hunger-striking students has aroused the indignation of the people all over the country ....

2. Given the performance of State Chairman Yang Shangkun and Premier Li Peng in dealing with the students' hunger strike, we believe that they [are no longer qualified to be either] Communist party members or state leaders. Thus, we suggest that the Standing Committee of the National People's Congress immediately remove them from all their governmental positions, and that the

---

[1]The sixteen scholars who signed the declaration were Jin Guantao, Liu Qingfeng, Chen Fangzheng, Dong Xiuyu, Chen Wanxiong, Yan Jiaqi, Long Pu, Liu Shuxian, Liu Dong, Chen Danchen, Zhang Gang, Shen Dade, Wu Tingjia, Mao Yushi, Gu Jianfen, and Ye Xiaoqing.

party's Central Committee . . . expel them from the party. Article 187 of the Criminal Code . . . stipulates that "A state employee who through dereliction of duty damages either public property or the interests of the state and people shall be punished." The behavior of both Yang Shangkun and Li Peng constitutes dereliction of duty, so we hereby lodge a complaint against Yang Shangkun and Li Peng with the Supreme People's Procuratorate and ask it to institute proceedings against them.

As the chairman of the Central Military Commission, Deng Xiaoping has placed himself above the state and party, thus fundamentally violating Article 10, Section 3, of the party constitution, which stipulates that "The highest leading organ of the party is the National Party Congress and the Central Committee that it elects." By imposing feudal rule and one-man dictatorship, Deng Xiaoping has also violated Article 16 of the party constitution, which stipulates that "No leader may make arbitrary decisions or place himself above the organization." In dealing with the student hunger strike petition, Deng plotted to mobilize the armed forces to suppress the people and the revolution. He thus violated Article 131 of the Criminal Code . . . which stipulates that "Personal rights, democratic rights, and other citizen rights are protected and may not be violated by any person or any government institution . . . ." We therefore propose that the party Central Committee remove Deng from all his party positions and expel him. We also hereby lodge a complaint against Deng Xiaoping with the Supreme People's Procuratorate and request that it institute proceedings against him.

3. The student movement is a great democratic, patriotic movement. The only goal of over 100,000 college and university students is to establish a republic based on democracy. We seek nothing but the prosperity and strength of China. . . . Now, as the situation continues to deteriorate, we appeal to the people to maintain calm and order . . . .

4. We do not want to involve ourselves in any factional struggle within the party. We believe that the most urgent task to be done in today's China is to build a political system based on full democracy and legality. We do not need to stake China's future on one or two men. The traditional mentality of hoping for "Upright Judge Bao"[1] must be totally abandoned. Hence, we earnestly call upon all Chinese intellectuals, workers, and city residents of every stratum to unite and form an autonomous organization based on democracy. Such an organization will completely conform to the constitution and will fully represent the will of the people. It will play an effective role of supervising . . . the government and the governing party. Only then can we say that the students' struggle for democracy has achieved its goal.

---

[1]"Upright Judge Bao" (Baogong) was a local official known in traditional China for defending the poor.

113

Letter to the Capital Workers

COMMITTEE IN SUPPORT OF STUDENTS' ACTION
BY THE CHINESE WORKERS' MOVEMENT COLLEGE
AND THE TEMPORARY COMMAND CENTER OF THE
CAPITAL WORKERS' PICKET GROUP

Around May 21, 1989

Source: *ORSD*, 1:31.

To the great capital worker comrades:

Democracy and dictatorship have arrived at the hour of a struggle to death. The Li Peng government has become isolated and reactionary by publicly hoisting the banner of opposing the people and democracy. Now the Li Peng government is moving a large number of armed troops into Beijing. We can see that this grand democratic movement is going to be swept away. This morning, 300,000 university students declared a general hunger strike. Most of the students are facing the threat of a strong and brutal suppression. Only the capital's working class can save this great democratic movement. We urgently appeal to capital workers and citizens to take immediate actions.

1. Use nonviolent means to prevent the troops from entering the city and publicize to the troops the truth of this patriotic democratic movement and its great historical significance. Also, try to win support from the troops.

2. Organize workers' picket groups immediately to maintain order in the capital. Prevent illegal behavior like beating, smashing, robbing, and burning so as to ensure the continuation of the struggle of the students' hunger strike.

114

A Statement to the Soldiers

AUTONOMOUS STUDENTS' ASSOCIATION OF
BEIJING NORMAL UNIVERSITY

May 21, 1989

Source: *ORSD*, 1:38.

Hello, all soldiers in the People's Liberation Army!

We must first of all point out that the army is the army of the people and the country. Its responsibility is to protect the welfare of the people and the country. Do you know the real purpose of your being sent to the capital? It is to become the tool for suppressing the people. However, people in the capital trust you and welcome you to have a look at reality.

In fact, who are the "small minority"? What you are seeing now is the clearest picture: People are suffering and crying and are concerned with the future of our nation. Those university students have not eaten anything for seven complete days while under the fierce sunlight. All citizens in the country are worried about them. We have been trying to help them by forming picket lines to maintain orderly traffic in the capital. Where are the [traffic] police? Why does the government not reply to the two minimum demands made by the students? (Negate the April 26 editorial of *People's Daily* and admit that the student movement is patriotic and democratic; also, top leaders should hold dialogues with the students on an equal basis and a live broadcast.) Several thousand students are holding a hunger strike aimed at these two minimum demands. But we have been kept waiting and waiting. More than three thousand [hunger strike] students have fainted. The strong appeal and support of the people are met with arms. We have cried out in the voice of the people to get rid of corruption and official profiteering, to promote democracy and a legal system. What is wrong with this? The rally and demonstration of one million people in the capital together with the students' petitioning during this month have been conducted with systematic organization and with cool-minded restraint and rationality. There has not been one single disastrous incident. The government has delayed its reply many times. For the saying that "There is anarchy," we have to ask, "Where is the government?"

At last, the government came out after a struggle at the top. There is no excuse for turmoil. They are using you—brother army nurtured by the people— to suppress the people in the interest of a few!

Soldiers, we love you. The people love you. Your hands must not be stained with the people's blood!

115

An Open Letter to All Officers and Soldiers of the Liberation Army

A WITNESS OF THE STUDENT MOVEMENT

May 21, 1989

Source: *ORSD*, 1:39.

To all soldiers and officials in the Liberation Army:

From mid-April onward, in Beijing and in many places in this country, thousands of students have held rallies, written big-character posters, and held class boycotts and hunger strikes aimed at urging the government to get rid of corruption, the excessive use of power, profiteering by bureaucrats, inflation, and other problems. These actions are supported by people in the capital and people in other places in the country. In the last few days, genuine reports have been read or heard or watched in newspapers and on television. Have you noticed this? Why are you not allowed to know this? It is because the government is afraid of letting you know the truth. The truth is that all workers, peasants as well as ordinary people, support the students by donating money and delivering food and water to them. In the last few days, thousands upon thousands of people, including cadres from central organizations, ministries under the State Council, *People's Daily*, the Central Party School, the Central Broadcast Station, and even some of the People's Police and PLA soldiers have joined them. Also, there are people from all over the country here to support the students.

Soldiers and officials, you are the hands and feet of the workers, peasants, and people from all walks [of life] in the country. You are our brothers and sisters. The purpose of this movement is to petition [the government] for the people and the country. The students have sacrificed a lot in the interests of the people and the country by holding a hunger strike, which up to the present has lasted for eight days. More than two thousand have fainted, and there are more whose lives are in danger. Kindhearted people expected the government to show some sympathy, but [it did not]. The government does not agree with the two demands of (1) admitting this movement is patriotic; and (2) [holding]a dialogue on an equal basis. On the contrary, they have sent you to suppress the movement. They use you as tools and make it possible to let people kill each other in order to protect their existing advantages.

Soldiers and officials, people all over China understand your situation. But striving for democracy and abolishing corruption is our common goal. The Thirty-eighth Army has refused the order to suppress the students and has retreated from Beijing. What are you going to do?

People all over the country are watching you! Do not do anything to sadden your parents, brothers, and sisters!

116
Beijing Workers' Autonomous Union Preparatory Program

BWAU PREPARATORY COMMITTEE

May 21, 1989

Source: *ORSD*, 1:30.

Since April 20, most Chinese workers have displayed a strong desire to participate in and discuss political issues. There is not yet an organization that can really represent the opinions and desires of the workers. Therefore, we think it is necessary to set up an autonomous organization.

Here is the program:

1. BWAU is an independent, autonomous organization joined by workers voluntarily. According to democratic procedures, it enjoys an equal relationship with other mass organizations and is not controlled by any other organization.

2. BWAU's fundamental principle is to propose political and economic ideas that are in accordance with the majority of workers. This organization should not only be a welfare organization.

3. This organization has the function of supervising the CCP.

4. It has the right to supervise entities of all state-owned and collectively owned enterprises through all legal and effective means so as to guarantee that workers are the real masters of enterprises. In enterprises other than state-owned and collectively owned ones, [BWAU] has the right to protect the interests of the workers by negotiating with enterprise owners . . . .

5. [BWAU] guarantees all legal rights of its members within the scope of the constitution and the [country's] laws.

117

Smash the Counterrevolutionary Coup Carried Out by Li Peng and Yang Shangkun

FACULTY MEMBERS, PARTY MEMBERS, AND
GRADUATE STUDENTS OF UNIVERSITIES IN BEIJING

May 21, 1989

Source: *October Review* (May–June 1989):25.

To all members of the NPC,
All members of the NPC of the various provinces and cities,
Directors of the various provincial and municipal governments as well as the various ministries under the State Council,
Directors of the various armies, various military regions, and the various field armies of the People's Liberation Army:

A well-planned counterrevolutionary coup by a small handful of conspirators headed by Li Peng and Yang Shangkun was carried out on May 19, 1989. They forced Comrade Zhao Ziyang, the party general secretary, to resign; shamefully grabbed the power of the party, state, and military; and ordered ten thousand soldiers to come to Beijing to enforce martial law in . . . the stable and peaceful capital of socialist China. [Further,] they ordered the PLA commanders and soldiers to point their guns at several hundred thousand patriotic students and city residents who lack weapons. This is a sheer fascist counterrevolutionary coup! Now we'd like you to focus on the following key facts:

1. The small handful headed by Li Peng and Yang Shangkun forced General Secretary Zhao Ziyang to resign without the approval of the Central Committee plenum that had been planned and was about to be held. And the small handful dared not publicize to the party the true facts of the enlarged conference of the Politburo. Isn't this a conspiracy opposed to the party's principle of collective leadership?

2. The small handful headed by Li Peng and Yang Shangkun ordered troops to come to Beijing without the Central Military Commission's collective approval, without the signature of Zhao Ziyang, the first deputy chairman of the Central Military Commission, and without reporting to the NPC. Isn't this an unconstitutional, counterrevolutionary coup for grabbing power over the military and the country?

3. The small handful headed by Li Peng and Yang Shangkun have, ever since the beginning of the student democratic movement, cheated both their

superior authorities and ordinary people by provoking turmoil and traffic jams in Beijing and some other provinces and cities so as to create a reason for their counterrevolutionary coup. But, from the beginning of May to the present, the masses have not employed force in the capital and other provinces and cities. There is absolutely no reason why martial law should be carried out in Beijing. Then what is their purpose in bringing army troops here? Is it to scatter the students and city residents who are engaged in delivering petitions, who are totally unarmed and have followed perfectly good order? Comrades! Anybody with political sense can see through their real purpose. Undoubtedly, the people at whom [Li Peng and Yang Shangkun] are aiming are high-level cadres in the Central Committee who support the party's principles and who oppose the conspiracy of the coup! And they also aim at patriotic cadres and soldiers at various levels of the party, the state, and the military! Yang Shangkun and the stubborn and counterrevolutionary Li Peng, who are ready to kill, have jumped out in front of the democratic movement to grab power. Their purpose, like the goal of Sima Zhao [a famous "conspirator" in the Han dynasty], is known by everybody.

Chairman Mao pointed out long ago that once the true rightists in the party come to power and carry out a despotic, fascist dictatorship, they are bound to be opposed by the entire party and the people of the whole country. Thus, one thing is certain: They will neither live in peace nor live a long life. Comrades, we mustn't allow Li Peng's and Yang Shangkun's conspiracy to be realized. And we must not allow our great socialist motherland to become a dark, feudal, fascist country ruled by the Li, the Yang, and other families! Dear comrades, can we allow the benefits provided by the life and blood of our numerous revolutionary forefathers and one billion people to be undone by Li Peng and Yang Shangkun? . . .

118

BWAU Public Notice

BWAU STANDING COMMITTEE

May 21, 1989

Source: *ORSD*, 1:29.

An emergency meeting on our future tasks in the present situation was held this afternoon by the BWAU Standing Committee. Standing Committee members . . . established a leading group, a secretariat, a publishing agency, a rear service agency, and a liaison agency.

    1. BWAU is an autonomous organization, and it complies with the present situation. Its purpose is to lead this democratic, patriotic movement according to democracy and under law.

    It welcomes all workers and workers' unions from various factories and coal mines in the capital to join actively in our union.

    2. According to the present situation, the meeting has decided that (1) the present job of the workers' picket groups is to cooperate closely with [ASUCUB] so as to guarantee the safety of the students and the stability of social order in Beijing; and (2) in the meantime, group members should guarantee the transportation of various kinds of materials and products of daily use, such as vegetables and grain, to Beijing.

119

The Purpose of the City Construction Workers' Autonomous Union [CCWAU]

CCWAU PRESIDENT

May 21, 1989

Source: *ORSD*, 1:32.

The City Construction Workers' Autonomous Union was formally founded on May 21, 1989, at 6:00 P.M.

Its purpose is the following:

We are not prison labor outside of prison, but legal citizens of the republic. We want democracy and freedom. The students are petitioning and are on hunger strike for the people. We are Chinese workers with a conscience. The government is wicked. We workers are in sympathy with student brothers and sisters. We, the workers, must support the students till the end.

A national crisis is ahead, and each individual has the responsibility [to save the nation]. The working class from all sections, from all professions, must unite together and protect our students. [Deng] Xiaoping and Li Peng do not know the right thing to do and should be thrown off the [political] stage.

120

Urgent News

ANONYMOUS

May 21, 1989

Source: Handbill passed out at Beijing University, HKFS.

We have just received the three resolutions of the bogus [puppet] government headed by Li Peng:

1. Suppression begins at 5:00 A.M. tomorrow at the latest. To maintain the so-called twenty years of stability, it is worth killing 200,000 people [a phrase often attributed to Deng Xiaoping].

2. All sanitation workers will be summoned to a meeting today, [where they will be told to] report to work as usual tomorrow. Their main task is to clean up Tiananmen Square.

3. Except for those who have committed capital crimes, all prisoners in Beijing will be evacuated. Many prisons have already done this.[1]

All the college students and the people in Tiananmen Square hereby solemnly swear:

We may die, our blood may flow, but freedom and democracy cannot be lost. We will give up our blood and lives in exchange for a beautiful tomorrow for the republic! . . .

---

[1]This probably referred to purported plans to make space in the prisons for those who would soon be arrested.

121

Some Thoughts

ANONYMOUS

May 21, 1989

Source: Big-character poster in Tiananmen Square, *ORSD*, 2:175–77.

. . . 2. The constitution should be respected as the foundation of the state. . . . We should begin preparing to revise it. . . .

It should be clearly stipulated that the constitution is the final and highest expression of the will and interests of Chinese citizens, and that no [single] political party has the power to represent the will of 1.1 billion Chinese nationals. (It seems that a few people today cannot even represent the will of forty million CCP members.)

Within the limits of the law, every citizen fully enjoys all the rights, [including] freedom of speech, publication, assembly, association, and demonstration granted to them by Article 2, Section 35, of the constitution (promulgated on December 4, 1982). Each of these rights should be . . . interpreted by the highest legal authority and made known to all.

All public servants in the government, especially high-ranking ones and those in charge of political affairs, should swear an oath of office before the constitution. The government should designate a day as Constitution Day, [so as to indicate to all] that our country is a "People's Republic," not a "party-state." . . .

5. . . . The pay for all party leaders (including staff workers) at all levels, except for those concurrently holding posts in state institutions, must be provided by the party itself and should not be treated as a state financial expense. . . .

6. . . . Permit [those] citizens concerned about state affairs who hold different opinions and views to form new political parties. As long as they have not committed treason, those seeking to organize new political parties should be permitted to do so. . . .

122

Declaration of Human Rights

CHINESE HUMAN RIGHTS MOVEMENT COMMITTEE, BEIJING

Around May 20, 1989

Source: *ORSD*, 2:92.

In view of the widespread ignorance and neglect of or even apathy toward human rights in Chinese society, in view of several thousand years of cruel interference in and the infringement of human rights by our rulers, and in view of the need to create a new society, a new order, and a new morality, we hereby solemnly declare the following to be the inviolable and inalienable natural rights of human beings:

1. Everyone is born free and equal, regardless of origin, status, age, sex, profession, level of schooling, religion, party affiliation, and ethnicity.

2. The right to life and security and to oppose oppression are humankind's inalienable natural rights.

3. There are no crimes of conscience. Everyone has freedom of speech, writing, publication, and advocacy.

4. . . . Everyone has the freedom to believe or not believe in a religion or in various theories [such as Marxism].

5. . . . Everyone has the right to travel and to reside inside or outside the country. . . .

6. Personal dignity shall not be infringed on because of criminal conviction.

7. The individual has the right to privacy. One's family, domicile, and correspondence are protected by law.

8. Everyone has the right to education. Higher education should be open to everyone based on achievement scores.

9. Private property acquired through one's [own] labor is sacred and inviolable.

10. Freedom of marriage between adult men and women shall not be interfered with by any outside force. Marriage must be voluntarily agreed upon by both parties.

11. Everyone has the right to assembly and association, whether openly or secretly.

12. The power of the government comes from the people. In the absence of free elections . . . , the people may rescind any power usurped either by force or under the guise of the will of the people by any individual or group (including any of the political parties).

13. Everyone has the right to either direct or indirect participation in government (through free elections of representatives).

14. The law is the embodiment of the popular will and cannot be changed arbitrarily by one individual or any one political party. Everyone is equal before the law.

15. The army is the defender of the interests of the people and of the state. It must strictly observe neutrality in political affairs and not [be subordinate to] an individual or a political party.

16. Democracy and freedom are the basic guarantees of social stability, people's well-being, and national prosperity. Therefore, each person has the right and the duty to establish and safeguard such a system and to oppose autocracy and tyranny.

123

Thoughts beneath the Monument

ANONYMOUS

After May 17, 1989

Source: *ORSD*, 1:94–95.

. . . Gazing at the heavily guarded defense lines under the Monument [to the People's Heroes][1] and all the busy people above it, everyone who really truly has a democratic consciousness will clearly realize that a potential crisis is brewing. The rotten smell of the existing political system and the obsolete ideas fast approaching death are now eroding our cradle of democracy . . . .

. . . [T]he waste in the gathering places of the college students in Tiananmen Square is astounding. Many high-quality nutrients are scattered on the ground; numerous bottles of drinking water . . . and a lot of food and bread have been discarded.

Under the monument, layer after layer of sentries and tight pickets [around the student leadership's headquarters] inspire awe and veneration. However, after one shows a special pass and goes through three checkpoints, one finds to one's great disappointment that the members of the Autonomous Student Union of Colleges and Universities in Beijing [ASUCUB] are "missing."

---

[1]This monument, which stands in the middle of Tiananmen Square, became the headquarters for the student leadership of the movement.

Time is passing quickly, and the Standing Committee of ASUCUB is embroiled in an endless quarrel, [which is contributing to] the loss of control in Tiananmen Square.

. . . Why have the heavy shadows of feudal bureaucrats and corrupt politics appeared in the very center of this democracy movement? Why under the banner of democracy can someone so skillfully play the role of a sheep before the wolves and of a wolf before the sheep? Why have hundreds of thousands of college students in Tiananmen Square turned such a blind eye to all of this or done nothing about it? This shows that we have neglected our own democratic consciousness, that we are blind to the profound, inner significance of this democracy movement, that our own obsolete ideas and feudal habits [have compromised our values]. Although young students have played the role of vanguards and fighters in this popular democracy movement, long-standing oppression by feudal autocracy has made us strangers to applying the consciousness and the rights of a citizen to judge our own actions. . . . Obviously, if we let [this] phenomenon go unchecked, the final result of this student movement will inevitably be the emergence of a new autocratic and bureaucratic stratum. . . . AS-UCUB will be pushed to slide in the opposite [direction] of the democracy movement. [This in turn] will exacerbate the blindness, perplexity, loss of purpose, and exhaustion already appearing among some students and residents. . . . [F]rom now on, all of us . . . should . . . examine our own behavior and the goals of this democracy movement. . . . The basis for this . . . self-examination should be: Has the work that we are engaged in, and what we have thought and done, really promoted the propagation of democratic ideas? . . .

. . . Human beings should have the right to choose independently their fate, the right to protect their dignity as human beings, and the consciousness and courage to be responsible for all their actions. At the same time, one has the obligation to respect all the rights and needs of others as human beings. Only when such a consciousness governs one's actions can one be considered a person with a democratic consciousness. . . . [Only thus] can all those participating in the movement rid themselves of the desire to control and command. . . .

Concretely speaking, we should first clearly recognize that city residents, workers, students, journalists, jurists, and all democratic parties are completely equal. . . . However, as relatively independent strata and as elements of a pluralistic democratic society, . . . they all have their own interests and demands that they rightfully seek. . . . This means that, whether spiritually or materially, people owe us nothing. No one should take on the airs of a hero and feel justified in asking or demanding people to make donations. . . .

Second, everyone participating in this movement should . . . be aware that it is a movement in which everyone realizes his/her own values and achieves and safeguards his/her own dignity as a human being. No one should sit idly and enjoy the fruits of others' work. No one should expect others to save or to make decisions for them. Particularly the college students who comprise the core of the

SLIDING TOWARD TRAGEDY 283

democracy movement . . . should try hard to get rid of the subconscious [attitude] of being either masters or slaves. They should not be willing to live under the shadow of self-created leaders, and they should not impose their demands and wishes upon others, making themselves the variant of a new bigwig living on the flesh and blood of the people. . . . They should . . . propagate a democratic spirit in order to lay the first solid cornerstone for building a modern society in China.

124

Open Letter to Deng Xiaoping: Concerning the Good Thing You Did for the Nation Last Year

COMMAND CENTER OF TIANANMEN SQUARE, RECOVERED
HUNGER- STRIKE LEADERS, ASUCUB, AND THE COMMAND
CENTER OF COLLEGE STUDENTS FROM OTHER PROVINCES

May 22, 1989

Source: *Tiananmen 1989*, pp. 337–38.

Xiaoping:[1] How are you?

[At] the call of college students, a great and unprecedented patriotic mass movement is now taking place in Beijing and throughout the country. Some leaders at the center are not following the popular will. [Rather than seeing that they themselves are part of the problem,] they view this patriotic movement as turmoil and are now mobilizing troops [to enter] Beijing. Nevertheless, more than one day after martial law was declared, there are still continuous demonstrations in Beijing, and the troops cannot enter the city. They are all blocked at the outskirts of the city by the . . . people. It is really unprecedented for an order from the central authorities to meet such strong resistance. You are a wise man and cannot fail to understand the present situation. . . . Although some in the demonstrations shouted some slogans unfavorable to you . . . [most of] these slogans were just [letting off steam]. There is no need to list your remarkable

---

[1]By addressing Deng Xiaoping only by his given name, the students committed an act of what the party old guard would consider *lèse majesté*: They were in effect claiming the status of close comrades (but without adding the appellation "comrade," commonly used when the top party leadership refer to each other by given names). Yet in the body of the text, the polite formal form of the second person pronoun is used in addressing Deng.

contributions to our country. The people will never forget them. The complaint that the people have about you, the powerful political leader of China commonly recognized as number one both at home and abroad, is that you still have not made the broadminded judgments of this patriotic democracy movement that [a man] with your sharp mind should have. We recognize that there appears to be a certain degree of confusion in Beijing, and we also . . . hope for a quick end to it. We are even more unwilling to see real turmoil caused by clashes between us and the people's army. The vast majority of the people . . . demand democracy and oppose corruption. They have already stood up and will not compromise with the present government that has opposed its will in wrongly judging the nature of this patriotic movement. So the confrontation between the present government and the people will continue. . . . The chances of restoring stability will be remote.

To conclude this democracy movement peacefully, the heavy burden (which could also be called an opportunity) of history has, since our country has not yet fully achieved true democracy, again fallen on your shoulders. We sincerely urge you to exercise your prestige and powerful influence in the party, government, and army to force some unpopular leaders to step down. . . . How this part of history is written has much to do with you. We sincerely hope that with your intervention the process of democratization in China will be advanced nonviolently. . . .

125
Letter to the Party Central Committee by Party Members in Shanghai

ABOUT 500 PARTY MEMBERS IN SHANGHAI'S
[MUNICIPAL COMMUNIST PARTY ORGANIZATION BUREAU]

May 22, 1989

Source: *Tiananmen 1989*, pp. 338–39.

To the party Central Committee:
    At present our country and party are at a critical juncture. As party members, we are extremely worried. . . . Hence we write this letter to the party Central Committee. . . . The great patriotic democracy movement now sweeping Beijing and the whole country essentially reflects the will of the whole party and the people of the whole country to revitalize China and realize the four modernizations. In

the speech made at the meeting attended by central government and Beijing party, government, and army cadres on May 19, however, Comrade Li Peng accused this movement of "creating turmoil." Based on this erroneous judgment, Comrade Li Peng ordered martial law and called the army into Beijing. After his speech, the people in Beijing and other areas witnessed a new tide of protest. . . . [T]he actual effect of Comrade Li Peng's "May 19" speech was very negative and will likely lead the party into an extremely dangerous situation. Party members should not allow the situation to deteriorate further.

For the past forty years, our party made many serious mistakes. . . . One . . . reason such mistakes are not prevented is the abnormal political life within the party. Most of the upright party members are not able to stand up and . . . effectively oppose wrong decisions. Historical tragedies should not be repeated. [W]e can no longer keep silent. We want to exercise the rights entrusted to us by the party constitution. . . .

We suggest that the party's Central Committee convene a special session . . . as soon as possible to discuss the current situation. . . .

We strongly demand that:

1. Comrade Li Peng's "May 19" speech be retracted and normal order in Beijing be restored as soon as possible. Bloodshed and a crackdown on the students and people are absolutely prohibited.

2. The April 26 *People's Daily* editorial be negated and a sincere dialogue be conducted by the government with the students on the basis of full equality. . . .

3. The news embargo be removed immediately. [Everyone] must know the truth. . . .

126
Urgent Appeal to the Citizens of the Capital

CAPITAL INTELLECTUALS

May 22, 1989

Source: Handbill in Beijing University, in *ORSD*, 1:19.

By declaring a military dictatorship, the ruling clique of the military government has outrageously trampled upon the constitution and openly launched a war against the people. The Chinese nation is at the most critical moment, a moment of life and death. Large-scale bloodshed and sacrifice of lives by the people in the capital, the young students and elite intellectuals, is likely, and bloody suppression is imminent. To save the republic, some intellectuals in the capital have issued the following urgent appeals to the people of the capital:

1. We urgently call for . . . the people to gather at Fuxingmen and Jianguomen at 1:30 on the afternoon of May 23. Then begin a big demonstration with the core slogans of "Lift martial law" and "Li Peng and Yang Shangkun step down."

2. . . . [S]trengthen propaganda work among the PLA soldiers. The . . . slogan is "Don't stain your hands with the blood of the people." Organize a propaganda offensive, including high school, elementary school, and kindergarten children to go to the heart of the garrison army quickly to weaken its morale and compel the soldiers to turn their weapons around, transfer their allegiance, and counterattack.

3. Convene an emergency special session of the Beijing People's Congress to impeach Chen Xitong [the mayor of Beijing] according to law, to declare martial law void, and to elect a new government. Restore and stabilize public transportation and public security, and create a new social order necessary for the people's livelihood. . . .

5. We should harbor no illusion about the ruling clique of the military government. We must clearly recognize the imminent danger of bloody clashes on a large scale and not slacken our vigilance. All the city residents need to organize themselves immediately and establish a unified communication network, a command and coordination center. We must be prepared for the military government to launch a focused attack against key sectors by concentrating troops . . . , and be prepared for bloodshed, for sacrificing lives, as well as organizing emergency needs, medical facilities, and medicine. . . .

6. If the military government risks universal condemnation by conducting bloody terror and imposing autocratic dictatorship regardless of large-scale bloodshed and death, the people in the capital should immediately evacuate the city, or disperse and protect the student leaders, the intellectuals, and many national elites. . . .

127

Urgent Suggestions

TEACHERS' SUPPORT GROUP OF BEIJING UNIVERSITY

May 22, 1989

Source: Courtesy of HKFS.

At the moment a considerable number of PLA soldiers and officers among the martial law troops have already been moved by our political propaganda work. They have begun to understand the democracy movement and show sympathy toward us. The soldiers and officers of the martial law troops are, however, living in a very difficult situation. Their supply of food, drinking water, and medicine is inadequate. To win the support of the soldiers, to win time, and to make the soldiers and officers feel the warmth of Beijing people, we, out of humanitarian consideration, hereby suggest that we should:

1. Arrange for some ambulances and medical workers now serving the hunger strikers to go to where martial law troops are stationed to provide medical service and give medicine to ailing soldiers and officers.

2. Call on the state-owned commercial networks and private vendors to sell food and drinks to the troops at a fair price;

3. Organize professional and amateur theater troupes, and those famous actors and actresses who have clearly shown their support for the students, to give special performances for the martial law troops; and

4. Continue to give newspapers, magazines, and journals of art and literature to the soldiers and officers to liven up their cultural and recreational activities.

128
Another Urgent Appeal

BEIJING ENTREPRENEURS ASSOCIATION

May 22, 1989

Source: *ORSD*, 2:67.

On May 18 we made an appeal in *China Youth* entitled "Lose no opportunity to prevent the situation from becoming more complicated. . . . " In view of recent developments, we make the following urgent appeals:

1. The government should try to solve the problems democratically and legally by immediately rescinding martial law and withdrawing the troops, and not let the situation deteriorate.

2. All directors (managers) and workers of all enterprises in the capital should stand fast at their posts and guarantee normal order for working within the enterprises, [thereby] safeguarding the economic life in the capital so as to support the patriotic movement of the students.

3. The workers' pickets already formed in the enterprises should support the patriotic movement of the students by helping the people's police and students maintain social order and public security, and prevent any illegal activities.

We appeal to the people of all walks of life throughout society to adopt a more sober, rational, and restrained attitude, as well as respect for order, in seeking success for the patriotic movement and in promoting the process of socialist democracy.

129

Introducing *Xinwen kuaixun*

XINWEN KUAIXUN

May 22, 1989

Source: *Xinwen kuaixun* (News express), May 22, 1989, no. 1, in *ORSD*, 2:201.

Given that the government is now tightly blocking news channels and . . . news reports are [grossly] inconsistent with the facts, all of us conscientious journalists and theoretical workers in the capital have decided to publish *News Express* so as to defend the solemn rights of "freedom of the press, speech, and publication" granted in the Constitution of the People's Republic of China, to guarantee the truth . . . of news reports, and the goal that "important issues should be known to the people."

The sole aim of *News Express* is quickly, truly, and accurately to report to the people in the capital, all over the country, and throughout the world about the great patriotic democracy movement by the students, workers, city residents, cadres, intellectuals, and the people of all walks of life in the capital as well as in other provinces of the country; and to report relevant news and views from [China] and the world.

Long live the people!
Long live freedom!
Long live democracy!
Long live the republic!

130

Letter to the Workers' Pickets

AUTONOMOUS STUDENTS' UNION OF BEIJING
NORMAL UNIVERSITY

May 28, 1989 [original document incorrectly stated April]

Source: *ORSD*, 1:34.

All workers, citizens, and comrades:

Thank you for your hard work. For more than a month, you have been giving wide support to this great patriotic movement, both materially and spiritually. We, the patriotic students have voiced your desires. The workers and students are closely linked together. When we have demonstrations on the streets, you applaud and cheer for us, deliver food and water, and even donate all your money unselfishly. When we protest against the government's shameful acts, you show us your passionate support. Without your support, we would not have been able to hold on till the present.

Li Peng's hypocritical government did not accept the students' righteous request and even contradicted itself in accusing the student movement of turmoil. It then ordered the troops to enter Beijing [to suppress the movement]. You have insisted on standing on the students' side, and have bravely, intelligently, and effectively blocked the troops from entering Beijing. Today is the fourth day under martial law. The hypocritical government vulgarly and treacherously organized something called the workers' picket group to help the troops enter Beijing. Do not think that workers and students will have conflicts and fight against one another so as to let the government fish in troubled waters. It is said that the government has ordered some plainclothes [police] to join the workers' pickets as agitators. Workers, comrades, and compatriots, you must open your eyes wide. Even so, we still believe that they are Chinese although they are plainclothes [police]. If they still lack a conscience, they will help Li Peng's hypocritical government.

131

Open Letter to the Students from an Old Soldier

A VETERAN OF THE PEOPLE'S LIBERATION ARMY

May 22, 1989

Source: *ORSD*, 1:43.

Dear students and citizens:

A salute to you from an old soldier!

Over the past period, I have paid attention to your struggle quietly and [now] would like to remind you that you have already achieved an unimaginable victory! I can't openly step out to support you, but I want to tell you some things:

1. *Strategy:* There are thousands upon thousands of people on Tiananmen Square. A small minority of soldiers cannot handle such a situation. Martial law has been imposed for many hours, but there has been no action taken on the square because there are insufficient soldiers and policemen in the city. The education received by the army is different from that of the policemen. It is difficult for them to point their guns at people. Ten million united Beijing people are unconquerable.

2. *Tactics:*

a. Road intersections: The people's spontaneous blocking of army vehicles is unprecedented. Never retreat. Even if some platoons succeed in entering from different directions, do not retreat. A few platoons cannot solve the problem and cannot carry out martial law on the square. It is victory if road junctions are successfully blocked. To reach this goal, it is a must to establish a stable command system at the road junctions and to improve the situation of poor organization.

b. Splitting: This is a commonly used tactic [by the army]. People can borrow this to oppose the army. Fully prepared, we can let two-thirds of the army enter but block the remaining one-third. Repeat this at the next road intersection. This will systematically cut the army into several unconnected parts. With this tactic, the power and initiative of the army will vanish.

c. Shooting and tear gas: For several hundred thousand people who are crowded together, shooting and using tear gas will cause much confusion, injuries, and death. We must warn the leaders of the army that whoever gives the order to kill will someday be sentenced to death by a military court. Even if Beijing can be controlled by a massacre, how can so many cities in the country be controlled? They do not have that many armies.

d. We should trust the basic qualities of the people's army. We must enforce deep and detailed ideological work. We must not only tell the soldiers not to enter the city, but also try to change their position and stand on the people's side. Victory to people in Beijing.

132

Seven Senior Army Leaders State Their Positions

ZHANG AIPING, XIAO KE, YE FEI, YANG DEZHI, SONG SHILUN, CHEN ZAIDAO, AND LI JUKUI

May 23, 1989

Source: Handbill, in *ORSD*, 2:84.

To the General Headquarters of the Martial Law Troops in Beijing and the Central Military Commission:

As the situation is extremely grave at present, we, as veteran soldiers, make the following demands:

The people's army belongs to the people. It cannot set itself against the people. Even less can it suppress the people. And it absolutely cannot open fire on the people. To prevent the situation from deteriorating further, the troops cannot enter the city. . . .

133

The Final Battle between Light and Darkness: Statement on the Current Situation

JOINT CONFERENCE OF PEOPLE FROM ALL
WALKS OF LIFE IN THE CAPITAL

May 23, 1989

Source: *ORSD*, 2:27.

Since April 1989, China has entered a totally new historical era. The great patriotic democracy movement initiated by the college students in Beijing and broadly participated in by people from all walks of life throughout the country is unprecedented in Chinese history.

All past Chinese revolutions were for the sake of providing people with adequate food and clothing, for seeking minimum subsistence. This makes past Chinese revolutions totally different from the Lutheran Reformation in the West, and from revolutionary movements such as the bourgeois revolution, which was idealistic and sought both basic living conditions and the development of human beings.

. . . Our struggle this time is for democracy, human rights, and the development of the human being. This movement has surpassed any revolution in Chinese history. Even the "May Fourth" Movement of 1919 and the "April 5" Movement of 1976 cannot match it. . . .

We only have our bare fists and are defenseless, yet violence against the people comes to nothing. . . . A new era now begins in which violence will be met with good will. The peaceful struggle for democracy and human rights is bound to succeed. This is a revolution by the people. It does not resort to terror, and it will not let those who impose terror succeed. The consciousness of the people is the goal of the struggle and the sign of victory.

. . . At present, due to the perverse acts of a handful of people like Li Peng, there is turmoil. These people have intentionally stopped normal public transportation, cut the normal supply of daily necessities of life, and exerted intense pressure on the leading cadres at various levels and on the workers. They have blocked the passage of information and controlled the news reports. They are confusing right and wrong and producing lies. They are trampling on legality and sabotaging democracy. They even cruelly and stupidly use the military to force the people to surrender.

Beijing people, however, have not been intimidated by all this. The struggle has now entered a stage of stalemate. The martial law order has been issued for several days, but not one single soldier of the martial law troops has been able to enter the city. . . .

It is not unlikely that we may suffer a defeat, but we really have no room for maneuver. If a few persons who oppose the people succeed, they will take revenge on the people, both those who were criticized in the so-called anti–spiritual pollution and anti–bourgeois liberalization campaigns, and the participants in this movement. The accomplishments of the ten years of reform and the open door will be totally lost.

When that time comes, the process of democratization in China will be halted and the reform and open-door policies will be abandoned. . . . Our people will again return to the status of being oppressed and powerless. Waiting for the people are bludgeons, labels,[1] prisons, or even butchers' knives.

We can only fight to win or die. For so many years under a consistently high-handed [government], so many of us have been accustomed to being worldly wise and playing safe, being forbearing and conciliatory. But now, facing a handful of insane government leaders who are against the people, we can no longer harbor illusions. If they can disregard the lives of several thousand student hunger strikers, how can we expect them to show kindness to the people?

Li Peng is fierce of mien but faint of heart. We should not mistake his attitude for strength. Li Peng and his ilk are beating a retreat not because they are restrained, but because they are incompetent. When he was chairman of the State Education Commission, Li Peng pushed Chinese education into a crisis. Since he has been premier, production has declined and prices have skyrocketed. His incompetence is obvious. . . .

Every Chinese with a conscience and sense of justice: let's unite and save our country from danger.

---

[1]Refers to political labels that follow people in their dossiers, affecting their and their children's opportunities for education, jobs, and so forth.

134

Some Viewpoints on the Current Situation

CHINESE SCIENCE AND TECHNOLOGY UNIVERSITY

May 23, 1989

Source: *ORSD*, 2:142.

. . . During the ten years of reform, because of the lack of feedback in the existing autocratic system, corruption [became] widespread and major mistakes in decisions were frequent. This has produced profound ideological, economic, and political crises. They have finally led to this widespread political movement . . . which is aimed at facilitating the Chinese political system's shift from autocracy to democracy in order to fit the needs of modernization.

As a political movement, this will either be settled by peaceful political means or end up in a violent crackdown. . . . [T]he situation has changed from a likely victory for Li Peng's high-handed policy to a stalemate between the government and the students and people. . . .

In view of the actual situation in China, it is not yet possible for democratic forces to occupy a position of overwhelming dominance. At the same time, it is equally impossible for the autocratic forces to be overwhelmingly dominant. We should recognize that there are still a large number of middle-of-the-road forces. Which way these forces lean will decide the final victory or failure of the two sides. As an example, take the central government: It has a democratic force with Zhao Ziyang and Wan Li as its representatives, and a despotic force with Li Peng as its representative. In between are some middle-of-the-road forces that have not yet directly taken their positions. How to win over the middle-of-the-road forces is the crucial question for the democracy movement at the moment.

The basic wishes of the middle-of-the-road forces are to restore order as soon as possible and solve problems in a stable environment. These forces don't want to set themselves against the people, nor do they want to damage the reputation of the Communist party. Hence, when the popular will is resolute and on the upsurge, and there is no time for hesitation, [the middle-of-the-roaders] will decisively stand by the democratic forces. . . . [T]hey will provide a counterforce to the high-handed policy of Li Peng, on the one hand, and intensify the struggle among various political forces, on the other. . . .

Based on the above analysis, we think the correct strategies to be adopted in the democracy movement are:

Goals of actions: Gradually isolating and forcing the collapse of the extreme autocratic forces, to try to win over the middle-of-the-road forces, and to protect and develop democratic forces.[1]

... *Contents of actions*: Continuing to hold sit-ins and demonstrations and, at the same time, holding large-scale petitioning demonstrations, trying to win over the soldiers in order to resist high-handed policy and to promote a peaceful solution of the problems. ...

135
Letter to the People of All Circles in Beijing

ANONYMOUS

Late May 1989

Source: Leaflet, in *ORSD*, 1:19.

Dear residents, workers, peasants, cadres, intellectuals, and PLA officers and soldiers:

... Democratic rights are the natural and inalienable social rights of every citizen: Every citizen has the right to express his or her opinion, to participate in making policies and laws, electing and removing state cadres, supervising state cadres' work, and implementing every policy. All citizens also have the right to defend themselves and the obligation to respect these same rights for all others. These rights are the sole basis on which we can become masters of our own country and overthrow dictatorial oppression. The time has come to abolish the autocratic system under which a small minority dictate to everyone and establish a true democratic system where all people have a say. We must not miss this opportunity.

Do you want corrupt officials to step down? Do you want those engaged in official profiteering to give back what they have grabbed from the people? Do you want to stop inflation, raise your wages, and have the right to defend your own interests? Do you want to banish the shadows of political persecution forever? If you do, then join this struggle. Democracy is everyone's concern. ... Do we want our children and grandchildren to live under a political system where the People's Congress is only a rubber stamp, and even the general secretary of the Communist party could not protect himself? ...

---

[1]This is strongly reminiscent of the Communist party's own formulation of united-front strategy.

136

Letter to the Residents of Beijing

AUTONOMOUS STUDENTS' UNION OF BEIJING
NORMAL UNIVERSITY

May 23, 1989

Source: Courtesy of HKFS.

Dear city residents:

. . . We hope residents will continue with the students to struggle and completely smash the martial law decree.

Our strategy is to choose important intersections with narrow roads and many residential homes and organize residents to take shifts around the clock. Once something unusual happens, summon nearby residents to block the roads and stop troops and other suspicious people. Use peaceful means, talk reasonably to the troops, and move them with emotion. Expose the true colors of Li Peng's bogus government that unfurls the banner of socialism to impose feudal fascist dictatorship. Unveil to the soldiers this great patriotic democracy movement's significance in order to divide them and shake the army's morale. Once martial law is smashed, Li's bogus government will soon fall.

137

Letter to the Officers and Soldiers Ordered to Enter Beijing to Impose Martial Law

AN ARMY MAJOR

May 23, 1989

Source: Handout at Beijing University, in *ORSD*, 1:41.

Dear soldiers:

I am also a serviceman and was born into a peasant's family. We are all brothers and comrades-in-arms. My unit is stationed in Beijing. Being a little older than you, I'd like to talk with you about our duty as soldiers.

The PLA is a people's army made up of sons of workers and peasants. The sole purpose of this army is to stand firmly by the people and serve the people wholeheartedly, which means that we are not the armed force of warlords or of some private families.

When enemies were invading our motherland, we fought courageously on the battlefield, never balking at any sacrifice, including our blood and lives. When people were suffering natural disasters, we immediately went forward to rescue them without regard for our own safety. We have enjoyed high esteem in the people's hearts. The relationship between the army and the people has been compared to that of fish and water.

With a broken heart, I'd like to tell you that the reason you were sent to Beijing this time is not to fight against the enemy, nor to provide disaster relief. As a matter of fact, you have been tricked and are being used. You have been sent to Beijing to suppress the students' patriotic movement. What's worse is that once you enter the capital, you might ignite a civil war.

The current movement, started by the students and participated in by intellectuals, workers, and civilians, has spread to the whole nation and aims at pushing forward the reforms, opposing corruption and official profiteering, and improving the people's living conditions. Millions of people in Beijing have participated in the demonstrations and have petitioned on a scale unprecedented in [Chinese] history. It can be compared with the May Fourth Movement in 1919 and will certainly be recorded forever in history. This movement has hit the vital point of the privileged class, the corrupt officials and the bureaucrats, and also that of the Yang family. Yang Shangkun was once persecuted by Mao Zedong and later cleared by the party's Central Committee, which announced his rehabilitation and entrusted him with an important position.[1] After he became executive vice-chairman of the Central Military Commission, he started seeking personal interests by abusing his power and began practicing nepotism by appointing his own brother, Yang Baibing, as chief of the General Political Department, and then his own son as chief of the Second Artillery Force.[2] The Military Commission meetings have almost become his family meetings!

Recently, the party Central Committee has many times considered the students' patriotic enthusiasm in a positive way. It has not agreed to label this mass movement as "turmoil." Don't you know that once labeled as "turmoil," it is equivalent to "counterrevolutionary?" No one would agree with this! The Central Committee supports the students' demands of "opposing bureaucracy and corruption." The Yang brothers feel that the more the movement grows, the less favorable it is to their own feudal privileges. Risking universal condemnation,

---

[1]Hu Yaobang is believed by some to have played a key role in clearing Yang Shangkun after the Cultural Revolution. Ruan Ming, "Hu Yaobang and I."

[2]This military unit was, in reality, a missile research operation located in Beijing.

they openly usurped supreme power by squeezing out Zhao Ziyang, the general secretary officially elected by the whole party, and by propping up Li Peng, a wicked careerist who has been making serious mistakes. It was also Yang Shangkun who secretly decided to send military forces to Beijing with the purposes of (1) suppressing the students' patriotic prodemocracy movement, shutting up the people's mouths, and therefore covering up his own scandals; (2) preparing to stage a military coup and establishing the Yang dynasty and fascist military dictatorship. What a heinous criminal plot! Now their conspiracy has been exposed and has met with strong opposition and silent resistance from many army officers and soldiers as well as senior army officials. Some even raised the slogan of "Down with the New Warlord!"

Just think: Why are such large and powerful military forces, including tanks and armored troops, proceeding to the peaceful capital? Is an armed turmoil taking place here? No! Are attacking, smashing, robbing, and burning going on here? No! What is happening is that the unarmed students are peacefully petitioning in the form of boycotting class, demonstrating on streets, sitting in, and participating in a hunger strike. If it is only for the purpose of dealing with a "handful of bad people," wouldn't the hundreds of thousands of Armed Police in Beijing be enough?

Dear brothers, you have probably understood the people's attitudes. They are blocking the army trucks at the risk of their lives to protect the students and teachers! Once again, the Chinese nation is at a crucial historical moment. We should not do anything foolish to break our family's hearts and to be cursed by the people forever. We should not become pawns of the Yang brothers and sinners of history. Your guns and fists should never target the students, teachers, and civilians. It is better to be dismissed from the army than to be used as a tool. Don't ever cause bloodshed! Remember, the students will never forget you, your parents will support you, and people will be grateful to you. That is the common wish of many of my comrades-in-arms as well as mine.

138

An Unpredictable Government Is Always Unpredictable

BEIJING UNIVERSITY

Late May 1989

Source: Handbill, in *ORSD*, 1:20.

On May 13, when three thousand Beijing college students went on a hunger strike in Tiananmen Square, many people believed that in two or three days the government would regain its conscience and show pity by satisfying some of the students' demands that the government agrees are "in line with the party Central Committee's wishes." These people were wrong.

During May 17, 18, and 19, when several million people, young and old, from all social strata, supported the students' cry for democracy, many people again believed that this time the government would have to listen to the people's wishes and act accordingly. . . . Again these people were wrong.

In the early morning of May 20, Li Peng's speech dealt a severe blow to those who still harbored illusions. . . . Before and after the demonstration of May 23 with its student slogan "We will march every day until Li Peng steps down," probably many people again congratulated each other, thinking that martial law would be aborted and Li Peng routed.

But wait!

A young woman yesterday tearfully told us how her husband was persecuted. He works in a certain army unit in Beijing. Because he and his colleagues demonstrated on May 17 and 18 in support of the students and brought back a few handbills to the unit, he was under investigation yesterday and his colleagues were under confinement. All Beijing enterprises are now pressured to "clean out" demonstrators. Even before "the harvest is over," they want to "settle accounts."

Good people: do you remember the big sticks on your backs during the anti-Rightist movement, the Cultural Revolution, and the "April 5" movement?

Do you feel safe because you have only brought back a few handbills or participated in a few demonstrations?

All good Chinese: It is time we woke up. We have no other choice. Compatriots: Unite! Only if we step forward bravely will Chinese people have a future. . . . Patriotic compatriots: Let's unite and fight to the end. We are willing to die for democracy and freedom. Let us march forward!

139

Some Views on the Current Situation and Our Tasks

YOUNG AND MIDDLE-AGED THEORETICAL WORKERS OF BEIJING

May 23, 1989

Source: Distributed by the Autonomous Student Union of Beijing Science and Technology University, HKFS.

Li Peng's appearance on behalf of the party's Central Committee and the State Council actually means that the party general secretary, Comrade Zhao Ziyang, has been deposed. Li Peng has overstepped his authority and usurped the power of the Standing Committee of the National People's Congress by secretly assembling the group armies to garrison the capital, and declaring martial law throughout Beijing. This seriously violates the state and party constitutions. It is indeed a military coup. . . . We must accurately and deeply understand this coup so we can correctly direct our actions.

2. Like Hitler's usurpation of power and Lin Biao's "Project 571" coup attempt,[1] Li Peng also created turmoil and then imposed emergency measures under the pretext of quelling the turmoil.

Li Peng and his ilk purposely delayed holding a dialogue with the petitioning students or meeting the hunger strikers. Several times they prevented General Secretary Zhao Ziyang, who from the beginning of the hunger strike wanted to have a sincere and direct dialogue with the students, from meeting the students. Li Peng time and again sent Yuan Mu and He Dongchang to play "good guy/bad guy" roles to conduct false and insincere dialogues with the students. They were simply acting in an opera. They wanted to use He Dongchang's feudal, narrow-minded, vengeful attitude to goad the students into taking radical actions and to create a social crisis, which they could use to weaken the general secretary, attack Zhao, and then replace him. This social crisis would justify the extraordinary and extreme measure of mobilizing troops and declaring martial law in the capital, Beijing, in peacetime. All these measures and methods are unprecedented since the founding of the People's Republic. They also shut down the

---

[1]"Project 571" refers to Lin Biao's putative conspiracy to assassinate Mao and take power in the fall of 1971. The Chinese pronunciation of "571" with the tones changed can also mean "armed uprising." The original document translated here appears to have misprinted the number as "5712."

subway, stopped bus transportation, and reduced the supply of daily necessities to create more turmoil and arouse the residents against the students. They believed that once they fully controlled the situation and consolidated their positions, they would restore the supply of daily necessities and perhaps draw funds from the state treasury to create the illusion of prosperity in Beijing. They probably would give everyone a pay hike[2] . . . to show the achievements of martial law and the "virtuous government." Such schemes are necessary elements in their coup. . . .

3. Li Peng's military coup has met strong resistance from residents and students who are the vanguard in fighting martial law. . . .

The inability of Li Peng's government to impose martial law shows its incompetence. Students and residents have used "people's war" to "glue" the armies entering Beijing to the suburbs by explaining events to the soldiers, persuading them, and showing them the facts . . . thereby reducing Li Peng's ability to use the good tradition of our party and army—that "the lower level is subordinate to the higher level and the whole party is subordinate to the Central Committee"—for his own purpose. Subordination must be based on the truth. . . .

4. Work we must do:

a. Organize the people to analyze theoretically the illegality and unconstitutionality of Li Peng's behavior . . . and appeal to all party and government organizations and all social groups to struggle resolutely against Li Peng. . . .

b. Organize student and basic-level party branches in colleges, universities, and cultural circles that have already taken a stand to refuse to recognize Li Peng's bogus regime. We should disseminate this widely to set an example for upper-level party organizations and those in other circles to follow.

c. Tell Beijing residents and people nationwide the truth: Without any "traffic obstruction," Beijing authorities shut down the subway, stopped the buses, and reduced the supply of daily necessities in order to create turmoil, incite hatred against the students, call troops into the city, and deceive people nationwide.

d. Appeal to the military to return to where they were originally stationed for the sake of the soldiers. The army should make it clear that it will not interfere in political disputes and will safeguard the constitution.

---

[2]The government reportedly did give across-the-board pay hikes after the June 4 crackdown, evidently to placate workers.

140

Statement in Support of the Patriotic Students

XI'AN MUNICIPAL FEDERATION OF THIEVES

May 23, 1989

Source: Poster spotted in Xi'an by a relative of William Hinton.

In support of the patriotic activities of our patriotic students, we have upon consideration decided to go on strike and suspend all thefts for the time being. We appreciate your compliance and implementation.

141

Aspirations of Thieves

LETTER BROADCAST BY THE VOICE OF BEIJING UNIVERSITY [RADIO STATION]

May 24, 1989

Source: *ORSD*, 2:68.

City residents and college students:

You have worked hard. We are a group of thieves. We have, however, decided to stop our stealing activities now in order to support the college students.

City residents, may you feel at ease in supporting the college students. Li Peng, the son of a bitch, is bound to be thrown out of office. He is a despicable creature. We are not good at making statements. May you college students make comments!

142

Circular of Teachers' Support Group of Beijing University

CHINESE LANGUAGE DEPARTMENT OF BEIJING
NORMAL UNIVERSITY

May 24, 1989

Source: Courtesy of HKFS.

Dear comrade city residents:
. . . Before and after the troops enter the city, it is very likely that some unidentified persons will disguise themselves as residents or students, attempt to beat, smash, loot, commit arson and other criminal acts, and provoke violent incidents to put the blame on residents and students as a pretext for martial law and suppression. Since the student movement began, and up to the date of the big demonstration by millions of Beijing residents [probably the march of May 23], the people have been highly rational and disciplined. Therefore, we must become highly vigilant about the above-mentioned possibility. We suggest:

1. Once criminal acts of beating, smashing, looting, and committing arson occur, we should immediately point out in our propaganda work that they are not done by the students.

2. We should not respond to those who provoke incidents and stir up strife. We should try to get their identification and send them to the Public Security Bureau.

3. We should affect social order as little as possible to avoid providing a pretext for the government to begin a crackdown.

4. We should definitely block the troops at the outskirts of the city. We should never believe that the troops are sent in for any reason other than to deal with the students and residents.

143

Letter of Beijing Residents to Provincial Party and Government Leaders

SOME BEIJING RESIDENTS, PRINTED BY INDEPENDENT
STUDENT UNION OF BEIJING NORMAL UNIVERSITY

May 24, 1989

Source: Handbill, HKFS.

Party and government leaders of Beijing and . . . the provinces:
   A strong, vibrant patriotic democracy movement has erupted in Beijing and areas nationwide. . . . The movement's method is peaceful and public order everywhere is good. . . . However, a handful of people headed by Li Peng have, with ulterior motives, vilified the movement for creating "turmoil" and . . . blocked domestic and foreign news reports. . . .
   In fact, there is no turmoil in Beijing. The people's normal work and life are not paralyzed. Only after an action unprecedented in the republic's history—the dispatch of a large number of troops into Beijing—did people begin spontaneously to set up barricades. . . . Because some plainclothes government agents were trying to penetrate the city in ambulances, people began to stop some suspicious cars for questioning. Residents have no complaints about these actions. Beijing's "turmoil" is really the obvious decrease in this month's traffic accidents and the unprecedentedly harmonious relations among people, and people's unanimous opposition to martial law. . . .
   Leading party and government comrades in other provinces: As the leading cadres at various levels, you are the people's public servants. . . . The handful of persons headed by Li Peng have not only distorted the facts: they have also ordered you, against your will, to support their measures. Hence, some of us Beijing residents must step forward to tell you the truth and ask you to choose between the people and a handful of persons headed by Li Peng. . . . We certainly know that some leaders, who could not get correct information and knew nothing about the truth, have expressed support for "antiturmoil" measures. We understand their situation. But after the whole truth has come to light, they should automatically change their positions and attitudes. We only hope you will think seriously about the interests of the party, state, and people; and think about party spirit and party conscience before taking positions. Only standing with the people makes you a wise and great leader. If, after knowing the truth, some people like running dogs still follow Li Peng and his handful, they will become the people's enemy and

will soon go before history's tribunal along with Li Peng and his ilk. . . . Please look at the people's strength and listen to the people's voice.

144

Open Letter to the Standing Committee of the NPC

SOME 200 INTELLECTUALS

May 24, 1989

Source: *Tiananmen 1989*, pp. 339–40.

Chairman, vice-chairmen, secretary general, and members of the Standing Committee of the NPC:

We are very pleased at the news that Mr. Wan Li, chairman of the Standing Committee, has returned early from his visit abroad. We see hope for solving China's current problem in line with democracy and the legal system. The Standing Committee of the NPC . . . has the power to repeal State Council administrative rules, resolutions, and orders that contravene the constitution and the law. We appeal to you to convene a special session of the Standing Committee immediately after Chairman Wan Li returns to Beijing in order to resolve China's present serious crisis.[1]

. . . Article 29 of the constitution stipulates that the military forces in our country belong to the people. . . . It violates the spirit of Article 29 to send troops into Beijing to "carry out the task of imposing martial law" under circumstances where there is neither foreign invasion nor riots. Hence, we strongly appeal to the Standing Committee of the NPC to convene a special session immediately to repeal martial law. We also hope students will withdraw from Tiananmen Square after martial law is repealed.

---

[1]Wan Li, chairman of the Standing Committee of the NPC and a leading reformer, had spoken favorably of the student movement while visiting Canada. He shortened his visit to the United States supposedly to convene the NPC Standing Committee. But upon landing in Shanghai on May 24, he was reportedly hospitalized; later stories suggest, as would be expected, that he received messages from Deng Xiaoping and Li Peng. Several days later he declared his support for the martial law decree.

145

Letter to Workers Nationwide

BEIJING WORKERS' AUTONOMOUS UNION

Mid-May 1989

Source: *ORSD*, 2:43.

Fellow workers nationwide:

The students' patriotic democracy movement has already ascended into a nationwide movement joined by all Chinese nationalities. . . . With the Chinese traditional spirit of not fearing death, we Beijing workers have bravely stood at the forefront of the struggle for democracy and civil rights.

Because of the shackles of feudal despotism in the past forty—or should we say several thousand—years, Chinese people have been ruthlessly and cruelly deprived of their human rights and personal dignity. In their minds, all rights and dignities were the exclusive property of emperors; the people could not fight for these rights, but only beg for some of them. . . . Whoever strove for these rights was beheaded and his entire family exterminated. All this has led to a baffling sense of fear among Chinese.

Now, enlightened by the student movement, we begin to understand the rights and dignity to which we as human beings are entitled; yet within a tightly controlled environment replete with highly oppressive politics, the dictators use the despicable weapons of administrative dismissal and economic sanctions to threaten us. So even though we know our rights and dignity are being trampled on, we dare not speak out or resist. How base and cruel the despotic regime is as it seeks to destroy our human nature. . . .

Brother workers: If our generation is destined to carry this national shame into the twenty-first century, let us fight to the death in the twentieth century.

Brother workers: Their politics of raw power is not frightening; what should be frightening is the eruption of anger generated by their power politics. Highly oppressive policies are even less frightening. What is frightening is the explosion of resistance their highly oppressive policies will generate.

Brother workers: Let's act with one heart and bear our generation's temporary, yet perhaps enormous, pains and exchange them for the next generation's pure, democratic air and the same rights and dignity as enjoyed by people worldwide.

The people are the majority and only the autocrats are "a handful." If we workers all stand up and march, even the dust kicked up by our footsteps will send the autocrats to hell!

146

The Most Enormous Case of Negligence Since the Founding of the Republic— Firmly Demand an Investigation of Li Peng's Criminal Responsibility

STUDY GROUP OF LI PENG'S LEGAL RESPONSIBILITY, CENTRAL SOUTH CHINA UNIVERSITY OF POLITICAL SCIENCE AND LAW

May 24, 1989

Source: Handbill, HKFS.

The People's Republic of China is now at a unique moment and has become the focus of world attention. . . . Who must be held responsible for these serious social consequences? . . .

According to Article 86 of the PRC Constitution, the State Council is the premier's responsibility. Therefore, Li Peng should have represented the people's interests and will, and properly solved problems pointed out by the students. Yet he goes against the people's will . . . thus worsening the situation, leading to very serious consequences. We therefore believe that Li Peng has violated Article 187 of the PRC Criminal Code by neglecting his duty. To enforce the law, this study group hereby suggests:

1. Based on Article 5 of the PRC Constitution, the Supreme People's Court should set up a special tribunal and according to law investigate Li Peng's criminal responsibility.

2. According to Article 62, Section 11 of the PRC Constitution, the NPC should repeal martial law . . . [and] according to Article 63 of the PRC Constitution remove Li Peng from his post as the premier. . . .

3. Li Peng should turn himself in as early as possible in order to seek lenient treatment.

147

The Popular Will Must Not Be Insulted!

ANONYMOUS

May 24, 1989

Source: Beijing University leaflet, in *ORSD*, 2:55.

Beijing's municipal government has ordered major factories and enterprises in Beijing to force workers to organize pickets, beginning on the afternoon of May 22. Their tasks are:
1. Safeguard order in the capital.
2. Remove the roadblocks.
Obviously, their fundamental aim is to clear the streets so troops can enter Beijing and impose martial law. Propaganda organs tightly controlled by Li Peng's government will then grandly declare worldwide that the capitals' workers and residents have cleared the streets and warmly welcomed the PLA troops into the city ... thus covering their dark rule and unjustified crackdown with a fig leaf. ...

But they have miscalculated and again underestimated the strength of the people and of justice. Listen to the workers' heartfelt wishes. A worker from Beijing Textile Mill said: "The organization of the so-called workers' pickets in our factory is a government scheme to get factory managers to buy worker support with twenty yuan and drinks. We must join the pickets or be severely punished. But we have our conscience. When we arrived at places where army trucks were blocked and helped students maintain order, students were a bit apprehensive. But we gave them straw hats and donations and always stood by them. The government cannot buy our support with money."[1]

Many work units in Beijing have done their utmost to refuse this imposed task of forming workers' pickets, pleading a lack of manpower. Anyone with a conscience is unwilling to do so, and the people's eyes are discerning. The government

---

[1]Bribing workers to remove students and roadblocks from the street succeeded in Shanghai, while the failure to remove Beijing's roadblocks on May 22 meant that military force would be necessary. Different outcomes in these two cities affected the postcrackdown political status of their respective leadership. Shanghai's first secretary, Jiang Zemin, became general secretary of the CCP, while Shanghai's mayor, Zhu Rongji, was widely rumored to be a possibility for the next premier. Li Ximing and Chen Xitong, first secretary and mayor of Beijing respectively, while highly active after the crackdown, received no promotions. According to rumors, Deng Xiaoping decided that no one with blood on his or her hands could be promoted.

also tried to organize "peasant pickets," but peasants could not be deceived either. They also stood by the students and told soldiers the truth, asking army trucks not to enter Beijing.[2]

Why has the government used both hard and soft tactics and material incentives? They have a guilty conscience! A just cause enjoys abundant support while an unjust cause finds little support.

The people's will must not be insulted!

"Xiaoping, You are so, so muddleheaded."

—Slogan from photo

148

An Official Denunciation of Deng Drafted for Marx

BEIJING UNIVERSITY

May 24, 1989

Source: Leaflet, in *ORSD*, 2:166–67.

The period for activities to rescue the Chinese Communist party has ended, while the call is sounded for a punitive expedition against Deng Xiaoping. This battle is a prerequisite for fighting feudalism and all such obstacles to establishing human beings as being most valuable.

After reviewing Deng's activities in the post-Mao era, we can easily list his ten major crimes:

1. Trampling on the [state] constitution. On numerous occasions, Deng Xiaoping has meddled in the policies and concrete decisions made by organs of state power at all levels. He has made the republic's highest organ of power—the National People's Congress—his own rubber stamp.

2. Disregarding the party constitution. He has totally destroyed intraparty democracy, placing sixty years of the party's organizational life in an extremely abnormal situation.

3. He has seized government and party power, dominated the army, and

---

[2]According to reports at the time, troops moving north from the city of Shijiazhuang to Beijing were repeatedly harassed by peasants.

exercised autocratic rule. He has become an actual emperor and overlord.

4. He is adept at creating impressions and empiricism. Everyone knows the campaign against "spiritual pollution" was the product of empiricism and conservatism.[1] "Bourgeois liberalization" is also a false accusation. His theoretical contributions to Marxism, revered by some flunkeys and annotators, amount only to such a meaningless phrase as "socialism with Chinese characteristics." . . . Because of these quotations, the emancipation of the Chinese people's individual spirit has been delayed for ten years or more.

5. Trampling on human rights. Deng deceived ordinary people and suppressed their thoughts. He is afraid of people marching and demonstrating, so time and again he emphasizes stability and unity, craftily conflating the richness of thought with loss of order and with social and organizational chaos. He has attempted to make 1.1 billion Chinese people follow only a few of his quotations and outdated socialist theories. He wants a big country with 1.1 billion people to follow his perceptions. He wants others to believe that only when people follow him will China have a future.

6. Cracking down on dissidents and appointing people through favoritism.

7. Allowing his son to engage in criminal acts.

8. Suppressing the patriotic democratic movement.

9. Standing high above the masses, swathed in mystery.

10. Openly plundering the people's wealth through deception and bullying. . . .

We can see that Deng Xiaoping, who once made great contributions to the party and the country, has brought great disaster to the Chinese people in the post-Mao era. These are not the failings of a human being but the crimes of a demon. Deng Xiaoping is a devil incarnate; an incarnation of brutality, despotism, feudalism, and ignorance. . . .

---

[1]The campaigns against spiritual pollution (1983) and bourgeois liberalization (1987) aimed at eliminating values and cultural trends that party conservatives believed had crept into China through the opening to the West. The author here is calling them the result of conservatism and empiricism because he feels that Deng and the conservatives invented the threat of spiritual pollution or bourgeois liberalization, having no basis in social reality.

149
I Want to Say a Few Words

TEACHER AT BEIJING UNIVERSITY

May 24, 1989

Source: *ORSD*, 2:146.

I am not optimistic about the situation improving after Wan Li returns from abroad. Everyone knows that China is still a feudal society where whoever controls the military becomes ruler and writes history. Deng [Xiaoping] and Yang [Shangkun] actually control the military. Li Peng is only the mouthpiece they put forward and whom they will sacrifice if necessary.

Last night I had the opportunity to talk with someone from the military. He said college students are too idealistic and unrealistic and in the end will fall victim to a power struggle at the top. He said the military generally has a poor opinion of Zhao Ziyang, believing that Zhao should be held responsible for the current governmental corruption and official profiteering . . . so it is wrong for the students to support Zhao. He also said that officers and soldiers have noticed the irregularity of promoting certain officers according to family ties, but they consider this quite natural in China. So they may be dissatisfied and complain but they will never mutiny because of this.

This student movement is very likely to fail. . . . But I think students will not suffer suppression or persecution. Those in danger are well-known intellectual elites who have dared to express their own views at this time.

I would like to say some encouraging words to boost morale, but I cannot.

150

Uproot Obscurantist Rule, Live Again as Chinese

A PERSON FROM THE LAND OF PLENTY[1]

May 24, 1989

Source: *ORSD*, 2:173.

Because of the obscurantist rule of several thousand years, the Chinese people are accustomed to pinning their hopes on leaders and hoping for upright judges and good government. They place no hope in themselves. Obscurantist rule has made our people slavish and apathetic, leading to the endless repetition of China's historical tragedies.

A mature Chinese national should not regard the party and the government as a god or a mother, nor should he regard what they give as a favor. The party and the government are merely one organizer of society. Everyone should have the consciousness and the right to criticize and supervise them. All Chinese should place hope on themselves and strive for democracy, freedom, and human rights, so as to be a worthy master of the country. Only thus can we develop a democratic, clean, and honest system of government and thoroughly eradicate obscurantist rule. Those unwilling to be hoodwinked and enslaved should persistently and resolutely struggle to eradicate obscurantist rule and feudal autocracy. The advance of history and the progress of humanity are always promoted by the mass of people.

There never has been a savior, nor can we rely on supernatural beings or emperors to save us. To create the well-being of humanity, we must depend entirely on ourselves.

"Our pen cannot write what we want to write;
Our mouth cannot say what we want to say."
—Slogan from photo

---

[1]The phrase "Land of Plenty" refers to Sichuan Province, suggesting that although this poster appeared in Tiananmen Square, it was written by someone from Sichuan.

151

Interviews on May 25

MU REN

May 25, 1989

Source: *Xinwen daobao* (News herald), no. 6, May 27, 1989.

On the afternoon of May 25, a *People's Daily* reporter who wishes to remain anonymous angrily told me at the northwest corner of Tiananmen Square: "What kind of people's government is this? Since May 20, the government has sent lots of PLA soldiers and Armed Police[1] to impose military control on us. When we enter or leave the newspaper office or go to the restroom, damn it, there's somebody following us and asking questions. . . . We all say that the newspaper is our home, but now that we do not even have our personal freedom, how can we talk about a home?"

. . . A colleague of this reporter told me: "Many journalists in our unit have continuously stood on the students' side, using various methods to support them. However, before the hunger strike, many of our objective reports about the student movement were put on ice and replaced with the government's teachings. . . .

"After the troops moved into our office building on May 20, the authorities began to show 'extra concern' for those who had participated in demonstrations, and warned us. Later they revised our reports at will. . . . The published reports were beyond recognition. Moreover, our 'heads' issued an explicit order forbidding us to report on the student movement and the people from all walks of life who support the students. They threaten to dock our pay and bonuses and impose administrative punishments. But who cares? When we go out every day, the only place we go is where the students are."[2]

Looking ashamed and helpless, the two reporters said: . . . "Our articles must

---

[1]The Armed Police are a special law enforcement unit carrying weapons. Ordinary police are unarmed.

[2]Some senior personnel at *People's Daily* who sympathized with the movement had toned down some articles to prevent younger reporters from exposing themselves in the event of a crackdown. Having been labeled as "rightists" in the 1950s, many older editors knew what could happen. The newspaper also ran stories without bylines to protect individual reporters. Computerized production also shielded reporters because those who composed directly on computer could not be identified by handwriting. Typesetters later "lost" handwritten drafts used in setting stories to type.

be submitted for approval at every level. Moreover, since martial law, scrutiny at each level must occur before articles are typeset. . . . Many people in our office who support the students still try to use every means to publish the reports about the movement. For instance, if "Down with Li Peng" is out, we use "Oppose the premier of the State Council." If that's not allowed, then we change it into "It is directly targeted at the premier of the State Council."

"Oppose Bureaucracy, Protect Human Rights!"
—Slogan from photo

152
Brief Introduction to the Union of People from All Circles in the Capital

CAPITAL UNION

May 25, 1989

Source: *ORSD*, 1:24.

1. The Union of People from All Circles in the Capital is called "Capital Union" for short.
2. The Capital Union is . . . a mass organization consisting mainly of workers, intellectuals, cadres of state institutions, students, patriotic democratic personages,[1] peasants, and entrepreneurs.
3. The purpose of the Capital Union is . . . to establish a broad patriotic and democratic united front to strengthen democratic forces continuously. . . .
4. The goals of the Capital Union in the near future are to mobilize the patriots in all circles in Beijing to cooperate actively and enthusiastically; and to

---

[1]"Patriotic democratic personages" in the past referred to nonparty dignitaries, mostly old members of noncommunist parties that were permitted to continue after 1949 provided they acknowledged the CCP's leading role. These parties were quite active in this movement, and some Chinese hoped they could use the fact that they were already legal, push them to become more independent, and then make them the basis of a competitive party system that could challenge the CCP (see Doc. 80). Since the crackdown, and particularly since the abrogation of Communist parties' leading role in most of Eastern Europe and the Soviet Union, their role has been highlighted, but only under the leadership of the CCP.

support ASUCUB and the autonomous organizations of other colleges and universities in completing the patriotic democratic movement.

5. The immediate tasks of the Capital Union are:

a. With help from most journalists, publish a nongovernmental newspaper—*People's Voice*—that can really voice the people's aspirations;

b. Organize residents' pickets to help the students maintain public order, normal life, and social stability in the capital;

c. Mobilize the masses as much as possible to resist martial law and completely foil the martial law scheme of a handful of autocrats;

d. Study the strategy and tactics of the patriotic democratic movement to provide all patriots and patriotic groups . . . with timely, accurate, and reliable information, substantial theories, and solutions to problems;

e. Coordinate patriots from all circles for well-aimed, well-prepared, organized, forceful, and unified actions that can deal a severe blow to the handful of autocrats and provide the greatest possible assistance to the students.

f. Invite criticisms and suggestions from patriots in all circles to make the Capital Union more mature and perfect.

6. The Capital Union consists of departments for theoretical research, strategy and countermeasures, information, fundraising, propaganda and agitation, liaison, coordination, reinforcements, editing, publishing the *People's Voice*, and security.

7. The Capital Union bases its code of conduct on the will of the vast majority of Chinese citizens. The Capital Union supports the constitution and acts within constitutional limits but believes that the constitution must be revised and perfected.

8. The condition for disbanding the Capital Union would occur only after an extensive survey of the popular will [indicated that] the vast majority of citizens believed it no longer necessary for the Capital Union to exist. No other forces or factor can dissolve it. . . .

9. The Capital Union is still in a formative stage, and we hope that patriots in all walks of life and patriotic groups will give us sincere help and guidance . . . including all kinds of material support. . . .

The Beijing University Liaison Office of the Liaison Department of the Capital Union is temporarily located on the second floor of Building No. 28 at Beijing University. Someone will be on duty in the office day and night.[1]

---

[2]This was the same building where some major student organizers lived and where the decision was taken to launch the hunger strike.

153

Letter to All People in Beijing

BEIJING UNIVERSITY

Late May 1989

Source: Handbill, courtesy of HKFS.

Backed by the diehards headed by Deng Xiaoping, the double-dealer Li Peng has declared war on 1.1 billion Chinese people, including 10 million people of Beijing. . . . Beijing is reporting an emergency! Every citizen living on this piece of land, every citizen who hates feudal autocracy, every citizen who loves democracy and freedom: stand up now! Flood out of the factories and government offices, residential lanes and alleys, villages and towns. Go to the city, the streets, and the square to stand side by side with your elders, your brothers, and your sisters. All must mobilize on their own[1] and defend every inch of land. . . . Use all peaceful means to oppose martial law. Stop the army trucks, tell soldiers the truth, and prevent the army from occupying the city. We call on all government office workers to join a general strike and paralyze this decadent, cruel regime. . . . Our goals are that Deng Xiaoping must resign and Li Peng must step down!

The most urgent task at present is to block the army trucks at the following spots: Dabeiyao, Hujialou, Muxuyuan, Xueyuan Road, Xinjiekou, 309 Hospital, Fengtai, Qing River, Wukesong, Gongzhufen, Wanshou Road, Shuangqing Road, Liuliqiao, and the subway stations.

Unite to defend Beijing with our concrete actions!

"Sell Mitsubishi to Pay Back the Foreign Debt!"
—Slogan from photo

---

[1]The Chinese phrase hearkens back to the War of Resistance against Japan (1937–45) when it was difficult to organize villages and individuals.

154

Why Are Troops Bearing Down on the City?

PROPAGANDA GROUP OF CHINESE UNIVERSITY OF
POLITICAL SCIENCE AND LAW

May 25, 1989

Source: Handbill, courtesy of HKFS.

. . . The aim of this mobilization of the army into the capital is a matter of great concern to people in all walks of life. All attention has focused on two aspects:

1. In terms of which armies are entering the city, the number of troops already exceeds the scale of eight group armies. According to the estimate of an inside source as many as nine group armies may be entering the capital. In addition to the armored cars equipped with heavy machine guns found on May 20, tanks equipped with heavy artillery were also found on May 21. The troops also include a new mobile and rapid deployment force—the 162d Division of the 54th Group Army. The troops assembled in Beijing's suburbs (in terms of numbers and firepower) far exceed anything needed for suppressing the student movement, dispersing demonstrators, maintaining the security of vital institutions, and restoring social order. This is the first question causing great concern among the people.

2. Regarding the origin of the troops entering Beijing, they are not merely from Beijing Garrison, nor from provincial military districts or subdistricts under the Beijing Military Region. Some troops were sent from Sichuan. According to sources from the troops arriving at Beijing Railway Station on May 21, they set out from Chengdu three or four days before. The troops also include five group armies from the Shenyang and Jinan military regions. . . . Why move troops from as far away as Chengdu? This is the second question causing great concern among us.

These two questions have us worried that this assembly of troops may be aimed at a problem more grim than the student movement . . . related to leadership changes in the [central leadership], or to preventing a military coup. . . . Not even when the Gang of Four were arrested several years ago[1] did so many troops from all over [China] enter the city. Faced with this, the people

---

[1]Members of the "Gang of Four" were arrested on October 6, 1976, a month after Mao's death. Their arrest was in many ways a military coup carried out by Marshal Ye Jianying, with the assistance of Hua Guofeng and Wang Dongxing.

cannot help asking: Why are they sending several hundred thousand fully equipped troops into the capital, in disregard of national security on the frontiers and powerful popular opposition? . . .

155
About Martial Law

ANONYMOUS

May 25, 1989

Source: Leaflet, HKFS.

1. The reasons for imposing martial law:

a. . . . The fundamental causes of the current so-called turmoil . . . in the capital are the corruption within the party and government and the stagnation of political reform. The direct cause is the government's erroneous evaluation of the democracy movement, its delays, deception, and high-handed policy. . . . This rapidly developing democratic movement was initiated by the students in a social context of compounded grievances and complaints. . . . In a situation in which a few government leaders with ulterior motives are trying sabotage, delay, and deception; and where we face brutal violence from the Armed Police and a large number of troops bearing down on the city, participants in the democracy movement maintain nonviolent, peaceful tactics. . . . During the period of petition, there was not a single incident of beating, smashing, looting, or burning. Incidence of crime, traffic accidents, and fire decreased greatly. The key sectors of the economy are stable, and social order has been maintained.

b. The real reason for declaring martial law is that this patriotic democratic movement has won the people's sympathy, understanding, and support both at home and abroad, particularly of intellectuals, journalists, city residents, and workers, thus striking at . . . the bureaucratic group and corrupt elements in the government, seriously weakening their vested interests. . . . A few government leaders have become desperate and recklessly imposed martial law on the people. . . .

c. Another possible danger is that the patriotic democratic movement has intensified the contradictions among different factions within the party. Certain persons, who monopolize power but are confounded by the people before truth and justice, have attempted to impose martial law and assemble troops in the capital, so as to intimidate their opponents and achieve ulterior purposes. If that's the case, then this is a counterrevolutionary military coup.

2. The evil consequences of martial law:

a. Military involvement in residents' political and normal lives, gravely damaging the environment of democracy and harmony, . . . is an extreme example of using unusual means to solve political problems. . . . It can only intensify the contradictions and create turmoil.

b. There are already a large number of military forces . . . in Beijing. . . . Now hundreds of thousands of troops are being sent to Beijing from all over the country, including armored units. This has created the potential for a military coup directed by a few, which could easily cause wars among warlords nationwide and bring about a national disaster and disintegration.

c. With the troops bearing down on the city . . . there emerges an atmosphere of terror putting very heavy psychological pressure on the people. This is extremely unfavorable to stability and unity, and to maintaining a peaceful and democratic political atmosphere. This has also damaged the environment for economic construction. . . .

d. The entry of hundreds of thousands of troops has created a new and heavy burden on the capital which already has ten million residents and a floating population of two million people from other provinces. In particular, the stationing of armored troops and large numbers of military trucks seriously disrupts traffic in the capital. . . .

e. To use the people's army to suppress the popular democratic movement will create much tension between the army and people, and will damage the PLA's image and prestige.

156
Watch Out for the New "Reichstag" Case

BEIJING NORMAL UNIVERSITY

May 25, 1989

Source: Leaflet, printed and distributed by Beijing Normal University, in *ORSD*, 2:107.

Early on May 23, the Beijing Party Committee organized a group of people to welcome troops at Fengtai and remove the roadblocks. They clashed with local residents, who were then beaten by well-equipped riot police.

That afternoon, students discovered a truck full of armed personnel near the Capital Steel Works who pretended to be hunger strikers. They had weapons in their bags. But for the students who tried to stop the crowd and maintain order, these armed personnel would have been torn to pieces by thousands of angry people.

At 2:00 P.M., three unidentified people defiled the portrait of Chairman Mao on Tiananmen.[1] When captured by the students, these three repeatedly said: "You'd better send us to the Public Security Bureau." Their identity is still being investigated.

Aside from this, armed personnel inside the *People's Daily* office building were in plainclothes and had guns sent in by old, beat-up trucks.

We must be vigilant. Li Peng's government and the Beijing municipal government are using every means to incite the masses to fight each other. They even sent disguised agents to foment disturbances and confusion as a pretext for imposing martial law. Residents citywide must watch out.

157
What Do Factional Disputes Reveal?

MENG ZHONGXING,[1a] AUTONOMOUS STUDENT UNION OF
BEIJING SCIENCE AND TECHNOLOGY UNIVERSITY

May 25, 1989

Source: Courtesy of Robin Munro.

The abnormal phenomena prevailing on the present political scene prompt people to believe that there are factional disputes within the central government. Such an analysis is not at all unfounded. But the problem is, what do these disputes indicate?

Our party's history is filled with factional disputes. From Chen Duxiu, Zhang Guotao, and Wang Ming, to Liu Shaoqi, Deng Xiaoping, and Zhou Enlai, to Lin Biao and Jiang Qing's group, to the present, disputes are like sticking in our party's history. What is worse is that no one can guarantee the prevention of new wounds and new scars. Those scars are records of the tremendous price paid by the party and the people. What do those scars reveal? They reveal the lack of democracy in the party!

The invincibility of Mao Zedong in the revolutionary struggle has created in

---

[1]They splattered paint on the giant portrait. It remains unclear whether they were provocateurs or angry citizens, reportedly from Liuyang County, Hu Yaobang's birthplace in Hunan Province, Mao's home province. These men were eventually sentenced to twenty years' imprisonment.

[1a]This is a pen name meaning "Dreaming of China's Rise."

people a psychological dependence: to defend one's position in the revolutionary line-up and make sure of one's survival by relying on an able or powerful leader. Under the spell of such psychological dependence, people lose their ability to think independently and critically. All they can do is to swear allegiance to whomever is in power. This dependence, in turn, allows those who possess a certain degree of authority to consolidate their own power, thereby causing the emergence of factions.

Factional struggles can only be avoided if people in power respect democratic procedure. Without a truly democratic structure, it is impossible for any political party or organization to reach a unified goal. Even if rules and regulations are written down, giving the impression of unity, it can only be superficial. Crises constantly recur. This is particularly true in our traditional culture of officialdom (by which I mean the traditional practice in which the intellectual's sole aim in studying is to take part in the official examination through which government officials are selected). Officials are tempted to satisfy their desire for power. Under these circumstances, coups and usurpation of power are almost inevitable. Our party has a lot of such painful experiences. Some of the coups may be good and necessary, but the political ground necessitating them is certainly unhealthy. The only way to eliminate factional disputes is to practice genuine democracy in the party.

Without democracy, factional disputes will be inevitable, and one-man rule will not be overcome. Factional struggles have serious consequences, such as internal burnout and chaos from top to bottom, as can be witnessed everywhere in our country. Therefore, to practice genuine democracy and promote a democratic atmosphere in work is necessary for the elimination of factional struggles and a commitment on the part of people to strengthening the country.

Long Live Democracy! Long Live the People!

158
Why We Have Initiated this Democracy Movement

BEIJING UNIVERSITY

Mid-May 1989

Source: Leaflet, in *ORSD*, 1:18.

The reasons we initiated the largest democratic movement in Chinese history are:

1. The three-thousand-year-old feudal autocracy in China still exists. . . . Bureaucrats shield one another according to feudal "coat-tail" relationships, while others are only interested in scrambling for power and profit. . . .

2. Ideological control and coverups of internal stories and scandals. The government . . . has implemented news censorship to block the flow of information. . . . The news media have been unable to play their supervisory role, so corruption is increasingly widespread.

3. Because the legal system is unsound and the legislative, judicial, and administrative powers are not separated, corrupt officials do whatever they like and manipulate the laws for their own purposes. Since high-ranking officials are not punished for crimes, . . . official profiteering is rampant.

4. Some people in government are incompetent and have made one mistake after another. In the forty years since the Republic was founded, forty million people have been purged. Now the whole country becomes a testing ground, the economy is frequently in crisis, and prices are skyrocketing.

5. Our country is among the poorest in the world, with low government revenues and heavy debts. Bureaucrats eat and drink at government expense all the time, build many office buildings, hotels, restaurants, and villas, and buy up all the luxury cars. No wonder there is no money to invest in education. Educational expenditure as a proportion of GNP is much lower than the world average. "Poor professors" and "foolish-looking doctors" are China's special product. Since the founding of the Republic, the campaign to eliminate illiteracy has helped 150 million people. But recently, 200 million more have become illiterate. Science and education are facing a crisis. These fundamental pillars of the republic are verging on collapse.

Compatriots: Without democracy, [there is] no hope; without reform, [there is] no hope. Retreat leads to destruction. . . . Our democratic movement's maximum goal is preliminary political democracy (people's participation, democratic supervision, democratic election, separation of legislative, judicial, and administrative powers, and freedom of demonstration, assembly, association, and the press). The breakthrough point is press freedom. Our minimum goal is: Li Peng must step down.

With Li Peng gone, stability will return under heaven.

159

Declaration of the Hunger Strike Group Formed Jointly by People of All Nationalities, Workers, and Well-known People of All Walks of Life in Society

PREPARATORY COMMITTEE OF THE HUNGER STRIKERS' PETITION GROUP

May 26, 1989

Source: HKFS.

In the past month or two, the democratic movement . . . has generated profound responses at home and abroad. The movement's essence is to eradicate official corruption and profiteering, lift news censorship, defend freedom of speech, and oppose dictatorship and autocracy so as to administer the country through people's democracy, rescue our motherland from a survival crisis caused by widespread difficulties and accumulated by age-old misdeeds, guarantee smooth progress in reform, and reinvigorate China.

. . . We are determined to take the place of all college students who continue their struggle in Tiananmen Square.[1] To express the wishes and demands of people nationwide, we have decided to organize a "Hunger Strike Petition Group" of people of all nationalities and well-known people of all walks of life in society and make this declaration:

1. Organizational and concrete matters:

a. The number of petitioning hunger strikers: one to five thousand. . . .

d. Place of hunger strike: two places at the Great Hall of the People and the Xinhua Gate.

e. Place for application: on the second level of the front side of the Monument to the People's Heroes.

f. Time for application: from May 28 to May 29. The hunger strike begins on May 30. . . .

h. Sponsors: Some leading cadres and office workers from the ministries and commissions of the central government, well-known people from all parts of society, workers, peasants, city residents, students who have studied abroad, soldiers, etc.

---

[1]The first hunger strike ended on May 19, after the martial law declaration made it clear that the authorities would not meet the hunger strikers' demand for a dialogue.

i. The termination date depends on the development of the situation.

2. *Concrete agenda and contents of the hunger strikers' petition:*

a. Demand that the government withdraw the troops immediately and repeal "martial law" and the "military curfew."

b. Demand that false accusations against the students' patriotic democratic movement be removed. They are "rescuing the country," not "creating turmoil." . . . No suppression and crackdown under any pretext is permissible.

c. Demand freedom of the press and speech, and a general pardon of political prisoners who are in prison for speaking out.

d. Demand that ill-gotten wealth be handed over immediately to the state treasury. Sons and daughters of high-ranking officials engaged in "official profiteering" must be prosecuted. . . .

e. Demand an immediate cleanup of personal cliques in the central government.

f. Demand an immediate reorganization of the central government. Old officials should retire and incompetent, corrupt, and bad officials must step down. True servants of the people will be elected to manage state affairs.

g. Demand the impeachment or removal of Li Peng, Yang Shangkun, and their ilk who have abused their power and neglected their duties, and who are fatuous and incompetent. They are welcome to step down voluntarily.

h. The country cannot go on without a leader. We demand that Comrade Zhao Ziyang, who can represent the people's interests, take charge of the work.

i. Demand an immediate revision of the constitution.

j. Oppose those political tricksters and opportunists who are taking advantage of the situation to launch a military coup or political coup.

k. Demand protection of the democratic rights of people nationwide. No crackdown or "postmovement revenge" is allowed.

. . . We are not afraid of expulsion from the party or dismissal from work positions; we are not afraid of being expelled from the rank of the cadres and losing our official power; we are not afraid of being beheaded or being put in prison. . . .

"The people will decide who is right and who is wrong!"
—Slogan from photo

160

Mobilize Immediately and Capture the Bastille of the Eighties—Our Appeal

BEIJING WORKERS' AUTONOMOUS UNION AND YOUNG CHINA
COMMUNICATION SOCIETY

May 26, 1989

Source: *ORSD*, 2:45.

. . . The fascist government and Stalinist dictatorial system do not and will not retreat voluntarily from the stage of history. . . . Li Peng and his backstage boss along with a handful of diehards are still acting hysterically and are likely to stake everything on a single throw of the dice. Isn't it true that someone [suggesting Deng Xiaoping] was quoted as saying, "What's 200,000 deaths if it buys twenty years of stability?" No one with an ounce of sense harbors any illusions about a regime that Beijing citizens spit on and curse as "a government of hooligans" and "a dictatorship by rascals." No one will be so naive as to believe their promises of "not seeking revenge after the harvest." . . .

Give me liberty or give me death!

We want to live like human beings!

Two hundred years ago, with the ideas of freedom and revolutionary enthusiasm aroused by the Enlightenment, the brave French people created a historical miracle with their bare fists by capturing the Bastille—the last stronghold of feudal despotism—thus making a unique contribution to human civilization. With the spirit of self-sacrifice, rationality, and enthusiasm, and with an indomitable, tenacious, and dutiful spirit edified by a culture of five thousand years and a democratic revolutionary tradition of 150 years, the brave, honest, and ingenious Chinese people are today waging a final battle against the Bastille of the 1980s—the last Stalinist stronghold in the world. . . . Our future generations will be forever proud of the epoch-making contributions their predecessors are making to the development of human civilization. . . .

"Wipe out the fascists! Freedom belongs to the people!"
—Slogan from photo

161

Who Will Swallow the Disastrous Results? Brief Discussion on the Severe Consequences of Martial Law

COMMENTATOR OF QINGHUA UNIVERSITY

May 24, 1989

Source: Big-character poster, in *ORSD*, 2:147–48.

The antiparty and antipeople clique of Li Peng and Yang Shangkun has flown in the face of the people's will, brazenly declaring martial law. . . . Their mean tricks have had, and will continue to have, an adverse impact on the political, economic, ideological, and cultural life in China and on the psychology of the Chinese people. . . .

1. *The grave political consequences are mainly as follows:*

a. The disappointment, hopelessness, dissension, and discord of the people.

. . . Recently, reform and the open door have brought people together under the banner of invigorating China. However, good times don't last long. Corruption, bribery, and chaotic political programs have again sapped the people's hopes. . . . Chinese are certainly accustomed to being silent and docile, but the wounds in their heart of hearts can hardly be concealed. One billion Chinese are again shrouded in the shadow of disappointment. . . .

b. The return of feudalism and Stalinism.

. . . Personality cults, absolute power, military control by a political group (instead of by the state), and factional struggles in palace politics are all manifestations of political feudalism. One important characteristic of Stalinism is "Might makes right," which always requires that at crucial moments military force be resorted to in order to suppress the people. . . . The fundamental reason for government leaders to use military terror when confronting popular cries for democracy and freedom is their fear of democracy and the weakening of their absolute power. This is a vivid manifestation of feudalism and Stalinism. As one philosopher put it so well: "Power corrupts, and absolute power corrupts absolutely." Without the precondition of democracy, conducting so-called honest and clean government is no different from expecting prostitutes to be chaste. . . .

c. Political reform has become a mere scrap of paper.

. . . Obviously, feudalism and the political system we seek are as incompatible as fire and water. Even if "reform" of the political system is carried out now, it is only feudalism under the cloak of "reform." . . .

d. The Chinese people have lost trust in the party and government. Efforts at unifying the country will fail.

. . . Why did unprecedentedly large demonstrations occur in Hong Kong? Because in just a few years Hong Kong will revert to the mainland. Hong Kong people are concerned about their future. Premier Zhou Enlai once proudly said that "We Chinese mean what we say." But in most cases, the Chinese leaders do not mean what they say. . . . It is obvious that the government has prepared high-pressure hoses, tear gas, and many tanks and guns, yet it has solemnly vowed that these are not for cracking down on the students but for maintaining social order and security. Have troops entered Beijing simply for city residents to gawk at? Under such circumstances, how can Hong Kong people believe in your "no change for fifty years?"[1] How can Taiwanese compatriots support your "one country, two systems?"[2] Poor China, how much longer do you have to be divided?

2. *The final economic consequence is an economic recession.*

The stock index in Hong Kong is declining, and foreign investment will be reduced. (Two American companies in China have already withdrawn their employees.) Economic reform will be blocked, and worker and peasant enthusiasm will be severely dampened. All this means that there will be a recession. . . . Moreover, since Li Peng came to power, he has talked only of adjusting and reorganizing, showing no interest in economic reform.

After the 1984 Sino-British Agreement [on the Future of Hong Kong] was proclaimed, a lot of capital was transferred out of Hong Kong (because of distrust of the Chinese government). The number of Hong Kong migrants to Taiwan and foreign countries has increased rapidly. This gives us another signal. We can imagine, after this crackdown, how much more manpower and capital will be drained away from Hong Kong. . . .

Foreign investors need a good and stable political environment. Foreign business people are not afraid of demonstrations and marches by Chinese students, but fear China imposing dictatorship. . . .

All kinds of official profiteering, rising inflation, and using "IOUs" to buy grain from peasants have already dampened the enthusiasm of the workers and peasants.[3] Imposing martial law makes most honest people passive. If the government uses treasury bonds to buy tear gas to crack down on the people, how

---

[1]This phrase refers to China's promise that Hong Kong would be able to keep its own social and economic system for fifty years after national reunification scheduled for 1997.

[2]"One country, two systems" was a concept devised by Deng Xiaoping under which both Hong Kong and Taiwan would be incorporated into a socialist country but be able to maintain their capitalist systems.

[3]Due to a shortfall in the state budget, the Chinese government began in fall 1988 to buy peasant grain with IOUs, or what the Chinese called "white paper" (*bai tiaozi*). This decision created great instability in the rural markets and angered many peasants who needed money to buy agricultural inputs. This tactic continued after 1989.

can they expect the people to "tighten their belts" and "work hard"? In a word . . . it is very difficult for the economy to take a turn for the better within a year or two.

3. *The ideological and cultural consequences are simple:* continuation of the campaign against bourgeois liberalization, of the monopoly on interpreting truth, of the suppression of intellectuals (because "a handful" and "extremely small number of people" are all in intellectual circles . . .). What's more, under gunpoint, the apathetic atmosphere where "ten thousand horses are all mute" will be graver if Li Peng's clique continues to set limits on thought and suppresses freedom of speech. Intellectuals will be shrouded in disappointments and evasion. . . .

The last ray of hope lies in further awakening the people, overthrowing the Li Peng clique, and letting reformers like Zhao Ziyang lead the country.

The final way out: Political and economic reform, and removing the institutional conditions allowing tragedies to recur.

162

Statement on the Current Situation

JOINT CONFERENCE ON DEFENDING THE CONSTITUTION,
AUTONOMOUS STUDENT UNION OF COLLEGES AND
UNIVERSITIES IN BEIJING, BEIJING WORKERS' AUTONOMOUS
UNION, FEDERATION OF COLLEGE STUDENTS FROM OTHER
PROVINCES TO BEIJING, DARE-TO-DIE CORPS OF BEIJING WORKERS,
COMMAND CENTER FOR DEFENDING TIANANMEN SQUARE,
BEIJING WORKERS' PICKETS, CONFEDERATION OF INTELLECTUAL
CIRCLES, DARE-TO-DIE CORPS OF BEIJING RESIDENTS

May 27, 1989

Source: Joint Conference of People from All Walks of Life in the Capital, in *ORSD*, 2:29–30.

On behalf of the Autonomous Student Union of Colleges and Universities of Beijing, the Joint Conference of People from All Walks of Life in the Capital . . . Wang Dan has issued the following joint ten-point statement:

1. From the very beginning, this "student movement" and "popular movement" has been a purely spontaneous, massive, and great patriotic democratic movement. . . . Its greatness lies in the fact that this movement . . . is absolutely not subject to changes in the internal struggle within the ruling party. No leader or political group in the ruling party and the government has the power to control this democratic movement. . . .

2. The basic starting point of this student and popular movement is to promote political reform in today's China by speeding up the process of democratization. Only thus can we effectively wipe out the serious corruption in the ruling party and the government and truly eliminate "official profiteering." . . .

3. Because of this, attitudes toward this great student and popular movement have become a litmus test for the political ideologies and positions of every Chinese, particularly every political leader. . . . Whoever negates and opposes this democratic movement negates and opposes the process of democratization in China. . . .

4. The fundamental reason Premier Li Peng, He Dongchang, Li Ximing, Chen Xitong, and other leaders are so unpopular in this movement is that they disregarded the popular will from the very beginning. . . . The extremely irrational martial law order issued by Li Peng on May 20 is a fascist, terrorist tool for sabotaging democracy and legality. This makes all the people feel strongly that so long as Li Peng and his ilk are in power, the personal safety of all the students, workers, city residents, cadres, party members, and intellectuals who have participated in or supported this movement is threatened. Thus, after martial law was declared, all the people made the totally reasonable and legitimate demand that Li Peng, He Dongchang, and their ilk be removed from the official leading positions.

5. As general secretary of the ruling party, Zhao Ziyang is undoubtedly responsible for the corruption and official profiteering in the ruling party and government. However, after returning from North Korea, he called for calm, rationality, restraint, and order, and for "solving the problems along the lines of democracy and the legal system," thus showing the correct attitude that a political leader should adopt toward this movement. . . . This makes the masses adopt a more positive attitude toward Zhao Ziyang. . . .

6. From this we can see that the attitude of the people toward any political leader totally depends on the leader's attitude toward this movement. If someone thinks that this democracy movement is aimed at supporting certain political leaders and knocking down certain political leaders from the very beginning, then he has greatly underestimated the level of this movement and the people's desires for democracy and a legal system. . . .

7. Regrettably, some political leaders in China still use traditional ways of thinking to look at the problems. They completely lack the political quality of "new thinking."[1] They always treat popular movements merely as tools and reflections of intraparty struggle. They always take it for granted that there are "behind-the-screen" people running this democracy movement . . . [and] that this

---

[1]"New thinking" (*xin siwei*) is a direct reference to Mikhail Gorbachev's call for treating social, political, and economic problems in a new way. It also reflects Wang Dan's attraction to the Eastern European reforms. For his views on Eastern Europe, see Doc. 7.

movement must be backed by certain high-ranking leaders within the party. Therefore, they have gone to the extreme of believing that settling the intraparty struggle will solve the problem. Once the "behind-the-screen backer" is found, this movement will automatically vanish like mist and smoke. Such views are too outdated. They underestimate the people's political quality. . . . The end of the intraparty struggle does not mean the end of this great democracy movement. . . . It is not the intraparty struggle that determines the democracy movement, but the democracy movement that ultimately determines the outcome of the intraparty struggle. . . .

8. . . . Here we reaffirm our short-term and concrete goals.

First, the suspension of martial law and the withdrawal of troops.

Second, repudiation of the "April 26" editorial of the *People's Daily* and of Li Peng's "May 20" speech;[2] public affirmation that this movement is a great patriotic democratic movement and recognition of the legitimacy of the masses' autonomous organizations and of the truly representative civil autonomous organizations.

Third, immediate convocation of an emergency session of the NPC to discuss the appeals by all the people for removing Li Peng from his position, so as to create a propitious atmosphere for solving problems by democratic and legal procedures. . . . If an emergency session of the NPC is not convened soon, the large, peaceful petition activities in Tiananmen Square will continue at least until June 20 when the Eighth Session of the NPC convenes.

9. The greatness of the mass movement and democratic movement lies in the fact that it has been a highly rational, calm, restrained, orderly, and peaceful petition from the very beginning. . . . Whoever dares to order the armies to suppress the student movement and the popular, patriotic democratic movement is pushing the ruling party, the government, and the army toward destruction. For if such circumstances arise, it means that the nature of the ruling party, the government, and the army has fundamentally changed. The consequences are too dreadful to contemplate.

10. The great "April 27" peaceful petition march is the most glorious chapter in the annals of Chinese contemporary history. On the one-month anniversary of the April 27 demonstration, we are making the above special statement to commemorate this great day. We also suggest to people nationwide that "April 27" be designated as "Freedom and Democracy Day" in China.

"Seek democracy, oppose privilege!"
—Slogan from photo

---

[2]Li Peng, "The Order of the State Council on Enforcing Martial Law in Part of Beijing Municipality," May 20, 1989, in *Beijing Spring*, ed. Oksenberg, et al., Doc. 47.

163

Letter to All Officers and Soldiers of the People's Liberation Army

ANONYMOUS

Late May 1989

Source: Leaflet distributed at Liuliqiao, a southwestern suburb in Beijing where some troops were stationed; in *ORSD*, 1:40.

Dear PLA soldiers and officers:

The People's Liberation Army soldiers are the sons and brothers of the people. You are defenders of the republic, and you should defend the people, not just a few persons. When the republic is at a life-or-death moment, you should take the will of the people as your highest command . . . .

The soldiers and officers of the Thirty-eighth Army have refused to carry out the erroneous [order] to suppress the people. They are outstanding representatives of the PLA . . . .

Dear soldiers and officers: You are facing your own brothers and sisters, your own elders and compatriots. You should never do anything wrong that will sadden your parents and gladden a few oligarchs. The people are watching you closely and are expecting so much of you.

Stand by the people!

Defend the constitution!

Struggle for democracy!

Continue the reform!

164

Reflections on the Student Movement

ANONYMOUS

May 27, 1989

Source: Courtesy of HKFS.

It is beyond what we could have originally imagined that . . . we seem to have gained nothing while the conservative group [in the CCP] has taken advantage of the situation to purge a large number of reformers. China has entered a dark period full of fierce undercurrents.

The lessons of this student movement are:

1. There is no systematic and appealing platform to direct the student movement, and no strong leading body. Achieving democratization in China requires a political party with a clear political platform (as in the bourgeois democratic revolutions [of Europe]). This is the most urgent matter at the moment. . . . China must undergo a bourgeois revolution. The Communist party is a party of the feudal class and represents the interests of a small handful of leaders (feudal aristocrats). . . . The new and old democratic revolutions led by the CCP in the past were, in fact, peasant uprisings. [The CCP] achieved victory only because of the coincidence of conditions in the international arena (the Japanese invasion) and domestic circumstances (the corruption of the Chiang [Kai-shek] dynasty). Mao Zedong was just another Zhu Yuanzhang.[1]

2. We must clearly understand the difficult and complicated nature of the situation and strategically conduct a protracted war.[2] The feudal conservative forces are still very strong at this time, and the political quality of the army is still very low. Therefore, we cannot hope to change the situation overnight. Strategically, we must retreat and turn our efforts to the propaganda work of emancipating the people's minds by popularizing the ideas of democracy, freedom, and human rights. I believe these efforts will bear fruit within the next

---

[1]Zhu Yuanzhang was founder of the Ming dynasty (1368–1644) and is considered a tyrannical emperor. Mao Zedong was often compared to him. For the treatment of Zhu in recent Chinese historiography, see Lawrence R. Sullivan, "The Controversy Over 'Feudal Despotism': Politics and Historiography in China 1978–82," *The Australian Journal of Chinese Affairs*, no. 23 (January 1990): 1–31.

[2]After criticizing Mao this article ironically then quotes one of his most famous writings. See "On Protracted War," May 1938, *Selected Works of Mao Tse-tung* (Beijing: Foreign Languages Press, 1965), 2:113–94.

decade, or within several decades. We should not forget that the Communist party also fought for several decades [before victory]. . . .

3. This student movement should produce a group of revolutionaries with the qualities of political leaders. Aside from having a strong sense of justice and devotion to the mission, they should not have too many illusions, be too kindhearted, or be gullible. In the meantime, they should commit themselves to certain beliefs and be willing to make sacrifices. In addition to having good organizational and leadership skills, they should also be wise, courageous, resolute, firm, and tenacious. And they must be ruthless toward the enemy. All this can be learned from the history of Western bourgeois revolutions.

4. We must not be afraid of bloodshed. We must mobilize workers, peasants, merchants, students, and soldiers to go on strike to resist taxation and grain procurement, and to conduct uprisings. . . . We should never pin our hopes on factional struggles within the party or on certain enlightened leaders. This can be learned from the democratic struggles in Hungary, Poland, the Philippines, and South Korea. Only when one or two generations sacrifice their interests can we achieve the long-term interests of China. . . .

165
Additional Comments on the Direction of the Student Movement

SOME [QINGHUA UNIVERSITY] TEACHERS WORRIED
ABOUT THE STUDENT MOVEMENT

May 27, 1989

Source: Handbill, courtesy of HKFS.

This great patriotic movement has been going on continuously for more than a month. . . . In this movement, the vast majority of the students of Qinghua University are indeed our teachers, from whom we have received a profound education. We have deeply felt your patriotic enthusiasm. We have seen your fearless actions in defense of the republic. We are very proud of you. . . .

For more than a month, the students have held a hunger strike and sit-in or organized pickets. . . . The students are much too tired. With such a fatigued army, it is obviously impossible to wage a new and more powerful struggle. The students should take a good rest. . . . We all know that [you] are not afraid of bloodshed and sacrificing your lives. . . . Taking a good rest now is not just for the sake of your own health, or even for the health of Beijing residents, but also for the victory of this struggle.

. . . Obviously, the government has adopted a completely erroneous attitude toward the student movement. It stands on the opposite side of the overwhelming majority of the people and regards the students as great scourges, accusing the students of creating turmoil. . . . The students should not be criticized for demanding that the government correct its wrong judgment and make a correct evaluation of the movement. But to achieve this goal is a very complicated problem. Here we have a problem of balance of forces. If we make the mistake of miscalculating the balance of forces and suggesting unrealistic slogans for the struggle, we will not be able to achieve our goal. So the movement will abort or have difficulty continuing. For example, we think that slogans shouted in the demonstrations like "We will come to demonstrate every day until Li Peng steps down" or "Convene the National People's Congress to impeach Li Peng" are unrealistic, although they represent the heartfelt wishes of the people. Li Peng continues to ignore the demands of the students, but if the students actually demonstrate every day, isn't it like asking a fatigued army to attack a well-rested king? It will be impossible for the students to go on like this for a long time. As to the convening of the NPC, we should have even less hope. Under the present system in China, it is easy to know how the deputies to the NPC are elected, and whether the majority of them can truly represent the people in casting their votes. It is certainly possible that the NPC would convene and refuse to impeach Li Peng.

Another issue concerns whether the sit-in groups on Tiananmen Square should be withdrawn. Under the present circumstances, since the government has not lifted martial law, it will be very difficult emotionally for the students to accept a withdrawal. For if you [the government] say that the troops are not sent in to deal with the students, then why have you forced the troops to bear down on the city where there is no sign of turmoil? If the troops are not meant to attack the students, then why not withdraw them? . . . Seven days after the declaration of martial law, the troops are still stationed at the outskirts of the city, and the whole city is in good order. Obviously, more profound political factors and reasons are involved here. The troops are connected with factional struggles among the central authorities. Since the present Chinese political system is completely closed and there is no transparency or openness, it is very difficult for the students to know exactly what is going on behind the scenes. In political movements in the past, political struggles were reflected in the factional struggles within the party. The people could not grab the initiative. Under these circumstances, it is impossible for the students to get directly involved in these struggles. So we think that the student movement should keep its independence and purity; we should maintain the nature of our movement. . . .

We should reaffirm the goal of the democratic movement of the students, again demanding that the government correctly reevaluate the student movement and accept the students' demands for continuing the reform, particularly of the political system. We should clearly express our views that the student movement supports the reformers in the party and opposes the conservative forces, and that the students have the right to struggle again in various ways for achieving the goal of the democracy movement at an appropriate time.

We should withdraw the sit-in and petitioning groups on Tiananmen Square in order to show that we are taking the big picture into consideration. In the meantime, we should make it clear that this is only a change of form in the struggle. During this period, the students can calmly observe and analyze the situation, reorganize their forces, and watch the development of the internal struggle at the center. Irrespective of who takes charge of the work of the central authorities, the students will support him only if he stands by them and supports reform. Otherwise, the students have the right and the energy to launch a new struggle.

We believe that such struggles are reasonable, advantageous, and restrained. Otherwise, if the sit-in persists, the number of students participating will decline, and so will the number of city residents supporting the students. And the entire movement may actually end up fizzling out. To maintain our strength and keep the initiative, we should combine work with rest, and combine attack with withdrawal. The idea of accomplishing the whole task at one stroke is not only unrealistic and unacceptable, but also harmful to the movement.

. . . Furthermore, we are even more worried at seeing the students of the Preparatory Committee call on students to go to other provinces. This is like walking right into a trap and making unnecessary sacrifices, which should never be done.

166

Announcement Concerning the Protest March by Chinese All over the World on May 28

ANONYMOUS

May 28, 1989

Source: Mimeograph, in *Tiananmen 1989* and *ORSD*, 2:30.

Time: 10:00 A.M., May 28.
 Sponsors: Overseas Chinese Students' Union in France and Overseas Chinese.
 The Joint Conference of People From All Walks of Life in the Capital,

ASUCUB, the City Residents' Union, and the Workers' Autonomous Union have decided to respond.

Goals:

1. Lift martial law, oppose violence, defend peace, and call for Chinese all over the world to stand up!

2. Freedom of the press. Remove news censorship, increase the transparency of the government process, open the political process, and let people know about major events.

3. Defend the constitution and human rights. Long live democracy! Long live freedom! The Chinese people all over the world should fight for democracy and freedom.

4. It is not shameful to be patriotic. "Those who make criticisms are not guilty, and those who are being criticized should listen carefully."[1] Demand a solution to problems along democratic and legal lines.

5. Chinese people all over the world, strive together to knock down autocracy! Li Peng must step down, and Deng Xiaoping must retire from political life. Oppose autocracy, oppose using guns to control politics, and oppose power politics.

6. Down with official profiteering. Wipe out corruption and severely punish corrupt officials.

7. The soldiers are one part of the people, and they share the same fate as the people. Treatment of the officers and soldiers should be improved, and extended service in the army should be opposed.[2] The people's army must not fall prey to the political struggle.

People of the whole city, unite and strive for a beautiful life to come.

167

The Republic Is Not Private Property

XX OF BEIJING UNIVERSITY

May 28, 1989

Source: *ORSD*, 2:171.

Recently, someone has trotted out a viewpoint: The Communist party sacrificed more than twenty million people in exchange for a new China, and so it will

---

[1]This is a quotation of Mao Zedong's from the Cultural Revolution.

[2]This unpopular measure was introduced to deal with severe problems of retention in the army as the commercial economy in rural areas lured army men back to civilian life.

never give way meekly. This viewpoint is tantamount to saying, "I have fought for this country so I must rule this country."

Such a view has provided a "strong" justification for those who abuse their power. . . . When China was in the dark old days, the Chinese people were seeking an equal and fair world even at the price of sacrificing their own lives. They finally found an organization that could unite all the oppressed people—the Chinese Communist party. The people gave all they had to the party, not to help those who later became rulers to accumulate [power] for their own ease and comfort, but to form a mighty torrent with their flesh and blood to break through the old world. They also did this so as to put their own light and heat into the burning flames that could light the way for later generations. Certain "Communists" now want to dominate that blazing prairie fire because they were once the tinder of this fire, but the people will not allow them to use their flesh and blood as bargaining chips. Those twenty million lives sacrificed are not the private property of any individual or small group, but a price paid by the whole Chinese people. This glorious republic belongs to the people.

The People's Republic will never forget many Communists who shed their last drop of blood for the people. However, certain living persons think it only natural to seize the honor of the martyrs, claiming that they represent the deceased heroes and hoping to build, like a feudal emperor, a path to the throne with the dead bodies of tens of thousands of people. They will never succeed! Once the people have awakened, the doom for the conspirators comes.

Even if the twenty million lives exchanged for the republic could be credited to those self-proclaimed "founding fathers" as political capital, they should repay the debt for the countless ghosts of those victims of injustice who died during the Great Leap Forward, the three years of natural disasters, and the whole series of political persecutions.[1] They owe a debt of blood to the people. And the people will no longer let these parasites suck the blood of the people.

On several occasions, China has been tossed backward by the torrents of world developments because the Chinese people have been bound hand and foot by the feudal patriarchal system. The awakened Chinese people can no longer allow anyone to turn this democracy movement into a change of feudal dynasties. The feudal autocrats must return power to the people. The *Internationale* has significance for our times.[2] Let's unite and thoroughly smash the shackles of feudal rule in our march toward brightness.

---

[1]Recent estimates by Western demographers based on the Chinese census of 1982 indicate an absolute drop in China's population from 654 million in 1959 to 644 million in 1961 following the peak year of famine induced by Great Leap Forward policies.

[2]This probably refers to that segment in the *Internationale* that calls on people never to "rely on saviors."

168

Letter to People Throughout the World

SOME MEDICAL PERSONNEL IN BEIJING

Late May 1989

Source: *ORSD*, 2:64.

To all the world's peace-loving people:

In the last month, a democracy movement of unprecedented proportions has taken place in China. The whole world is focusing its attention on China and Beijing. The world's people have shown sincere sympathy for the Chinese people in their struggle for democracy. . . . Now hundreds of thousands of students and several million city residents who have participated in this legal struggle in Beijing are facing an imminent threat of a bloody crackdown and loss of freedom.

. . . On May 20, Li Peng issued the martial law order to be carried out in the urban areas of Beijing, whereupon the authorities for a time cut off the water supply to Tiananmen Square and strictly forbade any units to send food or drink to the square. They thereby caused hunger and thirst for 200,000 college students, who had already been peacefully petitioning on the square for seven days and nights and had been plagued by illness. The inhumane authorities have even given the following orders to all hospitals in Beijing:

1. Any ambulances taking students to hospitals may not return to the square.

2. Outpatient treatment only to students; students may not be hospitalized.

3. Emergency rooms may not use expensive medicines.

4. No medicine may be distributed to students on the square.

5. No drink or food may be provided to the students.

The three thousand college students who have been on a hunger strike for seven days and are plagued with illness are on the verge of death. It is only because of the desperate efforts by many medical workers that medical care has been maintained at all on the square.

Is this the humanitarianism that Li Peng talked about? When troops attempting to enter the city were blocked by millions of city residents in all quarters, the authorities ordered ambulances for the troops so they could sneak into the city.

Hence, we issue this urgent appeal to all people who love peace and cherish humanity, asking you to show your sympathy and to exert your influence to mobilize the world community to use every means possible in preventing this human tragedy in which human rights are trampled on and people are murdered. Long live humanitarianism!

169

A Moving Story: The Removal from Duty of Commander Xu of the Thirty-eighth Army

A SOLDIER FROM THE BEIJING MILITARY REGION

May 29, 1989

Source: *ORSD*, 2:152.

One day at the end of March [1989], Commander Xu and newly recruited soldiers were conducting military drills throwing hand grenades. Unfortunately, the commander broke his leg and was sent to the General Army Hospital of the Beijing Military Region for treatment.

During more than forty days of treatment from early April to mid-May, Commander Xu was lucky enough to have a chance to witness the student movement taking place in Beijing.[1] When reading newspapers or watching television, he was moved to tears by the students' spirit of self-sacrifice for national salvation. Commander Xu always loved listening to the news from medical workers and patients, and to their views about the student movement. According to people close to him, "Commander Xu became quite reticent."

One day in mid-May, the commander was suddenly summoned to the headquarters of the Beijing Military Region where Zhou Yibing, the regional commander, transmitted an order from the Central Military Commission signed by Deng Xiaoping, which ordered the Thirty-eighth Army to enter Beijing immediately to curb the turmoil.[2] Commander Xu showed no intention of violating the order and immediately carried it back to Thirty-eighth Army headquarters on

---

[1]The hospital is located in the Chaoyang section of Beijing where the commander may have personally viewed the demonstrations.

[2]At the time, Deng Xiaoping was still chairman of the Central Military Commission (a post from which he resigned after the June 4 crackdown), and Zhao Ziyang was vice-chairman. Yang Shangkun defended Deng's authority to order troop movements personally without the "collective" approval of all Central Military Commission members in a critical speech to the commission on May 24. General Zhou Yibing, commander of the

crutches.

There Commander Xu summoned the officers of all levels for an urgent mobilization before the battle. He personally arranged troop deployments and set the schedule for the army's entry into Beijing. After all was set, he telephoned the Beijing Military Region [headquarters], saying he could not lead the troops into Beijing because of illness. [Informed by Zhou Yibing] that this was a violation of a military order, Commander Xu answered that no matter what kind of charges his superiors might lodge against him, he would not lead the army's advance. Then the commander [checked into] the General Army Hospital in Beijing on the pretext of seeking medical treatment. (Indeed, his broken leg was not fully recovered.) . . .

On hearing this, Yang Shangkun was furious and could not sleep for several nights. He personally issued a Central Military Commission order to relieve Commander Xu of his command and to arrest him to face immediate court martial.

A deputy director of the political department of the headquarters of the military region carried this order to the hospital accompanied by security guards. After showing the commission's order to Commander Xu, they asked, "Do you have anything to say?" The commander calmly answered, "I have thought about it [for a long time], and I am fully prepared in my mind. I am a soldier and if I don't follow orders, I should be punished. You can carry out your orders now. As for the student movement, I have my own views. It is too early to reach a conclusion about the student movement." Afterward, the commander was put in a police car under escort.

While detained for court martial . . . , Commander Xu told his interrogators, "The people's army does not have a history of suppressing the people. I cannot stain this history."

Students, this is a true, moving story. Let's always remember this national hero. . . .

Commander Xu, your soldiers will never let you down. The people all over the country will always remember you.

High respect to the national hero, Commander Xu!

"Democracy means that everyone enjoys freedom of speech and has the right to manage the country!"
—Slogan from photo

---

entire Beijing Military Region and Commander Xu's immediate superior, was reportedly replaced after the crackdown for not being "resolute enough" in crushing the prodemocracy movement. Oksenberg et al., eds., *Beijing Spring*, p. 296, and *South China Morning Post*, May 29, 1990, p. 9.

170

Declaration of Eight Institutes of Art in the Capital

EIGHT [*sic*] INSTITUTES OF ART IN BEIJING (CENTRAL INSTITUTE OF
FINE ARTS AND CRAFTS, CENTRAL DRAMA INSTITUTE,
CENTRAL MUSIC CONSERVATORY, BEIJING FILM INSTITUTE,
BEIJING DANCE INSTITUTE, CHINESE INSTITUTE OF
TRADITIONAL OPERA, CHINESE MUSIC CONSERVATORY)

May 30, 1989

Source: *ORSD*, 2:107.

Dear comrades and students:

Our great and dignified Chinese people have finally broken through autocracy and forged an upsurge of democracy in 1989. . . .

Now this utterly inhuman, bestial, and despotic government has resorted to scurrilous attacks, violence, and deceit to destroy the goddess of democracy in the cradle. The fall of [feudal] darkness simply shows that they have already reached a dead end and will soon meet their doom. The people will definitely put them on trial.

At this critical moment, we need to keep calm and unified. We need an enormous coalescing force all the more—the Goddess of Democracy (*Minzhu zhi nüshen*).

How long since we have met, Goddess of Democracy!

You, for whom the Chinese people, suffering several thousand years of oppression by feudal despotism, have longed from the bottom of their hearts!

You, who are the symbol of the ideals of tens of thousands of students on the square and tens of millions of Chinese people!

You, who are the spirit of the 1989 Chinese democratic tide!

You, who are the hope of rescuing the Chinese nation!

Today on the square of the people stands the statue of the people's Goddess of Democracy. She declares to the world that the great awakening of the Chinese people to democratic ideas has reached a new stage. The trees of democracy and freedom are being planted in this ancient land, and they will blossom most splendidly and bear the richest fruit.

Made of plaster, the Goddess of Democracy cannot stand here forever, but she is a symbol in the minds of the people and is sacred and inviolable. Whoever dares to sully her will be punished by the people.

We firmly believe that this dark night will soon be over and the dawn of victory will surely arrive. When true democracy and freedom arrive, we will erect an even more magnificent, great, and permanent Goddess of Democracy. . . .

We hope even more that the Chinese people will keep this "Goddess of Democracy" in their hearts permanently.

Long live the people! Long live freedom! Long live democracy!

171
Our Task Is Hard and the Road Is Long

ANONYMOUS

Late May 1989

Source: courtesy of HKFS.

What we are now facing is not Li Peng alone, but a bureaucratic stratum with vested interests. This stratum has profoundly felt that the students and the people will deprive them of their privileges, which are usually kept out of public view, so they are now gradually joining together to deal with the people. This stratum includes the old leaders headed by Yang Shangkun and the new conservatives headed by Li Peng. In their minds there is no democratic idea. They are accustomed to deceiving the people and imposing a brutal regime on the people.

Li Peng is backed by a group of stubborn old leaders. Among them there is no open and aboveboard political leader like George Washington. Chinese government circles even lack the democratic atmosphere of George Washington's time. They do not allow any transparency because their despicable desire for power and wealth, their low intelligence and incompetence, and their inhumanity cannot be exposed to the light of day.

. . . We have waited and waited. The old bureaucrats are gone, but the new bureaucrats remain to rule us. Should we wait for the total destruction of China? No! We are the sons and daughters of China, and we cannot keep silent. . . . Maybe it will take several generations to achieve democracy in China. But this movement tells us, as long as we unite and struggle persistently with everyone trying his best, we can gradually succeed. Someday, in the dark night we will see the first light of democracy in China.

172

I Was Willing to Sacrifice Myself to Allow More Students to Live On

CHAI LING

Late May 1989

Source: *Singtao Evening Post*, Hong Kong.

[Introduction:] This essay was written by Chai Ling before and after the hunger strike. When she had finished it, she gave it to reporters in Beijing. The last bits of the essay are almost illegible because she was then physically very weak. Thus, the editor of *Singtao Evening Post* [Hong Kong] has filled in the blanks and refined the sentences before producing the following published version.

Question: Is this the darkest day of the movement?

The darkest day has not yet come. Many students did not understand that staying on the square is the only way left for us. Our retreat will make the government happy. I am the chief commander. I will never make any compromises—the Autonomous Student Union of Non-Beijing Universities and the faction that supports surrender compete with ASUCUB for power and authority. There are quite a few people who intend to use the movement to rebuild their own images, like Liu Xiaobo. . . .

I think the government will retaliate against every one of us in a crazy way. This is because Chinese have a strong tendency to take revenge. I bear no unrealistic hopes. After the first dialogue was suspended midway, I read aloud our declaration of a hunger strike. At that time, I hoped it could be broadcast live so that people all over the country could know what was in the students' minds concerning the hunger strike. We still thought we could move them.

Many people have joined the movement; but they hold no beliefs. Their thoughts are very confused. This movement reveals the extent to which we understand and are concerned about "democracy." The body of intellectuals and theorists are lagging far behind. They have not put forward any well-completed theory. I think the significance of this movement is that it is a great spontaneous movement joined by [ordinary] people.

I believe in inevitability. I don't believe in the existing theories. As an individual, I am willing to live on. I believe a great revolution will soon break out. I must preserve the seed and the strength of our revolution. If I am still alive, I desire to "stand up" again in the next movement and let the people of China really "stand up."

Such reform has pushed intellectuals to an impasse and without a sense of security. This country is bound to come to an end. Only the people can save themselves. Repression. On May 25, I chatted with a plainclothes policeman. He said that the arrested might be sentenced to jail for either three, five, seven, or seventeen years. When released from jail, I would be forty years of age. I cannot willingly accept this. I believe it will benefit everyone to establish a system of democracy and to make use of science to save the country. Of course, we can go to study abroad; but if our country can solve its problems, why should we spend our youth abroad and contribute our talents to overseas countries? My mother country is too poor, and she needs people who are willing to struggle and sacrifice for her, she needs lots of them. Regrettably, with such a political system, people regardless of class can only try to secure green cards.

Someone must continue with this task—because this is not a personal issue, it concerns the ultimate fate of the country.

173

Solemn Statement

STUDENTS AND TEACHERS OF THE CENTRAL
INSTITUTE OF FINE ARTS AND CRAFTS

June 1, 1989

Source: *ORSD*, 2:108.

A statement by the Management Bureau of Tiananmen Square said that a "so-called statue of a goddess has been erected on this place; this insults and tramples on the national dignity and the image of the Chinese nation."

We solemnly give the following response:

1. It is an insult to the image of the Chinese nation for the Management Bureau to hurl abuse at the statue of the Goddess of Democracy and Freedom. Why can't she belong to the Chinese people? We all know that during the Anti-Japanese War, there was a famous song entitled "We Are on Taihang Mountain," [with] such words as "The red sun is shining all over the east and the god of freedom is singing heartily." How many of our forefathers unhesitatingly marched to the battlefield of national salvation! The blood of the young people was spattered all over the land of China.

2. The Urban Sculpture Planning Group has also accused us of not applying for permission to erect the statue. Anyone with a little professional knowledge will tell you that this group is in charge of planning for permanent sculptures in

the city, and our work is just a temporary model. This can be seen from the materials used, namely, ordinary foam plastics rather than plaster or stone. It is always permissible to erect model statues for temporary purposes during gatherings or demonstrations by the people either in China or foreign countries. . . . Once the student movement concludes, this statue will naturally be removed from Tiananmen Square.

3. A very few people mortally fear and hate the statue of the Goddess of Democracy and Freedom, so they only dare to refer to it as a statue of *a* goddess. You may order the troops to remove the statue by force, but you cannot remove the people's longing for democracy and freedom.

Long live a democratic, free socialist motherland!

Footnote: During the celebration of National Day on October 1, 1988, some model statues of animals, such as panda bears, dragons, and cattle, were also erected on Tiananmen Square. Have they become permanent statues? Did they represent an insult or a lack of respect to the revolutionary martyrs?

174

You Would Have to Wait Ten Thousand Years

JI NAN

No date

Source: *ORSD*, 1:92.

> Wait until a monkey becomes a man
> An ordinary man becomes a god
> Quotations become a sea
> White bones become a ghost.
>
> Wait until a monkey becomes Darwin
> An ordinary man becomes Stalin
> Quotations become Zhongnanhai
> White bones become successors.
>
> Wait until red flags become shrouds
> Fresh blood becomes the tree of life
> Love becomes dry melon
> Ambition becomes [filthy] soil.

Wait until facts become a book
Lies become a map of many miles
A landlord becomes a private businessman
Life becomes a real grave.

Wait until sworn words become clouds
False masks become real things
Mountains become pictures
A cold heart becomes spring.

Wait until blood becomes a tree of love
Ah Q becomes the god of the sun[1]
The future becomes a piece of paper
Truth becomes two pieces of clouds.

175

Proposals for Organizing a Beijing College Student Propaganda Corps for a Long March

AUTONOMOUS STUDENT UNION OF BEIJING
AGRICULTURAL UNIVERSITY

June 2, 1989

Source: *ORSD*, 2:109.

We propose that thousands of college students of the capital conduct a long march south to demonstrate peacefully and propagandize so as to bring about a new upsurge in the democracy movement.

1. Goals and necessary actions:

a. The long march is a statement. It will declare to people throughout China that democratization and the tide of reform are irreversible. It will call upon the people to rise up to oppose corruption and official profiteering, and to win democracy. It will support the people's defense of their interests. It

---

[1]Ah Q is the central character—a symbol of Chinese fecklessness and incapacity to recognize and acknowledge one's own defeat—in a famous short story by China's best-known writer in the first half of the twentieth century.

will also exert certain pressure on the government and create a good atmosphere for the convening of the NPC.

b. The Long March Propaganda Corps is also a seed-spreading machine. It will tell the people throughout the country the truth and significance of this patriotic movement and will mobilize them in forging a powerful tide advancing toward democracy. The people alone are the fundamental force in pushing history forward.

c. The Long March Propaganda Corps is also a support corps. Along the way, college and university students will join us one after another. The ranks will grow ever stronger and become a force of thousands, even tens of thousands of people. . . . It is a very powerful corps supporting the students who are still on Tiananmen Square, supporting the hunger strike and petition struggle about to be initiated by the intellectuals. It will also support 1,200 brave students who are marching north from Nanjing.[1]

d. This long march will turn around the present low tide of the democracy movement and push the movement forward.

2. Feasibility:

a. The people are more awakened daily and good examples have been set by the students. . . .

b. Democratization has become a great and irreversible tide all over the world. Strong support from world opinion also provides us with a global context for the long march.

c. ASUCUB and patriotic people of all walks of life in Beijing have decided to stand fast on Tiananmen until June 20, when the NPC will convene.

d. The hunger strike and petition soon to be initiated by the famous scholars and intellectuals headed by Yan Jiaqi will also provide a good opportunity for this long march to be carried out.

e. Twelve hundred people in Nanjing and elsewhere have initiated a march north in support of Beijing students. With Beijing students going south, another upsurge of the democracy movement is inevitable.

3. Concrete planning:

a. Routes: South along the Beijing-Shanghai railway. (We suggest that other colleges and universities might take different routes, such as the Beijing-Guangzhou railway and the Northeast railway.)

b. Time: Departure from Beijing in early June. Agricultural University students are ready to depart before June 5.

c. Methods: Riding on bicycle. . . .

d. Organization: Militarized. All participating colleges and universities will

---

[1]Beijing student leaders initially exhibited considerable distrust of students from other cities, as recently noted by Nanjing student leader Li Lu, who ultimately became a close associate of Chai Ling. Li Lu, *Moving the Mountain: My Life in China from the Cultural Revolution to Tiananmen Square* (London: Macmillan, 1990).

form an organizing committee that takes full responsibility for managing the long march.

e. Work along the way: Posting handbills, delivering speeches, doing other propaganda activities, fundraising, and coordinating work in colleges and universities along the way.

f. The organizing committee may decide to adopt a relay method. At some places, the advance group of students may return [to Beijing]. They are to be followed by succeeding groups of students to continue to go down south.

4. Preparatory work:

Mobilization and propaganda work must be done well among the students in all the colleges and universities. The hardships of the long march should be fully considered. Bicycles (there will be bicycle-repair groups) and camping tents must be prepared.

We appeal to ASUCUB and all the other colleges and universities to give serious consideration to the significance of this long march and to get actively involved in the preparatory work while strengthening contacts.

Long live democracy! Long live the people!

176

The Biggest Mistake of the CCP Is Its Undemocratic Attitude: A Dialogue between Wu'er Kaixi and Another Student Leader

WU'ER KAIXI

June 3, 1989

Source: *Ming pao* (Enlightenment), Hong Kong, June 17, 1989, p. 1, based on interview of June 3; translated in FBIS, *Daily Report: China*, June 20, 1989, pp. 24–27 [edited].

... *Q:* What is your view on the death of Hu Yaobang?

A: ... That the death of a democratic leader could cause such great turmoil is itself a problem, which shows the Chinese people's extreme dissatisfaction with the current situation in their country.

Q: What did you expect to get when you first joined the movement?

A: I expected improvement in two aspects. First, as far as democratic consciousness was concerned, I hoped that we could get the same effects of enlightenment as did the May Fourth Movement. Actually, although the Chinese people strongly desire democracy, they lack consciousness of democracy and do not understand it. I hope that through the student movement, we will progress in our work toward enlightening the people. Second, I hoped that we could set a good example with regard to the skills for promoting democracy. At the beginning, I hoped that our Student Self-Government Federation's legal status would be recognized, and it could play its role in government administration as an opposition group.

Q: To your mind, what mistakes has the government made in dealing with the student movement? What basic problems have these mistakes reflected?

A: For example, before the massive demonstration on April 22, the majority of young students ... presented a petition [to the government]. At that time, students only lodged their appeal. There was no organization. The government could have taken the initiative to solve the problem, and easily handled the student movement.

Q: If the government had handled the student movement at that time, what results would you have expected?

A: This would have been determined by our own efforts. I didn't think that the situation would become so chaotic.

Q: What was the second mistake of the government in its policy?

A: On April 22, the government sent public security police and soldiers to beat up students. Actually, [this use of] force enabled the students to become more united and gave rise to the establishment of the temporary student federation. On April 27, I initiated the establishment of the federation [ASUCUB]. As a result, the student movement is greatly different from the past. Massive student organizations have been formed.

Q: In your mind, what problems have the government's mistakes reflected? Did you expect these problems? What do you expect in the future?

A: I think that the key to all these mistakes is that the government is not democratic. It is not accustomed to listening to opinions.

Basically, it is not accustomed to such democratic actions as demonstrations, sit-ins, and so on. The decision-making process of the government itself is not democratic. In fact, in the government everything is decided by one person. Li Peng himself has said: In our government, actually it is Deng Xiaoping who has the final say. Lacking democracy and being unaccustomed to democratic life are the main factors contributing to the current situation. In the meantime, another problem is the poor quality of many high-ranking officials of the government.

Q: What are your main motives for leading the student movement? What theories and convictions do you follow to understand democracy and the current situation of Chinese society?

A: Actually, my motives are quite simple. I am very dissatisfied with society. ... When I assess education in China, I discover that the problems of education are very serious. At first, my attention was focused on education. After thinking over the matter further, I realized that it is the political system that blocks the improvement of education. Therefore, my first purpose in establishing a students' federation was actively to promote political reform, to protect citizens' rights and freedom contained in the [state] constitution, and to ensure that economic reform could be truly implemented. In addition, freedom of the press is, of course, also my goal. I believe that the main reasons contributing to the many problems in China's system, including corruption, bureaucracy, undemocratic practices, and so on, [are] that the people cannot independently exercise their political rights, or exercise control over their own political and economic life. . . . Actually, we can say that it is a democratic movement of human rights.

Q: Through constant dialogue with the government and participating in such a massive social movement, do you think that you have enhanced your understanding, or accumulated more experiences?

A: Of course I have. In particular, as far as I myself am concerned, I have greatly enhanced my capability to think over and observe things. What I have learned in this regard is greater than what I had achieved in the classroom on the mainland. I understand the practical problems of the government and the society. People in general cannot understand this. One of the things that I have realized is that consciousness of democracy is inseparable from the environment and the people. Just as I said in the past, the greatest obstacles to reform in China are its population of one billion and its five-thousand-year history.

Q: According to the organizational and political experiences you have gained from participating in the current student movement, what will be the main problems facing China on its path toward democracy?

A: There are mainly two problems in this regard. First, consciousness of democracy by the masses. When we are promoting the democracy movement, people are shouting slogans of overthrowing Li Peng. This shows that we are unable to promote democratic ideas. This is a great obstacle to the consciousness of democracy. Second, the system itself is also an obstacle. If the government persists in the system of prohibiting the existence of an opposition party, and if there are no real checks and balances, there will be no hope of success for reform and democracy in China.

Q: If your idea can be smoothly spread throughout society, what will be the response of the government and the [chance] of success?

A: I think that we will succeed. It is difficult to predict the result in the short run. However, in the long run, democracy in China will gradually advance. Our actions are speeding it up. At present, we are not powerful enough, and we must exert greater efforts.

Q: As far as the system is concerned, what obstacles will you encounter?

A: In view of the situation in Beijing over the past two days, no one is too optimistic about it. We must face reality. As far as the development of democracy in China is concerned, retrogression could occur.

. . . *Q:* Apart from the obstacles erected by the government, do you think there are also problems concerning the students and masses who have participated in the movement?

A: We lack experience in fighting for democracy. In the meantime, we our-selves are maliciously poisoned by the bureaucratic system. Actually, many student leaders are also influenced by bureaucratic style. This is a very big obstacle.

Q: Now I want to ask you: How much do you understand the nature of previous political movements over the past forty years in China? Let us take . . . the democracy wall movement in 1986 and 1987 [*sic*] as an example. Can you compare it with the current movement, and tell us their similarities and differ-ences?

A: I think that basically there is no difference between the previous student movements and the current one. However, the previous student movements lacked organization. They did not extensively involve people [of] various strata, and fewer people participated in them. In the meantime, they did not evoke the common understanding and responses of the masses.

The greatest success of the current movement is that it has evoked the com-mon understanding and response of Beijing residents. An organized and power-ful opposition force has been developed. Although we are not completely satisfied with it, [this understanding and response] is hard to come by. Even if we fail in our action, I believe that a greater student or social movement will occur soon. At that time, we will achieve greater success.

People of our generation have witnessed the opening up of China, and the contributions made by Hu Yaobang and others have further enlightened us ideo-logically. I believe that through the current democratic movement, university students of the 1990s will have a stronger consciousness of democracy.

Q: From newspapers I learn that many noted intellectuals have supported you. They are also active in disseminating their political ideas. I do not know whether you have contacted them. If you have, what is your appraisal of them? Can you tell me the similarities and differences between you and them?

A: In China, a small number of persons have made very great contributions to democracy, . . . [or] at least great efforts in this regard. I believe that the quality of people of the younger generation is better than that of people of the older generation. Young people are also purer. Due to the restrictions of the environ-ment and the feudal system which lasted several thousand years, Chinese intel-lectuals are generally weak and prone to compromise. Yet many of their proposals that [could be called] protests are worth mentioning. . . .

Q: . . . Do you think that the political and democratic ideas of intellectuals who demand democracy, freedom, and cultural values . . . are disconnected with our social foundation?

A: Yes. Very often their theories are attached to the so-called reformers. But I do not believe we need reform. The reform movement has been around for a long time. It started in the Qing dynasty but never truly succeeded. Experiences have told us that reform is useless in foreign countries. However, our intellectuals have continued to stick to reform, [when] what China needs is revolution. Of course, I do not favor violent revolution. What I mean is that some people believe that power only resides in the highest stratum. But I don't think that it resides in the highest stratum alone. It also resides in the people.

Q: I wish to ask you: What are the differences between your concept of the people and that of the government? How do you define the word "people"?

A: First of all, people must not be regarded as an organic whole. They are individuals, or a group of citizens. According to an old concept, people are regarded as a pile of [homogeneous] beings. This is actually an insult to the people. People are complicated. Regarding people as being one billion individual citizens is different from regarding them as an organic whole.

177

The First Lesson of Democracy for the People on the Mainland: An Interview with Fang Lizhi by *Lianho Pao* on June 2 in Beijing

FANG LIZHI

June 2, 1989

Source: *Lianho pao* (United daily), June 3, 1989, in *Tiananmen 1989*, pp. 260–62.

Q: . . . Would you comment on the student movement in terms of the interactions between the government and students and all the participants?

A: From a short-term or realistic perspective, this seems like a tragedy of historical development. After all, martial law has been imposed. But from a long-term perspective, this movement is definitely advantageous to the development of democracy in China. It is just like the May Fourth Movement. Although the concrete aims of the May Fourth Movement were somewhat problematic at that time, the profound significance of the May Fourth Movement did not merely lie in its concrete aims. In other words, the success of today's student movement does not depend on whether or not it achieves its proposed aims. Rather, it lies in the fact that this movement has made intellectuals, students, and ordinary people understand that they have the right to make their own choice. If they don't like certain leaders, they have the right to demand that they step down, and they can do so openly. They will no longer regard government leaders as the saviors of the Chinese nation, but as its servants.

The achievement of this student movement that we can directly feel is the participation of millions of people. They have gone through the baptism of the movement and developed something of a democratic consciousness. Tiananmen Square is like a school. Whoever goes to Tiananmen will be affected, either emotionally or ideologically. In fact, the whole atmosphere of democracy makes people feel quite differently. For instance, human relationships were at their best during the May 17 large demonstration. When two cars bumped into each other, both drivers apologized to each other due to the general atmosphere of May 17. This shows that once they have gotten rid of their fear of dictatorship, people become very good and honest. We may say that the present-day phenomenon in the mainland of people fearing others or losing their tempers with others all comes from the fear of autocracy. Once their fear is removed, the people will have a sense of security. Once there is democracy, it can change their ugly side, now seen as the [basic] nature of the Chinese people.[1] The people will taste what it feels like as a human being.

Q: Hasn't the enthusiasm of the people and students conspicuously declined in the past few days?

A: That is because the government has exerted strict control and done a lot of work to keep the people from having any way to express their enthusiasm. The Chinese regime has been maintained over the past forty years by a reign of terror. The regime not only has used ideology to control people's thinking, but has also controlled all social resources. The reform of the political system should start right here.

Q: Will there be many changes of personnel and power structure at the top of the CCP because of the student movement?

A: It is not very easy for us at the bottom to comprehend the changes at the top. This is mainly because politics [in China] is not open or transparent. We have no way to know their views on each other. Even less do we know what is happening in the course of the power struggle. However, this student movement has provided a chance for everyone to see clearly that in the past the relationship between the people and the leaders has been stood on its head. The people do not have to depend on or thank the CCP for everything. Deng Xiaoping is no longer a paramount state leader. He is a servant, too. People have the right to criticize him and suggest that he should retire. People have adopted an independent attitude toward the government, and they have the right to be the masters. Today people have seen very clearly whether the decisions should be made according to the will of the people or according to the views of a few leaders. In the past, the government used to say that socialist democracy was better than bourgeois democracy. After this democracy movement, when they compare the popular will with the government's use of martial law to confront it, everyone will clearly comprehend the attitude and nature of the authorities.

---

[1]A reference to the vitriolic representation of the Chinese national character in Bo Yang's *The Ugly Chinese.*

Q: Will the Chinese Communist regime and the party be affected by this movement?

A: It has affected the nature of the Chinese Communist regime, which already shows signs of qualitative change. This isn't happening only in China. Socialist countries in recent years have been changing. Nobody thinks they can sustain themselves as in the past. The greatest changes have occurred in East Germany and Hungary; secondarily, in Poland; and then the Soviet Union is changing too. This shows that after forty years' trial, the socialism of Lenin, Stalin, and Mao Zedong has proved a failure.

At present, we do not see evidence that the nature of the Chinese Communist regime is changing. Nevertheless, the demands of the intellectuals and students have been made. Socialism reached its peak at the end of World War II. Now it has declined. It is a disease that infected human beings in this century, but by now it has proved that it does not work. I can optimistically predict that this disease will be gone by the next century.

Q: From another point of view, when the students boycott classes, they are taking a course on democracy in the social education program. Will this have some other impact too?

A: The students' progress in study depends on each individual student because each one is different. As a result of this student movement, some students will become political leaders by engaging themselves in politics. Others will return to class and study even harder, finally becoming intellectuals and scholars. The crucial issue is that we no longer need those scholars and political leaders who can only recite the teachings of Marxism.

Q: Some worry that the Chinese Communist party may retrogress because the impact of this student movement is too great.

A: This is quite possible. History has never developed in a linear fashion. If Li Peng can consolidate his power after the movement, he is bound to regress to the centrally planned economy. He has more than once affirmed [the importance] of central planning. However, Li Peng's ideas have no chance of succeeding and will inevitably fail. Ultimately, they will be forced to go the open-door route again. But the Chinese people will see some bad days. The general trend is independent of Li Peng's will.

Q: Have you yourself clearly avoided involvement in this movement?

A: I have done so mainly so that the student movement's development would not be misinterpreted or misunderstood because of my personal involvement, and so that the authorities could find no pretext to suppress this spontaneous movement. Morally and spiritually, there certainly exists some influence of mine on the students. From my point of view, I have expressed all my support for the speeches of the student movement. But if the students are left to act independently on Tiananmen Square, they should be even more powerful.

Q: Have you had any trouble personally?

A: They have already carried out [police] surveillance on me. Last week when

I went to Shanxi to attend a meeting, there were [easily identifiable] lookouts all the way. There is always a possibility that they will arrest me.

Q: What role will you likely play in the democracy movement in the future?

A: It's hard to say. It all depends on the future development of the situation. The authorities can take action against me at any time, but they may suffer an even bigger loss. I have been named in several party documents. Also, when they refer to "the famous scholar XXX," they are actually referring to me.

Q: Do you think the authorities' revenge will be extensive?

A: This depends on the strength of the resistance by the intellectuals and on the pressures both inside and outside the party. The more pressure and the more resistance, the fewer actions the Communist party dares to take. As a matter of fact, as far as I am concerned, my criticism of the CCP is not the sharpest, but I am the most independent. That is what they want to eradicate. No matter how sharply you criticize the Communist party, as long as you have "a second kind of loyalty," the Communist party can more or less tolerate you.[2]

Q: Will reports and criticism by world opinion have some influence?

A: Democracy and human rights are international issues; they cannot be treated simply as foreign interference into one's domestic affairs. Wasn't the CCP involved in issuing statements condemning the human rights problems in South Africa, and in meeting with the Soviet Union on Cambodia? Isn't that also interference? In a word, human rights in the international community can have only one standard, which should also be applied to China.

Q: The Guomindang in Taiwan has already expressed its support of the student movement, but it has also felt considerable embarrassment. What do you think?

A: Well, the Guomindang is not without difficult problems. These can more or less push Taiwan to be more democratic.

---

[2]This refers to the superficial loyalty of CCP members, which nevertheless allows the party to tolerate its members' frequent deviations from official policies. See Liu Binyan, *A Higher Kind of Loyalty*, trans. Zhu Hong (New York: Pantheon, 1990).

178

June 2 Declaration of a Hunger Strike

LIU XIAOBO, ZHOU DUO, HOU DEJIAN, AND GAO XIN

June 2, 1989

Source: *Tiananmen 1989*, pp. 288–90.

We are going on a hunger strike![1] We protest! We appeal! We confess! We are not seeking death. We are seeking true life. Under the irrational military violence and pressure exerted by the Li Peng government, Chinese intellectuals must end their weak-kneed behavior of all talk and no action, passed down for several thousand years. With our actions, we must protest martial law and call for the birth of a new political culture. We must confess to the errors that we have made because of our old habit of weakness. Every one of us is responsible for the backwardness of the Chinese nation.

1. This unprecedented democracy movement has consistently adopted legal, nonviolent, rational, and peaceful means to strive for freedom, democracy, and human rights. But the Li Peng government has gone so far as to assemble hundreds of thousands of troops to crack down on the defenseless students and people from all walks of life. Hence, we are going on a hunger strike not to petition again, but to protest martial law and the military curfew! We suggest that peaceful means be adopted to promote the democratization process in China. We oppose any form of violence, but we are not afraid of brutal violence [against us]. We want to use peaceful means to display the strength of our democratic forces in civil society and to smash the undemocratic order maintained only by bayonets and lies. It is extremely absurd and foolish to impose martial law and a military curfew on the peaceful petitioning students and the people. . . . This has created an extremely bad precedent in the history of the PRC, making the Communist party, the government, and the military subject to great humiliation. All the achievements of ten years of reform and the open door are destroyed in one day.

2. Several millennia of Chinese history are full of cases of violence against

---

[1]This is the declaration issued for a seventy-two-hour hunger strike in Tiananmen Square by four well-known personages: Liu Xiaobo, a lecturer at Beijing Normal University, best known for his criticism of Chinese traditional culture; Zhou Duo, formerly a sociology teacher at Beijing University and later a department head at the Stone Company; Hou Dejian, a rock star originally from Taiwan; and Gao Xin, former chief editor of *Normal University Weekly* and a CCP member.

violence and mutual hatred. Right up to the present, animosity has been a Chinese tradition. Since 1949, the slogan of "taking class struggle as the key link" has pushed to even greater extremes the traditional mindset of hatred, animosity, and violence against violence. Martial law is another manifestation of the political culture of class struggle. Hence, our hunger strike calls on the Chinese from now on gradually to abandon and eliminate animosity and the mindset of hatred. We must thoroughly give up the political culture of "class struggle," because hatred can only produce violence and autocracy. We must begin democratic construction in China with a new democratic spirit of tolerance and cooperative consciousness. Democratic politics is a politics without an enemy and hatred. It is composed of consultation, discussion, and voting on the basis of mutual respect, mutual tolerance, and mutual compromise. Li Peng as premier has made serious mistakes and should resign according to democratic procedure. But Li Peng is not our enemy. Even if he steps down, he still enjoys his rights as does any citizen. He may even have the right to stick to his wrong views. We appeal to everyone . . . to give up the old political culture and begin a new one. We demand that the government immediately end martial law. We appeal to both the students and the government to begin anew, through peaceful negotiation and consultative dialogue, to settle the confrontation between the two sides.

3. This student movement has won unprecedented sympathy, understanding, and support. The imposition of martial law has changed this student movement into a popular democratic movement. But undeniably, many people support the students out of humanitarian sympathy for them and dissatisfaction with the government. They lack a civic consciousness of political responsibility. Hence, we appeal to the entire society to give up gradually the attitudes of onlookers and simple sympathy and to build up a civic consciousness. Civic consciousness is first and foremost a consciousness of the equality of political rights. Every citizen should have the confidence that his political rights are equal to the rights of the premier. Second, civic consciousness is not merely a sense of justice and sympathy, but even more a rationalized consciousness of participation; that is, also a sense of political responsibility. Everyone should not merely sympathize and support, but also directly participate in building democracy. Finally, civic consciousness is a self-awareness in assuming responsibilities and obligations. If social politics is rational and legal, it is to everyone's credit; if social politics is irrational and illegal, then everyone bears the responsibility. . . . Everyone must clearly understand that in democratic politics, one is first and foremost a citizen, and only secondarily a student, professor, worker, cadre, soldier, or whatever.

4. For several thousand years, Chinese society has been living in a vicious cycle of a new emperor replacing an old emperor. History has proven that the stepping down of some unpopular leader and the assumption of power by some very popular leader cannot solve the essential problems of Chinese politics. What we need is not a perfect savior, but a perfect democratic system. Hence, we

appeal: First, the whole society should use every means to establish legal and popular autonomous organizations, and gradually form popular political power to counterbalance the government's decision making . . . because the essence of democracy is checks and balances. We would rather have ten mutually balancing devils than one angel with absolute power.[2] Second, we should gradually establish a sound impeachment system whereby leaders guilty of serious mistakes can be impeached. It is not important who assumes or steps down from power, but how one does it. Appointment or removal through undemocratic procedures can only lead to dictatorship.

5. During this movement, both the government and students have made mistakes. The main mistake of the government is to confront the students and city residents under the guidance of the old way of political thinking of "class struggle," thus making the conflict continually intensify. The main mistake of the students is the unsoundness of their own organizational construction. In the process of striving for democracy, many undemocratic factors have appeared. Hence, we appeal: Both the government and students should conduct a sober self-examination. We consider that, as far as the whole situation is concerned, the major errors have been made by the government. Actions, like demonstrations and hunger strikes, are the democratic way for the people to express their wishes, and they are completely legal and rational. They are not creating turmoil. The government has ignored the basic rights granted to every citizen by the constitution, and with an autocratic political mindset it has defined this movement as turmoil. Thus, it has led to a series of even more erroneous decisions and made the movement frequently escalate and the confrontation become even more intense. . . . These mistakes are no less grave than the wrong decisions in the "Cultural Revolution." It is only due to the restraint of the students and city residents, and the strong appeals made by people from all walks of life—including all people of insight in the party, the government, and the army—that no large-scale bloodshed has happened. In view of this, the government must recognize and examine itself concerning these mistakes. We believe it is still not too late to do so. This government should learn a bitter lesson from this large-scale democratic movement: to get accustomed to listening attentively to the voice of the people, and to people using their constitutional rights to express their will. They must learn how to run the country in a democratic way. The popular democratic movement is now teaching the people how to manage society with democracy and legality.

The mistakes by the students are mainly manifested in the confusion of their internal organization and a lack of efficiency and democratic procedure. For instance, the goals are democratic, but the means and processes are

---

[2]The authors are both calling for a system of checks and balances and rejecting proposals for a "Neo-authoritarianism" in which a single leader would be given extraordinary power to transform the system, as previously advocated by Zhao Ziyang's supporters.

undemocratic. The theories are democratic, but the methods of handling concrete problems are undemocratic. The lack of a cooperative spirit and the rights that cancel each other out[3] produced zero efficiency of decision making, financial chaos, and material waste. There is too much emotion and not enough rationality, too much awareness of privileges and not enough of equality. For about one hundred years, the Chinese people's struggle for democracy has largely remained at the level of ideology and sloganeering. There was an emphasis on enlightenment of thought, not practical operations; an emphasis on ends, not on means, process, and procedure. We believe that the actual realization of democratic politics is the democratization of the operational process, means, and procedures. Hence, we appeal: The Chinese should abandon the traditional, empty democracy of simple ideologies, slogans, and goals, and begin constructing the democracy of operational processes, means, and procedures, thus changing the core element of the democracy movement from the enlightenment of thought to the actual operation of democracy. The construction of democracy should start from every concrete thing. We appeal: The students should conduct a self-examination centering on the reorganization of the student ranks on Tiananmen Square.

6. The grave mistakes of the government are also reflected in the wording of "a handful." Through our hunger strike, we want to tell the country and world opinion that the so-called handful are such people: They are not the students, but citizens with a sense of political responsibility who have actively participated in this popular democratic movement in which the students have played a key role. Everything they have done is rational and legal. . . .

We must admit that running the country democratically is new to every Chinese citizen. All Chinese citizens must learn from the beginning, including the highest leaders of party and state. In this process, errors by both the government and the people are inevitable. The key lies in recognizing mistakes and correcting them. . . . Through the process of continually correcting mistakes, we will gradually learn how to run our country democratically.

Our basic slogans are:

1. We have no enemy! Don't let hatred and violence poison our wisdom and the process of China's democratization!

2. We all need to examine ourselves. China's backwardness is everyone's responsibility!

3. We are first and foremost citizens.

---

[3]One feature often criticized was the student organizations' decision rule on the square: All decisions required unanimity. This gave each unit veto power. Thus, even when a majority favored withdrawal from the square, one group could prevent such a decision. Student leader Shen Tong defended this rule, however, as a respect for minority views in contrast to the CCP principle that the "minority obeys the majority," which effectively robs minority opinion groups in the party of any influence or rights. Interview, fall 1989.

4. We are not looking for death! We are seeking a true life!
The place, time, and rules of the hunger strike.
1. Place: Under the Monument to the People's Heroes on Tiananmen Square.
2. Time: Seventy-two hours, from 4:00 P.M. on June 2 to 4:00 P.M. on June 5.
(Special explanation: As Hou Dejian will go to make records in Hong Kong in six days, the hunger strike time for him is forty-eight hours. . . .)
3. Rules: Drink water only and [eat] no food. No other nutritious drinks. . . .

179

A Dialogue between a Student and a Corporal of the People's Liberation Army

Early Morning of June 3, 1989

Source: Translated by C. Y. Mok, courtesy of Robin Munro.

During the early morning of June 3, 1989, several tens of thousands of members of the PLA were moving toward Tiananmen Square. They were only a hundred meters away when they were stopped and turned back by a much larger number of unarmed Beijing citizens.

While the soldiers were resting on the roadside waiting for their retreat, countless numbers of students, workers, and government cadres were trying to explain to them the real situation in Beijing. . . . What follows is a dialogue between a student . . . and a corporal of the PLA:

Student: Do you know why you have come to Beijing?

Corporal: We have come here to enforce the order to maintain law and order in the capital.

S: There is no "turmoil" in Beijing. . . . You think you have come to maintain order, but in actual fact you have come to silence the masses. Go and fetch the newspapers published ten days or so ago and you will see that what was contained in the newspapers then is very different from what appears now. Look and listen. Remember the day when martial law was imposed? Everyone noticed the tone of the evening news announcer. He was almost crying. . . .

. . . Please think about this. Over the past month, there have been demonstrations on a mammoth scale, and yet there hasn't been any violence. . . . Of course, when a million or more people demonstrate in the streets, they will obstruct traffic. It's important for you to know why we march in the streets.

C: I read in the newspapers that there's a group called the Flying Tigers who run amok on their motorcycles, and their activities have certainly disrupted public order.

S: Why do the Flying Tigers run around? First of all, it's their way of expressing support and solidarity. Second, they carry messages for the people everywhere. . . .

Your arrival has stabilized the situation, but it is not the kind of stability we want. We want the stability of the national system and not the kind of stability that consists in suppressing the people.

The newspapers in Beijing admitted before that at the height of the demonstrations, when more than a million people in Beijing were participating, there was no police presence maintaining order. But during that period, fewer incidents occurred than at any other time in Beijing. . . .

It's true that the public buses caused traffic disruptions. But why were the buses used that way? They were driven by public transport workers to block you. They were doing their best out of their own free will. . . . Right now the newspapers are openly raping and distorting public opinion. Every unit has now been forced to come out in support of the government. Who dares to dissent? The government has organized 200,000 peasants in marches to support it. . . . Now every factory has received instructions. If you don't go [to a progovernment demonstration] as directed, you are considered to have missed a day's work and the penalty is forty yuan deducted from your pay packet. If you go, you are given ten yuan plus the wage bonus. . . . A new occupation has been born: to go on demonstrations. Anyone can join. They give you money and wages. This sure would solve the problem of unemployed youth. (Laughter from bystanders.)

C: What's the state of law and order and production in the city of Beijing? I've heard that it's been brought to a standstill.

S: . . . The stoppages in production have not been forced on the workers. They're all voluntary and supported by the people. This is a kind of protest. . . .

C: Aren't unlawful elements taking advantage of the situation to stir up trouble?

Bystanders: No! No!

S: Let me put it this way. Certain unlawful incidents have taken place. There were three people who splashed paint on the portrait of Mao Zedong. They were grabbed by the students and sent to the police station. The students also grabbed two pickpockets and sent them to the police. But the students were beaten bloody. A Japanese reporter happened to be taking photographs and the police charged him, hitting him on the face. . . . This is no rebellion. Furthermore, it's not the PLA's business to maintain social order. It should be the work of the police. What is the purpose of your presence? I think you've come to suppress a coup. . . .

Haven't the newspapers reported that everything is very orderly? There are fewer fights, less abusive language, fewer traffic accidents, less criminal activity.

The police force is a people's force. Off-duty, they come to join the demonstrations to support us.

C: After our troops entered the city to enforce martial law, weren't members of the PLA wounded? . . . The *Liberation Army Daily* reported that some of our [soldiers] have been beaten up and sent to the hospital. . . .

S: You can see some leaflets with pictures being circulated around Beijing. In the leaflet are six consecutive photos. We've run off a lot of copies. You can see that the Armed Police were beating people up. Finally they were chased by the people, who threw bricks at them. The police went up to the PLA vehicles, and the people were angry. They would have fought anyone who came forward. This was because those Armed Police had beaten up and injured a lot of people. . . .

A nonstudent bystander: Why are so many ordinary people taking part? They've been moved by the actions of the students. Really, the students maintain excellent order.

C: When you were hunger striking on Tiananmen Square, the Russian leader Gorbachev was paying a state visit. It was the most important meeting between China and Russia for thirty years. Were you aware of the international implications?

S: We took that into consideration and moved to the side [of the square]. Furthermore, the government could have agreed to a dialogue, or they could have said they would talk to us after the Gorbachev visit. . . . The government was heartless and continued to ignore us. It didn't even say, "You stop the hunger strike, please, and we'll discuss a way to work things out." There was no response whatsoever! . . .

Some people are extremely angry with anyone wearing a military uniform. They want to fight them. Many of these ordinary folks haven't had much education. They just feel that the PLA shouldn't be doing what it's doing, and they're prepared to fight. The students are more rational. Just now a few soldiers were grabbed at Tiananmen Square, and the people were yelling for them to be beaten up. But all the student marshals helped to get them released, because we didn't want an outbreak of violence. . . .

C: What is happening in Beijing will affect the whole country. Have you thought of the economic losses to the nation?

S: Right now our hard-earned money has been turned to the profit of officials. When the workers come to support us, they're not working in the factories. But the industrial production lines didn't stop. We haven't run out of daily necessities. To be sure, public transportation is at a standstill. But why? The buses have all been driven to the city outskirts to block the PLA from entering the city. The subway has been closed to the public because the authorities are using it to transport troops. . . .

As far as losses are concerned, the May Fourth Movement seventy years ago led to losses. . . . Forty years ago when the Communist party was making revolution, the workers went out into the streets and assembly lines ceased operations. Didn't the Communist party organize strikes? The Communists then in opposition knew that strikes would affect production. Why didn't they listen to the Guomindang's advice "not to disrupt the economy?" . . .

C: Is it true that a so-called Goddess of Democracy has been erected in Tiananmen Square? . . .

S: Think about this. . . . Why don't [the newspapers] dare to let the statue appear on television? If you say that the erection of the statue violates the urban planning laws, then we must point out that those laws apply only to the erection of permanent structures. If the statue is regarded as debasing the Monument [to the People's Heroes], then wouldn't the dragon dances and exhibitions of pandas in celebration of the New Year and festivals in past years have had the same debasing effect? . . .

C: You erected a statue of a goddess, and according to the newspapers you did not consult the people. That is raping public opinion.

S: What is meant by "raping public opinion"? You can see that more than a million people came out to march in the streets and the population of Beijing is only a few million. . . .

C: Don't your activities constitute turmoil? Isn't the capital in turmoil?

S: Yes, it is in turmoil. It is turmoil initiated by a handful of people.[1] But do you know how much crime there was in Beijing before this? . . . During this particular period of time, compared to other times during the past few years, the number of crimes was the smallest. . . .

An ordinary citizen: During this time, even the pickpockets have gone on strike!

S: . . . The actions you've undertaken have generated tremendous animosity among the people. If Beijing were really in a state of turmoil, the people would welcome your entry into the city to help restore order. Why would they want to drive you away? . . .

C: Why don't you let us enter the city?

S: Didn't I explain it just now? When you enter the city, "order" will be improved. Those maniacs will say: Now social order has been improved. . . . There will be arrests in every unit. And when that happens, we will have to shut up. There will now be no convocation of the NPC. Even the chairman of the NPC has remained silent since his return.

C: Li Peng, Yang Shangkun, and other leaders of the country have said that the PLA hasn't come to suppress the students.

S: You are bringing tanks, airplanes, and artillery. These are totally unnecessary. Why can't they mobilize the PLA of the Beijing Military Region? You've been lied to. China has a very strange phenomenon: The general secretaries of the party are antiparty! And two general secretaries lost their power suddenly. Some say that it's a coup. . . .

C: I understand that the Beijing Military Region has sent its troops. . . . They are the ones who arrived first.

---

[1]This undoubtedly refers to the party hardliners who ordered martial law.

S: That must be the Thirty-eighth Army! But the commander of the Thirty-eighth Army has been court-martialed and is no longer able to exercise command. Even if the Beijing Military Region's troops are moving, it means that power over [the BMR's troops] has been seized. . . .

C (to foreign reporters): No photographs! (*Other soldiers were also raising objections.*) It is shameful to the nation to allow foreigners to see this.

S: The foreign and Hong Kong reporters . . . have reported only the present situation of the students. There has been no insult at all. . . .

We are now regular listeners to the "Voice of America." The radio station is quite objective, not agitational. . . . The foreigners are helping us to dispel rumors. For example, not long ago, there was a rumor circulating on Tiananmen Square that Deng Xiaoping had lost power. . . . But after about twenty minutes of this, the "Voice of America" broadcast that the news was false. The Chinese government never acted to dispel similar rumors. . . .

Under martial law, the newspapers only reported that you [soldiers] have been beaten up by students. Why don't they report that we've been feeding you? You were ordered to come here as an emergency matter and didn't bring any food. . . .

C: When Hu Yaobang died, the newspaper reported that people were shouting slogans like "Down with the Communist party!" Is that so?

S: I can't say whether or not there was such a slogan shouted. I personally didn't hear it. There were several million people. However, certain measures and actions of the Communist party were extremely disappointing to the people. So we often hear slogans like "Down with Deng Xiaoping!" and "Down with Li Peng!" It's not just a few people saying that. . . .

C: Don't you think that Deng Xiaoping has contributed a lot to the reforms over the past ten years?

S: I can tell you that if Deng Xiaoping had resigned in 1985, he would have been a great leader. But what he has done over the past several years has been awfully disappointing. He's just a remake of Mao Zedong.

C: Hasn't Zhao Ziyang resigned?

S: No, not resigned. He has lost power. . . . Zhao Ziyang was asked to make a speech denouncing the turmoil, but he refused.

C: Don't you agree that there should be martial law in some areas of Beijing?

S: We disagree, because it's unnecessary. What is meant by "some areas"? Now all [government] departments and newspaper offices have come under the control of the military. "Some areas" embraces the entire city. When the hunger strike began, I was opposed to it. But the government kept stalling its response and telling lies to our faces. . . . I was very angry. All the reformers have been eliminated and, up to now, there has been no emergency meeting of the NPC. The *People's Daily* yesterday reported that the Standing Committee of the NPC reported to Li Peng and studied Li Peng's report. They also had to declare their own position. Why should the Standing Committee of the NPC declare their position to the government? It should be the government explaining its actions to the NPC! The NPC is empowered to dismiss Li Peng. Why should they be making a declaration to him! This simply shows that there is something wrong with the state system. . . . The NPC meets every year and the members, I suppose, simply go to the banquets, put up their hands, and then go home. Why should the people be feeding such NPC deputies? . . .

C: The martial law order has been promulgated with legal sanctions. It's the same as the martial law imposed in Lhasa.

S: That was a rebellion. The PLA has two responsibilities. [Someone] said this at a . . . meeting of divisional commanders: The PLA's first responsibility is to protect the border and another is to deal with rebellion. . . . The whole country backed the imposition of martial law in Lhasa. . . . But the two situations are different, entirely different.[2]

C: We received orders from above that martial law has to be enforced. We soldiers have to obey orders.

S: This I know. We understand. That's why we're providing you with food and water. . . . But, truly, I would rather have you beat me up than allow you to march into the city. . . .

C: Weren't you told that you should go back to class, and that all the matters can be resolved through direct dialogue? (*Bystanders laugh mockingly.*) If you prolong the occupation [of the square], we will see another Cultural Revolution.

S: First of all, [Li Peng] didn't offer dialogue. Second, he opposed dialogue before, and if he wants dialogue now, will it be sincere? . . . Promises were made many times, but have they been realized? Not once. And then before any dialogue began, you were sent for. They let the PLA have a dialogue with us. What can the students' representatives say then?

C: If they refuse dialogue and you continue your sit-in, it will have a bad effect on the country. . . .

S: Then who should be held responsible? Should we be held responsible? This is why the government is so despicable.

C: If our country is to die, both the government and the students should be held responsible, half and half.

S: Listen, it's like under Guomindang rule. When both the party and the nation were dying then, the students rose up. If a government is like that, let it die. . . . If the government doesn't let the people act and doesn't do anything for the people itself, then the government should go.

C: The government still does a lot of good things.

S: Yeah, some good things. But those who did the good things were relieved

---

[2]By this point in the popular movement, and certainly after the crackdown began, some of those involved began rethinking the Tibet question, recognizing that the situations were perhaps not so very different, and that suppression was no more justified in Lhasa than in Beijing. But the view expressed by this student was probably the dominant one, even among most political dissidents, who are Han Chinese.

of their power. . . . What good things has Li Peng done? He has neither qualifications nor abilities. He has been in a high position for quite some time, and what has he done? . . . China's education deteriorated while he was chairman of the [State] Education Commission. Then when he became premier the country deteriorated. Now he wants to succeed Zhao Ziyang as general secretary of the party. Then the party will be done for! . . . You cannot use the philosophy of the gangster: I've come to kill you, to suppress you, and you are to blame because you've resisted me. Yes, we all have a noose around our neck, but if we didn't resist, we would be choked to death. . . . The government dismisses a general secretary and sacks a state chairman tomorrow. And if we don't give a damn, the situation will be pacified.

VI

June 3–4
The Beijing Massacre and
Its Aftermath

Lawrence R. Sullivan

"Faxisi Yeshou!" (Fascist Beasts!)

Documents in this final section portray the military crackdown from the perspective of students, Beijing residents, and foreign eyewitnesses in the capital and in Chengdu, Sichuan, where security forces also inflicted substantial civilian casualties. These sources capture the intense anger, shock, and despair created by the Chinese government's resort to a homicidal policy of using overwhelming military force to end the political crisis by invading its own capital. Individual acts of courage are also described as students, average citizens, and especially medical personnel sought to minimize casualties, even among captured soldiers whom students protected from enraged crowds. Overall, however, these documents reflect the incredible brutality of an ill-disciplined army unleashed against an unarmed citizenry.

The description of the violence in these materials is very emotional and often graphic as Beijing citizens reacted with horror to the army's assault (Doc. 181). Many of the accounts written by Chinese do not, however, provide an accurate historical record of the June 4 massacre. In the midst of the chaotic army attack, it was exceedingly difficult to estimate actual casualties. Prodemocracy participants also had an obvious political reason for inflating the count of dead and wounded, though official government accounts of heavy casualties among troops were undoubtedly fabrications.[1]

---

[1]The Chinese Red Cross issued a civilian death count of 2,600 immediately after the crackdown, but a few days later the Chinese government only acknowledged the death of 300 nonmilitary people. Amnesty International estimated that between 700 and 3,000 died, though some Chinese democratic activists suggested that the death toll was less than

Many documents also claim that the army massacred large numbers of students in Tiananmen Square near the Monument to the People's Heroes. According to an account by the Beijing student union (ASUCUB), soldiers and riot policemen rushing into the square "ruthlessly used machine guns and submachine guns to shoot at the defenseless students and city residents around them" (Doc. 183). But Robin Munro's eyewitness account argues that students occupying the monument were actually allowed to leave. The vast majority of casualties occurred, instead, among ordinary citizens defending the streets leading into the square.[2] "[T]he geography of the killing reveals much about the government's cold political logic and its choice of targets," Munro suggests (Doc. 190). While students were largely spared, soldiers concentrated on terrorizing the "common people" (*laobaixing*), even admitting in one instance that "it is you common people we are out to kill."[3] Citing other Chinese eyewitnesses, however, professors Anita Chan and Jonathan Unger challenge Munro's account by suggesting that "quite terrible events . . . occurred in the square that night" (Doc. 191). As these and other contradictory accounts indicate, much remains unclear about the events of June 3–4 in Beijing. We simply cannot say with certainty what happened.

Origins of the Crackdown

Why did the central Chinese leadership, absent Zhao Ziyang, decide to launch a military crackdown on June 4? From the beginning of the demonstrations on April 18, the Beijing spring movement had been remarkably nonviolent. Some groups had advocated more militant action, but the vast majority of participants remained committed to peaceful protest. Following the imposition of martial law on May 20, citizens seemed collectively aware that any violence, especially against the blockaded troops, would be totally counterproductive. Not one violent incident provoked by demonstrators was recorded in Beijing from May 20 to June 3, even by CCP-controlled media. The government also exercised restraint by allowing students to remain in Tiananmen long after the declaration of martial law. Perhaps this reflected the reluctance of military and police commanders to

---

a thousand. Beijing Mayor Chen Xitong's NPC report claimed that troops and police suffered "several dozens" dead and "6,000" wounded. But the fact that fewer than ten soldiers were posthumously honored after June 4 probably indicates the true death count. See Amnesty International, *People's Republic of China: Preliminary Findings of Killings of Unarmed Civilians, Arbitrary Arrests, and Summary Executions since June 3, 1989* (New York, August 1989), and Oksenberg et al., eds., *Beijing Spring*, Doc. 2.

[2]Robin Munro, an eyewitness to the events on the square until 6:15 A.M. on June 4, believes, however, that lethal force certainly would have been used against the students if they had not voted to leave the monument. Student accusations that martial law troops burned corpses on the square to remove evidence of the massacre have not been confirmed, although sources verify heavy black smoke there early on June 4 (Doc. 191).

[3]This statement was heard from troops chasing citizens into an alleyway between Xidan and Liubukou near the square. Interview, Beijing resident, 1989.

attack the students. But it may have also been part of the hardliners' overall strategy to, Chinese say, "attract more fish to bite the hook" (*yinyu shanggou'er*), that is, to give people more time to reveal their "counterrevolutionary" character by joining the prohibited demonstrations.[4]

By June 3, however, it was evident that the student and popular movement was running out of steam. The numbers of students occupying the square had decreased substantially as some groups had apparently voted to return to campus on June 5. Professor Rudolf Wagner speculates in his eyewitness acount that "if the government was willing to wait two more days, it would achieve its purpose to clear Tiananmen without bloodshed, although the social challenge certainly would not have been over" (Doc. 193).[5] The government's subsequent justification of the crackdown claimed that "a serious counterrevolutionary rebellion" and "riot" had broken out on the night of June 3 to which military action was merely a reaction. Beijing Mayor Chen Xitong even contended that "[mobs] planned to incite people to take to the streets . . . to stage a violent rebellion in an attempt to overthrow the government."[6] Yet nothing in the documents reproduced here, or any other reputable evidence, supports this assertion. The mood in the city had definitely turned anxious as crowds interpreted the death of four citizens in an accident involving a speeding People's Armed Police (PAP) vehicle on June 2 as a harbinger of further military action. But except for some suspected undercover police being roughed up on the streets, nothing approaching an organized, violent revolution preceded the army's forced entry into the city.[7]

---

[4]Mao Zedong employed this strategy in the 1957 Hundred Flowers campaign when, after luring liberal intellectuals into voicing public criticisms of the CCP, he crushed them in the subsequent anti-Rightist campaign. Many veteran intellectuals warned students throughout spring 1989, often to no avail, that a government led by Deng Xiaoping (who had prosecuted "Rightists" in 1957) was replicating Mao's strategy. Interview, Beijing intellectual, 1989.

[5]Some students had also voted to remain in Tiananmen until June 20 in order to present a petition to the scheduled meeting of the NPC Standing Committee. By June 3, however, less than five thousand students were on the square. Yi and Thompson, *Crisis at Tiananmen*, p. 71.

[6]Chen continued: "At this critical juncture, the party's Central Committee, the State Council, and the Central Military Commission decided to order troops poised on the outskirts of the capital to enforce martial law and quell the counterrevolutionary rebellion." Oksenberg et al., eds., *Beijing Spring*, Doc. 2.

[7]No evidence of an organized uprising—caches of weapons or pamphlets exhorting the population to take up arms—was ever presented by the government in the Chinese media. Even official accounts of the "turmoil" presented virtually no corroborating evidence of an organized conspiracy or preemptive violence even by the so-called hooligans the government accused of orchestrating the movement. See Shi Wei, "What Has Happened in Beijing," *Beijing Review*, no. 26, June 26–July 2, 1989, p. 11. After the Soviet military's bloody crackdown in Vilnius, Lithuania, in January 1991, Soviet officials, including President Mikhail Gorbachev, similarly blamed the Lithuanians, rather than the Soviet army, for initiating the violence. *New York Times*, January 14, 1991.

Several of the following documents attempt to explain the government's decision to use military force. Robin Munro believes that "the logic of the massacre . . . is clear." Despite dwindling numbers of students in Tiananmen, the active participation of workers and other urban residents in the movement in Beijing and many other cities posed a mortal threat to the regime, similar to the political crisis that would bring down Eastern European Communist regimes several months later. With the *laobaixing* "beginning to articulate their own grievances" and to organize "autonomous" organizations, the "party's alarm," Munro suggests, "was real." Unlike earlier prodemocracy demonstrations in China, the government now confronted a popular movement involving large numbers of unified workers.[8] The popular movement "had to be crushed," Munro argues, to preserve the regime from a popular revolt, which is why the *laobaixing*, rather than students, suffered the greatest number of casualties (Doc. 190).

Sharp divisions within the CCP and even security organs also impelled conservative leaders to take radical action. Unprecedented public protests had occurred among party members in Shanghai and other cities against the hardline leadership.[9] As some police and even military units joined the demonstrations, hardliners were rapidly losing support within the critical organizations of the Communist dictatorship. "The rapidly defecting party apparatus," Munro concludes, "had to be frightened and shocked back into line." Military force was the last resort for conservative leaders to maintain their control over the Communist party and Chinese society.

Other accounts from Western and Chinese sources reproduced here suggest an alternate interpretation of the conservative leadership's decision to crackdown. In this scenario, hardline leaders were concerned not so much with the objective threat to the regime—which seemed to be declining—but rather with a peaceful outcome to the crisis that may have bolstered the position of the recently deposed Zhao Ziyang. To undermine Zhao's proposals for a peaceful end to the crisis, conservative leaders actually intensified the crisis to justify purging the party of reformists. Rather than being frightened by the mass demonstrations, as Munro argues, this interpretation suggests the government took provocative actions, including the crackdown, just as the movement appeared to be subsiding in a manner predicted by the general secretary.

---

[8]Workers emerged as a unified force in 1989 in response to the economic and social dislocations caused by the reforms in conjunction with the absence of institutional means to challenge newly empowered factory managers. The elimination in 1978 of political labels, which had divided workers ever since 1949, also enhanced working class unity. Wang, "Analyzing the Role of Chinese Workers," in *China: The Crisis of 1989*, ed. DesForges et al.

[9]See Doc. 125. Also, Roy Forward, "Letter from Shanghai," in *The Australian Journal of Chinese Affairs*, no. 24 (July 1990): 287.

This pattern had, in fact, occurred from the very beginning of the demonstrations. Perceptible declines in popular activity were often immediately followed by provocative government actions. Rudolf Wagner notes, for instance, that the April 26 editorial appeared just when "things [had] calmed down" (Doc. 193). So, too, did the government declare martial law immediately after the students had voted to end the hunger strike on May 19.[10] The dramatic upsurges in the movement that followed these decisions effectively prevented a peaceful end to the crisis as proposed by Zhao Ziyang earlier on May 4. "It looked as if someone in the center needed some massive outpouring of public criticism and sentiment," Wagner argues, "to prop up his own position."

That *People's Daily* admitted on June 3 that "normal order has largely been restored in Beijing" strengthens this interpretation of the crackdown.[11] Although students remained in the square, the city suffered little serious disruption, with few, if any, strikes or other crippling actions.[12] Launching a military assault on the square was not primarily a response to "chaos" on the streets and the purported threat to "social stability" posed by the popular movement. The attack was, instead, carried out to ensure that the ousted Zhao and his supporters were linked to a "counterrevolutionary rebellion" that never really existed. Military action was necessary to "prove" Zhao's association with politically treasonable elements, especially to party rank-and-file who may have now found Zhao's moderate proposals for ending the crisis eminently reasonable.

Exaggerating the threat of the crisis to the regime was also decisively important to the conservative leadership of Li Peng, Yang Shangkun, and Beijing First Party Secretary Li Ximing. With their political positions apparently weakened by party member protests against their hard line, the last thing these highly unpopular

---

[10]China Central TV announced the students' decision to end the hunger strike on May 19 at 9:20 P.M. Three hours later, Li Peng declared martial law at what appeared to be a hastily arranged meeting held at the abnormal hour of 12:00 midnight. This sudden decision to introduce troops may have been taken to further antagonize the city, undermine Zhao, and destroy the popular movement with brute force just when the crisis seemed to be ebbing, as was believed by many Beijing residents. Other observers suggest, however, that martial law was a reaction to the possible decision by the government's own All-China Federation of Trade Unions to call a general strike on May 20, which hardliners feared would threaten the very existence of the regime. Interview, Beijing resident, 1989, and Wang, "Analyzing the Role of Chinese Workers," in *China: The Crisis of 1989*, ed. DesForges et al., p. 247.

[11]The article also claimed that "[t]he district where the party Central Committee and State Council are located is still being surrounded," though it admitted that normalcy had been largely restored elsewhere in the city. Oksenberg et al., eds., *Beijing Spring*, Doc. 55.

[12]Workers evidently joined the demonstrations during their nonworking hours rather than risking strikes. Beijing residents reported the city's transportation to be nearly back to normal on June 3, leaving the *People's Daily* report of the same day with little evidence of "chaos," except for a purported theft from a milk truck and attempted robberies in rural Hebei by "bandits" who supposedly used the situation in the capital as an excuse for their actions! Ibid.

leaders could tolerate was a petering out of the popular movement without a direct confrontation with proreform forces in the party.[13] Previous student demonstrations in 1986–87 had not substantially improved the hardliners' political position, as Zhao Ziyang had replaced Hu Yaobang as general secretary and ordered an early halt to the conservative "anti–bourgeois liberalization" campaign. A more profound crisis was needed this time to ensure an unequivocal victory for the conservatives. The unprecedented popular movement in China thus ultimately became a pawn in a high-level political struggle that essentially ended with a conservative coup against reformers.[14] As one veteran CCP member commented, the crackdown aimed "to destroy the forces of enlightened party leaders" (Doc. 200).

The Assault on Beijing

Signs of an impending crackdown appeared in early June.[15] Tension rose dramatically on the streets as plainclothes police increasingly tried to infiltrate groups on the square (Doc. 193). Contrary to cautious police tactics adopted since mid-April, demonstrators were now arrested on the spot, often in highly provocative fashion.[16] Perhaps frustrated by the movement's nonviolence, government hardliners apparently ordered the military to provoke public "disturbances" in order to justify a resort to force. In one instance, rifles and machine guns were abandoned in a vehicle accompanying a formation of unarmed troops who had literally jogged into the city on June 2.[17] It is possible that sympathetic

---

[13]The Central Committee was reportedly inundated with telegrams from party officials throughout the country calling on the leadership to negotiate with the students as Zhao had proposed. Sullivan interview of Chinese intellectual with contacts in the PLA, 1989.

[14]The entire crisis is, in this sense, reminiscent of Mao Zedong's tactics in the Cultural Revolution when he provoked violent political struggle to prosecute high-level CCP leaders, most notably Liu Shaoqi, whose prestige and popularity had challenged the Chairman's political authority and personal control of China's political agenda.

[15]Following Yang Shangkun's critical speech to the Central Military Commission on May 24, nominally "retired" party leaders, such as Peng Zhen, issued declarations supporting martial law, as did the commanders of all seven military regions, including Beijing's. Whether such pledges included explicit support for the ensuing crackdown is unknown.

[16]Demonstrators apprehended by police in the square were quickly taken to the Great Hall of the People and Zhongnanhai, where crowds attempting to rescue them were filmed. This footage later showed up on government propaganda programs that described "ruffians" as "storming" the leadership headquarters. Other ominous developments included the occupation by troops of key installations, such as the *People's Daily* compound, and the arrest of demonstrating workers in late May. Huang Yasheng, lecture at Fairbank Center for East Asian Research (hereafter FCEAR), Harvard University, summer 1989.

[17]Abandoning guns on the street violated one of the PLA's most absolute rules requiring soldiers to guard their weapons with their lives. A foreign military attaché interviewed in Beijing described the introduction of unarmed soldiers into the city center as a conventional military tactic for testing potential resistance on the street to an all-out assault. Interview conducted by Robin Munro, June 7, 1989.

soldiers were trying to provide arms to the demonstrators to combat the coming crackdown. But as Chai Ling later explained, students suspected the government of deliberately delivering weapons into the hands of demonstrators to "prove" the threat of an armed rebellion—a pretext the students quickly counteracted by turning the arms over to local authorities (Doc. 198).

The situation was further agitated by the deaths in the PAP vehicle accident described above, and the unprecedented use of tear gas in Beijing against peaceful crowds on the afternoon of June 3. Once armored personnel carriers (APCs) began roaring through the streets later that evening, it was obvious that the long-awaited crackdown had begun. Yet, contrary to government assertions of a "planned conspiracy," troops were met not by well-organized, armed "rebels," but by a highly spontaneous and disorganized popular resistance totally incapable of fighting a professional army equipped with AK–47s and battlefield tanks (Doc. 193).

The most startling aspect of the crackdown was the troops' indiscriminate firing and outright savagery against an unarmed populace. "[S]tudents and city residents who were trying to hide in lanes" were fired at. So, too, were crowds who taunted the troops as "bandits," as were individuals attempting to aid the wounded (docs. 183, 195). Tanks and APCs sprayed bullets into buildings and down alleyways, taking a heavy toll of citizens, especially in Muxudi (west of the square), where, it is claimed, "four hundred people [were] instantly killed or wounded" (Doc. 183). Victims included children and the elderly who remained in their homes that came under indiscriminate fire. Buildings housing high-level cadres were even shot up, such as Building No. 22 near Muxudi, the home of Liu Shaoqi's widow, Wang Guangmei, where a relative of a high-ranking State Council official was killed.[18] Most shocking was the use of highly destructive explosive shells and dumdum bullets outlawed by international conventions governing war. And in a pattern repeating the April 20 clash outside Zhongnanhai, security forces once again engaged in flagrant assaults on women. Medical personnel in Beijing and Chengdu were also shot, apparently causing the death of several doctors (docs. 185, 197).

The Twenty-seventh Army from Hebei Province acted with particular ferocity (Doc. 187). Commanded by a reputed relative of Yang Shangkun, it readily obeyed orders evidently issued by Li Peng on June 3 authorizing the use of lethal force against the citizenry (Doc. 198). Both Munro and Wagner speculate that the Twenty-seventh Army's experience in China's 1979 war with Vietnam contributed to the troops' savage behavior, although events on June 3–4 also apparently provoked some soldiers to seek revenge for the death of an officer near Muxudi. For whatever reasons, the frenzied, "crazy" state of many troops led

---

[18]The son-in-law of the deputy director of the State Procuracy was fatally wounded in Building No. 22. Several relatives of former CCP leader Li Lisan, and Bo Yibo's chauffeur, were also reported killed in other parts of the city.

many Beijing residents to believe that the soldiers had been injected with drugs.[19] But since security forces in Chengdu were also exceedingly cruel, a more general pattern was probably at work: Confronted with mass protests and government propaganda about an imminent "counterrevolutionary rebellion," soldiers, police, and even some armed workers were given a free hand to crush the mass movement at any cost (Doc. 197).[20] CCP hardliners evidently believed that the authority of the Communist party could only be restored by unleashing such raw, violent power that some Chinese thought fascism had taken hold. Swastikas scrawled on burned-out PLA tanks and public yearnings for foreign military intervention from Taiwan and even the United States indicated just how seriously the CCP had alienated its own people (Doc. 193).

The following accounts of June 3–4 also testify to the complexity of the situation as it unfolded in the early morning hours of June 4. While Twenty-seventh Army soldiers in Muxudi and the shopping area of Wangfujing (immediately east of the square) cut down unarmed civilians, troops deployed in other parts of the city, such as the Thirty-eighth Army from the city of Baoding (Hebei Province) and the Fortieth Army from China's Northeast, exercised considerable restraint (Doc. 183).[21] Troops retaking the Monument to the People's Heroes also acted professionally, although the students' refusal to accept "bricks and gasoline" offered by local residents eliminated any pretext for a wholesale slaughter of unarmed teenagers (docs. 181, 194).[22] Despite the horrendous violence, Beijing citizens reacted calmly even when given the opportunity to exact revenge against captured or isolated soldiers. Most people apparently wanted to inaugurate a new political movement without resorting to the hatred and violence frequently promoted by the CCP under the rubric of "class struggle." As Chai Ling claimed, "If we had lost our senses, as those soldiers did, and used sticks

---

[19]Hou Dejian's eyewitness account reinforces this image of the troops' frenzied state: "[The soldiers] were furious. . . . They began to load their machine guns and shouted loudly. Some became so impatient that they continuously trampled the smashed bottles on the ground." Cited in Yi and Thompson, *Crisis at Tiananmen*, p. 245. Many Beijing citizens readily accepted the drug theory after hearing that soldiers had laughed while shooting people.

[20]Workers carrying makeshift arms in Beijing's eastern district indicated they had been offered thirty yuan each by the government to beat up students on the night of the crackdown. Interview, Beijing resident, 1989.

[21]According to conversations with troops stationed in a local Beijing park, Thirty-eighth Army soldiers were denied bullets evidently to avoid open clashes with the Twenty-seventh Army. Later testimony from Chinese sources indicates, however, that some soldiers from the Thirty-eighth Army also opened fire in Muxudi. Fortieth Army soldiers deployed in Dongzhimen northeast of the square generally avoided civilian casualties by firing in the air. Interview, Beijing resident, 1989, and personal communication from David Zweig.

[22]Dressed in camouflaged uniforms, troops seizing the monument were apparently supported by a special paratroop unit.

and other 'weapons' to fight against their machine guns, it would have been the greatest tragedy" (Doc. 198).

Such restraint was not, however, exhibited by all the populace, including some students. Some fought pitched battles with oncoming troops into the morning hours. Once the army broke the long nonviolent standoff that had followed the May 19 declaration of martial law, many in the city engaged in an "uprising" against an invading force no different, they believed, from the Japanese in World War II. Workers and other ordinary people used Molotov cocktails, stones, and captured weapons to fight the army. Meanwhile, they berated nonviolent students for rescuing soldiers from enraged crowds even after their classmates had been killed. Construction workers were particularly willing to fight. So, too, were truck drivers, who suffered casualties after using such vehicles as heavy coal trucks from Shanxi Province to block tanks and APCs at key intersections in the city.

Much of the violence was a response to outrageous army actions. When a speeding APC crushed a man to death near Jianguomenwai in the eastern section of Beijing, residents chased the vehicle all the way to Tiananmen where it was burned, although students apparently saved the driver.[23] One soldier cornered in a Beijing alleyway was surrounded and summarily killed after he had bragged of killing thirteen people. Another was lynched from a bridge in Chongwenmen (southeast of the square), after shooting three defenseless women who had begged for their lives.[24] Large crowds also quickly set upon vulnerable military targets, including a loaded troop truck overturned in the square, and an armed paratroop unit was pelted with stones by crowds near Qianmen just south of Tiananmen. Despite their palpable hatred for the "people's army," however, Beijing citizens lacked the weapons and organization to carry on a sustained battle commensurate with successful popular uprisings in other countries.

The Aftermath

The violence in Beijing did not end with the army's takeover of Tiananmen on the morning of June 4. Citizens confronted soldiers throughout the day at the northern end of the square where troops fired several salvos inflicting numerous casualties.[25] Army units cut off from the main force in other parts of the city were surrounded by citizens who burned their vehicles. Many troops also apparently torched their own equipment, either as an act of rebellion or to provide

---

[23]Human Rights in China, ed., *Children of the Dragon: The Story of Tiananmen Square* (New York: Macmillan, 1990), p. 72, and interview, Beijing resident, 1989.

[24]Interview, Beijing resident, 1989.

[25]William Hinton, an eyewitness to these clashes on June 4 near the Beijing Hotel (east of the square), claims two hundred civilians were shot, with about fifty killed. Lecture at FCEAR, June 29, 1989. BBC and Hong Kong television crews both captured this event on film. See, "China . . . The Awakening," Independent Hong Kong TV production.

provocative scenes for propaganda cameras filming the "riot" (Doc. 195).[26] Although the army quickly gained control of the square, government authority seemed to vanish elsewhere in the city. Residents freely posted stark descriptions of the previous evening's massacre on neighborhood bulletin boards, scrawled death threats on the walls near Li Peng's residential compound, and openly carried the dead through the streets.

As troops and tanks maneuvered into what appeared to be defensive positions with armies facing each other, some observers speculated that China might be heading for civil war. This possibility was probably overestimated. But in bringing some 350,000 troops to surround Beijing, hardline leaders were apparently girding for a conflict with more than just a few thousand students in Tiananmen.[27] Postcrackdown rationalizations by the government claim that protesters had planned to kill "all the forty-eight million Communists of the country" (Doc. 193). Zhao Ziyang was also accused in a secret party document of a plan to carry out a coup on June 4, which the military crackdown successfully preempted.[28] Whether China confronted a Romanian-style rebellion within military ranks, as Robin Munro suggests, remains unknown (Doc. 190). But the following documents clearly indicate that China still lacks an integrated national army, making future internecine warfare a real threat. Troops surrounded by hostile crowds in Beijing were often ignored by nearby military units that could easily have come to their rescue. "Obviously, the rule in this army" Rudolf Wagner observed, "is, everyone for himself" (Doc. 193).

Late in the afternoon on June 4, a summer storm drenched Beijing. "Heaven is crying" the city's residents were heard to comment. Within days, the army regained control of the city, pursuing alleged "counterrevolutionaries" into the capital's alleyways where summary executions of suspects evidently occurred

---

[26]Yang Shangkun attempted to control insubordination in military ranks by warning that he would personally punish "any troops who do not obey orders." Yet discipline was a problem during the crackdown, as even Yang's direct orders were reportedly disobeyed by many commanders. This led to considerable postcrackdown punishments of rank-and-file troops and major shakeups in the command structure of the PAP and the PLA, where the commanders of the Thirty-eighth and Twenty-eighth armies were dismissed. Oksenberg et al., eds., *Beijing Spring*, Doc. 50; Lawrence R. Sullivan, "The Chinese Communist Party and the Beijing Massacre: The Crisis in Authority," in *China in the Nineties: Crisis Management and Beyond*, ed. David S. G. Goodman and Gerald Segal (London: Oxford Clarendon Press, 1991); and Chuan Wen, "Liusi: Zhonggong jundui de beiju" (June 4: The tragedy of the Chinese Communist Army), in *Kaifang zazhi* (Open magazine), Hong Kong (June 1990): 31.

[27]Donald Morrison, ed., *Massacre in Beijing: China's Struggle for Democracy* (New York: Time Inc., 1989), p. 31.

[28]Interview, Beijing CCP member, 1990. Zhao purportedly planned to use four thousand elite troops under his direct authority to execute his "coup." The document was read to party members over the phone to ensure against its duplication and probably to allow subsequent deniability of such trumped up charges if Zhao or other reformers ever return to power.

(Doc. 190). The government warned all citizens to turn in captured army weapons, but some individuals, outraged over the death of family members or friends, killed soldiers isolated from their units. Ironically, since the Twenty-seventh Army had been pulled out of the city soon after June 4, the victims had probably not participated in the massacre.

The government also called on citizens to track down student leaders now wanted as "criminals." In one celebrated case, a woman in Xi'an turned her brother into authorities. But most student leaders escaped Beijing and then the country, in part because police evidently made only halfhearted efforts to capture them. This undoubtedly reflected the anger of Public and State Security officials over the killing of plainclothes policemen who had remained on Beijing's streets during the crackdown.[29] Hospital personnel also refused the demands of martial law authorities to provide lists of wounded patients and, often at their own peril, even withheld names of the dead.[30]

Within a week, Beijing's citizenry returned to work. But fearing reprisals, the city's residents conspicuously avoided troops, now scurrilously referred to as "green devils." "The ghosts have entered the village," city residents were heard to comment in a phrase resuscitated from the Anti-Japanese War period. Yet any provocation of soldiers was dealt with swiftly. One old man shouting "Down with Fascists!" at troops in Beijing's eastern district was summarily gunned down. Foreigners were also targeted as PLA units shot up the diplomatic compound in Jianguomenwai, while APCs circled in front of Beijing's International Hotel on the night of June 6 firing menacingly into the air.[31] Meanwhile, CCP members who joined the government in declaring the crackdown a "great victory" were systematically shunned by their Beijing neighbors and coworkers.

The Unending Political Struggle

Deng Xiaoping's reappearance on June 9 ended rumors of his death or incapacitation, thus halting prospects of radical changes in the top leadership. Yet intellectuals, such as the dissident newsreporter Dai Qing, still voiced opposition by withdrawing from the party—this despite the fact that she had initially supported

---

[29]Interview, Beijing resident with contacts inside China's security organs. The fact that plainclothes police (indistinguishable from residents) were not pulled off the streets prior to the crackdown indicates that the leadership's orders were apparently a closely guarded secret. For a description of the "Yellow Bird Operation," which assisted fleeing demonstrators, see the *Washington Post*, June 2, 1991.

[30]Interview, Beijing medical personnel, 1989. Despite efforts to protect injured citizens, two to three were reportedly lynched by troops outside a Beijing hospital. Thanks to Professor Tony Saich of the University of Leiden for this information.

[31]Interview, Beijing resident, 1989, and Robin Munro, personal communication, 1989. The U.S. Embassy's official investigation of the shootings at the diplomatic compound concluded: "There is no doubt . . . that certain apartments [in the compound] were deliberately targeted by the army." Cited in Morrison, *Massacre in Beijing*, p. 200.

martial law out of fear that army commanders opposing the demonstrations might become "independent" if the civilian leadership had not taken decisive action (Doc. 199).[32] Students in Beijing and other cities also frantically appealed to workers to stage a "general strike" as some Guangzhou workers reacted to the massacre by forming a local union (Doc. 184). But like the students' futile wish that Thirty-eighth Army units would attack the Twenty-seventh Army, major strikes by workers did not occur, except in the northern city of Shenyang (Doc. 193). Besides their fear of losing jobs, workers were prevented from taking significant action by the army's preemptive occupation of such major industrial installations as the Capital Iron and Steel plant in Beijing's western suburbs.[33] Harsh punishment meted out to arrested workers (and prominently portrayed on national television) also undoubtedly deterred strikes. The 1989 prodemocracy movement in Beijing and other cities was the most spontaneous mass movement in China's post-1949 history, but it did not compare in grass-roots organization and popular support to Poland's Solidarity.

Students were more successful, however, in challenging the official government account of the "June 4 incident" (liusi shibian). Even in cities where major demonstrations had not occurred, such as Changchun (Jilin Province), student-organized rallies and propaganda teams spread the word about the Beijing massacre, countering officially sanctioned reports on television and by soldiers visiting factories and other work units.[34] Students also canonized their martyrs from Tiananmen to win public sympathy (Doc. 182). But in propagandizing to the public about their heroic "sacrifices," the students generally underplayed the more serious loses suffered by the laobaixing. Despite the unprecedented unity of the popular movement, the military crackdown did not eliminate longstanding

---

[32]Dai Qing was later detained for several months. *People's Daily* also indirectly resisted the hardliners immediately after the crackdown by, for instance, running a story on June 8 ostensibly about South Korea titled "Fascist clique wantonly kills students and civilians." This subversive resistance continued until June 11 when the paper's chief editor and director were both replaced by hardliners who reimposed strict ideological control, aided by military personnel deployed in the *People's Daily* compound. Frank Tan, "The *People's Daily* and the Epiphany of Press Reform: How the Organ of the Chinese Communist Party Subverted the Party During the Spring of 1989," in *China: The Crisis of 1989*, ed. DesForges et al., pp. 168, 178.

[33]The popular Chinese saying that "The whole country watches the capital [i.e., Beijing] and the capital watches the [steel] corporation" made government control of that facility a high priority, though no evidence exists that a major strike occurred there. Sympathetic strikes in Shenyang went on for several days and were only halted after military action was threatened. Gunn, "Tell the World About Us," p. 257.

[34]Roger W. Howard, "The Student Democracy Movement in Changchun," in *The Australian Journal of Chinese Affairs*, no. 24 (July 1990): 240. The most fervent response to the Beijing massacre was in Shanghai, where disorders lasted for three days until the city government not only threatened to cut off food supplies, but also mobilized large numbers of workers to reimpose control over the streets. John H. Maier, "Tian'anmen 1989: The View from Shanghai," *China Information* 5, 1 (Summer 1990): 10.

divisions between the educated elite and the average citizen. Yet the impact of the popular movement and the violent crackdown was undoubtedly profound, not only in Beijing, but in countless areas where similar protests had evidently occurred. A letter written by a county party secretary from China's hinterland, which ends this collection, indicates the possible long-term impact (Doc. 200). Receiving news of the crackdown by international radio broadcasts and China's pervasive word-of-mouth "small-channel news network" (*xiaodao xiaoxi*), this CCP member proclaimed that a "democratic consciousness has already found its way into the minds of the people."[35] His commitment to "an unshirkable share of responsibility for the fate of the country," if widely shared throughout CCP ranks, promises that the democracy movement in China did not end in Tiananmen Square on June 4, 1989.[36]

---

[35]Visiting remote mountainous regions of Yunnan Province in summer 1989, Michael Gasster of Rutgers University found similar widespread knowledge of the massacre and disbelief of government propaganda among local residents. Personal communication. The *xiaodao xiaoxi* is so pervasive that even the Chinese government relies on leaks to test popular reactions to proposed policy changes. Interview, Beijing CCP member, 1989.

[36]The apparent inability of CCP hardliners to carry out widespread purges of democratic sympathizers because of lower-level resistance to central government plans since June 4, 1989, leaves the party with a substantial social base of support for future political liberalization. This is especially true among well-educated members whose numbers have grown substantially in recent years to 29 percent of total membership. Stanley Rosen, "The Chinese Communist Party and Chinese Society: Popular Attitudes Toward Party Membership and the Party's Image," in *The Australian Journal of Chinese Affairs*, no. 24 (July 1990): 57–58, and Sullivan, "The CCP and the Beijing Massacre," in *China in the Nineties*, ed. Goodman and Segal.

Punish the murders! Pay back the debt of blood!
—Placard from photo

There has never been a world savior,
nor do we rely on a divine emperor to create happiness for
    mankind.
We rely entirely on ourselves.
We want to take back the fruits of our labor
and let our thoughts break down our prison.
Quick, heat the furnace red-hot
so that we can strike the iron when it's hot!
—The *Internationale*, second stanza

180
Letter to World Compatriots

BEIJING UNIVERSITY PREPARATORY COMMITTEE

June 4, 1989

Source: *ORSD*, 2:17.

Compatriots:
    We want to report the sad news about an atrocity of unparalleled savagery. Between the late evening of June [3] and the early morning of June 4, 1989, a large-scale massacre occurred in Beijing. The armies were ordered to enter Tiananmen Square. They used tanks, armored vehicles, machine guns, and sub-machine guns to slaughter innocent city residents and students along the way. By the morning of June 4, the number of the dead had already reached about five thousand. All the victims were defenseless students and people. The government mobilized a large number of riot policemen and soldiers who wantonly vented their barbarity. Machine-gun shooting went beyond the streets into residential areas. Many residents could not escape the massacre even when they stayed at

home. The blood is floating along East and West Chang'an Boulevard. What is more, the [government] did not even allow medical workers from the hospitals to rescue the victims. As soon as ambulances appeared, they were shot at by machine guns. Many medical workers failed to survive the massacre.

On Tiananmen Square, the students were prepared to stand fast to their posts until death. The armies and policemen, however, were killing people on their way to the square. They surrounded the square and the announcement by the Martial Law Command Center (*jieyan budui*) was repeatedly broadcast, demanding that the students withdraw; otherwise the students themselves would bear the consequences. Nonetheless, a few students who withdrew were shot by machine guns. Later the army troops no longer allowed the students to withdraw. They sent in tanks that crushed the people into pieces. Those who were not crushed were killed by bayonets. Military policemen then used forklifts to pull the dead bodies into piles and burned them on the spot . . . to do away with any evidence. They would not allow any person alive to become a witness to their crimes. It is estimated that as many as two thousand people were killed on the square. The government said this was a suppression of a counterrevolutionary riot.

We urge all the Chinese people to hold a general strike led by the workers, a boycott of classes by the students, and a shoppers' strike in opposing the brutal government. We strongly appeal to compatriots throughout the whole world to condemn the shameful massacre by the Chinese government and ask the United Nations to impose sanctions against the Chinese government for its inhuman acts.

181
Urgent Appeal of June 4

BEIJING UNIVERSITY

June 4, 1989

Source: Courtesy of HKFS.

Fellow students and compatriots:

Our blood is floating like a river. The streets and lanes are covered with a mixture of flesh and blood. The cruel, fascist-style killing is absolutely intolerable. Blood must not be shed in vain and the struggle must not stop. . . . Our view is that we cannot use violence against violence. A river of blood should not become a sea of blood. We have already [had to] make too heavy a sacrifice proving that the Li Peng government has become the total enemy of the people. Its demise can be expected soon.

We do not have armed force. We are defenseless in front of a well-equipped and modern army. But the power of our peaceful struggle cannot be underestimated. What we must do immediately is to tell the whole truth of the massacre to the world, call for a general strike by workers and shoppers in the city and throughout the country, and appeal for support from the international community.

President Ding [Shisun] of our university returned to campus last night, and we must urge and help the university authorities to make a correct response.

This is an extremely unusual and critical moment. More bloodshed can happen at any time. Angry people are just like a runaway wild horse. Fellow students and countrymen: From the beginning to the end, we have always used reason and wisdom to influence and lead the masses. At this crucial moment, we bear an even more important responsibility.

The best memorial ceremony for the dead is not to shed more blood but to strive for final victory!

Peaceful struggle and victory to the people!

Eternal glory to the martyrs who laid down their lives for democracy!

182

June 3 "Joan of Arc"

BEIJING UNIVERSITY

June 4, 1989

Source: Leaflet, in *ORSD*, 2:18.

One survivor of the "June 3" massacre told us the story about the heroic actions of a "Joan of Arc"–like girl student.

At midnight, a young girl in her twenties with long hair down to her shoulders rescued wounded and dying students on the square. Just when reactionary policemen opened fire and some people were shot down one after another while others were forced to retreat, she determinedly held high a flag and bravely dashed toward the gunpoints of the policemen. About twenty meters behind her followed people moved by her brave behavior. Then several explosions of gunshots were heard. She was still bravely dashing forward even after being shot several times. Finally she fell down after being hit by six bullets. Because she was too near the reactionary armies, the people behind her could not take her body back.

This unknown girl "Joan of Arc" is our goddess of democracy.

183

Letter to World Compatriots Regarding the Truth of the Beijing Massacre

ASUCUB

June 4, 1989

Source: *ORSD*, 1:22–23.

. . . On June 2, a speeding army truck hit and killed three people and seriously injured one at Muxudi. Thus started the bloody crackdown on the patriotic people by the reactionary government.

On the early morning of June 3, army soldiers in plainclothes moved into the downtown areas by bus. The students and residents all rose to block them. The army troops then fired tear-gas shells and rubber bullets into Qianmen, Liubukou, Xidan, etc. Many students and city residents were injured. One seven-year-old child was trampled to death on the spot by the soldiers at Liubukou.

On the evening of June 3, army troops accompanied by armored vehicles and riot policemen with tear gas suddenly started to rush onto Tiananmen Square from all directions. Along the way, they ruthlessly used machine guns and sub-machine guns to shoot at the defenseless students and city residents around them. Four hundred people were instantly killed or wounded around Muxudi. The army troops even opened fire at those trying to rescue the wounded.

Just after midnight on June 4, three armored vehicles headed south through the Xidan intersection at a very high speed. They knocked over a public trolley bus parked on the road. Soon, the rumble of trucks and continuous shots were heard from the direction of the Military Museum [near Muxudi]. According to one student who fled the shooting, a large number of students and city residents had already been killed or wounded in the areas between Xidan and the Military Museum.

At 12:40 A.M. army troops at a distance of five hundred meters from the Xidan Road intersection at first fired large quantities of tear gas. People [on the street] could hardly open their eyes and had to squat on their heels. Just then, several buses simultaneously burst into flames. It was obvious that it was a deliberate act of arson by plainclothes agents of the government, targeted at putting the blame on the students and city residents, to provide a pretext for the authorities to use violence in massacring the people.

At 12:50 A.M., large groups of riot police appeared, shouted "Fire!" and then fired many times at the unprepared and defenseless students and city residents in the streets. Several lines of students and residents instantly fell. Dozens were killed, and several hundred were wounded. Those killed included bypassers. As soon as they found the students and city residents who were trying to hide themselves in lanes (*hutong*), the soldiers continued to fire at them. In a lane on the east side of Xidan, four people were wounded. From small children to old men, no one in the streets could escape the massacre.

At a little past 1:00 A.M., a large number of army trucks full of soldiers arrived at the Xidan intersection. Many people stood along the road or in front of the lanes, watching quietly. Large numbers of soldiers, however, continued shooting at the people, who fell in groups. The soldiers not only shot at people, but also pursued and beat residents and students who were unable to escape. . . . A student from the Beijing Second Foreign Languages Institute was bleeding profusely from both feet. He described how he and his classmates were trying to go forward to rescue a girl student. Five of them instantly fell following several shots. Three hours later, when the army troops finished passing through the Xidan intersection, many of the surviving students and city residents tried to go to Tiananmen Square. However, the roads leading to Tiananmen Square were blocked by army troops who without hesitation fired at anyone appearing in the streets. They did not even spare those trying to retreat. Shots were even more intense when people shouted slogans.

From 11:00 P.M. on June 3 to 6:00 A.M. on June 4, continuous gun-shots resounded all over Tiananmen Square, the east and west sides of Chang'an Boulevard and in the area around Qianmen Street [south of the square]. Wherever the army troops passed, blood splashes appeared, with innumerable dead and wounded. Along the streets the people cried. It was really too horrible to see all this. On Tiananmen Square, there were many army trucks, and tanks dashed around madly. By 6:00 A.M., according to an incomplete figure, more than seven thousand people were injured, and more than three thousand people had been killed. The massacre is continuing, and casualties are increasing. Innumerable city residents and students lay in pools of blood. . . . They were not able to escape the bullets. They had, however, carried towels and gauze masks, because they thought that the army troops would at most fire tear gas and rubber bullets. The innocent, kind students and city residents had absolutely not expected Li Peng's government to be so crazy and inhumane. . . . These innocent citizens of the People's Republic who were longing for democracy were the so-called counterrevolutionary rioters according to the Li Peng government. . . .

184
Declaration of the Guangzhou Independent Workers' Union

June 4, 1989

Source: *ORSD*, 1:32.

The Guangdong Workers' Autonomous Union [GWAU] was established today. It is a perfectly patriotic organization that developed out of the nationwide patriotic democratic movement. GWAU is an organization initiated by Guangdong workers and is supervised by Guangzhou residents to whom we are responsible. Our objective is to unite all the possible [sources of] strength that can be united. Freedom, democracy, and wealth for a sorrowful China depend on pushing forward the democratic movement.

Now, troops have opened fire in Beijing. The people are shedding blood, the nation confronts a critical moment, with the historical burden falling on the shoulders of every worker. Down with violence, support the students, promote democracy and science, there is no other choice!

The nation is confused, disordered, tossed to and fro, flooded with bureaucracy and a spoiled political and economic system. The rise and fall of the nation affects the welfare of every individual worker. We Guangzhou workers can no longer tolerate this. GWAU urgently appeals to people from all walks of life to support and participate in this nationwide . . . movement.

185
Remember! This Dark Day of June 4

MEDICAL WORKER

June 4, 1989

Source: Leaflet at Beijing University, June 4, 1989, courtesy of HKFS.

The following is an eyewitness account by a medical worker who was among the last group to withdraw from the square:

A little past 5:00 A.M. on June 4, the students began to withdraw from Tiananmen

Square. Some students did not leave, either because they were too weak to walk, were strong-willed, were seriously wounded, or could not crawl out of their tents in time. Behind them armored vehicles were catching up with them at a very fast speed. The brutal policemen began beating everyone. Many students were beaten unconscious and fell to the ground. The military policemen even attacked medical workers who had dashed ahead to rescue the students risking their own safety. We rescued three students from being beaten by wood clubs. After pulling them aside, these same students were lying on the ground, and military policemen continued to use leather shoes, wood, electric and iron clubs, and even machine guns to massacre our students. After that, armored vehicles ran over the students' bodies, covering the ground with a mixture of flesh and blood. A few minutes later, they organized many military policemen to use brooms and forklifts to heap the mixture of flesh and blood and pieces of the bodies of the students onto piles. Then they burned them into ashes along with tents, quilts, blankets, and other things. Several criminally lit fires were burning in Tiananmen Square.

In one tent, a student was awakened just as an armored vehicle ran over his tent. Instantly, a youth full of patriotic zeal became a mixture of flesh and blood.

During the night, we also rescued five soldiers, among whom three were sent to the hospital and the other two recovered from shock. When sending these two soldiers back to their units, however, they abruptly said [to us]: "We are only carrying out orders, and you yourselves will bear the consequences if you do not leave [the square]." Among us, one doctor from Xiehe Hospital [near Dongdan, east of the square] was killed, and one doctor from the Sino-Japanese Friendship Hospital was shot in the side.

We left the square at about 7:00 A.M. The students in the square who shed their blood for the motherland were turned into crumbled bodies and burned into ashes!

186

Chinese Alliance for the Protection of Human Rights

June 4, 1989

Source: Leaflet distributed on June 8, 1989, at People's University, Beijing. Courtesy of Rudolf G. Wagner.

To the people of the entire nation:

Workers, peasants, intellectuals, and soldiers of the Liberation Army of the entire country:

All members of the Communist party, of the different democratic parties, and nonparty personalities:

On June 3 there occurred in Beijing a gruesome massacre; we are deeply grieved by this incident. All people concerned with recent developments ask themselves why the soldiers, the sons of the people, opened fire on the people, why the Chinese Communist party went so far as to become the enemy of the people!? The fact is that traitors emerged within the party and the army, that a counterrevolutionary military coup occurred in the center, the chief criminals of which are Yang Shangkun and Li Peng.

Since Yang Shangkun last year climbed to the position of vice-chairman of the Military Commission and that of head of state, he tightened and developed with unceasing cunning his reactionary influence. His younger brother Yang Baibing took over the chairmanship of the [army's] General Political Department and his son-in-law Chi Haotian became chief-of-staff. They installed their relatives and confidants, removed those who disagreed with them, and gradually usurped the main leading positions within the army.

In April and May the patriotic and democratic movement of the entire people gave Yang Shangkun's reactionary clique a shock, because once the country pursues democratic policies, their prerogatives would inevitably be in jeopardy, and [would] shake the basis for their plan to establish autocratic control over the entire country. Thereupon, like a [cornered] dog who will leap over a wall, they used the power they had usurped in the army to initiate a counterrevolutionary military coup.

1. They put comrades Deng Xiaoping and Zhao Ziyang under house arrest and, waving the flag of Comrade Deng Xiaoping, made believe that they were acting in his name.

2. They proclaimed martial law in Beijing, used military means to prevent the center from publicizing its opinions, and pressed the provinces, cities, and self-administered districts to express their support in a desperate attempt to create a fait accompli.

3. They committed a brutal, bloody massacre against the people to pave the way for a despotic autocracy.

4. They stifled public opinion, blocked information channels, and deceived the people of the entire world.

In view of the above facts, the Chinese Alliance for the Protection of Human Rights calls on the nation's workers, peasants, intellectuals, and officers and soldiers of the Liberation Army to unite and struggle for the suppression of the counterrevolutionary coup.

1. It calls on those members of the Thirteenth Central Committee, on those delegates of the Seventh People's Congress, and on those members of the Political Consultative Conference, who can still move freely to hurry to Guangzhou, set up a provisional central government, and lead the people of the country in the suppression of this counterrevolutionary military coup.

2. It calls on the officers and soldiers of the Liberation Army to stand on the side of the people in the interest of the people and for the future of the party and the state. It calls on the military regions and on the different branches of the armed forces to unite and proceed to Beijing to subdue the traitors.

3. It calls on the members of the Chinese Communist party, members of the democratic parties, and on nonparty personalities as well as the people of the entire nation to unite, wage a struggle using a variety of forms (strikes, closing shops, boycotting of classes), and smash the plans of the coup clique to control China.

Compatriots of the entire country, the Chinese nation has come to a life-and-death juncture: let us unite and fight for a socialist, democratic, and free China.

187
The Twenty-seventh Army: Murderers in the Massacre

ANONYMOUS

June 5, 1989

Source: Beijing University handbill, in *ORSD*, 2:18.

From late June 3 to the early morning of June 4, only soldiers of the Twenty-seventh Army were insanely massacring innocent people and students.

The Twenty-seventh Army is under the direct control of the third son of Yang Shangkun [Yang Jianhua]. Before the massacre, the soldiers received [drug] injections that contained stimulants. They were told that they were being given prophylactic inoculations to prevent themselves from being infected by the pestilence on Tiananmen Square. That is why these soldiers killed people without blinking an eye.

The Twenty-eighth Army [*sic*, here the author probably is referring to the Thirty-eighth Army as written below] soldiers followed the Twenty-seventh Army but refused to shoot even when they were surrounded. Shots from machine guns on the roof of the air force building at Gongzhufen tried to provoke the Twenty-eighth Army [*sic*] to respond, and the helicopters directed its soldiers to open fire, but it resolutely refused to do so.

On the early morning of June 4, west of Muxudi, about thirty armored vehicles and one hundred army trucks were burned, some of which were set on fire by the soldiers of the armored force themselves. . . .

Finally, the Thirty-eighth Army had reached an agreement with the masses that they would retreat into the Military Museum. The Thirty-eighth Army also refused to open fire on the people. One division commander of the Thirty-eighth Army said: "We would rather face court-martial than shoot the people."

Up to this time, the troops under the direct control of the damned Yang Shangkun suffered no losses. Those soldiers who did not fight back and were captured and killed by the people mostly belonged to other armies.

188

Foreword

FUNERAL COMMITTEE

June 5, 1989

Source: Beijing University handbill, in *ORSD*, 2:20.

On the evening of June 3, 1989, in the capital of the People's Republic, Li Peng's government used hundreds of thousands of modern soldiers to massacre our patriotic residents and young students. The casualties were higher than 4,600 people.

May you, the brave people who have died, rest in peace!

Those of us who have survived will make the Li Peng government pay its blood debt. We will hold a memorial ceremony for your heroic spirit with our victory!

Eternal glory to the heroes who laid down their lives for democracy and freedom in China!

189

The People Will Never Forgive You

ANONYMOUS

June 6, 1989

Source: Beijing University handbill, in *ORSD*, 2:21.

What is the old method? Isn't that the method of suppressing the people? Why can't you talk to the people? Are you afraid of hearing the truth? Because you have set yourselves against the people, you are only seemingly powerful, but in reality you are timid as a mouse. Were you supported by the people? At Xinhua Gate and on Chang'an Boulevard, I saw irrefutable evidence of the army troops massacring the people everywhere . . . the bloody marks of the tank treads, the pools of blood, and the bullet holes! You opened fire and used tear gas, attempting to conceal your weakness. The people oppose you, and your shameful legacy will ultimately suffer in history.

You have lost minimal humanitarianism by ignoring the masses wounded by your guns and by stopping the doctors who tried to rescue them. All the hospitals in Beijing are now packed with the wounded. For example, fifty-three people died in Tongren Hospital, forty-one died in Fuxing Hospital, thirty died in the Post and Telecommunications Hospital, seven died in People's Hospital, and seventeen died in the navy's General Hospital. One doctor said that about six hundred died in all the hospitals. Moreover, there are many more who cannot be included, particularly those who died in Tiananmen Square and around the entrances. . . .

The news media controlled by you has mixed black and white and has distorted public opinion. You said that there were only a handful of rioters. Then why not publicize the number of rioters? You said that "more than one thousand army commanders and soldiers were killed or wounded," but weren't they fully armed? Were they not driving tanks and armored vehicles toward the city residents? If more than a thousand among them were killed or wounded, then how many thousand more were killed or wounded among the city residents and students who could only use stones and bricks to resist weakly? How many old people, women, and small children died at gunpoint? No wonder beasts like you had said with a murderous look on your face that "there is absolutely no guarantee of safety. Those who resist will have to bear the consequences."[1]

Deng Xiaoping, Li Peng, Yang Shangkun, Qiao Shi, and Chen Yun: You are beasts who would kill your father to marry your mother. You are utterly devoid of conscience and totally inhumane. You have publicly set yourselves against the people. You bastards are the public enemy of the Chinese nation, of all the people in the world who are pursuing justice, democracy, and peace. You are autocrats and traitors to the people. I wonder how long you can last? People will not forgive you. . . .

Fellow countrymen and forty million party members: You were originally Chinese with a conscience who longed for democracy. Now an extremely small number of party bandits in the hypocritical government of Li Peng have taken the republic as their private property, which was established by the blood sacrifice of twenty million Chinese. And they have just destroyed the republic in a moment, because they have not only strengthened the supreme power of the

---

[1]This is a quote from the official announcement broadcast on China Central TV on the evening of June 3.

People's Republic, but also used the republic's most powerful state machinery to crack down on the people. Their criminal acts have not only trampled on your solemn party constitution, but also stained your belief in communism—[an ideology] that contains a strong sense of humanitarianism and justice. What's more, they have destroyed the republic of 1.1 billion people. The majority of Chinese will never recognize the legitimacy of the hypocritical government headed by Deng Xiaoping. All the political parties and the people of all the nationalities will work together to denounce this fascist, hypocritical government. Let's unite and again uphold justice in order to establish a democratic government and rebuild a republic. This is the unshirkable duty of every Chinese citizen, the bound duty of all children of China, and the ultimate wishes of all the people who are pursuing justice and democracy. . . .

190

Remembering Tiananmen Square: Who Died in Beijing, and Why

ROBIN MUNRO

Source: Robin Munro, "Remembering Tiananmen Square: Who Died, and Why." *The Nation* magazine/The Nation Company, Inc., © 1990.

Among the revolts that ignited the Communist world in 1989, China's was the greatest failure. On the night of June 3–4 the Chinese Communist party showed the world that it would stop at nothing to maintain its monopoly of power.[1]

But what exactly did happen that night? Few modern events have been covered as intensively by the Western news media as the Tiananmen Square democracy movement. Yet in critical respects the denouement remains shrouded in myth. In the immediate aftermath, some basic notions took hold: Journalists spoke routinely of the slaughter of students, of "the massacre in Tiananmen Square." A year later, that phrase has become the official shorthand for what happened in Beijing.

A "revisionist" trend currently emerging in some Western circles maintains that there was no massacre. That is preposterous. A massacre did take place—but not in Tiananmen Square, and not predominantly of students. The great majority

---

[1]Robin Munro, research associate on China for Asia Watch, a New York–based human rights organization, has been a close observer of China's democracy and human rights movement since 1978. He gratefully acknowledges the cooperation of Richard Nations in making available interview material, and research assistance by Deborah Schwartz.

of those who died (perhaps as many as a thousand in all) were workers, or *laobaixing* ("common folk," or "old hundred names"), and they died mainly on the approach roads in western Beijing. Several dozen people died in the immediate environs of the square itself. But to speak of that as the real massacre distorts the citywide nature of the carnage and diminishes the real political drama that unfolded in Tiananmen Square.

Hundreds of reporters were in Beijing that night, but very few were present for the climactic clearing of the square by the army. Many were on the real killing grounds of western Beijing, along Chang'an Boulevard and Fuxingmen Boulevard, and reported vividly and accurately on what they saw. Some had been arrested, and others were pinned down behind roadblocks. Others still were back in their hotels for early morning filing deadlines. Most who were in the vicinity of the square when the army arrived, however, left quickly and out of legitimate fear for their safety.

But there were also more profound questions about how the Western media saw their role in the events in Beijing. The whole world was watching, and reporters often saw themselves as guarantors of the students' safety. There was something in the pacific idealism of the students that triggered memories of the 1960s and the civil rights movement, riveting Western attention on the students and causing the crucial role of the *laobaixing* to be largely overlooked.

And there was more: some predisposition, perhaps, on the media's part to believe in a massacre in the square as the necessary consummation of an allegory of innocence, sacrifice, and redemption. The students' own language may have contributed to this. On May 13 the hunger strikers in the square declared, "Our bodies are still tender and not full grown, and the prospect of dying frightens us all; but history calls us and we must go." Writer Ross Terrill, interviewed on a June 29 ABC special by Ted Koppel, recalled one student telling him, "We are now ready to face death, and we don't want you to have to be part of that. Please go home." And the reporters, for the most part, did so. Into the resulting vacuum rushed the most lurid tales of what then supposedly took place.

This account seeks to explain why the real massacre took the shape it did. It points to the regime's relative tolerance of the students and to its horror of the working-class unrest that threatened to turn the protests into a full-fledged insurrection. It also looks at the critical implications of the fact that sections of the Chinese army were clearly not prepared to carry out orders on the night of June 3–4.

Some people do accept that the bulk of the killing took place outside Tiananmen Square. Koppel, for example, in his June 29 special, noted the distinction but downplayed it as a "loophole" to be exploited by the Chinese government. But insisting on factual precision is not just a matter of splitting hairs. For the geography of the killing reveals much about the government's cold political logic and its choice of targets—as well as the likely scenario of the next round of prodemocracy struggles in China. The regime squandered its remaining popular legitimacy in a single night of bloodshed, and unless it can somehow learn the art of compromise, the fact that a sizable section of the "masses" was ready to fight back, together with the potential unreliability of the army, provides the ingredients for a possible replay of a Romanian-style revolt.

Journalism may be only the rough draft of history, but if left uncorrected it can forever distort the future course of events. Nothing serves the cause of China's students and *laobaixing* better than the unvarnished truth, for it speaks eloquently of their heroism and of the regime's cowardice and brutality. But Western criticisms based on a false version of the clearing of Tiananmen Square have handed the butchers of Beijing needless propaganda victories in the United Nations and elsewhere. They have also distracted attention from the main target of the continuing repression: the mass movement that eventually superseded the students' protest action. The credit for inspiring the movement and upholding the banner of nonviolence will always belong to the students. But only by refocusing attention on the *laobaixing* will we understand why China, a year later, continues to be ruled by the jackboot, the rifle, and the thought police.

On April 26, 1989, the *People's Daily* [Doc. 43] published its now infamous editorial condemning the student protest movement in Beijing as being, in essence, "a planned conspiracy, a riot, whose real nature was to fundamentally negate the leadership of the Chinese Communist party and to negate the socialist system." The editorial was the first definitive statement by the Chinese leadership on the student movement since its inception on April 15, the day reform-minded party leader Hu Yaobang had died.

But if a conspiracy to overthrow the socialist system had been launched in the Chinese capital, whom did the party point to as the main culprits? Surprisingly, not to the students. According to the editorial, "The party and government [take] a tolerant, restrained attitude to certain inappropriate words and actions of emotionally excited young students." On the other hand, "these facts demonstrate that an extremely small number of people were not involved in mourning Comrade Hu Yaobang. . . . Their goal was to poison people's minds, to create turmoil throughout the country, to destroy political stability and unity." As the official conspiracy theory developed, the authorities charged that the students were being manipulated by "outside elements" with "ulterior motives." This meant, first of all, dissident Chinese workers and (to a lesser extent) intellectuals, and second, foreign "reactionaries." This line of analysis was upheld during the military crackdown of June 3–4, and it underpins the repression that continues to this day.

Chinese political tradition has long conferred a limited degree of tolerance and immunity on students, a certain latitude of action not shared by other groups—and especially not by the workers. This relative privilege was enhanced during the decade of reform in the 1980s, as Deng Xiaoping moved rapidly toward a historic compromise with the intelligentsia (whom Mao Zedong had ruthlessly persecuted) in order to advance China's modernization program and facilitate the economic opening to the West. This official stance was fraught with problems, of course, since greater freedom for the students and intellectuals inevitably brought with it the danger of corrosive "bourgeois liberal" ideas from the West.

But that was nothing compared with the other danger that had preoccupied the party since the start of the reform process. This was the prospect of organized unrest and dissent among the urban working class, along the lines of Poland's Solidarity. Above all, it was the rapid trend toward just such a movement—what China's leaders call the "Polish disease"—in Beijing and other major cities last spring that determined the uncompromising character of the crackdown when it finally came. The students had initiated the movement and brilliantly out-maneuvered the government; but with the intervention of broader social forces on Tiananmen Square, the students soon lost control of the situation, and their leadership became chronically divided.

The other major factor behind the crackdown was the increasing ideological defection of the party apparatus itself to the students' cause. By mid-May, even sections of the public security service, law courts, and military—the very back-bone of the dictatorship of the proletariat—were beginning to appear in the square in open support of the prodemocracy movement. On June 14, in an illustration of the party's paranoid vision of events, the Beijing Propaganda Department concluded that "a certain small group of people" had "plotted to arrest party and state leaders and seize power in a 'Bastille'-style attack."

In retrospect, the logic of the massacre of June 3–4 is clear. The students responded to the draconian *People's Daily* editorial not, as expected, by retreat-ing to their campuses but by stepping up their protests. The demonstrations drew massive public support, and the authorities were thrown into a state of confusion and paralysis from which they did not emerge until after June 4. On May 13, after a brief hiatus of failed "dialogue" with the government, the students launched a mass hunger strike at Tiananmen Square. By May 17, the sight of as many as two thousand idealistic young students collapsing from heat and starva-tion brought more than a million ordinary Beijing citizens into the square in a moving display of human solidarity. "The students speak on behalf of all of us," they would tell any foreigner who cared to listen. Having been passive specta-tors, the *laobaixing* now began to act as a bastion of active support for the students, bringing food and other supplies to the square on an around-the-clock basis.

This specter of emerging cross-class solidarity led directly to the authorities' decision to impose martial law in Beijing on May 20. But again, the strength of the popular response caught China's leaders unawares: The tanks and troop columns were halted at all major points of entry to the city by a human wall of peaceful protesters, and after a few days the soldiers were forced to withdraw to their barracks in the suburbs. Action groups formed spontaneously throughout Beijing. These included "dare-to-die squads" of workers and other *laobaixing*, who vowed to die rather than let the army into the city; the workers' pickets,

who, together with formidably organized contingents of student pickets, pa-
trolled the neighborhoods and maintained order (the public security forces and
traffic police were nowhere to be seen after May 20); and the "little flying
tigers," large groups of youths on motorcycles who sped around the city on
liaison missions for the movement. The *laobaixing* were now in a posture of
peaceful, nonviolent, but direct confrontation with the government and the army,
and similar "turmoil"—to use the party's term—rapidly emerged in dozens of
other cities.

Moreover, the *laobaixing* were beginning to articulate their own grievances.
These were mostly a product of the decade-long economic reforms, which,
though broadly popular, had also generated a range of serious social tensions:
sharp income polarization, spiraling commodity prices, an acute shortage of
acceptable housing, and—last but by no means least—rampant corruption, speculation, and profiteering by government and party officials. The authorities probably overestimated the political challenge that these new workers' and citizens'
groups posed. The groups were spontaneous, and while their visible impact and
propaganda effect were considerable, they lacked any distinct ideological framework or program. But the party's alarm was real.

However, the birth of the Beijing Workers' Autonomous Union a few days
after the abortive imposition of martial law posed a much greater threat. That is
because this group, headquartered in a couple of scruffy tents in the northwest
corner of Tiananmen Square, raised an issue that had been taboo in China since
1949: the right of workers to engage in independent labor organization and
self-representation. Such a demand struck at the very core of the Chinese Communist state, for the party's main claim to legitimacy is that it rules in the name
and interests of the "laboring masses." Although its active membership remained
relatively small, its formal membership soared during the first few days of June,
reaching a peak of more than ten thousand enrollments after three of its leaders
were secretly arrested on May 29. Autonomous workers' groups quickly sprang
up in most of China's major cities.

This was the "cancer cell" that the authorities had feared from the outset
would appear if legal recognition were ever to be conferred on the student
organizations. In the government's eye, if the statue of the Goddess of Democracy, erected in the square at the end of May, represented the arrogant defiance
by the students and the symbolic intrusion of "bourgeois liberalism" and "Western subversion" into the sacred heart of Communist rule, the crude red-and-black
banner of the Beijing Workers' Autonomous Union, not a hundred yards away
from the goddess, represented the terrifying power of the workers awakened.
Both had to be crushed, and the rapidly defecting party apparatus had to be
frightened and shocked back into line.

In the spirit of the April 26 editorial, the students and intellectuals would, by
and large, be spared. The *laobaixing*, on the other hand, would be mercilessly
punished in order to eradicate organized popular unrest for a generation. The

arenas of conflict on the night of June 3–4 overlapped, but they were essentially separate. The real killing grounds, the theater of the popular uprising and massacre, lay mainly on the periphery, above all along western Chang'an Boulevard and out to the western suburbs. Here, the *laobaixing* fought and died to defend the center: Tiananmen Square. The prodemocracy movement stayed firm in its commitment to the principles of dialogue and nonviolence, and it resorted to force on that final night only out of desperation and rage. Once the army had embarked on the rape of Beijing, it was clear that all was lost. In the eye of the storm, around the Monument to the People's Heroes, stood the students—brave, resolute but ultimately protected within a charmed circle. At the last minute, in the square itself, with its most lethal resources arrayed against the moral authority of youth, the government stepped back from the brink of a slaughter of incalculable proportions.

The Bloody Road to Tiananmen

There were more than one thousand foreign journalists in Beijing on the night of the army's final drive to clear Tiananmen Square, and many of them followed the advance of the main People's Liberation Army assault force through the western suburbs as it plowed murderously through the crowds of *laobaixing* that formed at all points to block its path. Most of the foreign film footage of the massacre was shot in this sector of the city, in neighborhoods like Muxudi, Fuxingmen, and Liubukou, where hundreds of unarmed protesters and innocent bystanders were mowed down by random gunfire from semi-automatic weapons. The troops apparently made no distinction between these people and the small number who hurled stones, rocks, and Molotov cocktails or set fire to vehicles that had been used as roadblocks. Since this main theater of the massacre was by and large well covered by the foreign news media, I will focus here on some less-known aspects of the action along western Chang'an and Fuxingmen—subsequently dubbed "Blood Boulevard" by the people of Beijing.

As far as is known, the first violence came at around 10:30 P.M. on June 3 at Gongzhufen, some two miles west of Muxudi, where vanguard contingents of the assault force used about twenty armored personnel carriers to crash through bus barricades that were blocking the circular intersection. A West German student living in Beijing at the time witnessed the incident and reported that many people were crushed to death as the APCs went through and soldiers fired indiscriminately at the crowd. A Finnish journalist who was also standing nearby reported seeing two soldiers with AK–47 assault rifles suddenly descend from the tenth truck of a convoy of fifty or so that drove through the gaps in the barricades. "They were torn to pieces" by the crowd, she says. "It was a horrible sight." The pattern of the night's conflict, then, was set from the start: Random and brutal killings by the army came first, followed swiftly by a small number of revenge killings of troops by distraught, and increasingly insurgent, citizens.

Why did the troops behave with such savagery? At Gongzhufen they had been alerted to the lethal realities of mass resistance, provoked by their violent invasion of the city and by their evident determination this time (in contrast to the halfhearted effort of May 20) to retake Tiananmen Square. Once they saw that terror tactics had conspicuously failed to subdue the crowds, the troops were fearful for their lives, and as they advanced slowly toward Muxudi, they responded by escalating the level of terror. From there on, the PLA acted almost as if it were confronting General Vo Nguyen Giap's battle-hardened armies in the hills along the Sino-Vietnamese border rather than unarmed civilians. Local resident and Western journalists who visited the hospitals in western Beijing that night describe them as resembling abattoirs.

Accidental factors, too, may partially explain the army's paroxysm of killing. The troops had intended to meet up at Muxudi with a unit of six hundred local officers of the People's Armed Police (PAP). (They may well have expected major resistance, for three people had been crushed to death by a PAP jeep at Muxudi the previous night, provoking angry protests.) But the PAP detachment, which was familiar with the layout of Beijing and was supposed to spearhead the army assault and lead the troops into the square, never made the rendezvous: it had been surrounded, blocked, and in the end dispersed by the *laobaixing* as it made its way through the alleyways around Yuetan park, about a mile and a half northeast of Muxudi. This unexpectedly deprived the troops of their paramilitary escort.

For political reasons, also, the army had its reasons for not being found wanting. As early as May 24 or 25, General Xu Qinxian, commanding officer of China's elite Thirty-eighth Army, had been arrested for failing to carry out martial-law orders (he was later court-martialed). This no doubt left other units eager to prove their zeal against the "counterrevolutionary rebellion." It is still widely believed in the West that most of the carnage was inflicted by the Twenty-seventh Army. But according to military sources, the deputy commander of the Twenty-seventh was booed when he appeared at a high-level Beijing conference on "propaganda theory" last September. He is said to have thrown down his cap in anger and frustration and exclaimed, "We in the Twenty-seventh are being saddled with the blame for what our army brothers in other units did. Yes, we opened fire, but I guarantee that we didn't kill any of the *laobaixing*!"

China may have come closer to a Romanian-style military revolt than is generally recognized. According to a report in the *South China Morning Post* on December 28, PLA Chief Political Commissar Yang Baibing revealed in a confidential speech earlier that month that "21 officers and cadres with ranks of divisional commander or above, 36 officers with ranks of regimental or battalion commander, and 54 officers with the rank of company chief 'breached discipline in a serious manner during the struggle to crush the counterrevolutionary rebellion' in June. In addition, 1,400 soldiers 'shed their weapons and ran away.' "

In the days that followed the massacre, the Chinese authorities repeatedly televised an astonishing piece of footage that showed dozens of APCs being torched by the crowd in the vicinity of the Military Museum, just west of Muxudi. The commentary said that many of the occupants had preferred to be burned alive rather than open fire on their compatriots; it also clearly implied that this had occurred in the early evening of June 3, before nightfall. This footage was a cornerstone of the government's "Big Lie," evidence of the "counterrevolutionary rebellion" that had obliged the government to respond with force.

The reality was different. At about 9:00 A.M. on Sunday, June 4, several foreign witnesses, inspecting the devastation of the previous night, were stunned to see a column of some three dozen APCs suddenly appear from the west and come to a halt at the Muxudi intersection. The first vehicle had struck the remnants of a barricade; a second had run into its rear, bringing the convoy to a halt. A large crowd materialized from the neighboring alleyways and surrounded the now silent armored column. The first troops to emerge were beaten, and at least one is thought to have been killed. Only the intervention of student pickets, who negotiated safe passage for the troops, headed off a pitched battle and, perhaps, a fresh round of killing. Several hundred soldiers simply walked away, leaving behind their lethal hardware for the crowd to muse over. Within half an hour, all the APCs had been set on fire, and a towering column of black smoke could be seen for miles.

It may be no coincidence that this incident took place right outside the main offices of China Central TV, from whose rooftop the scene was exhaustively videotaped. But a more significant explanation is that the troops actually deserted. A prominent West German Sinologist who was present described seeing soldiers escorted away from their vehicles. One APC, he says, "opened the top lids, and a hand appeared waving a white piece of cloth. Soldiers emerged and gave their automatic rifles to the young men receiving them. They hugged."

I witnessed a somewhat similar scene on the night of June 3 to the east of Tiananmen Square, at the Jianguomen overpass, where a column of several dozen troop trucks was halted by large crowds as it tried to cross Chang'an Boulevard. Several foreign witnesses saw soldiers openly fraternizing with civilians and even posing for photographs. Just after midnight I saw one group of soldiers climb down from their truck and wander off slowly with tears in their eyes. Minutes later an APC came charging at full speed across the overpass from the east and smashed through the line of PLA trucks, lifting one of them several feet into the air and splashing a young man's brain on the ground. Evidently the troops on the overpass had been identified as traitorous by the high command.

II

Tiananmen Square is the largest public space in the world. It extends over 100 acres, and no single eyewitness could hope to encompass the complex and confusing sequence of events that unfolded there on the night of June 3–4. My own account, therefore, is supplemented by the testimony of others who saw what happened at crucial moments.

I arrived at the square at about 1:15 A.M. Large crowds were fleeing eastward along Chang'an Boulevard. Continuous gunfire sounded from the northwest sector of the square, and a crippled APC lay blazing in the northeast corner, set afire by Molotov cocktails. Its tracks had been jammed with steel bars and traffic dividers. A CNN film unit and a number of British journalists were on the scene. According to John Simpson of the BBC, three APC crew members had been beaten to death and a fourth escorted to safety by student pickets. Jonathan Mirsky of the *London Observer*, who was beaten by armed policemen with truncheons just before I arrived, says he saw several people shot dead near the huge portrait of Mao on Tiananmen Gate.

Looking over to the northwest corner of the square, I saw with horror that the tents of the Beijing Workers' Autonomous Union were in flames, and I ran over to see if any of my friends from the union were dead or wounded. Twenty yards away, a menacing group of about two hundred heavily armed troops stood facing the tents. This was the advance party of the main invasion force of the PLA, which would arrive at the square at around 2 A.M. after smashing its way along western Chang'an. By now the crowds had fled from this area. Only the figure of a young man was visible, wandering slowly around the burning tents and gathering up piles of documents, which he implored me to take to the students on the Monument to the People's Heroes. This I did. Nearly all the students had withdrawn by now to the three tiers of the monument: three thousand to five thousand of them, perhaps, huddled tightly together. Their makeshift tent encampment, which sprawled over an area of several hundred square yards to the north of the monument, was virtually deserted. The students seemed calm, almost resigned. There was no panic, though the stutter of gunfire could be heard on the fringes of the square and beyond. Abruptly the government loudspeakers boomed into life with an endlessly repeated message: Everyone was to leave the square immediately; a "serious counterrevolutionary rebellion" had broken out, and the martial-law troops were empowered to clear Tiananmen Square by any means necessary.

At about this time, an American freelance journalist named Richard Nations was ducking gunfire in the far southwest corner of the square, where a major confrontation between troops and citizens had been underway since around 12:30 A.M. His notes were scribbled at the time: "Approximately 1:00 A.M.: Southwest corner, on Qianmen West Street in front of Kentucky Fried Chicken. Barricade of several burning buses blocks the intersection. Riot police are forced into the street under a shower of rocks and glass. Student pickets or organizers seem to intervene to evacuate about twenty-odd unarmed police/soldiers with shields and staves caught near burning buses. A tank races through, breaking up a roadblock, and a busload of troops disembark. Tracer bullets and sustained volleys." Several people were killed by troops in this confrontation.

Another witness to the clashes in the south was the renowned writer Lao Gui. At about 1:30 he wrote, "There was a continuous sound of gunfire coming from Zhushikou (about half a mile south of the square). Red flares were going up all around. I met a Western reporter at the cypress trees by the Mao Memorial Hall who told me, 'I saw three people killed with my own eyes, their stomachs were blown open, down at Zhushikou.' " Other accounts suggest that at least several dozen people were killed by troops as the army forced its way up through the southern neighborhoods. Close to 2:00 a force of about a hundred troops tried to enter the square from the southwest corner. "Suddenly there was intense firing and bullets flying all over the place," says NBC cameraman Tony Wasserman, who was there. "And somewhere along the way someone gets it in the stomach and someone in the ankle. Before this, the crowd grabs some soldiers from the southwest corner again and they beat the shit out of them." A little later, according to CBS cameraman Derek Williams, "In came the paratroopers.... They were real shitkickers."

Meanwhile, in the northern part of the square, the main invasion force had begun to arrive from the west. I watched them arrive from a position to the west of the Goddess of Democracy. The first column of troop-transport trucks entered the square hesitantly, at a walking pace. Groups of infantry escorted them, at first just a thin line, but quickly increasing to a dense column, thousands of them, all wearing steel helmets and carrying assault rifles. They took about an hour to deploy fully along the northern edge of the square. Many more troops and vehicles were backed up, invisible to me, all the way down Chang'an to the west.

After the arrival of this main force, only a sprinkling of people—apparently not students but ordinary residents and workers—remained in the northern part of the square, between Chang'an and the monument. The statue of democracy looked more dramatic than ever, facing Mao's portrait and the troops beneath it through the flames and smoke that still billowed from the crippled APC. At around 2:15, there was a terrific burst of AK–47 fire, lasting several minutes, from the vicinity of Tiananmen Gate. I hit the deck. Most of the crowd fled southward, toward the monument, but I saw no one injured.

At more or less the same moment, just a few hundred yards away, several hundred troops moved across from Tiananmen Gate to seal off the northeast entrance to the square, blocking off eastern Chang'an Boulevard to the north of the History Museum. A student named Ke Feng, one of the main organizers of the statue of democracy project, was hiding in a small park nearby. In the first five minutes or so, he saw about twenty people in the vicinity of the pedestrian underpass hit by "stray bullets," including "five people who fell and couldn't get up again." Some five hundred troops emerged from behind the History Museum, although these did not appear to be carrying rifles. As another two hundred to three hundred advanced from the direction of Tiananmen Gate, the crowd began shouting, "Fascists!" and "General Strike!"; others sang the *Internationale*. Ke Feng, still hiding nearby, tells of the soldiers "jumping for joy, as if playing a game. . . . An officer kept shouting through a megaphone for about fifteen minutes, 'Leave immediately, we'll shoot to kill!' "

In an extraordinary, suicidal act of defiance, someone drove an articulated twin-carriage bus at full speed straight at the soldiers. In the words of Kenneth Qiang, a council member of the Hong Kong Student Federation, "The driver was dragged out by soldiers and clubbed to the ground with their rifle butts. The crowd was incensed, and they ran forward to within fifty meters of the troops, throwing glass bottles at them. I heard two separate gunshots. The driver fell to the ground dead."

It was now around 2:30. The entire square had fallen silent, though gunfire was still audible in the distance. Taking advantage of the lull, I walked back to the workers' tents, which by now were a smoldering ruin. A young man pressed a small bundle of student leaflets into my hand. The emergency medical tent of the Beijing United Medical College, to the southeast of the statue of democracy, was a grim but heroic sight. The tent, staffed by some twenty volunteer doctors and medical students, stood virtually alone in this vast, deserted sector of the square. A small crowd of student pickets sat in a thin, wide circle around it, forming a "protective" perimeter. I spent perhaps a quarter of an hour inside, enough time to see four or five badly wounded people brought in on makeshift stretchers. One boy, probably a student, had taken a bullet in the side of his head and was clearly dying. One doctor said five people had died in his hands in the previous hour or so.

By 3:00 I could see no other foreigners anywhere in the square. The foreign television crews had apparently evacuated the place. "I now feel guilty about the decision," the BBC's Simpson wrote later in *Granta*. "It was wrong: we ought to have stayed in the square, even though the other camera crews had already left and it might have cost us our lives." Simpson's decision was to have a crucial impact on his reporting during the rest of the night.

I decided to find a vantage point on the raised area in front of the History Museum, thinking this would give me a clear view of the action while removing me from the scene of combat. But as I rounded the trees at the side of the museum and turned to climb the broad staircase in front of it, I froze. Several thousand steel-helmeted troops, each carrying an AK–47 and a long wooden cudgel, were sitting quietly on the steps. Across the square, in front of the Great Hall of the People, the same thing. If anything, there were even more soldiers on that side. I found myself thinking, "They've sealed off the square on all sides; they must be planning to kill us all," and I hastily returned to the shelter of the trees.

The square was lit by eerie white light. The silence was broken only by distant gunfire and the surreal echo of the government loudspeakers. At approximately this moment, Richard Nations was several hundred yards away at the monument. He described the scene in his notebook: "Monument seems surrounded by infantry with display of overwhelming armed force to north. Students seem to be stoically waiting for final hour—assault which now seems inevitable." The entry continues, "Meet Robin sitting in front of bushes on fence."

I later discovered that there were in fact about ten foreign journalists left in the square at 3:00, but I could have found no more resourceful a companion than Richard. Together we set out to explore the southern part of the square, which was littered with burning buses and cars but entirely empty of troops. (Access to the square was possible here until just after 6 A.M.) Unknown to us at the time, we passed within a stone's throw of the hiding place of a Hong Kong ATV television crew, who remained perched atop the public latrines in the southwest corner of the square until 4:30, when they judged the situation to be too dangerous and left.

The Darkness before Dawn

Abruptly, on the stroke of 4 o'clock, all the lights in Tiananmen Square went out. Back at the southeast corner of the monument, we waited anxiously, but the assault did not come. The students remained seated on the monument, just as before. No one made any move to leave. Noiselessly, as if in a dream, two busloads of student reinforcements appeared in the square from the southeast, coming to a halt yards from where we stood. The student loudspeakers crackled back to life and a voice announced—deadpan, as if reading a railroad schedule— "We will now play the *Internationale*, to raise our fighting spirit." I wondered what the soldiers were feeling, out there in the dark. Were the students counting on the embarrassment factor to save them if all else failed?

But still the attack did not materialize. When some people set fire to the abandoned tents and piles of garbage to the west of the monument—perhaps so the assault would not take place in darkness—the student leadership rebuked them: "Keep order, stay calm. We must create no pretext whatsoever for them."

At about 4:15 an array of lights, like fairy lights on a Christmas tree, suddenly came on all across the front of the Great Hall of the People, filling the west side of the square with a soft, luminous glow. At the same time, floodlights went on along the facade of the Forbidden City. Next, the southernmost doors of the Great Hall swung open, disgorging a human river of gun-toting troops, many with fixed bayonets. According to CBS's Derek Williams, who was close by, "They came around and joined a large blocking force which stretched in an L-shape down the west side of the street and then cut across the square in front of the Mao Mausoleum." Troops now began firing at the monument from the History Museum steps, and we could see the sparks flying from the obelisk, high above head level.

It was now just after 4:30. The square was empty of people, and scattered with forlorn debris of the abandoned encampment. The three thousand or so students remained huddled on the steps and the three levels of the monument. Again, the student loudspeakers crackled to life, and someone who announced himself as a leader of the Beijing Students' Autonomous Union took the microphone: "Students! We must on no account quit the square. We will now pay the highest price possible for the sake of securing democracy in China. Our blood shall be the consecration." My heart sank. After a few minutes, someone else spoke, this time a leader of the Beijing Workers' Autonomous Union: "We must all leave here immediately, for a terrible bloodbath is about to take place. There are troops surrounding us on all sides, and the situation is now extraordinarily dangerous. To wish to die here is no more than an immature fantasy." A lengthy silence ensued. Then Hou Dejian spoke. (Hou, a Taiwan-born popular singer, was one of four people who had begun a hunger strike on the monument on June 2.) "We have won a great victory," he said. "But now we must leave this place. We have shed too much of our blood. We cannot afford to lose any more. . . . We four hunger strikers will remain on the monument until everyone else has left safely, and then we will leave."

As Hou spoke, Richard and I decided to make one final trip to the monument. We picked our way slowly up the steps toward the hunger strikers' tent on the top level, through the tight ranks of seated students, who seemed largely oblivious of our presence (many were writing out their wills and farewell letters to their families). There was no hysteria, only courageous resolve. As we descended again by the steps on the east side, the loudspeakers had fallen silent. But a distant rumbling came from the northern sector of the square: The tanks had started up their engines.

Minutes passed, with nothing to break the spell. In the end, it took an obvious, even mundane move to break the tension: Someone took the microphone and proposed a voice vote. Opinions vary as to whether the shouts of "Stand firm!" were louder than the shouts of "Evacuate!" In any event, it was announced that the democratic decision had been in favor of leaving the square.

The question of what happened next has probably been the single biggest point of controversy in the reporting of the events of June 3–4 in Beijing. Correspondent Richard Roth of CBS had time to file one last report before soldiers arrested him and took him into the Great Hall of the People. "Soldiers have spotted CBS News cameraman Derek Williams and myself and are angrily dragging us away. And a moment later it begins: powerful bursts of automatic weapons, raging gunfire for a minute and a half that lasts as long as a nightmare. And we see no more." The film was confiscated. Roth's dramatic commentary, aired on the June 4 CBS Evening News and accompanied by footage shot two hours earlier, left the clear impression that troops had opened fire on the students as they evacuated the monument.

But there was no slaughter. Fermin Rodriguez and Jose Luis Marquez, a film crew from Television Espanola, shot the only known footage of the entire evacuation. Like Roth, they heard the sound of semi-automatic rifle fire as soldiers stormed the monument, but they say it was aimed at knocking out the student loudspeakers. Interviewed by Richard Nations, both men say they left the monument with the last of the students and saw no deaths. "There was absolutely nobody killed at the monument," said Rodriguez. "Everyone left and no one was killed."

What Nations and I saw, from our position twenty-five yards southeast of the monument, was unforgettable. For an agonizing minute, it seemed as if the students might not comply with the decision to leave. Then, slowly, they began to stand up and descend from the monument. As the first group filed past us, heading toward the open southeast corner of the square, we burst into spontaneous applause. Many in the ten-deep column, each contingent following the banners of its college, had tears rolling down their cheeks. All looked shaken; many were trembling or unsteady on their feet. But all looked proud and unbeaten. One group shouted, "Down with the Communist Party!"—the first time I had ever heard this openly said in China. Richard, ever the professional, continued to take notes. In his notebook, he remarks, "The students' leaders had pulled off the most difficult maneuver in politics of any human enterprise, an orderly retreat."

The Journalists

But according to a widely reprinted "eyewitness" account, which first ran in a Hong Kong paper and was purportedly written by a student from Beijing's Qinghua University, nearly all of us had already been killed, mowed down at point-blank range by a bank of a dozen machine guns just after 4:00. The survivors were then either chased across the square by tanks and crushed or else beaten to death with clubs. This story was picked up by, among others, *The New York Times* (although reporter Nicholas Kristof quickly challenged it), *The Washington Post*, and *The San Francisco Examiner*. In terms of lurid invention, it was in a class of its own. Astonishingly, however, it is only one of several such accounts, most of which say the mass slayings took place just before 5:00. Wu'er Kaixi, one of the principal student leaders, said he had seen "about two hundred students" cut down by gunfire in the predawn assault. But he was not there: He had been driven to safety in a van several hours earlier. How could these fabrications have gained so much acceptance?

There were, by my count, ten Western journalists in the vicinity of the monument at the time in question, as well as a handful of diplomats and Hong Kong Chinese. At least two of the reporters—Claudia Rosett of *The Asian Wall Street Journal* and John Pomfret of the Associated Press—filed accurate accounts of the evacuation, but these were isolated paragraphs buried in long reports from other parts of the city. With Roth and Williams of CBS under arrest in the Great Hall of the People, not to emerge until 5:30, the only foreign film footage of the evacuation is that taken by the Spanish TV crew, who insist they saw no killing.

In an interesting footnote, their reporter, Juan Restrepo, who was separated from his crew all night, says that their film of the night's events was garbled by his editors at Television Espanola in Madrid, creating the false impression that killings had taken place during the evacuation of the square.

Of all the comments by TV reporters who left the square, perhaps the most telling are those of John Simpson, whose BBC news team won a raft of awards for its coverage of events in Beijing. Simpson felt remorseful about leaving, but his account for *Granta* reveals how the sense of impending disaster led the news media to believe that the worst then actually happened: "Someone should have been there when the massacre took place, filming what happened, showing the courage of the students as they were surrounded by tanks and the army advancing, firing as it went." As dawn drew near on June 4, from a safe but very incomplete vantage point half a mile away on an upper floor of the Beijing Hotel (from which the Monument to the People's Heroes is completely hidden from view), Simpson wrote, "We filmed the tanks as they drove over the tents. . . . Dozens of people seem to have died in that way, and those who saw it said they could hear the screams of the people inside the tents over the noise of the tanks. We filmed as the lights in the square were switched off at 4:00 A.M. They were switched on again forty minutes later, when the troops and the tanks moved toward the monument itself, shooting first in the air and then, again, directly at the students themselves, so that the steps of the monument and the heroic reliefs which decorated it were smashed by bullets."

As Simpson's crew was filming, Japanese photojournalist Imaeda Koichi reports seeing no killing there, although he also says, "I did see some students in the tents, not many, only in three of the tents." Restrepo of Television Espanola had earlier checked all the tents in the vicinity of the Goddess of Democracy and says, "I can assure you that there were not more than five people inside the tents at around 3 A.M." Richard Nations and I also witnessed the army's advance from the north. At 5:00, from a position next to the monument, where the evacuation was continuing, we saw that the goddess had vanished. We headed back north to investigate, walking for several hundred yards through the deserted tent encampment. A long line of tanks and APC's was rumbling toward the monument, crushing everything in its path—tents, railings, boxes of provisions, bicycles. The possibility remains that a handful of students were still in the tents. The Chinese government claims soldiers checked the tents for sick or exhausted students, but we clearly saw that the advancing infantrymen walked behind the tanks.

Back at the monument again, five minutes later, we saw that the top level was now swarming with soldiers, their guns pointed skyward. In our absence, the writer Lao Gui had witnessed what happened: "A small detachment of soldiers dressed in camouflage uniforms rushed up to the monument, occupied the top of it, and fired incessantly into the air. . . . Soon, there was no more sound from the broadcast station. The soldiers had shot the loudspeakers apart." The Spanish crew was also there when the commandos stormed the top level; they saw no killings. Claudia Rosett and Imaeda Koichi concur, although Kenneth Qiang told me later that one student on the second level had been shot in the leg. (A widely circulated Hong Kong magazine, *Chai Ling zibai shu* [Chai Ling's testimony], quoted Qiang as saying he had seen "twenty to thirty students in a row at the front mowed down by gunfire"; this, he says, was pure invention by the magazine.) By 5:30, the students had left the square. Moving back at precisely the same speed as the advancing APCs, they extracted every last ounce of moral victory from their retreat. Lingering doubts about a small group of students who may have remained on the top level of the monument are dispelled by a remarkable eyewitness account by Yu Shuo, a former professor at People's University who now lives in exile in Paris. "As I was talking to [an army] officer," she says, "I suddenly realized that I was the last person left at the monument. As I walked down the terrace, I saw a line of characters on the relief: 'On June 4, 1989, the Chinese people shed their blood and died for democracy.' As I turned around, I saw that a soldier was about to pierce a bed with his bayonet. I saw two feet sticking out from it. . . . I rushed forward and dragged the feet. A boy fell down from the bed; he was not completely awake yet. He was the last student to leave the square."

It will probably never be firmly established what happened to the only two other significant groups of people left in the square at that late hour. One was the medical team from Beijing United Medical College; they were the last people seen by a South American diplomat as he left the square at 5:20. The second was a small crowd of *laobaixing* outside the Great Hall of the People. Richard Roth and Derek Williams were amazed to see these people still there when the journalists were brought out at 5:30.

The two Americans were driven by jeep directly across the square to the Children's Cultural Palace just to the northeast, where they were detained for about eighteen hours. "We saw no bodies in the square," Williams recollects. His account of this short ride is crucial: It seems inconceivable that the troops would have taken foreign journalists through the square if, as was widely rumored, they were busy covertly disposing of dead bodies at the time. By now it was broad daylight; the evacuation was complete. At the southern end of the square, Nations and I witnessed one final skirmish between stone throwers and soldiers who opened fire before running off with the crowd on their heels. We finally decided it was time to get the hell out. As far as we can ascertain, we were the last foreigners to leave Tiananmen Square. It was 6:15.

Epilogue

After fifty days of occupation by the prodemocracy movement, the square had finally been "returned to the people." But still the killing did not stop. As the student column wound its way slowly to the northwest, about half a mile from the square at the Liubukou intersection, four tanks came hurtling down Chang'an

Boulevard and crushed eleven of them to death. Shortly afterward, troops repeatedly fired on unarmed protesters just west of the Beijing Hotel, killing dozens. An unknown number of *laobaixing* were summarily executed in the days that followed, as troops combed the alleyways of Beijing looking for "hidden counterrevolutionaries."

To conclude, we should turn to two Chinese activists from last year's democracy movement, both of whom witnessed the final clearing of the square, for an answer to the question posed at the outset: Why does it matter where the massacre took place? Kong Jiesheng, a famous novelist and essayist, says: "Now, when the power-holding clique in Beijing is still unrepentant about the June 4 massacre but also sorely vexed by the criticisms and sanctions imposed by numerous countries, rebukes from outside China based on ill-founded concepts have given those vicious thugs precisely the 'spiritual shield' they so desperately need. It makes plausible their lengthy refutations of outside criticisms as being mere 'stuff and nonsense' and 'much ado about nothing' "—the very phrase used by General Secretary Jiang Zemin when asked by Barbara Walters, on ABC's *20/20* on May 18, about "the massacre in Tiananmen Square."

But Lao Gui should have the last word: "Because of hatred of the murderer, one sometimes cannot resist exaggerating the severity of the crime. This is understandable. . . . But those butchers then take advantage of this opportunity 'to clarify the truth,' using one truth to cover up ten falsehoods. They exploit the fact that no one died during the clearing of Tiananmen Square to conceal the truth that some deaths and injuries did occur there earlier. And they use the fact that there was no bloodbath in Tiananmen Square to cover up the truth about the bloodbaths in Muxudi, Nanchizi, and Liubukou. Why do we give them such an opportunity?"

191

Killing Their Children

ANITA CHAN AND JONATHAN UNGER

Source: Anita Chan and Jonathan Unger, "Killing Their Children." *The Nation* magazine/The Nation Company, Inc. © 1990.

Canberra, New South Wales, Australia

Robin Munro's excellent description of the Tiananmen massacre provides a carefully reasoned account of the many events of that night. We do not question Munro's eyewitness observations, nor his analysis that the government made a sharp distinction between students and workers and singled out the working class for the terror of that night. . . . We are convinced, though, that Munro is in error on one essential point. Strong evidence is available that students retreating south through Tiananmen Square were set upon by troops sometime between 5:00 and 5:30 A.M., and that a substantial number of young people were killed or wounded.

By Munro's account, he and journalist Richard Nations had been watching the first contingents of students peacefully leaving the Monument to the People's Heroes at the center of the square at 5 A.M. when the journalists noticed that the statue of the Goddess of Democracy had disappeared from view. They walked north several hundred yards through the tent city to investigate. Munro writes that a phalanx of tanks rolled past them toward the monument, crushing everything in its way. By the time Munro and Nations had returned to the vicinity of the monument, it was aswarm with soldiers, and students no longer were in evidence. Munro apparently was on the northern side of the monument, trapped amid the milling troops and the cacophony of many dozens of tanks, entirely out of sight and sound of the students retreating hundreds of yards to the southeast.

Accounts of what Munro missed are revealed in a tape recording taped later that morning by an Australian student at one of Beijing's universities as his Chinese schoolmates returned to campus from the square. A dozen voices spontaneously recount to one another the horrors they have just experienced. Very similar accounts were provided in mid-June 1989 by Hong Kong university students who were among the last group of evacuees from the square.

These eyewitness accounts agree that impatient troops stormed the monument to evict the students who remained, most of whom were on the northern steps and atop the monument, either waiting their turn or determined never to leave. At first the troops climbing the monument steps shot over the students' heads at the student loudspeaker system, but some of the soldiers soon lowered their sights. One of the students from Hong Kong had seen a student shot next to him, and as he clambered down the southern steps of the monument desperately trying to help carry the dying student, a second student fell wounded beside him.

Several of the students on the tape had already left the monument but were near the tail end of the column. They were attacked and beaten by troops, and in the melee students fell and were trampled by those behind. As one of the student voices notes, "A lot of people were stampeded to death at the end. During the retreat from the square there was chaos." The assault by the troops soon escalated into gunfire. One of the accounts on the tape tells a harrowing story:

"At 4:00 A.M., the lights in the square had been turned off. Then the troops surrounded us. When the lights went on again, many of the students heaved a sigh of relief and let down their vigilance. Some even returned to their tents to catch a nap. But then tanks moved into formation in a solid row and rapidly rolled right over the tents. The students who'd gone into the tents must all have been crushed. Then soldiers picked up the poles from the collapsed tents and rushed toward us and started beating us.

"I was at the edge of the column, trailing behind. There were also a lot of female students at the back. Their heads had been beaten bloody and they were screaming and crying. When the soldiers came at us they struck at our heads with their rifle butts. . . .

"I started running, alongside a huge fellow from Beijing University. He stopped to help pull some students to their feet so they wouldn't get squashed. This was because in front of us a lot of students had already fallen to the ground, and the ones at the back were stomping on them. Many were already dead. From the sides, the soldiers were shooting. A lot of students fell with the shots. Then, in order to avoid more casualties, we tried to hold back the students coming from behind [and] told them not to rush forward. Then we saw the military police coming up close behind. They were slashing their way through. I was chased over to a place where there was a pile of dead bodies."

The Chinese government, confident that there were no outside witnesses to these events, has claimed repeatedly to the world that no students were killed during their withdrawal from the square. The eyewitness accounts presented here, and many others that we have in our files, give the lie to such claims. Quite terrible events, it is clear, occurred in the square that night.

192

[Robin] Munro Replies

Source: Robin Munro, "Munro Replies." *The Nation* magazine/The Nation Company, Inc., © 1990.

Beijing

The new evidence presented by Anita Chan and Jonathan Unger of killings of students by troops during the final clearing of the square must be carefully and seriously considered. These accounts are flatly contradicted, however, by what Richard Nations and I actually saw, and also by all the eyewitness evidence—which comes from trained observers, Chinese as well as Western journalists—that we have since been able to piece together. The student accounts cited by Chan and Unger are indeed harrowing; but for the most part they are clearly not true.

First, the notion that Nations and I "missed" the alleged atrocities is wrong. We were absent from the monument for no more than five minutes. We were not "trapped" behind troop lines, "entirely out of sight and sound of the students retreating." Nor were we cut off by tanks. We arrived back at the monument well ahead of the approaching armored line. And contrary to what Chan and Unger assume, several hundred students were still on the monument at that time; only the top level was in fact "aswarm with soldiers."

412 PART VI: JUNE 3-4

Second, journalists who witnessed, from all angles, the events on and around the monument during our five-minute absence to the north (these included Claudia Rosett of *The Asian Wall Street Journal*, Fermin Rodriguez and Jose Luis Marquez of Television Espanola, and Chinese writer and journalist Lao Gui) all agree that no killing, panic, "trampling-to-death stampede," or even serious injury occurred—although like ourselves it was their expectation of just such an eventuality that led them to remain on the scene in the first place. If Chan and Unger's claim of killings on the monument is correct, then they need to explain an improbable conspiracy of silence on the part not only of these journalists but also of the students themselves. Some students certainly were pushed and beaten as the troops stormed the top level. But upon our return to the monument, from where the evacuation was still slowly proceeding, Nations and I talked to numerous students, including picket marshals who were actually organizing the retreat. Not one of them reported that any students had just been killed.

Third, Nations and I retreated to the east side of the Mao Mausoleum, from where we finally lost sight of the monument, just in back of the single picket line that was protecting the last of the student evacuees. We remained there for a further half-hour, long after the departing student column had left the square entirely, by which time it was daylight and only a small crowd of some fifty to one hundred people still stood around. Since the only exit from the square at this time was through the southeast corner, via the east side of the mausoleum, any student survivors of the alleged killings would necessarily have passed right by us. Chan and Unger specify that the killings occurred "sometime between 5:00 and 5:30 A.M." But Nations and I did not leave the square until 6:15. Even if we had missed seeing the fleeing survivors, it is scarcely possible that no one else in the small crowd, which remained remarkably relaxed, would have seen them.

Chan and Unger insist that "quite terrible events" occurred in the square during the student evacuation. As a longstanding and outspoken critic of the Chinese authorities' appalling human rights record, I find it invidious to have to record otherwise. A massacre certainly occurred elsewhere in Beijing that night. But Nations and I were in the square. Chan and Unger were not.

"It's no use trying to reason with them [i.e., PLA troops]."
—Army officer, night of June 3

193

A Dry and Factual Account of Things Witnessed or Heard Firsthand from Other Witnesses

RUDOLF G. WAGNER (UNIVERSITY OF HEIDELBERG)
AND CATHERINE LANCE YEH (HARVARD UNIVERSITY)

June 3–4, 1989

On June 3, we heard that troops had stormed into town in the morning and killed some people on the way. In the morning the [government] street loudspeakers took great pains to refute what they called rumors, such as Li Peng cursing the students commemorating Hu Yaobang's death and the like. The mood of this refutation was very defensive, and the credibility of some of the rumors was in fact enhanced by the rebuttal. Arriving at Muxudi, I saw a small transporter on the side of the street with a big dent in its side. In the early hours of the morning, a large number of trucks and armored vehicles had driven down this avenue into town at breakneck speed, at last to enforce martial law. It seems that the lead vehicle crashed into this small transporter, killing the four people inside. The action of the four people killed was seen by many as an act of resistance. The government declared on the radio that people had used this mere accident to fan up resentment by organizing a big funeral for them.

As I rode up the main avenue toward Tiananmen, I saw two army buses blocked there, the first with about twenty soldiers, the other with about fifty soldiers. Their vehicles had been incapacitated, and they must have been sitting there since early morning in a sweltering heat. As I passed I saw many of the people talking with the soldiers, and I saw one entire pack of ice cream bars being handed to them through the broken windows. Obviously, the men of the Twenty-seventh Army to whom these buses seemed to belong saw no need to come to the rescue of their stranded comrades. These soldiers—at the complete mercy of the surrounding people—were treated nonetheless with the utmost restraint.

About six hundred yards ahead, the street was blocked by about two hundred soldiers at the corner of Chang'an Boulevard and the walled compound housing the party and government center, Zhongnanhai. The soldiers were confronting the large crowd of several tens of thousands of people, mostly young, but with many middle-aged men among them. People were in light summer attire, completely unprepared for any confrontation. They were shouting slogans against Prime Minister Li Peng and trying to get through to Tiananmen. The soldiers had a similar crowd behind them and were clearly in a difficult position. They shot tear gas toward the crowd but obviously were unexperienced in this moderate form of "riot control." As the wind blew toward the soldiers, the crowds on my side were unaffected. People reacted with great shock to the tear gas salvoes. Many came running up to me in disbelief, asking whether there was a single government in the world that would treat its own citizens this way. I had to answer, sadly but in truth, that there were all too many governments in the world doing this and more. They had never seen tear gas and kept asking me whether it was poisonous and did long-term damage. People were obviously shocked and outraged that the army should use such measures against them. The constantly repeated phrase was, "How can a government of the people shoot tear gas at its own people!"

After about an hour of stalemate, a very small contingent of students from Beijing University arrived with their flag. Originally, a big demonstration had been planned for 2:00 P.M. to protest the morning's attack and the killing of the four citizens, but only about 150 people were in this group. The Beida students, however, sized up the situation, closed their ranks, and marched straight onto the line of soldiers. A great number of people joined, altogether perhaps five thousand. Within two minutes they had broken through the line, and the entire body of soldiers had retreated into the Central Committee compound. I do not know whether the soldiers had gas masks, but from a distance it appeared to me that they did not and consequently had gassed themselves for a while.

I went on to Tiananmen Square, which was perfectly calm. There were perhaps some one hundred tents there, many of them in orderly rows. Great efforts must have been made to keep the place clean and, apart from some cloth and bamboo sticks from abandoned tents lying around, there was little debris. Compared to reports about a few days earlier, the numbers had dramatically dwindled. On Friday, I heard, there had been a vote to return to campus by Monday, and it seemed that if the government was willing to wait two more days, it would achieve its purpose of clearing Tiananmen without bloodshed, although the social challenge certainly would not have been over. This seemed to be a constant pattern.

The crowds on the square were small in comparison. Most people were around the Monument to the People's Heroes, because a new hunger strike had begun there two days before with the famous political scientist Yan Jiaqi participating. The statue of the Goddess of Democracy erected by the students from the Central Fine Arts Academy had been completed right on the central axis of Tiananmen, facing north and thus confronting the leadership looking south from Tiananmen gate with its demands. Many people were reading the appeal for the statue inscribed on a streamer and were having themselves photographed in front of the statue.

I heard the ongoing battle between the students and the government propaganda group set up by Li Peng and headed by Yuan Mu. The government controlled the huge, high-quality loudspeakers on and around the square, while the students had a small generator with which they could broadcast their own news when the official loudspeakers were silent. On this day, the official loud-speakers were never silent; they broadcast a stern editorial about the necessity of martial law in Beijing, and then an anonymous letter from a student who had been on Tiananmen and had left. This letter claimed that the students there were trying to get away from the stress of studying, were looking for a free ride to Beijing, or were politicos building their own careers on the backs of the naive students who followed them. The loudspeakers, two per pole, were connected with two little outside wires each. On Tiananmen Square itself, these wires had long been cut, but on Chang'an Boulevard along Tiananmen they were still blaring. As I passed by, a man climbed up one of the poles and cut the wires amidst cheers from a rapidly growing crowd. The same process was repeated by him and then others with the other poles, so that within a few minutes all loudspeakers were dead except for those stationed inside the compound of the Great Hall of the People.

As I walked past this hall to the west of Tiananmen, I saw big crowds running into a small street. About 1,500 soldiers who had gotten in during the night or had come in through a reported underground tunnel leading straight from there to the Western Hills (built originally during the late 1960s in case of attack) had left their temporary abode in the Great Hall and had proceeded outside into the street to march on Tiananmen. The demonstration mentioned earlier had marched straight into this street, now packed with people. Just before I came, there had been a confrontation between the troops and the demonstrators with a number of people being beaten severely. Instead of fleeing the scene, people streamed in even greater numbers. The soldiers were surrounded by people on all sides, five to thirty deep, and seemed to have been standing in the street for several hours. It was now about 3:00 P.M. This stalemate was eventually broken by two very small groups, one consisting of medical school students, the other of about thirty people with a banner reading *"Gongren zizhi gongrenhui,"* the Chinese equiva-lent of Solidarity [and referred to as the "Workers' Autonomous Union" in this book's documents]. They showed up at the fringe of the surrounding masses. Instantly, amid loud cheers, a corridor was opened for them and they rushed straight toward the soldiers. The commanding officer gave orders that [the sol-diers] should leave. Another corridor was instantly opened by students against the protest of many people who wanted to have some revenge for the beatings, and the soldiers climbed one after the other over a fence back into the Great Hall. Again the beating by the soldiers had been met with surprising restraint, enforced by the seemingly great authority of the students and, in this case, the workers from the newly organized union. The soldiers, too, showed restraint.

Later that evening when we returned home, the television broadcast a stern editorial that underlined the absolute necessity of martial law. We heard Li Peng himself had gone on the 7:00 P.M. television news to declare the army would now do what it had to do and everybody should stay home. The people out in the streets, old and young, men and women, most in light sandals, certainly did not look as if they would confront tanks and armored personnel carriers [APCs] a short while later. But in fact they were sitting there waiting, in order to oppose the troops' entry into the city.

At about 11:30 P.M., XXX, Cathy's relative, called to report he had heard gunshots to the south and proceeded to go there. We could hear the sharp reports of gunfire on the balcony. Only at about 1:00 A.M. did XXX return and call. He had been at Muxudi when suddenly gunfire broke out everywhere. Tanks, APCs, and heavily armed soldiers, opposed by unarmed people, opened fire. Most of the shots were over their heads, but many went directly into the crowds. XXX saw many people dead or wounded. The military's advance was very slow: The tanks had to stop every few meters to get over or around obstacles. During the ninety minutes when XXX watched, they made just under two hundred meters' headway. Eventually the tanks got to the bridge and then onto the broad Chang'an Boulevard with not much else to prevent them from getting to Tiananmen, although the next morning evidence of fierce resistance was visible here, too. He saw one student with a bullet straight through his head. His neighbor, who had been at the same corner, was speaking to a stranger there when the man suddenly sank down with a bullet through his neck. He saw people who transport goods through town on three-wheeled platforms appended to a bicycle volunteering to take the wounded and dying to the hospitals.

In the morning of June 4, XXX telephoned us around 6:30 A.M. He had been out on the streets. Blood was everywhere. Most of the victims had been brought to hospitals. He saw near Baitasi, just northwest of Tiananmen, two people lying in the middle of the street, one dead, the other dying. They had been beaten to death by infuriated citizens who claimed they were undercover police. Already by Saturday, June 3, on Tiananmen Square the number of people in ostentatiously inconspicuous dress eagerly taking notes and photographing had been amazing. Many leaflets during the following days detailed the use of undercover police and soldiers disguised as civilians to penetrate the city.

We rode into town after listening to the BBC's 7:00 A.M. news. The streets were full of people. Right outside our place on [XX] Road in the direction of the Friendship Hotel, two army trucks were burning. Among the crowd there was numb furor, a sense of suspense and disbelief. Wherever we turned, there were destroyed vehicles and smoke. When we arrived at People's University, small jeeps, small transporters, and trucks were burning. It seems that any vehicle with an army number was being stopped and burned. As we passed People's University, we saw on the other side of the street a group of about two hundred students from Beijing University returning from Tiananmen. They were in rags, resembling an army that was withdrawing after heavy losses. The marchers were calling for a nationwide strike to protest what had happened. One of them gave a short report about the events on Tiananmen. They were carrying bullets, helmets, hand grenades, and other equipment used by the military against them, as well as blood-stained cloth. One student walked up to us and told us with a subdued voice that 2,500 people had been killed on the square during the preceding night, and this did not include the people killed during the approach of the army units. People stopped to voice support for the students and to listen to the report. Emotion was vivid on their faces. Many wept. In front of People's University many people clogged the streets. Through their loudspeaker, students were giving reports about the events in Beijing. This loudspeaker system played an important role in breaking the news monopoly of the government.

We rode on into the city. A man cycling behind us with a friend said he was going into town to look for his two children, both graduate students. A young man cycled next to us and addressed us in English. His face was pale with anger. "This is a fascist government! Fascist!" The open emotionalism among the people on the streets was overwhelming. "You have to tell your people and government all that happened here," the young man continued, "they have opened fire on their own people!"

We finally came to Muxudi. The scenes that follow were filmed by a secret government agent from the top of a nearby house and have been shown time and again on Chinese TV as proof of the "counterrevolutionaries' actions." We were eyewitnesses here most of the time when this film was turned; our own detailed description follows.

As we approached, we saw several dozen APCs, their lids closed, standing in line on the bridge. The first APC had crashed into a long bus that stood across the street, a second had crashed into the first one. The bus was already burned out, and the first APC was burning. Alongside the banks of the canal and around burning vehicles there were thousands of people. The street and the sidewalks were covered with stones people had picked out of the sidewalks to throw at the tanks during the previous night. The street was spattered with blood.

A soldier suddenly emerged from under the bridge together with another young person. When he was discovered, the crowd's mood quickly flared. Cries of "Beat him!" and "Kill him!" were heard, and some people began throwing stones. On the other side of the canal (where the soldier was), a large and threatening crowd gathered to see him coming up the embankment. He was obviously wounded or burned. The man seemed doomed. The other person, however, kept waving and explaining something. Cries were heard: "Don't throw stones!" "Don't beat him!" Eventually he was led out of sight, probably to a large compound hugging the canal to the south of the bridge.

In addition to the APCs on the bridge, there were perhaps a dozen or so trucks and another six or seven jeeps on the street. These lighter vehicles were all empty and burning. Further in the background was another group of trucks which was not burning. But as the people there had white shirts on, it seemed clear that those trucks were not held by the military.

We assumed that all those APCs must be empty. They have a heavy and a light machine gun mounted on the top, and usually carry up to ten fully armed soldiers and great amounts of ammunition. Suddenly there was movement in the APCs. Several started their engines. One got out of the line and swung around, its machine gun in a threatening level position. Completely surprised that these APCs were full of soldiers, we hid behind a tree and looked for better cover. People started running. The vehicle, however, did not fire a shot and seemed to try to make its way west back to where it had originally come from. (All this can be seen in part three of the PRC propaganda film *Baoluan zhengxian* [True face of the disturbances].)

The entire convoy had come to Muxudi at 6:00 A.M. The units that had broken through here late in the preceding evening and had begun the massacre on Tiananmen were from the Twenty-seventh Army. This army is commanded by the son of State President Yang Shangkun who, together with Li Peng, declared martial law. As we heard later, the Twenty-seventh Army had been to Vietnam. Their experience was thus with a well-entrenched, well-armed, and stubborn opponent, with very small and mobile units wielding high fire power, an opponent that relied on popular support (at least in its opposition to the Chinese), and large numbers of irregulars. In the eyes of the leadership around Yang Shangkun and Li Peng, these experiences qualified this army for taking an active role in the suppression of the democracy movement.

Units of this army had broken off here to go to Tiananmen, but had not kept the line behind themselves open. The convoy coming in at 6:00 A.M. was from another army, the Thirty-eighth, normally stationed in Baoding. Already once before, directly after the imposition of martial law, they had refused to shoot at people when ordered to get into the town.

The one APC that tried to get away stopped shortly down the road west, blocked by many burning vehicles. A short while thereafter, a young man climbed on another APC that was standing next to a burning vehicle and must have already been quite heated up. He tapped at one of the top doors, speaking to the soldiers inside. A few minutes later, the top doors were opened and six or seven soldiers emerged. They took off their helmets and handed over their weapons. Cries "Kill them, kill them!" were again heard, and people rushed over. But there was also opposition. Some people shouted "Do not hit them!" The young man waved away the crowd, and the soldiers were guided away to the building on the other side. A few minutes later, an APC next to the first one opened the top lid, and a hand appeared waving a white piece of cloth. Soldiers emerged and gave their automatic rifles to the young men receiving them. They hugged. From what we heard afterward, the guns were not loaded. Whether this was by a decision of the army leadership or by the Thirty-eighth Army, we don't know. In rapid succession, the other APCs' lids opened, and more soldiers emerged. They were all quickly guided away from the crowd by what seemed to be a student group, into buildings beyond the street.

The first two or three APCs were burning in a long succession of explosions. They obviously had all sorts of ammunition, including tracer ammunition. The explosions continued throughout the day.

We left and rode in the direction of Tiananmen. Everywhere groups of people had gathered to share their grief, news, and information. Chang'an Boulevard was a battlefield. The street is divided in the middle by a sort of fence. The fence had been moved to cross the entire street in a futile attempt to stop the tanks, which simply rolled over them.

Burned military vehicles and public buses were everywhere. The surface of Chang'an was torn up by tank treads. Right at Muxudi, an old woman who had looked out of the window on one of the upper floors of a building lining the street had been shot. Further down, in the building west of the Yanjing Hotel, a machine gun volley had grazed the walls just below the upper windows.

As we advanced, we saw a crowd near the Minzu Hotel standing around what turned out to be the body of a dead soldier, naked. People had been extremely restrained and considerate at Muxudi toward the soldiers who had not fired, but showed no trace of sympathy for this young man.

At the corner of Zhongnanhai and Chang'an Boulevard a few hundred meters away, the street was blocked by seven tanks lined up side by side with their guns pointed in our direction. Soldiers were standing on them in defiant postures. Infantry soldiers (about three hundred to four hundred) were massed in front of them, confronting a crowd about fifty to one hundred meters away that consisted of young men throwing stones at them. A little further behind were many more people milling around, young women sitting on the back seats of their boyfriends' bikes in dazzling clothes and high heels, young and old men from out of town on their three-wheeled transport bikes, people walking, even a few children. The mood was one of sadness, anger, and defiance. Black smoke was rising from the direction of Tiananmen Square. Repeatedly, a big unarmed transport helicopter was flying to the square, then a few minutes later flying back to the west, returning a quarter of an hour later to repeat the pattern. He did not seem to fly surveillance, but to transport things. Considering the huge convoy of APCs at Muxudi, it still is a puzzle why no units were dispatched to get these vehicles and soldiers out. There is always the possibility that the command was trying to get the proper footage for the postfestum legitimation of the massacre.

On Chang'an Boulevard, the crowd would advance with some throwing of stones and bottles. This would be followed by the sortie of fifty or a hundred soldiers who, however, stopped after some fifty meters while the crowd fled. The scene was different [from Saturday, June 3,] however. These soldiers, it turned out, had no tear gas, just live ammunition. We only heard the reports of guns but could not see what and where they were shooting. They used live ammunition on the people there. As we observed the confrontation from some distance, a young man dashed by with a friend on the back seat of his bike, yelling "They are using bullets!" The friend was bleeding from a head wound. On the evening BBC news, a similar confrontation was reported as seen by the BBC reporter stationed in the Beijing Hotel on the eastern side of Tiananmen. The soldiers opened fire on the crowd in the afternoon, and thirty to forty people were left dead or wounded on the ground.[1] There was, however, absolutely no communication, organization, or leadership visible to organize anything like a struggle. We eventually left this place, for many people ran up and urged us to leave, as foreigners might be in a particularly bad situation vis-à-vis these trigger-happy soldiers.

We returned to Muxudi where all the rest of the vehicles were now burning. It seemed that the soldiers were still in the compound directly to the south, as crowds were pressing over there to look over the walls. In marked contrast to the morning, there were no bursts from the APCs now burning. This means either that they had no ammunition stored, or that it had been removed. What happened to the arms is a matter of speculation. One possibility is of course that they were transported away by the one APC driven through the streets by students toward Beijing University. The various popular groups also had enough trucks to transport such things.

In the evening news on June 4, the martial law command demanded that all arms captured should be returned immediately. The next day it reported that some guns and other arms had been returned. In these APCs, however, had been quantities of arms and ammunition considerably larger than the very small government figures of returned arms.

The streets were still covered with blood. A number of troops had been disarmed and remained in the house on the other side of the bridge. On the street, about eighty heavy and light military vehicles had gone up in flames since morning. They were standing at the main entry road for the Twenty-seventh Army, which might at any moment make another run into the city with tanks. However, no one seemed to assume that the Twenty-seventh Army would care what happened to the Thirty-eighth Army. People seemed united in a nearly suicidal defiance of the threat they were under. They spoke openly of their anger and wanted to know if there was any government in the world today that would handle their own citizens in such a way. One student said we should report what had happened to the Committee on Human Rights of the United Nations. "The problem is," he said later, "there is no real organization or leadership to this movement which we could now follow."

On the Muxudi site, important decisions had to be made: What to do with those vehicles that were still closed; how to treat the individual soldier who emerged; how to treat the soldiers when they came out; what to do with the arms and vehicles—destroy or keep, return or use? A sort of spontaneous leadership by on-the-spot acclamation, based on a common philosophy, sprung up to decide these matters. Even the people who had just clamored for killing the soldiers would quickly calm down once the person on the APC waved to ward them off,

---

[1]William Hinton also witnessed this scene, which was filmed by the BBC.

and as others shouted "Don't hurt them!" A common philosophy prevailed that they should use peaceful means, try to win over the soldiers who did not shoot at them, and not mistreat "prisoners." People apparently did not want to mar the new hope for political change with blind violence and rigid new organizational structures. Altogether the scene at Muxudi had been one of extreme restraint by an amassed group of people who were extremely angry with the army for the action of the preceding night.

On the next morning, June 5, stories poured in from all over the city that soldiers were shooting at random in the center of town, that they obviously lacked organization and discipline. They seemed to behave as if surrounded by enemies (which was not entirely wrong as public opinion was violently against them). Perhaps the experience of their officers from the Vietnam War, where both sides had confronted each other with unmitigated hatred, and even mothers with children might suddenly pull out hand grenades, had formed their perspective on "people's war." The only way to impose their will on the populace was by terror. The television clip from the evening of June 5, repeated in the official series *True Face of the Disturbances*, about an army car that stalled on the road and was attacked by stone-throwing youths, with the driver probably killed, indicated why soldiers might be anxious. During this stone throwing, other military vehicles, including APCs, sped by completely unconcerned. Obviously, the rule in this army is, everyone for himself.

Rumors were also flying that the universities would be occupied by the military authorities. We rode our bikes over to Beijing University. There was no trace of the military, nor of tank treads on any street in the area. The Beida campus seemed half empty. A few hundred people had congregated in the area around the loudspeakers. Upon hearing the news that Taiwan had put its army on alert, some people cheered. The loudspeakers broadcast appeals by parents who had come to Beijing to look for their children. "ZZZ from Nanjing, please come to Building 28, your father and mother have come to look for you." "YYY please come to the announcer's station, your fellow students from MMM are looking for you."

Apparently, two hundred people were missing at Beida (among whom were fifty doctoral students), but only one person was confirmed dead at Tiananmen. No one knew how many students had left for home during the past few days. The different departments were trying to establish a name list of people missing to begin tracing them. If things were that difficult to trace in Beijing, they must have been much harder for the tens of thousands of students from other universities who had come to Beijing.

After we left Beida, we noticed a crowd waiting in front of a small factory entrance. One of its workers had been killed, and people went in one by one to pay their respects. After returning home we noticed that a tailor downstairs from our apartment seemed to have made a mistake and cut a skirt for a woman so short that it had become a mini skirt. She complained, and within a few minutes the happiest row was on with much barking and laughter, negotiation and satire. The triviality of daily life in the midst of a tense expectation of tanks moving into the district was overpowering.

As the evening darkened, all waited anxiously to hear tanks and APCs rolling toward the universities. But there was complete silence. We went out and saw photographs on a wall of dead citizens lying on the street. A young man came by and glued a computer-written eyewitness account of the Tiananmen massacre to a little cubicle on the street. Instantly a crowd assembled to read it [see Doc. 194]. One man said the soldiers were using *zhazi* (explosive bullets) on the students, and that these were imported from Germany. Many reports indicated that the wounds of the victims were much larger than regular bullets would have made. The entrance opening caused by these wounds was small, but the internal destruction was enormous.

The evening TV news came on with an announcer dressed in black for a few seconds. Then a very harsh letter by the Central Committee and the State Council was read, followed by an even sterner announcement from the army's high command. The Central Committee letter maintained that the counter-revolutionaries were out to kill all the forty-eight million Communist party members in the country, and that now was the hour to unite the party leadership (whoever that might have been). The army communiqué said that the victory at Tiananmen was but the first battle, and that the situation continued to be critical. Surprisingly, it claimed that the rumor that army action was imminent, and that people should stay at home, was unfounded. This definitely had not been a rumor, but some important change must have occurred to prevent the army from marching into Haidianqu, the university district.

In the evening, Beijing TV Station No. 1 interrupted its regular program to broadcast a Peking opera from the *Three Kingdoms* cycle. The entire action revolved around the extremely emotional mourning of the main protagonist's two brothers. A memorial service was held in the center of the stage, where a huge Chinese-language character, *ji* (honor the dead), was located. The voices rang with anger and despair. Seemingly, the station broadcast this opera as a memorial tribute to the victims of Tiananmen; for as a "counterrevolutionary mob," they were not entitled to a formal burial. A Chinese opera buff watching it with us alerted us to the double meaning of this play.

In the late evening, tanks were getting into position as if defending themselves against a force coming at them from outside. Their guns were turned outward. They began to position themselves with much space between each other, hugging walls. Rumors spread that we were heading for civil war between different armies right in Beijing.

On the morning of June 6, one of Cathy's relatives telephoned to say that some people had remained alive on Tiananmen Square until June 5, when they were then shot, burned, and their bones transported away by helicopter. A German neighbor said that actual fighting between military units had broken out somewhere about twenty kilometers to the south.

In the afternoon, news began streaming in that the "civil war had actually started." American news agencies were quoted as saying this. Everything was perfectly calm where we were, however. Later, we heard some twenty blasts from the west that sounded like artillery (or perhaps some work site where explosions were required). On the day before in the morning we had heard similar sounds from the same direction—the Western Hills, where the secret headquarters of the center are reported to have been installed in the late 1960s.

We met our friend XX. His driver had been on Tiananmen during the massacre. He feigned to be dead. When the shooting was over, he crawled behind the History Museum, got into the car, and drove away. According to what he said, on June 4 in Tiananmen Square, the tanks and APCs had rolled over the tents and the students in them. They were crushed. Afterward the army pushed the tents, clothes, and dead bodies into a pile, poured gasoline over them, and set fire to it with a flame thrower.

On Wednesday June 7, everyone started to leave in a flurry. It seemed, however, that the threat of a confrontation between two or more armies in Beijing had subsided. When we rode past People's University, it seemed almost deserted. No loudspeakers were outside. The explanation given for this was that the students feared many people would get killed if the army marched in, and there were crowds listening to the news.

At the Second Ring Road, a group of young people told us that during the night there had been some confrontation at the military airport in the northwest of the city on the way to the Summer Palace. The airport, they said, was controlled by the Thirty-eighth Army, which had its arms depot there. The Twenty-seventh contested that control, and during the night put people into uniforms of the Thirty-eighth. They were to take the airport and blow up their ammunition so as to prevent the Thirty-eighth from attacking the Twenty-seventh. The commandos had been discovered and killed.

They also told us that during the preceding night the secretary of the defense minister [Qin Jiwei] was reported to have gone to the campuses at Beida and Qinghua. The defense minister was supposed to be a supporter of Zhao Ziyang and opposed to the use of the military in the city. The secretary had asked the students not to prevent the troops from entering the city as they were to attack the Twenty-seventh Army. This news had been broadcast over the loudspeakers, they said, at Beida and Qinghua, and students had been out until late at night to greet the incoming troops. But none had come.

On our way home, we passed around the corner from Daozuomiao Road and saw blood on the sidewalk. The people standing there said that the night before around 1:00 A.M., two men had been sitting on the sidewalk drinking a beer. A military truck drove by and a soldier shot a volley of bullets at the two men and drove off. Neighbors brought the wounded to the hospital. One shoe was left on the sidewalk. Ants were crawling in the drying blood. Unawares, a small child trotted into the blood, and the mother pulled her back with a harsh word. This was about three hundred yards from where we lived. We decided to leave [the country].

194

Blood? Blood? Blood!!! A Factual Report about the Blood on Tiananmen

ANONYMOUS

June 7, 1989

Source: Computer-written account posted to a booth on Haidian Road near Zhong-guancun South Road, courtesy of Rudolf G. Wagner and Catherine Lance Yeh.

June 4, 2:40 A.M.

Several thousand helmeted riot police with see-through shields in their hands came under repeated volleys of gunfire [as written] from the west along Chang'an Boulevard, shooting toward Tiananmen. Immediately before this, they had used machine guns to drive away the citizens and students blocking their advance. Countless citizens and students lost their lives. . . . But of this nothing was known to the orderlies [among the people] around Tiananmen. The students lit a fire barricade across Chang'an Boulevard in order to block the [riot police] advance. At the western entrance of the street underpass from Tiananmen [to the other side of Chang'an Boulevard] an orderly who was less than a meter away from me suddenly collapsed. In his neck there was a bullet hole of about 3 centimeters in diameter. Blood gushed out. I was stunned. When I brought him to the emergency station, there was no sign of life in him. At the emergency station there were about ten to twenty people wounded, some hit by bullets in the stomach, others in the chest or head. I don't know whether they survived or not. According to the testimony of doctors on the scene, they were definitely killed or wounded by deadly military bullets; these were absolutely not rubber bullets.

We retreated to where Chang'an Boulevard faces Tiananmen. Because many costudents did not know that the military police had already opened fire with real bullets, the casualties were even more tragic because no one sought cover. Next to me five or six students went down. . . . We were forced to retreat back to the square. At this time, Chang'an Boulevard was already entirely under the control of the military police, and they fired away without scruples toward the square. Many students and people were hit, being completely taken by surprise. A student next to me was just about to drink something, when he suddenly gripped his stomach and collapsed. When I lifted his coat, he had a large hole in his stomach that was bleeding incessantly. Within less than a minute, five other students around me were carried away. All over Tiananmen Square were ambulance sirens and the students' wailing cries for help. Every few steps one could see traces of red blood. It made your hair stand up on end.

June 4, 4:15 A.M.

Two cars driven by citizens, full of broken bricks and gasoline bottles, were driven onto the square. The plan was to establish a defense line there. However, the students urged them to leave. They said: "Already too much of our blood and that of citizens has been spilled; we don't want any more of these meaningless sacrifices. We must make propaganda in every street and lane of the city, telling the masses everything that happened on Tiananmen. We have to call on the people to go on strike, close shops, and boycott classes." The citizens [with the car] left with tears streaming down their faces. At this time, the lamps on Tiananmen suddenly went out, and from all sides the sound of gunfire rose up. The students and citizens retreated in the darkness toward the Monument to the People's Heroes, and over the [government's] loudspeakers came the order to clear the square.

June 4, 4:50 A.M.

The lights went on again on the square. The Monument to the People's Heroes was surrounded by special troops wearing camouflage uniforms and carrying a mini-assault rifle [probably an Israeli Uzi later carried by Chinese units stationed in front of the U.S. Embassy].[1] With the muzzles of their guns they dispersed people. From time to time, the special unit shot into the air; when they heard that the students whom they had dispersed sang the *Internationale*, . . . they instantly started shooting at the loudspeaker of the "Beijing [Independent] Student Association" mounted on top of the monument. [The bullets] left scars at the top of the monument (an extreme form of insult to the revolutionary martyrs). After a short while, the loudspeaker fell silent, and at the same moment some twenty APCs advanced at high speed side by side from north to south, crushing the tents of the students. (Prior to this, the troops had not checked whether there were students in the tents or not. I cannot say with certainty whether there were or not, because at that time the troops did not let anyone walk around. We sat down wherever we had been standing.) In less than a minute, they had broken through to the fence surrounding the monument. The square was leveled to the ground!!!

June 4, 5:10 A.M.

Ten hunger strikers like Hou Dejian were driven from the third level of the monument. (Before this, they had reasonably called on the students and citizens

---

[1]A U.S. government source has cited Israel as a major supplier of arms to the PRC.

to evacuate the square quickly; but [the hunger strikers also proclaimed that if even one single student on the square would not leave, they would not leave the monument]. At this time, the ASUCUB decided that: "To avoid bloodshed and conserve our forces, the entire body of students will make an organized retreat." Upon hearing this, there was a great emotional upheaval among the crowd. Many students insisted on not leaving. They stood and sang the *Internationale*. After all, this had been the place where they had lived and fought . . . , where they had spent their sweat and fresh blood. Four men and many students tearfully urged them to leave. Mr. Hou Dejian pulled up one after the other. Organized by the student orderlies, the students left.

During this process, many helmeted military police carrying night sticks and electrical sticks (most of them PLA) pressed in from all sides. Therefore, the opening through which the students left was becoming very narrow, and this led to much chaos. Many people were trampled and hurt. From their midst constantly rose cries of pain. Countless people were wounded. Some students who insisted on not leaving were forcibly carried away by other students. All students left Tiananmen Square. From among the students rose many sobs and cries. Because [at that time] the military police did not permit ambulances onto the square, the place in front of the Museum of [Revolutionary] History [about 200 meters in length] was filled with many wounded people. (Their number is not known.) The students drove in a bus blackened by fire. When the wounded who had only received the most primitive bandages were brought onto this bus, they gave off heart-rending groans of pain. Everyone on the square changed their countenance in reaction to this. (Among the wounded, there were PLA soldiers. The students tended to them also.) Amidst the APCs and the night sticks of the military police, the students left the square in an organized fashion. At about 6:00 A.M. the students had all left the square through the southeastern corner.

195

Eyewitness Account

HOU TIANMING

Early June

Source: Anonymous.

At about 5:00 P.M. Saturday [June 3], I returned to Xinhua Gate, the front entrance to Communist party headquarters. People gathered there were angrily talking about what had happened that afternoon. There was an old woman among them, leaning on her son, tearfully telling the soldiers: "You shouldn't use guns against students. How will you explain it to your parents?" The soldiers were only eighteen or nineteen years old. They weren't permitted to respond, but they couldn't shut out what people said either. Several soldiers burst out crying. An officer who stood behind them removed anyone who wept.

As I walked westward away from the square, I saw people on bicycles rushing toward it, shouting hysterically, "Soldiers are killing civilians!" No one could believe the killing had started. Everyone stood in the middle of the streets and on the sidewalks, waiting for the army to arrive.

By 1:00 A.M., the army had arrived at Xidan [shopping district west of Tiananmen], spearheaded by armed police. They moved in a reversed-V formation, constantly throwing something at the crowds. It could have been tear gas. Because I was so shocked, I didn't feel anything. People nervously moved aside to allow the army to pass. The troops advanced slowly as if fighting in the jungle. Many were shooting, sometimes in the air, but more often at the crowd. When the armed police were about fifty meters away from the blockade, a courageous young man stood in the middle of the road holding high a red banner. As a bus behind him blazed violently, the man fell to the ground. The army was delayed by the fire, but continued shooting at the crowds. I hid behind a bus ticket office. A young man next to me was gunned down. I couldn't see where he was shot, but he was covered with blood. Another young man asked if we should hide in nearby houses. We didn't move. He left alone, walking closely against a wall. At that moment, a group of armed police rushed toward us with submachine guns and big clubs. One of them tried to drive us away with a club, but he didn't hit us. About twenty of us ran to one of the houses for protection, leaving behind the poor man who had been shot.

Inside the house, we found that the man who had asked us to join him was lying in a pool of blood. The courtyard was full of people, and the ground was sticky with blood. It was pitch black. I could feel that people were on the verge of going mad. Because of the tear gas, we couldn't keep our eyes open. Tears were streaming down our faces. We kept cursing the soldiers. We made a stretcher from a board—which I had torn off a telephone booth—and two iron bars and put the wounded man on it, even though I thought he might already be dead. We just needed to feel that there was something we could do. We ran with the stretcher, keeping against the wall, toward a hospital near the Minzu Hotel. The troops' faces under the street lights were a terrifying red. They spotted us. While some fired at us, others cheered. A car stopped to take the wounded man to the hospital. I left to hide inside the Minzu Hotel.

With army vehicles still in sight, Beijing residents resurfaced in the thousands. Chang'an Boulevard was packed with angry people. Everyone was weeping. They followed the troops, and shouted "Bandits! Bandits!" The soldiers turned around and shot at them. As soon as the gunfire stopped, however, people removed the wounded and marched on.

Trails of blood stains led me to two nearby hospitals. Through the window, I saw some wounded on stretchers in the hallway, as a doctor shook his head back and forth.

By 6:00 A.M., I had returned to Chang'an Boulevard. The gunshots from the east had not stopped. I headed west on a bike. There were burned vehicles in the middle of the streets everywhere I went. The air was full of smoke and fumes.

At the south side of Chang'an—near Muxudi—an army minibus had been overturned by civilians, who then threw stones at the disabled vehicle. Four or five bleeding soldiers emerged from the bus. Protected by other armed soldiers, they were led away to another army vehicle.

At Cuiwei Road [west of Muxudi], several army vehicles were still burning. One had dead bodies inside. One of the many onlookers told me that in the confusion, two army vehicles had collided with each other and one exploded. The civilians had not set fire to the vehicle, but they had cheered the collision.

I went back home but couldn't sleep. I couldn't believe what had happened. There was a phone call. One of my best friends, a student at Beijing University, had been shot. No one knew if he was still alive.

I went to Fuxing Hospital [near Muxudi] to look for him. I counted nineteen dead bodies on the ground, waiting for identification. I forced myself to look at every one of them. Nearly all of them were young. One had the left part of its head missing. As sickening as it was, I was relieved that I couldn't find my friend.

I met a middle-aged man at the entrance who told me that his brother had been murdered by the army. A few minutes later, he saw a young man carrying a machine gun. He grabbed the gun from him and walked out without a word.

Later, I found out that my friend had been killed after all. The next day, several of us went to the hospital to bid him farewell. Someone put a fresh flower on his body and touched his face for the last time. He was just twenty-two years old.

196

Television Transcript

BEIJING RESIDENT

June 3–4, 1989

Source: In *The Awakening . . . China*, Hong Kong Independent Television production, Summer 1989.

. . . They shot toward whichever window was lit. They shot all people, old and young. In our area, a nine-year-old child was shot dead with seven holes in his body. A doctor from Xiehe Hospital went to rescue people and was shot. They don't care who you are. A student was shot down. Four other students ran and asked a soldier nearby to let them go and rescue the wounded student. The soldier nodded. The four students went to take the wounded student with their hands up. Just as they bent down the soldier shot his entire clip and all four went down.

Hou Dejian and some other people were holding a sit-in and hunger strike. They negotiated with the troops to let the students withdraw [from the square]. The troops agreed. Students from Qinghua [University] were the last of the students to leave. Before they finished withdrawing, tanks came toward them. Seven students tried to block a tank hand in hand. The tank, however, drove over them once and then backed up to crush them again. All seven were crushed to death.

197

Eyewitness: The Chengdu Massacre

KARL HUTTERER

June 2–5, 1989

Source: *China Update*, no. 1 (August 1989): 4–5.

I was in Chengdu, Sichuan, from June 2 to June 7, 1989, and experienced the main period of disturbances and violence. . . . The . . . [following] report relies both on my own observations and experiences as well as on eyewitness reports by Chinese and Americans in Chengdu with whom I spoke.

Friday, June 2

. . . The number of students on the streets had been declining. Eighty percent of the students had returned to their classes. . . . Tensions had increased, however, during the last few days. For one, although Chinese media kept a complete blackout on what was going on in Beijing or elsewhere, a private information network was active. It transmitted reports that army units had moved in on Tiananmen Square but either were inactive or had perhaps been disarmed or partially disarmed by the students there. It was expected that the government would take sterner measures, and tensions were therefore quite high.

Perhaps more important, two days earlier a group of students had staged a sit-in on a major road [near Chengdu] to disrupt traffic (and probably to prevent trucks carrying troops from moving through). Some trucks did come through, however, and rolled over about six or seven demonstrators, injuring them gravely. Two of them died the next day. Memorial wreaths and posters were displayed on the steps of the Exhibition Center. . . .

Sunday, June 4

Quite early on Sunday morning, news began to trickle through about the massacre in Beijing. . . . The VOA, BBC World News, and private contacts were the major sources. . . . I spent a good portion of the day outside of town, where life went its normal way. . . . However, in those sections where the students and crowds of people were concentrated, tensions rose precipitously. By afternoon, rumors were rife that a national crackdown had been ordered and that by night-fall the PLA would attack all the provincial capitals where student demonstrations had been held.[1] By late afternoon and early evening, the first sounds of exploding tear-gas canisters and the dull, cannon-like reports of concussion grenades could be heard from the direction of the Exhibition Center. I tried to visit the place of action but was unable to get closer than one block. At that time the action was limited largely to tear gas and concussion grenades. Nevertheless, some people were hurt, and ambulances laboriously made their way back and forth through the crowds. Every time an ambulance came through with the wounded, the crowd broke out in applause and cheers in support of those being carried away. . . . Later, around 8:00 P.M., I went to the ninth-floor restaurant of the Jin Jiang Hotel to observe the action from there. Throughout that period, the intensity of the volleys increased to the point where the impression was of a city

---

[1] A government order authorized provincial officials to declare student demonstrations "riots," thereby legitimating the use of force.

under heavy cannon fire. In spite of this, however, the crowds did not disperse. With the onset of darkness, the security forces moved in in large numbers, wielding truncheons, knives, and electric cattle prods. I heard some isolated fire from automatic rifles. Much of the action consisted of [the army] isolating groups of demonstrators, stabbing them, and beating them to the ground. There is no question that none of the demonstrators were armed. The work of the security forces, on the other hand, was brutal in the extreme. Even after they had beaten down demonstrators, they would continue working on them with truncheons and knives until they were motionless. There was a pattern to it: With males, the preferred area of attack was the head, with females it was the abdomen. Numerous individual acts of brutality occurred. . . . The police and army violence was random. Even people who lay on the ground and pleaded for mercy were clubbed.

In the confrontation, demonstrators retaliated by throwing pieces of ripped-up asphalt and other things they could grab, and setting fire to buses, trucks, and APCs. Between ten and eleven at night, there was also evidence of a major fire at the "People's Market." . . . Essentially the whole block burned to the ground and was still smoldering for much of the next day. The security forces and fire brigades did not move in on the arson scene until about two hours after the fire had been set.

It was at first impossible to get reliable figures on the number of dead and wounded. . . . Only slowly did some more reliable information emerge. A doctor from one of the four major hospitals in Chengdu reported privately that twenty-seven people had died in her hospital. One may assume that similar numbers apply to the other hospitals. The situation was complicated because the army had given orders to the hospitals not to accept any wounded students. This order was particularly enforced at the two university hospitals, and I heard that at least in one hospital some staff members were arrested for disobeying army orders. . . . In any event, a consensus emerged eventually that somewhere around three to four hundred people were killed and up to a thousand wounded.

Monday, June 5

About 6:30 P.M., some staff members of the Jin Jiang Hotel warned a few of the foreigners living there that they should not venture outside the building, as the hotel would be attacked that night. The crowds of people were solid on People's South Road through the four blocks from the Exhibition Center to the hotel. Nevertheless, the throng outside the hotel seemed peaceful enough. By around [8:00] P.M., one began hearing the explosions of tear gas and concussion grenades. . . . Around 8:30 or 9:00 P.M. a melee broke out between demonstrators and security forces. . . . [R]ocks were thrown, property in front of the building was demolished, some plate glass windows were broken, and fires were set in front of the hotel. . . . The hotel was reported under attack. The American consul general rounded up whatever Americans he could get a hold of, and they barricaded themselves inside his apartment on the second floor. Meanwhile, the security forces closed the wrought iron gates in front of the hotel, in the process isolating some one to two hundred demonstrators inside the compound [grounds], and then proceeded to give them the same treatment they had meted out the previous night. . . . An American watching the situation from his window was so shocked by what he saw that he was barely able to speak about it the next day. . . . Outside the front gates, the battle between the security forces and the demonstrators seesawed back and forth . . . until a large contingent of army troops arrived and cleared the street. At the Jin Jiang Hotel, about thirty to fifty people were critically wounded or killed. . . .

198

I'm Still Alive!

CHAI LING

June 10, 1989

Source: *Shijie ribao* (World journal), New York, June 11, 1989.

Chai Ling, general coordinator of student demonstrators in Tiananmen Square, spoke on Hong Kong television on June 10. Her voice repeatedly was interrupted by bitter crying. Chai Ling provided the following account of the June 4 Beijing massacre.

Soldiers Kicked Hard at Students' Stomachs

This is Chai Ling, general coordinator of student demonstrators in Tiananmen Square. I'm still alive. . . . I am making this tape to tell the whole world about the Beijing massacre. . . .

We had sensed a harsh crackdown would occur on the basis of three signs. First, at 10:30 P.M., June 2, a speeding army vehicle hit four people; three of them died. Second, some soldiers left their guns for the students. This made the students suspicious. They turned over the weapons to the Public Security Bureau and obtained receipts. Third, on June 3 around 2:10 P.M., when a student tried to stop soldiers from beating demonstrators by saying "The People's Army loves the people," some soldiers kicked hard at his stomach and cursed, "Who will love people of your kind!"

I was in the square broadcasting station before the massacre and received many emergency calls from fellow students. . . . From 7:00 to 8:00 P.M., our headquarters held a press conference to release news of our situation. Few foreign journalists were present because their hotels were under surveillance by soldiers and policemen. At that press conference, we raised the call "Down with the fake government of Li Peng. . . . "

At 9:00 P.M., all the sit-in students in the square stood up. We held up our right arms and pledged: "I will sacrifice my youthful life to guard Tiananmen Square. I am ready to lose my head and shed my blood, but will never give up the people's square. I will hold on to the last minute of my life."

This Is a Battle of Love and Hatred

At 10:00 P.M., the University of Democracy began their lessons under the Goddess of Democracy. The president of the university was Zhang Boli, vice-coordinator of the square's headquarters.

The situation was extremely serious. The Twenty-seventh Army had begun killing people with bayonets and machine guns on Chang'an Boulevard, and the street was flooded with blood and dead bodies. Students ran back from the street, their bodies covered with blood. We held them tightly in our arms.

After 10:30 P.M., our headquarters requested the students to be calm. We stressed that the principle of peaceful struggle enabled the student prodemocracy movement to be joined by all kinds of people. Many workers and civilians said that the soldiers were fully armed to kill, so we were justified to arm ourselves for self-protection. However, we insisted on peaceful struggle. The highest principle of such a struggle was to sacrifice our lives.

After listening to our broadcast, students walked out of their tents in steady steps and sat down in the square, ready to confront bullets and bayonets. We were fighting a battle of love and hate, but not violence against violence. If we had lost our senses, as those soldiers did, and used sticks and other "weapons" to fight against their machine guns, it would have been the greatest tragedy. We were only waiting for the moment to dedicate our lives.

A Child of Fifteen Wrote His Last Words

The song *Descendants of the Dragon* [see part I] was broadcast through our loudspeakers. The sit-in students held one another's hands and embraced one another. Then came the last moment.

Among us was a student named Wang Li, only fifteen years of age. He wrote down his last words. A child of fifteen was thinking about death! (Bitter crying by Chai Ling. She continues with difficulty.) The People's Republic, please remember your children who have fought for you!

At dawn [on June 4], the headquarters decided to give up the sit-in. We went around and tried to persuade the students to leave the square, but they wouldn't. They sat there in silence. Those in the first row were the most determined. Our fellow students were ready to shed their blood. I then told an ancient story. There was a swarm of ants, about 1.1 billion in number. One day, the hill on which they lived caught fire, forcing them to move. To save the lives of others, a group of ants were burned to death. For the rebirth of the republic, we had to sacrifice our lives.

Then the four hunger strikers—Hou Dejian, Liu Xiaobo, Zhou Duo, and Gao Xin—persuaded the students to leave the square. They said, "Little brothers and sisters, we cannot shed more blood. We have to live on."

These four hunger strikers had a dialogue with army officers, who agreed to guarantee the students' safety if we left the square peacefully. However, before we had time to announce this agreement to the students, soldiers with machine guns charged up to the third row of students sitting on the Monument [to the People's Heroes]. Most students started leaving the square, weeping as they went.

I only learned afterward that some students still entertained illusions about the government and remained on the square. They thought that at most the soldiers would arrest them. Nevertheless, tanks crushed them into meat pies. It is said that two hundred died; but others have said four thousand died in the whole square. (Bitter crying. [Chai Ling] could not continue [on this subject].)

Tanks Crushed Them into Meat Pies

At present, it is difficult to know exactly how many died in the square. What we do know is that not one member of the Workers' Autonomous Union standing in the square survived. They had long been prepared to sacrifice their lives to protect the student demonstrators.

I learned afterward that military tanks crushed the student tents in the square. The soldiers poured gasoline on them and set them on fire together with the bodies of our fellow students. Then they washed the square with water. These slaughterers wanted to destroy evidence that would reveal the truth of the massacre.

On our way west from the Mao Mausoleum, we saw soldiers, tanks, and armored vehicles heading wildly toward the square. Chang'an Boulevard was a bloody road, but no corpses were seen on the street. We were told by civilians along the road that while some soldiers fired machine guns toward the crowd, others followed behind and piled the bodies of victims onto buses and tricycles. Some wounded thereby suffocated to death.

They Are Still Very Young, But They Are Gone Forever

Out of anger, some of us suggested going back to the square for a sit-in protest. Yet some soldiers told us not to shed more blood, for the square was well guarded by machine guns. We then headed west to return to our campuses.

A civilian told us that the soldiers fired rocket guns toward the square, killing a number of children and elderly people. A woman said that around 2:00 A.M. on June 4, she was blocking a tank and witnessed a girl who, while doing the same thing, was crushed into a meat pie.

On our way back to our campuses, we saw some slogans, such as "Support the correct policy decision of the party Central Committee." Enraged, we tore them to pieces.

([Chai Ling] gets more and more excited.) The sit-in students killed in the square were said to be rioters. This is a great lie! Our fellow students were crushed under the tanks, and even their corpses could not be pieced back together. (Weeping. Pause.) They will never come back to life. They will remain forever on Chang'an Boulevard. . . .

Back at the campus, we heard that Li Peng gave three commands on the evening of June 3:

1. The troops can open fire; armored vehicles can head forward at full speed.
2. Tiananmen Square must be cleared by dawn on June 4.
3. All heads of illegal organizations should be killed.

After the bloodbath in Tiananmen Square, the frenzied slaughterers are going to start killing throughout the country. This is an era of darkness. Nevertheless, the first light of morning will rise out of darkness. A republic of democracy is sure to be born. This is a moment of life and death for our nation. Wake up, my countrymen!

Down with Fascism!

199

A Loss of a Whole Generation of Chinese Elites: Telephone Interview with Dai Qing on Her Quitting the Party after the Massacre

June 10, 1989

Source: *Lianho pao* (United daily), June 11, 1989, in *Tiananmen 1989*, pp. 262–64.

. . . *Question*: Why have you quit the party?[1] Will it have any impact?

Answer: This is my personal act. I don't want it to cause any campaign or

---

[1]Dai Qing was a reporter for *Guangming Daily*, where her investigative articles, for instance on Mao Zedong and Liang Shuming, irritated conservative regime stalwarts. As an adopted daughter of Ye Jianying, a former marshal and minister of national defense from southern China, deceased in 1986, she has often been accorded political protection.

bring any attention. I only want to distance myself from politics in which I will no longer participate. I have retreated in order to strengthen my personal integrity. My act of quitting the party should not be viewed as an anti-Communist one. I still hope the party will be in good shape.

Q: What is your motive for quitting the party? Has the party answered you?

A: I quit the party on June 4. I cannot condone the tragic episode that I witnessed on June 3–4. According to the party constitution, you only need to make an application in order to quit the party. Or perhaps they will ask me why, but so far they haven't.

Q: How do you feel now that you have quit the party?

A: Not much different. I long predicted all this. I tried to send warnings to [party leaders] but failed. No one took my words seriously.

Q: Will your quitting the party affect your work and life?

A: It should be all right as long as I am a law-abiding citizen. There may be some restrictions on my reporting and travel because I am no longer a party member. There are some places where I cannot go to make reports. Isn't it true that there are also some restrictions on those who have quit the Guomindang in Taiwan?

Q: It is said that more than four hundred "counterrevolutionaries" who participated in the "riot" have been arrested.

A: Up to today, the punishment by the government has been limited to those rioters. I haven't seen any intellectual arrested because of his or her expression of individual views and thoughts. I don't know whether this exemption will continue in the future.

Q: It seems that nowadays the intellectuals no longer maintain contact with each other, a situation unlike that of the previous days. Is it true?

A: Everyone suspects wiretapping, and it is inappropriate to contact each other now. Moreover, . . . it is rare if contact among intellectuals takes place these days. On the other hand, the environment today is totally unfit for intellectuals to engage in organized activities. After all, intellectuals can do nothing under martial law.

Q: Why do you think this situation developed?

A: I don't think that Deng Xiaoping and Li Peng deliberately wanted to push the country into such a situation, nor did the students deliberately want to create turmoil. The fatal element was that both sides insisted on their own ways of thinking and never took into consideration the positions of the other side. . . . The goals of both sides were quite similar, but their chosen means were totally different, so it became a life-and-death struggle. This is also the reason why I have decided to distance myself from politics. . . .

In the final days, the students advocated overthrowing the government, but what happens after the government is overthrown? Who is capable of replacing the government? From the perspective of the government, this advocacy is extremely counterrevolutionary, and there could be absolutely no forgiveness or accommodation. Thus the whole event was pushed to the extreme.

The level of this kind of political struggle is too low.

Q: Will China be able to recover from this disaster?

A: . . . The recovery has to await the passing away of governance by old men as practiced by the first generation of leaders. There is no hope for change as long as they are still alive. But the situation now is at least better than nationwide chaos. Everything that happened in Beijing in the past days was only in a few areas. The imposition of martial law can be seen as having prevented turmoil from occurring on an even larger scale such as might have happened if military men had acted independently with their forces. If Deng Xiaoping could not have controlled the situation, the military men would inevitably have become independent.

Q: Sooner or later Deng Xiaoping will pass away. Will a situation necessarily emerge in which the military becomes independent?

A: It depends on how the reform proceeds. We cannot resort to military force at every turn to solve problems. The whole world is entering a period of accommodation after the post–World War II cold war. . . . I hope that the present situation in China is only temporary. If the government depends on military force, how can there be any civilization in China. If so, the intellectuals can only wait.

Q: Do you have any feeling of being in danger, particularly after June 4?

A: I have continued in a normal spirit. I did not participate in any event currently listed in party materials about the turmoil published by the Beijing Municipal Party Committee. Since the end of April, I have been continuously urging people not to escalate the situation. If I am purged because of these efforts, they won't find any justification. Those who have fled either are afraid or know that they have violated martial law orders.

Q: According to your logic, how should the Tiananmen Square massacre be viewed?

A: Up to June 2, I supported martial law. I believed that Tiananmen Square should be under martial law. But I had not imagined that [military force] would be used. A whole generation of Chinese elites has been lost. This sacrifice is too heavy.

Q: In this atmosphere, the government and the people are standing on two opposite ends. How can they accommodate this?

A: It is too difficult to [recover] a normal relationship between the people and government. The government really should not have committed this act.

Q: Yesterday Deng Xiaoping even mourned the soldiers who died, but not the students, intellectuals, and people who died.

A: Today the mayor of Beijing, Chen Xitong, has already changed the tone. Now the dead on both sides are mourned. But already it is a totally different situation.

Q: There have been some materials accusing the Guomindang of instigating the turmoil. Is it possible?

A: No, Taiwan is too far away; but I still want to look at their evidence.
Q: Will you stay at home in the upcoming days?
A: I feel all right. I will probably stay home unless I feel like writing something. I don't think I will have trouble.
Q: Please take care.
A: Thank you. Thank you for this conversation. This is my first telephone call from Taipei [Taiwan].

200

Letter to Friends from a County-Level Party Official

ANONYMOUS

Shortly after June 4, 1989

Source: Anonymous.

I received your letter some time ago and am sorry for not writing to you sooner. . . .

In recent years in China, because the enlightened leaders within the party strongly supported the reform and opening to the world, a policy of loosening (*fangsong*) and tolerance had been implemented toward the intellectuals and in the theoretical and academic worlds. With the continuous impact of the democratic upsurge in the world, and especially because of the increasing corruption of the regime, a great patriotic democracy movement burst out in April this year in China, with patriotic college students as its core, and with support from all Chinese people. This movement was totally spontaneous and popular. It is one of the greatest feats in the history of the Chinese nation. . . .

Of course, this movement also made a few dictators and diehards within the party fly into a rage from shame. They brandished the party's big sticks and played the same old tricks, attempting again to destroy the forces of enlightened party leaders. They used arms and swaggered as they cracked down on the patriotic young students. They used threats and intimidation against party cadres, workers, and city residents, trying to force them to give up their support and sympathy for the student movement. They exaggerated things just to scare people and continued to distort the facts and deceive the people, totally disregarding the popular will and world opinion. They have gone against the historical trend and stuck to their way of doing things. They were rude and unreasonable and acted arbitrarily, all for the purpose of implementing and protecting their feudal autocratic rule, while flaunting the banner of socialism. It seems now that they have prevailed, but it is only temporary. The democracy movement was strangled, but the whole people have been enlightened in their thinking. The democratic consciousness has already found its way into the minds of the people. The final victory is bound to belong to the people.

Like people all over the country, the people in [XX] county also praised and supported the student movement wholeheartedly. When the students from colleges and technical schools here marched in the streets in support of Beijing students, the city residents cheered them all along the sidewalks. They set off fireworks to show their support. They were generous in making donations. The people here showed extremely high enthusiasm. Originally, the people had almost grown numb to and tired of politics, particularly when the major and minor newspapers, the radio and TV programs all had the same tone. In recent months, however, members of every family and household followed the news reports closely. Many people also listened to the radio stations of the VOA and BBC. For a few days, the news media had indeed smashed the trammels that had bound them, boldly, faithfully, and comprehensively reporting the student movement. Even the young journalists from the [local] *Daily* went to demonstrate in the streets, demanding freedom of the press and truthful news reporting. If the situation in a small, remote, and ill-informed city like [XX] was so exciting, it is not difficult to imagine the warm atmosphere in other middle and large cities. Among the people we contacted, none had refused to show support for and agreement to the political demands by the patriotic students for freedom of speech and press, for perfecting the legal system, punishing the officials engaged in profiteering, wiping out corruption, knocking down the diehards, and promoting reform. The people admired the students for being brave and selfless, for their strong will to struggle, for their reason and wisdom and skills in struggle. They praised the students as national elites and as the [embodiment] of the Chinese spirit. What has especially shocked heaven and earth and moved one to song and tears is the heroic act of three thousand young students on a hunger strike for seven days.

Now, under the pressure of high-handed policies, the student movement has temporarily receded. The authorities have again picked up the old methods of the "Gang of Four" from the past, forcing people to reveal their attitudes and to write letters of fealty in support of the authorities. Ordinary people must study in order to be brainwashed, so that they may be in line with the center. You know too well the social structure of China. It is an organization and system like a very tight net. The danger of losing jobs and the threats of survival make many people fearful. Fear also comes from the policy of implication, the personal dossiers, which are just like the shadows of devils, and the many startling political movements of purging people in the past. The people, therefore, can only try to cope with the situation by burying anger deep in their hearts. Such a morbid society and a twisted mentality of the people could never exist in a democratic country.

That is why we long for the realization of true democracy in China. We believe that democracy and human rights are concepts of rationality. They are a crystallization of one thousand years of human civilization. All people can and should enjoy democracy no matter whether they live in the West or East. It is both a tragedy and hope for the Chinese nation that today the Chinese youth have to reemphasize the slogans of democracy, human rights, science, and freedom that were put forward seventy years ago. You overseas Chinese students provide a ray of hope for us. In the future this country should be led by the elites among the modern college students and overseas students.

Everything remains the same for us. We are getting older everyday, but our hearts are not old, because we always think of the future of the country and the fate of the people. Although sometimes we feel that the words of the lowly carry little weight, we still have an unshirkable share of responsibility for the fate of the country.

Let me stop here and let's keep in touch. . . .

Bibliography

Amnesty International. *People's Republic of China: Preliminary Findings of Killings of Unarmed Civilians, Arbitrary Arrests, and Summary Executions since June 3, 1989.* New York, 1989.

Article 19: The Year of the Lie: Censorship and Disinformation in the PRC, 1989. London, August 1989.

Asia Watch. *The Case of Wang Juntao.* New York, March 1991.

———. *Chinese Workers Receive Harsh Sentences.* New York, March 1991.

———. *Punishment Season: Human Rights in China after Martial Law.* New York, February 1990.

———. *Repression in China since June 4, 1989.* New York, 1990.

———. *Repression in China since June 4, 1989: Cumulative Data.* New York, January 1991.

———. *Rough Justice in Beijing: Punishing the Black Hands of Tiananmen Square.* New York, January 1991.

———. *Updates on Arrests 1-3.* New York, January, February, April 1991.

Bachman, David, and Yang Dali, eds. and trans. *Yan Jiaqi and China's Struggle for Democracy.* Armonk, NY: M. E. Sharpe, 1991.

Barmé, Geremie. "Traveling Heavy: The Intellectual Baggage of the Chinese Diaspora," *Problems of Communism* (January–April 1991).

Beijing Publishing House. *The Truth about the Beijing Turmoil.* Beijing, 1989.

Beijing Review. *Student Unrest: What Is It All About?* Beijing: China in Focus, no. 23, 1990.

Calhoun, Craig. "Revolution and Repression in Tiananmen Square," *Society* (September–October 1989).

Chan, Anita, and Jonathan Unger. "Voices from the Protest Movement: Chongqing, Sichuan," *Australian Journal of Chinese Affairs*, no. 24 (July 1990).

Che Muqi. *Beijing Turmoil: More Than Meets the Eye.* Beijing: Foreign Languages Press, 1990.

Cheng, Chu-yuan. *Behind the Tiananmen Massacre: Social, Political and Economic Ferment in China.* Boulder: Westview Press, 1990.

Cheung, Tai Ming. "The PLA and Its Role between April–June 1989," in *China's Military: The PLA in 1990/1991*, ed. Richard Yang. Boulder: Westview Press, 1991.

Chong, W. L. "The Crackdown's Aftermath: Notes on Exiles, Elderly Officials 'On Leave,' and a Radio Ship," *China Information* 5, 2 (Autumn 1990).

———. "Fang Lizhi, Li Shuxian and the 1989 Student Demonstrations: The Supposed Connection," *China Information* 4, 1 (Summer 1989).

———. "Why the 1989 Student Demonstrations Failed: A Lecture by Su Xiaokang," *China Information* 4, 3 (Winter 1989–90).

Chow, Rey. "Violence in the Other Country: Preliminary Remarks on the China Crisis," *Radical America* 22, 4.

Christiansen, Flemming. "The 1989 Student Demonstrations and the Limits of the Chinese Bargaining Machine," *China Information* 4, 1 (Summer 1989).

Chua, Morgan. *Tiananmen*. Hong Kong: Chinatown Publications, 1989.

Des Forges, Roger, et al., eds. *China: The Crisis of 1989, Origins and Implications*. 2 vols. Buffalo: Council on International Studies, State University of New York, 1990.

Dittmer, Lowell. "The Tiananmen Massacre," *Problems of Communism* (September–October 1989).

Dreyer, June. "The PLA and the Power Struggle of 1989," *Problems of Communism* (September–October 1989).

———. "The Role of the Military," *World Policy Journal* (Fall 1989).

———. "Tiananmen and the PLA," in *China's Military: The PLA in 1990/1991*, ed. Richard Yang. Boulder: Westview Press, 1991.

Duke, Michael. *The Iron House: A Memoir of the Chinese Democracy Movement and the Tiananmen Massacre*. Layton, UT: Gibbs Smith, 1990.

Erbaugh, Mary S., and Richard Curt Kraus. "The 1989 Democracy Movement in Fujian and Its Aftermath," *Australian Journal of Chinese Affairs*, no. 23 (January 1990).

Esherick, Joseph W. "Xi'an Spring," *Australian Journal of Chinese Affairs*, no. 24 (July 1990).

Fang Lizhi. *Bringing Down the Great Wall: Writings on Science, Culture and Democracy in China*. New York: Knopf, 1991.

Fathers, Michael, and Andrew Higgins. *Tiananmen: The Rape of Peking*. London: The Independent, 1989.

Fei, John C. H. "A Cultural Approach to the 1989 Beijing Crisis," *Asian Affairs: An American Review* 11, 2 (Summer 1989).

Feigon, Lee. *China Rising: The Meaning of Tiananmen*. Chicago: Ivan R. Dee, 1990.

Fincher, John. "Zhao's Fall, China's Loss," *Foreign Policy* (Fall 1989).

Finkel, Donald. *A Splintered Mirror: Chinese Poetry from the Democracy Movement*. San Francisco: North Point Press, 1991.

Fletcher Forum of World Affairs. "The People's Unfinished Revolution: Communist China at Forty," 14, 1 (Winter 1990).

Forster, Keith. "Impressions of the Popular Protest in Hangzhou, April/June 1989," *Australian Journal of Chinese Affairs*, no. 23 (January 1990).

Forward, Roy. "Letter from Shanghai," *Australian Journal of Chinese Affairs*, no. 24 (July 1990).

Fox, Josephine. "The Movement for Democracy and Its Consequences in Tianjin," *Australian Journal of Chinese Affairs*, no. 23 (January 1990).

Francis, Corina-Barbara. "The Progress of Protest in China: The Spring of 1989," *Asian Survey* 29, 9 (September 1989).

Friedman, Edward. "Democratization in China," *Telos*, no. 80 (Summer 1989).

Furth, Charlotte. "Democracy in China: Some Historical Reflections on the June 1989 Movement," *China Report* 25, 4 (October–December 1989).

Galtung, Johan. "What Happened in Beijing, 3–4 June 1989: What Happened Now?" *China Report* 25, 4 (October–December 1989).

Gold, Thomas. "The Resurgence of Civil Society in China," *Journal of Democracy* 1, 1 (Winter 1990).

Goldman, Merle. "China's Great Leap Backward," *Journal of Democracy* 1, 1 (Winter 1990).

———. "Vengeance in China," *New York Review of Books*, November 9, 1989.

Gong, Gerrit. "Tiananmen: A Personal Account," *The Washington Quarterly* (Winter 1990).

Gunn, Anne. "Tell the World About Us: The Student Movement in Shenyang, 1989,"

Australian Journal of Chinese Affairs, no. 24 (July 1990).

Hai Langtao. "The Tiananmen Square Tragedy: (The Heavenly Peace Court) Dialogues and Reflections," *Asian Thought and Society* (May–October 1989).

Han Minzhu and Hua Sheng, eds. *Cries for Democracy: Writings and Speeches from the 1989 Chinese Democracy Movement*. Princeton: Princeton University Press, 1990.

He Xin, trans. and intro. by Geremie Barmé. "Word of Advice to the Politburo," *Australian Journal of Chinese Affairs*, no. 23 (January 1990).

Hicks, George, ed. *The Broken Mirror: China after Tiananmen*. Chicago: St. James Press, 1990.

Howard, Roger W. "The Student Democracy Movement in Changchun," *Australian Journal of Chinese Affairs*, no. 24 (July 1990).

Hsiung, James C. "From the Vantage of the Beijing Hotel: Peering into the 1989 Student Unrest in China," *Asian Affairs: An American Review* 16, 2 (Summer 1989).

Huan Guocang. "The Events of Tiananmen Square," *Orbis* (Fall 1989).

———. "The Roots of Political Crisis," *World Policy Journal* (Fall 1989).

Huang Yasheng. "The Origins of China's Pro-Democracy Movement and the Government's Response: A Tale of Two Reforms," *Fletcher Forum of World Affairs* (Winter 1990).

Human Rights in China, ed. *Children of the Dragon: The Story of Tiananmen Square*. New York: Macmillan, 1990).

International League for Human Rights. *Massacre in Beijing: The Events of 3-4 June 1989 and Their Aftermath*. New York, 1989.

Jakobson, Linda. " 'Lies in Ink, Truth in Blood': The Role and Impact of the Chinese Media during the Beijing Spring of 1989." Cambridge: Harvard University Barone Center of Press Politics and Public Policy, August 1990.

Jane's Information Group. *China's Crisis: The Role of the Military*. London, 1989.

Jia Hao, ed. *The Democracy Movement of 1989 and China's Future*. Washington, DC: Washington Center for Chinese Studies, 1990.

Jiang Zhifeng. *Countdown to Tiananmen: The View at the Top*. San Francisco: Democratic Books and Pacific News Services, 1990.

Johnson, Kay Ann. "The Revolutionary Tradition of Pro-Democracy Students," *Radical America* 22, 4.

Joffe, Ellis. "The Tiananmen Crisis and the Politics of the PLA," in *China's Military: The PLA in 1990/1991*, ed. Richard Yang. Boulder: Westview Press, 1991.

Kent, Ann. *Human Rights in the PRC*. Canberra: Legislative Research Service, 1989–90.

Klintworth, Gary, ed. *China's Crisis: The International Implications*. Canberra: Papers on Strategy and Defense, no. 57, 1989.

Kwan, Michael David. *Broken Portraits: Encounters with Chinese Students*. San Francisco: China Books and Periodicals, 1990.

Landsberger, Stefan. "The 1989 Student Demonstrations in Beijing: A Chronology of Events," *China Information* 4, 1 (Summer 1989).

Lee, Chin-chuan, ed. *Voices of China: The Interplay of Politics and Journalism*. New York: Guilford, 1990.

Lee, Ta-ling, and John F. Copper. *Failure of Democracy Movement: Human Rights in the PRC 1988/89*. Baltimore: Occasional Paper no. 2, University of Maryland School of Law, 1991.

Li Lu. *Moving the Mountain: My Life in China from the Cultural Revolution to Tiananmen Square*. London: Macmillan, 1990.

Li, Peter, et al., eds. *Culture and Politics in China: An Anatomy of Tiananmen Square*. New Brunswick, NJ: Transaction Books, 1990.

Liu, Alan P. L. "Aspects of Beijing's Crisis Management: The Tiananmen Square Demonstration," *Asian Survey* 30, 5 (May 1990).

Liu Binyan. *China's Crisis, China's Hope: Essays from an Intellectual in Exile.* Cambridge: Harvard University Press, 1990.

———. "Deng's Pyrrhic Victory: China after Tiananmen," *New Republic*, October 2, 1989.

———, with Ruan Ming and Xu Gang. *"Tell the World": What Happened in China and Why.* New York: Pantheon, 1989.

Liu, William T. "A Social Study of the 1989 Beijing Crisis," *Asian Affairs: An American Review* 16, 2 (Summer 1989).

Lord, Winston. "China's Big Chill," *Foreign Affairs* (Fall 1989).

Luo Qiping et al. "The 1989 Pro-Democracy Movement: Student Organizations and Strategies," *China Information* 5, 2 (Autumn 1990).

MacFarquhar, Roderick. "The End of the Chinese Revolution," *New York Review of Books* (June 1989).

Maier, John H. "Tian'anmen 1989: The View from Shanghai," *China Information* 5,1 (Summer 1990).

Martin, Brian. *China in Crisis: The Events of April–June 1989.* Canberra: Legislative Research Service, 1989–90.

Martin, Helmut. "China's Democracy Movement in 1989: A Selected Bibliography of Chinese Source Materials," 1990.

Morrison, Donald, ed. *Massacre in Beijing: China's Struggle for Democracy.* New York: Time Inc., 1989.

Ming Bao. *June Four: A Chronicle of the Chinese Democratic Uprising.* Fayetteville: University of Arkansas Press, 1989.

Nathan, Andrew. "China Democracy in 1989: Continuity and Change," *Problems of Communism* (September–October 1989).

———. *China's Crisis.* New York: Columbia University Press, 1990.

Oksenberg, Michel, Lawrence R. Sullivan, and Marc Lambert, eds. *Beijing Spring, 1989: Confrontation and Conflict, The Basic Documents.* Armonk, NY: M. E. Sharpe, 1990.

Ostergaard, Clemens Stubbe. "Citizens, Groups, and a Nascent Civil Society in China: Toward an Understanding of the 1989 Student Demonstrations," *China Information* 4, 2 (Autumn 1989).

Pang, Pang. *The Death of Hu Yaobang.* Honolulu: Center for Chinese Studies, University of Hawaii, 1990.

Pieke, Frank, and Fons Lamboo. *Inventory of the Collection of the Chinese People's Movement, Spring 1989.* Amsterdam: Institute of Social History, 1990.

Poll Work Group, Psychology Department, Beijing Normal University. "Beijing Public Opinion Poll on the Student Demonstrations, held on 1–2 and 7 May 1989," *China Information* 4, 1 (Summer 1989).

Porter, Edgar. *Journalism from Tiananmen.* Honolulu: University of Hawaii, 1990.

Pye, Lucian W. "Tiananmen and Chinese Political Culture: The Escalation of Confrontation from Moralizing to Revenge," *Asian Survey* 30, 4 (April 1990).

"Special Section: Documents from the Chinese Democratic Movement."*Radical America* 22, 4.

Saich, Tony, ed. *The Chinese People's Movement: Perspectives on Spring 1989.* Armonk, NY: M. E. Sharpe, 1990.

———. "The Rise and Fall of the Beijing People's Movement," *Australian Journal of Chinese Affairs*, no. 24 (July 1990).

Salisbury, Harrison. *Tiananmen Diary: Thirteen Days in June.* Boston: Little, Brown, 1989.

Schell, Orville. "Children of Tiananmen," *Rolling Stone*, December 14–28, 1989.

Segal, Gerald. "The Chances of a Coup d'Etat," in *China's Military in 1990/1991*, ed. Richard Yang. Boulder: Westview Press, 1991.

Shen Tong, with Marianne Yen. *Almost a Revolution*. Boston: Houghton Mifflin, 1990.

Simmie, Scott, and Bob Nixon. *Tiananmen Square: An Eyewitness Account of the Chinese People's Passionate Quest for Democracy*. Seattle: University of Washington Press, 1989.

Solinger, Dorothy. "Democracy with Chinese Characteristics," *World Policy Journal* (Fall 1989).

Stahle, Esbjorn, and Terho Uimonen, eds. *Electronic Mail on China*. 2 vols. Stockholm: Skrifter utgiver av Foreningen for Orientaliska Studier, 1989.

Strand, David. "Protest in Beijing: Civil Society and Public Sphere in China," *Problems of Communism* (May–June 1990).

Su Shaozhi. *The Origin and Consequences of the Chinese Democratic Movement of 1989* in *History: End of Beginning*. London: Spokesman, 1990.

———. *Understanding Democratic Reform in China*. Milwaukee: Bradley Institute for Democracy, 1990.

Sullivan, Lawrence. "The Chinese Democracy Movement of 1989," *Orbis* (Fall 1989).

Tong, James, ed. "Death at the Gate of Heavenly Peace: The Democracy Movement in Beijing," *Chinese Law and Goverment* (Spring 1990).

———, and Andrew Ma, eds. "Baptism by Fire: The Democracy Movement in Beijing," *Chinese Law and Government* (Summer 1990).

Tong, James, and Elaine Chen, eds. "Fire and Fury: The Democracy Movement in Beijing, April–June 1989 (III)," *Chinese Sociology and Anthropology* (Fall 1990).

Turnley, David and Peter. *Beijing Spring*. New York: Stewart, Tabori and Chang, 1989.

Wakeman, Frederic. "The June Fourth Movement in China," *Items* (September 1989).

Walder, Andrew. "Beyond the Deng Era: China's Political Dilemma," *Asian Affairs: An American Review* 16, 2 (Summer 1989).

———. "The Political Sociology of the Beijing Upheaval of 1989," *Problems of Communism* (September–October 1989).

Warner, Shelley. "Shanghai's Response to the Deluge," *Australian Journal of Chinese Affairs*, no. 24 (July 1990).

Wright, Kate. "The Political Fortunes of Shanghai's *World Economic Herald*," *Australian Journal of Chinese Affairs*, no. 23 (January 1990).

Yang, Richard, ed., *The PLA and the Tiananmen Crisis*. Kaohsiung: Sun Yat-sen Center for Policy Studies, 1989.

Yang, Winston, and Marsha Wagner, eds. *Tiananmen: China's Struggle for Democracy: Its Prelude, Development, Aftermath, and Impact*. Baltimore: Occasional Paper no. 2, University of Maryland School of Law, 1990.

Yi Mu and Mark V. Thompson. *Crisis at Tiananmen: Reform and Reality in Modern China*. San Francisco: China Books and Periodicals, 1990.

You Ji and Ian Wilson. *Leadership Politics in the Chinese Party-Army State: The Fall of Zhao Ziyang*. Canberra: Research School of Pacific Studies, 1989.

Index

About the Editors

Suzanne Ogden, senior editor and project director (Ph.D., Brown University), is professor and chairperson, Department of Political Science, Northeastern University. She is author of *China's Unresolved Issues: Politics, Development, and Culture* (1989, 1992); author and editor of *Global Studies: The People's Republic of China, Taiwan, and Hong Kong* (1984, 1989, 1991); author and editor of *Annual Editions: World Politics* (for nine editions since 1983); as well as the author of a wide variety of articles on China.

Kathleen Hartford (Ph.D., Stanford University) is associate professor and chairperson, Department of Political Science, University of Massachusetts at Boston. She is coeditor of *Single Sparks: China's Rural Revolutions* (1989), and she has published widely on socialist reforms and on revolutions and social movements in pre-1949 China. Currently she is completing a manuscript on the dilemmas of reform in post-Mao China.

Lawrence Sullivan (Ph.D., University of Michigan) is associate professor of political science, Adelphi University, and associate in research, Fairbank Center, Harvard University. He is coeditor of *Beijing Spring, 1989* (1990). He has traveled to China frequently and has published numerous articles on the history of the Chinese Communist party, political historiography, and China's foreign policy.

David Zweig (Ph.D., University of Michigan) is associate professor of international politics, Fletcher School of Law and Diplomacy. He is author of *Agrarian Radicalism in China, 1968-1981* (1989) and coeditor of *New Perspectives on the Cultural Revolution* (1991). During 1991–92 he is in China under a grant from the Committee on Scholarly Communications with the PRC, working on a book on the domestic impact of the open door policy.